CASE CLOSED

VOLUME 34

Gosho Aoyama

Case Briefing:

Subject:
Occupation:
Special Skills:
Equipment:

Jimmy Kudo, a.k.a. Conan Edogawa
High School Student/Detective
Analytical thinking and deductive reasoning, Soccer
Bow Tie Voice Transmitter, Super Sneakers,
Homing Glasses, Stretchy Suspenders

The subject is hot on the trail of a pair of suspicious men in black when he is attacked from behind and administered a strange substance which physically transforms him into a first grader. When the subject confides in the eccentric inventor Dr. Agasa, they decide to keep the subject's true identity a secret for the safety of everyone around him. Assuming the new identity of first-grader Conan Edogawa, the subject continues to assist the police force on their most baffling cases. The only problem is that most crime-solving professionals won't take a little kid's advice!

Table of Contents

CONFIDEN

CASE CLOSED
Volume 34
Shonen Sunday Edition

Story and Art by GOSHO AOYAMA

© 1994 Gosho AOYAMA/Shogakukan
All rights reserved.
Original Japanese edition "MEITANTEI CONAN" published by SHOGAKUKAN Inc.

Translation
Tetsuichiro Miyaki

Touch-up & Lettering
Freeman Wong

Cover & Graphic Design
Andrea Rice

Editor
Shaenon K. Garrity

Printed in the U.S.A.

Published by VIZ Media, LLC
P.O. Box 77010
San Francisco, CA 94107

10 9 8 7 6 5 4 3 2
First printing, April 2010
Second printing, February 2014

TIME TO PICK THE APPLE

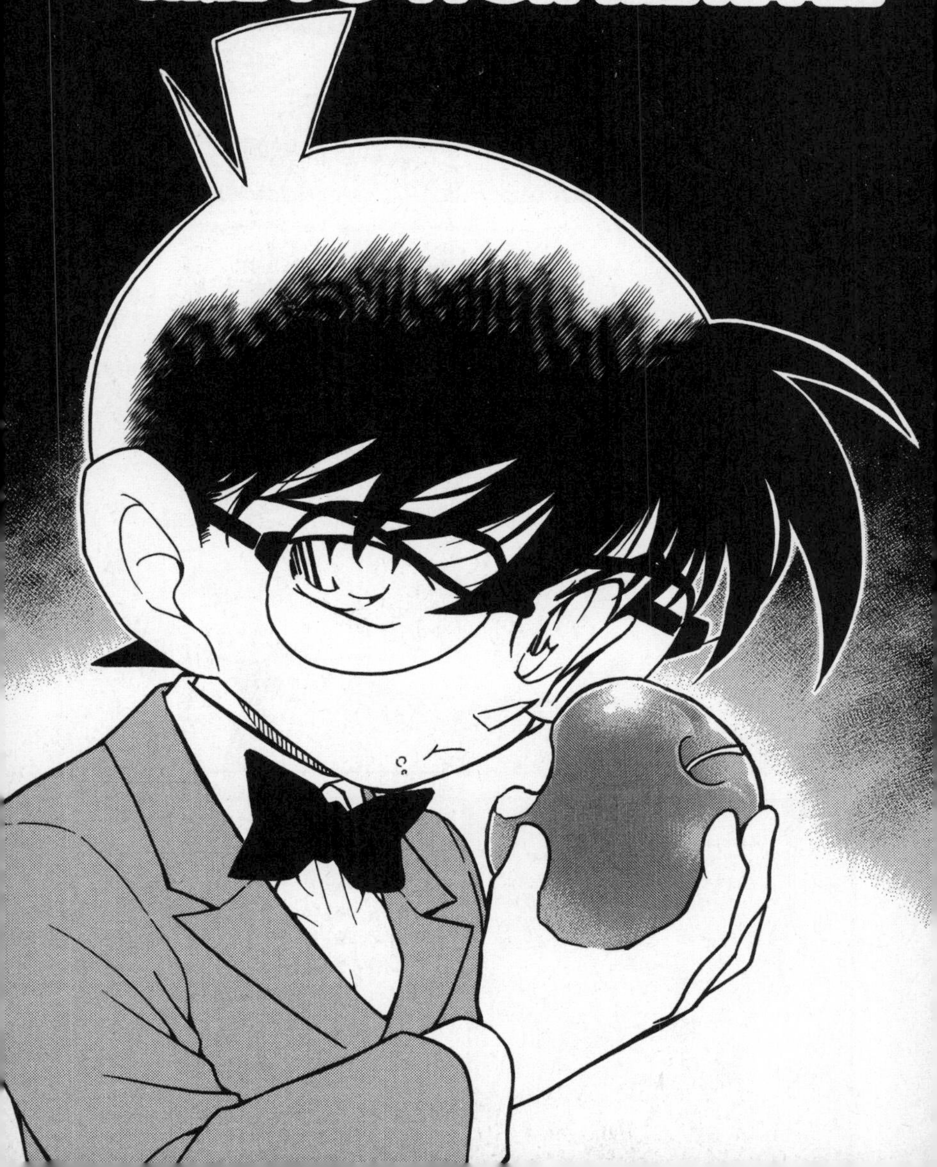

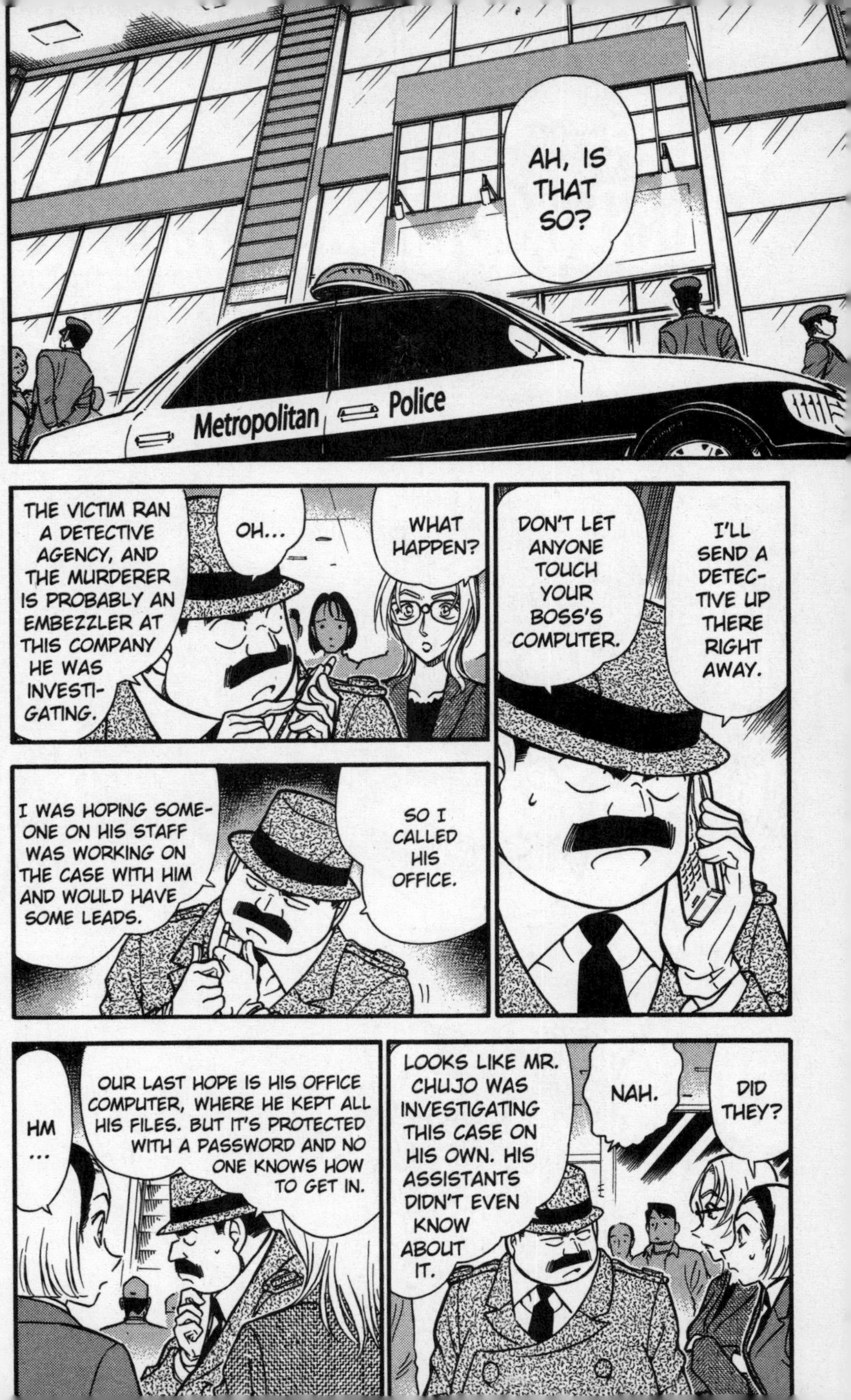
AH, IS THAT SO?
Metropolitan Police
I'LL SEND A DETECTIVE UP THERE RIGHT AWAY.
DON'T LET ANYONE TOUCH YOUR BOSS'S COMPUTER.
WHAT HAPPEN?
OH...
THE VICTIM RAN A DETECTIVE AGENCY, AND THE MURDERER IS PROBABLY AN EMBEZZLER AT THIS COMPANY HE WAS INVESTIGATING.
SO I CALLED HIS OFFICE.
I WAS HOPING SOMEONE ON HIS STAFF WAS WORKING ON THE CASE WITH HIM AND WOULD HAVE SOME LEADS.
DID THEY?
NAH.
LOOKS LIKE MR. CHUJO WAS INVESTIGATING THIS CASE ON HIS OWN. HIS ASSISTANTS DIDN'T EVEN KNOW ABOUT IT.
OUR LAST HOPE IS HIS OFFICE COMPUTER, WHERE HE KEPT ALL HIS FILES. BUT IT'S PROTECTED WITH A PASSWORD AND NO ONE KNOWS HOW TO GET IN.
HM ...

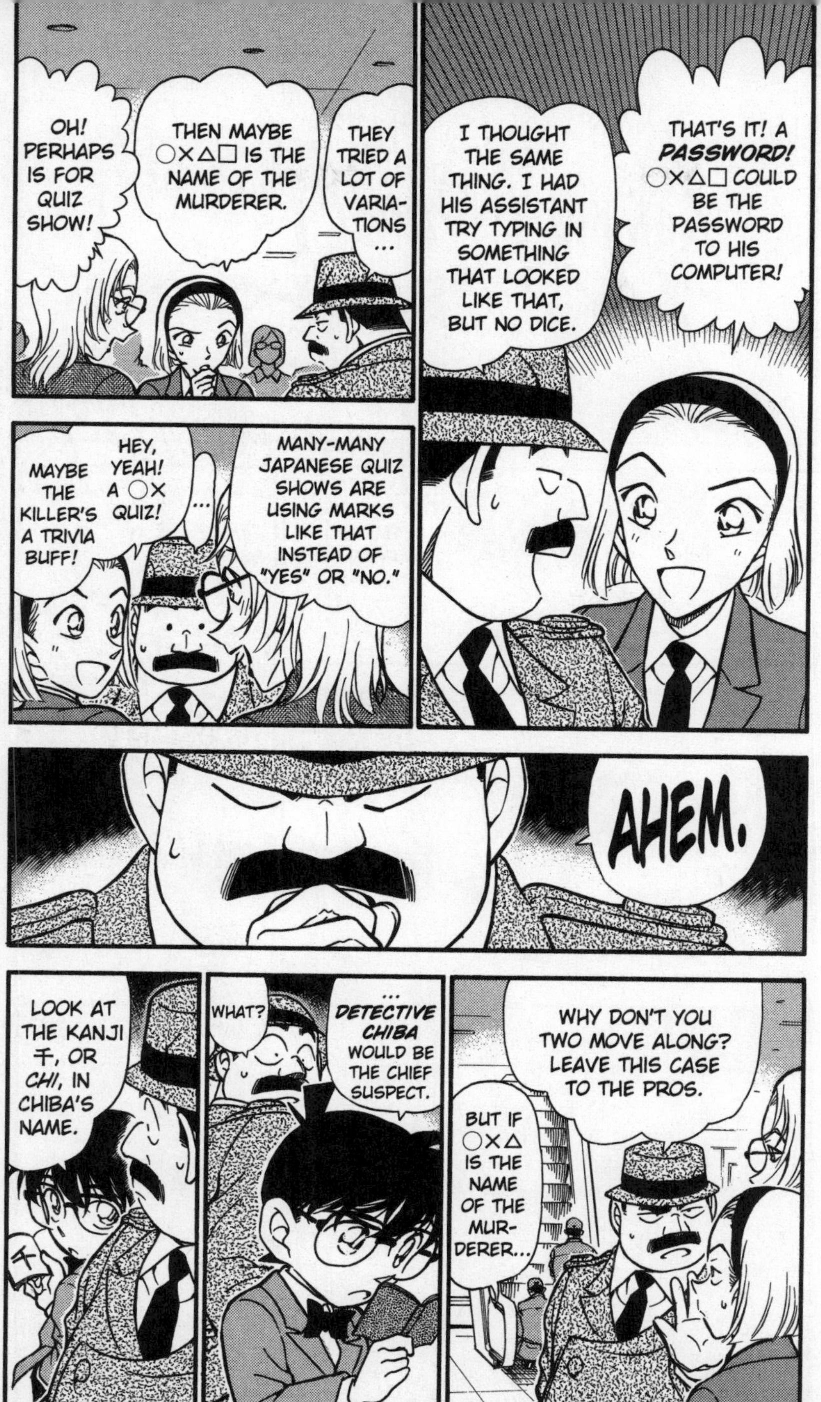
THAT'S IT! A ***PASSWORD!*** ○×△□ COULD BE THE PASSWORD TO HIS COMPUTER!
I THOUGHT THE SAME THING. I HAD HIS ASSISTANT TRY TYPING IN SOMETHING THAT LOOKED LIKE THAT, BUT NO DICE.
THEY TRIED A LOT OF VARIATIONS...
THEN MAYBE ○×△□ IS THE NAME OF THE MURDERER.
OH! PERHAPS IS FOR QUIZ SHOW!
MANY-MANY JAPANESE QUIZ SHOWS ARE USING MARKS LIKE THAT INSTEAD OF "YES" OR "NO."
...
HEY, YEAH! A ○× QUIZ!
MAYBE THE KILLER'S A TRIVIA BUFF!
AHEM.
WHY DON'T YOU TWO MOVE ALONG? LEAVE THIS CASE TO THE PROS.
BUT IF ○×△ IS THE NAME OF THE MURDERER...
... ***DETECTIVE CHIBA*** WOULD BE THE CHIEF SUSPECT.
WHAT?
LOOK AT THE KANJI 千, OR *CHI*, IN CHIBA'S NAME.
千

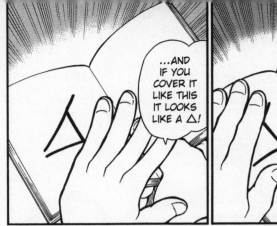

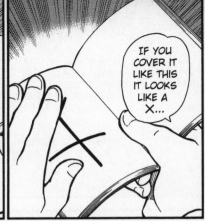

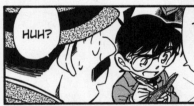

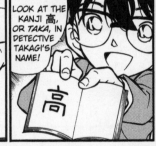

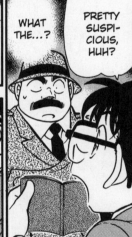

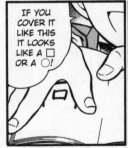

IF YOU COVER IT LIKE THIS IT LOOKS LIKE A ×...
...AND IF YOU COVER IT LIKE THIS IT LOOKS LIKE A △!
PRETTY SUSPICIOUS, HUH?
WHAT THE...?
HEY! BUT THAT'D MAKE DETECTIVE TAKAGI SUSPICIOUS TOO!
HUH?
LOOK AT THE KANJI 高, OR *TAKA*, IN DETECTIVE TAKAGI'S NAME!
IF YOU COVER IT LIKE THIS IT LOOKS LIKE A □ OR A ○!
I UNDERSTAND THE □, BUT WHY A ○?
SOME PEOPLE DRAW THE □ MARK AS A CIRCLE.
DR. AGASA DOES IT WHEN HE SIGNS HIS NAME.
BOT
HE SAYS IT'S OKAY TO ABBREVIATE THE KANJI A BIT WHEN YOU'RE IN A HURRY!
...

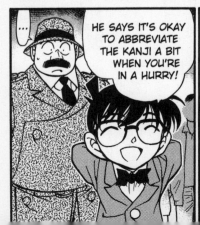

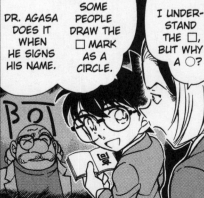

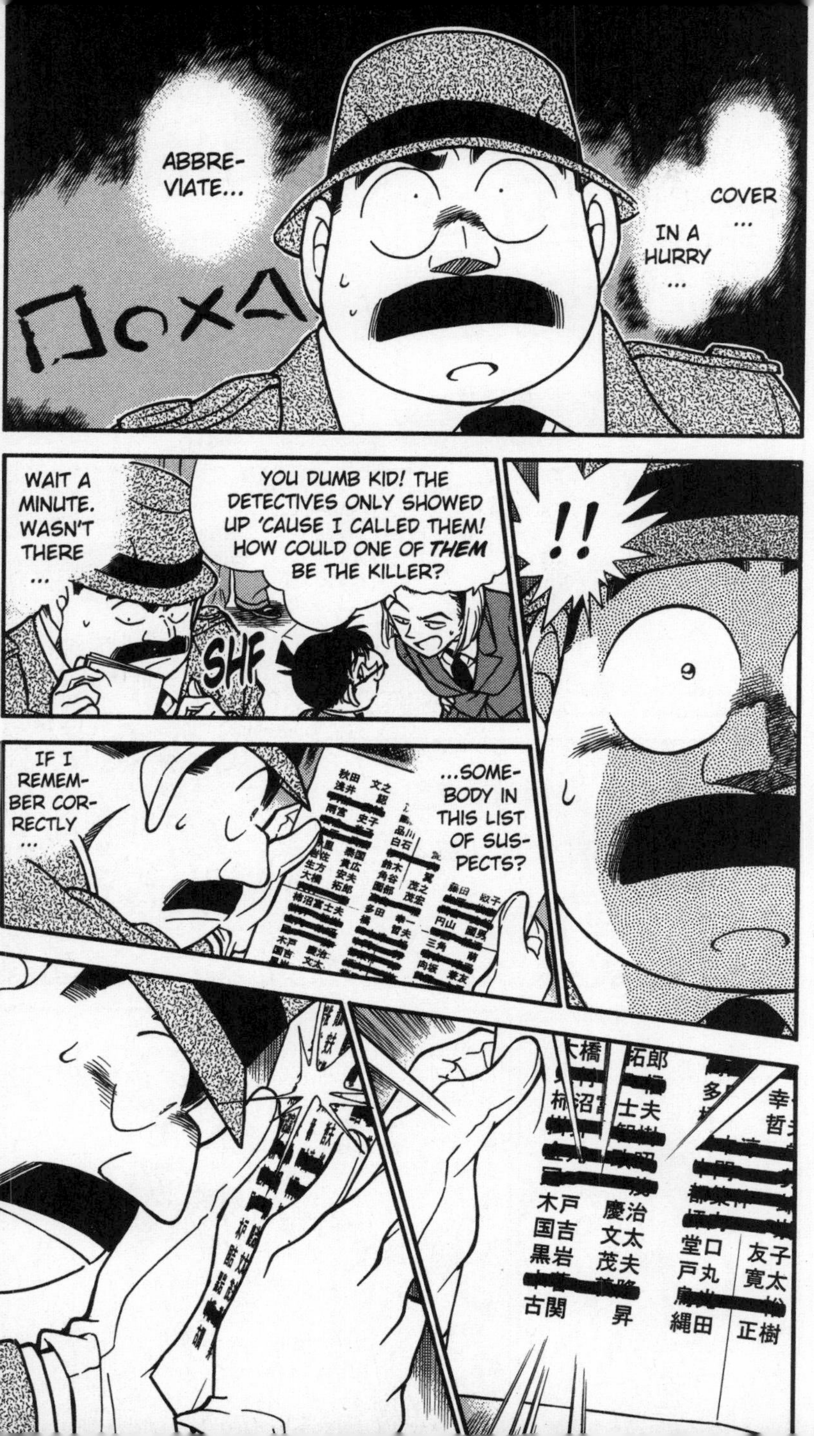
COVER ...
IN A HURRY ...
ABBRE-VIATE...
!!
YOU DUMB KID! THE DETECTIVES ONLY SHOWED UP 'CAUSE I CALLED THEM! HOW COULD ONE OF *THEM* BE THE KILLER?
WAIT A MINUTE. WASN'T THERE ...
SHF
IF I REMEMBER CORRECTLY ...
...SOMEBODY IN THIS LIST OF SUSPECTS?
大橋 拓郎
柿沼富 士夫
木戸 慶治
国吉 文太
黒岩 茂夫
古関 昇
堂口 友子
戸丸 寛太
縄田 正樹

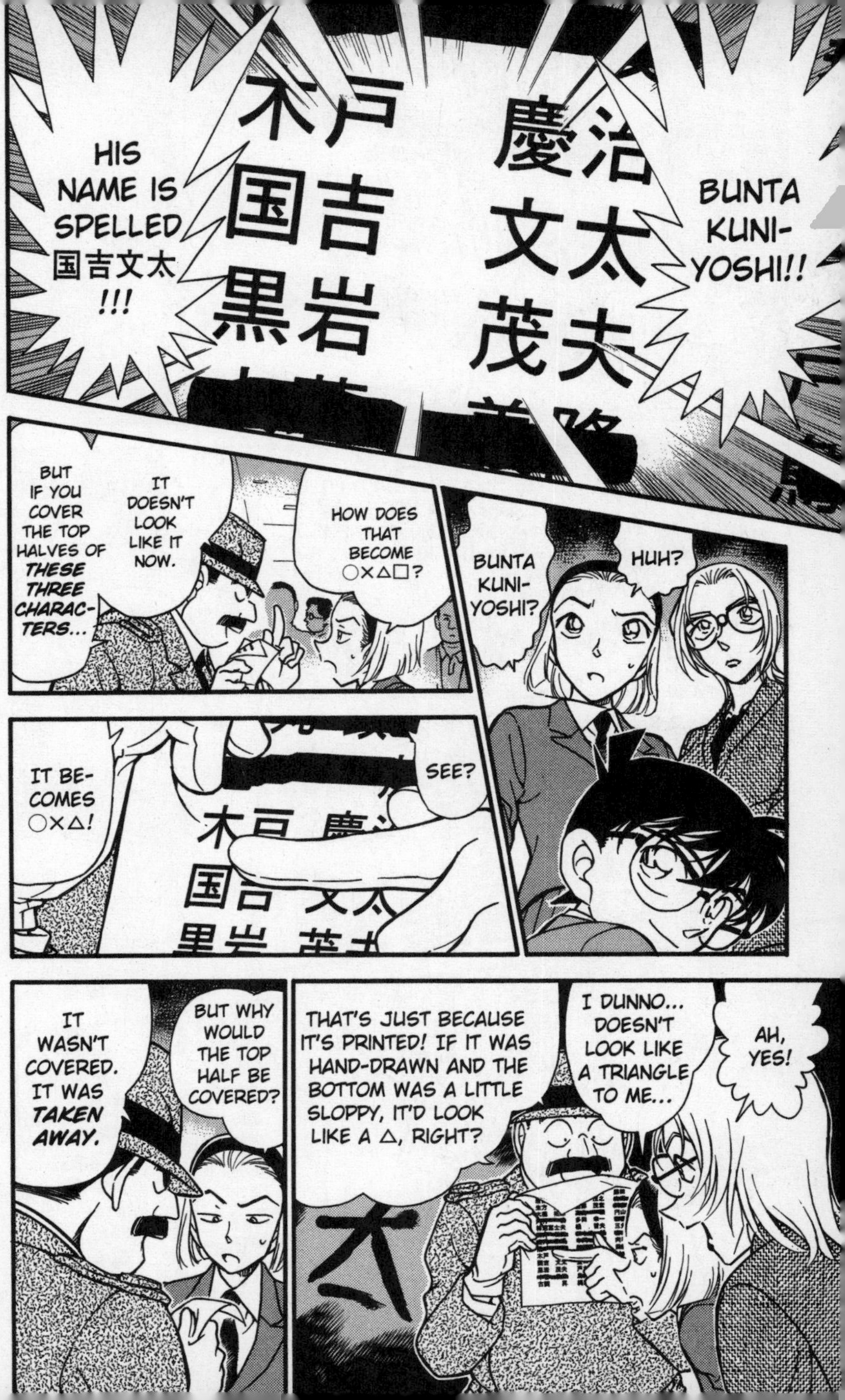
BUNTA KUNI-YOSHI!!
HIS NAME IS SPELLED 国吉文太 !!!
木戸 慶治
国吉 文太
黒岩 茂夫
HUH?
BUNTA KUNI-YOSHI?
HOW DOES THAT BECOME ○×△□?
IT DOESN'T LOOK LIKE IT NOW.
BUT IF YOU COVER THE TOP HALVES OF *THESE THREE CHARACTERS*...
SEE?
IT BE-COMES ○×△!
AH, YES!
I DUNNO... DOESN'T LOOK LIKE A TRIANGLE TO ME...
THAT'S JUST BECAUSE IT'S PRINTED! IF IT WAS HAND-DRAWN AND THE BOTTOM WAS A LITTLE SLOPPY, IT'D LOOK LIKE A △, RIGHT?
大
BUT WHY WOULD THE TOP HALF BE COVERED?
IT WASN'T COVERED. IT WAS *TAKEN AWAY.*

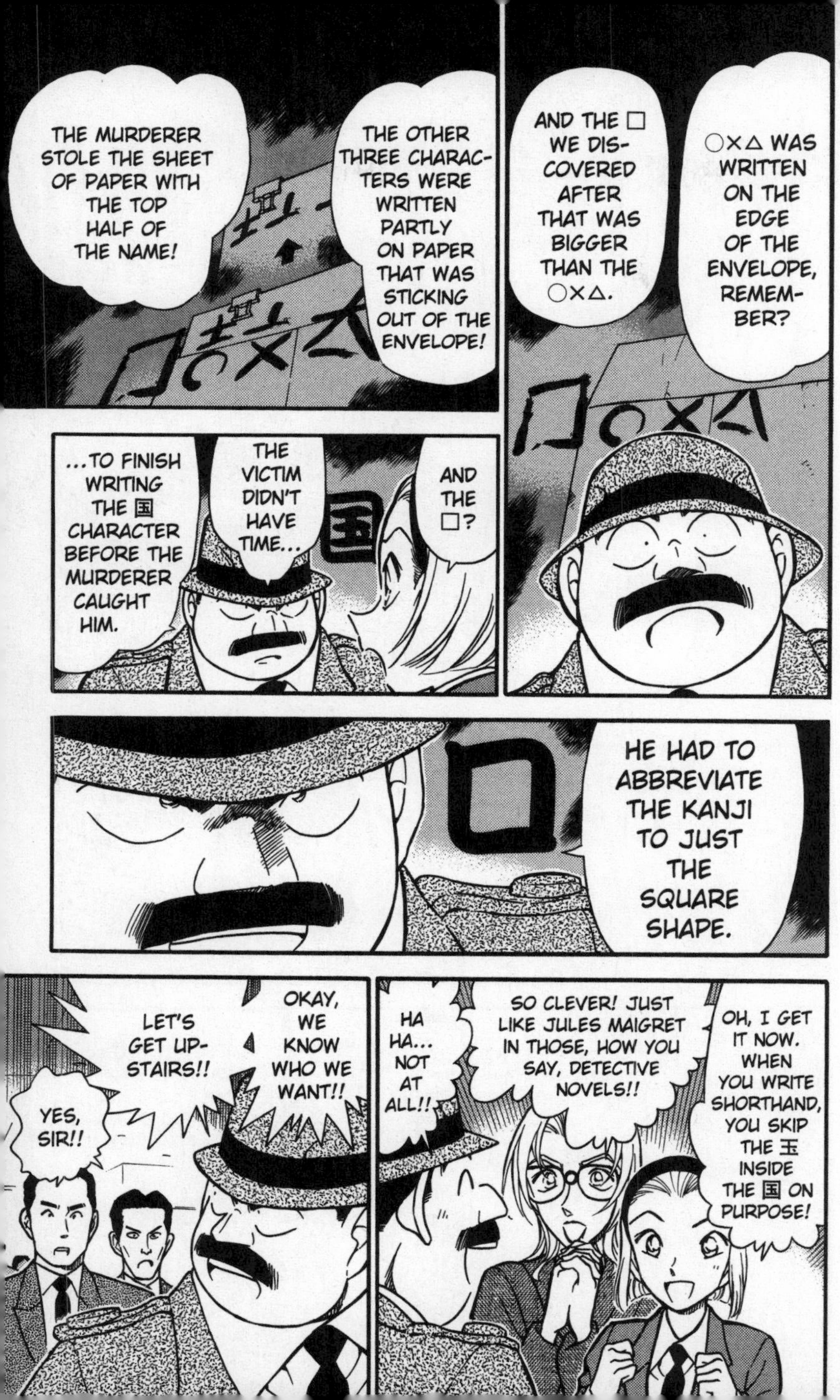
○×△ WAS WRITTEN ON THE EDGE OF THE ENVELOPE, REMEMBER?
AND THE □ WE DIS-COVERED AFTER THAT WAS BIGGER THAN THE ○×△.
THE OTHER THREE CHARAC-TERS WERE WRITTEN PARTLY ON PAPER THAT WAS STICKING OUT OF THE ENVELOPE!
THE MURDERER STOLE THE SHEET OF PAPER WITH THE TOP HALF OF THE NAME!
AND THE □?
THE VICTIM DIDN'T HAVE TIME...
...TO FINISH WRITING THE 国 CHARACTER BEFORE THE MURDERER CAUGHT HIM.
HE HAD TO ABBREVIATE THE KANJI TO JUST THE SQUARE SHAPE.
OH, I GET IT NOW. WHEN YOU WRITE SHORTHAND, YOU SKIP THE 玉 INSIDE THE 国 ON PURPOSE!
SO CLEVER! JUST LIKE JULES MAIGRET IN THOSE, HOW YOU SAY, DETECTIVE NOVELS!!
HA HA... NOT AT ALL!!
OKAY, WE KNOW WHO WE WANT!!
LET'S GET UP-STAIRS!!
YES, SIR!!

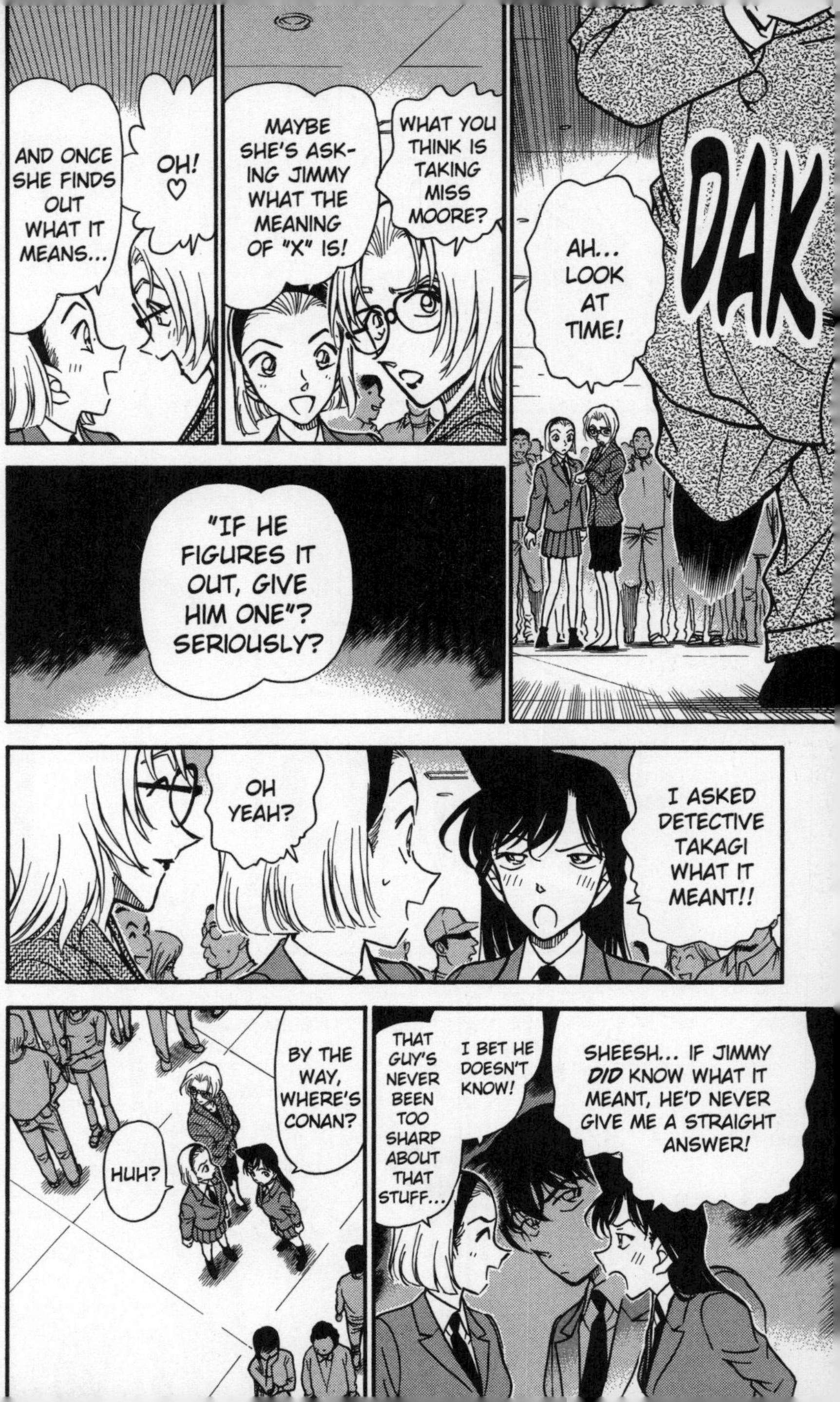
DAK
AH... LOOK AT TIME!
WHAT YOU THINK IS TAKING MISS MOORE?
MAYBE SHE'S ASK-ING JIMMY WHAT THE MEANING OF "X" IS!
OH! ♡
AND ONCE SHE FINDS OUT WHAT IT MEANS...
"IF HE FIGURES IT OUT, GIVE HIM ONE"? SERIOUSLY?
I ASKED DETECTIVE TAKAGI WHAT IT MEANT!!
OH YEAH?
SHEESH... IF JIMMY *DID* KNOW WHAT IT MEANT, HE'D NEVER GIVE ME A STRAIGHT ANSWER!
I BET HE DOESN'T KNOW!
THAT GUY'S NEVER BEEN TOO SHARP ABOUT THAT STUFF...
BY THE WAY, WHERE'S CONAN?
HUH?

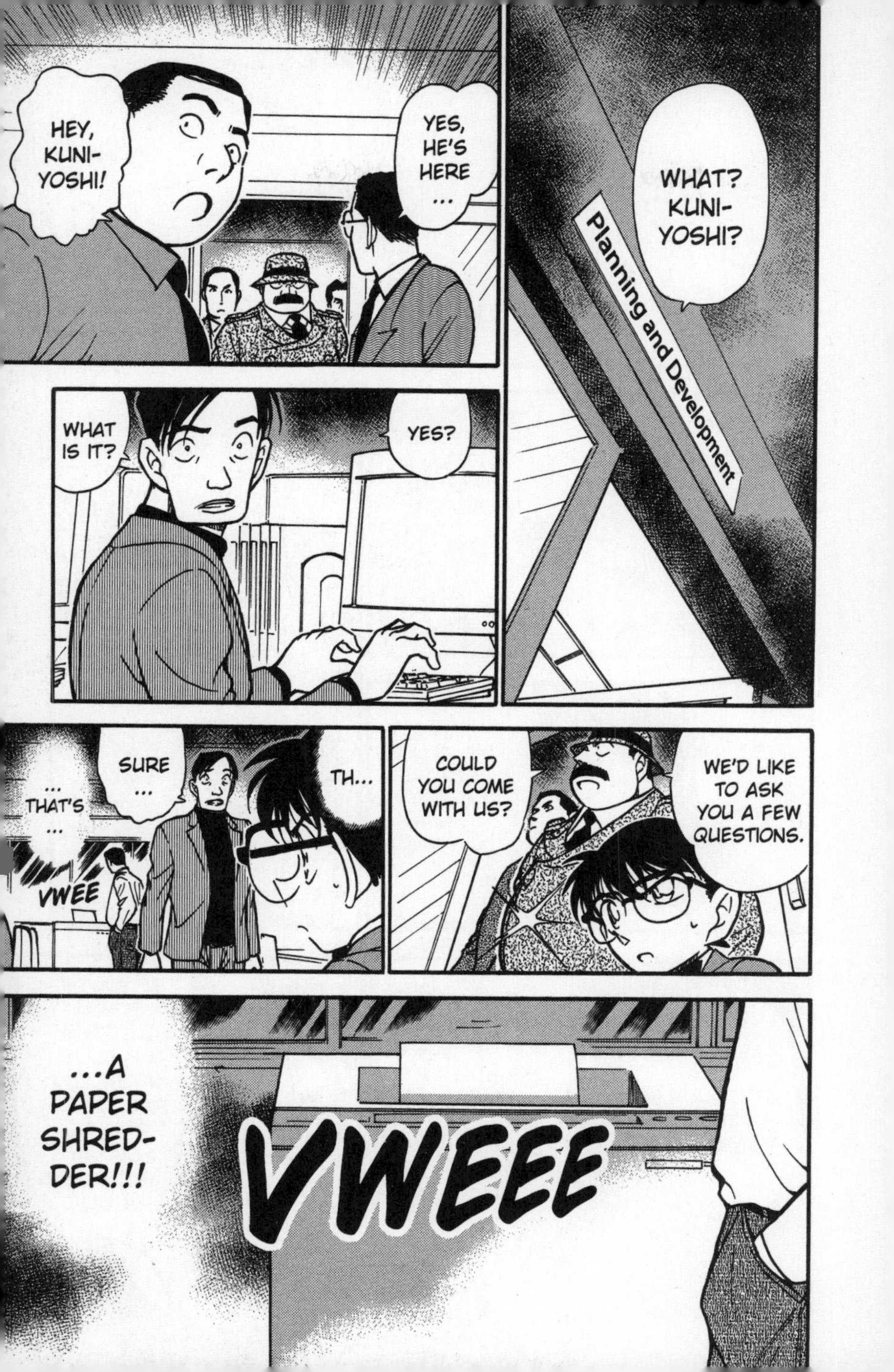
WHAT? KUNI-YOSHI?
Planning and Development
YES, HE'S HERE ...
HEY, KUNI-YOSHI!
YES?
WHAT IS IT?
WE'D LIKE TO ASK YOU A FEW QUESTIONS.
COULD YOU COME WITH US?
TH...
SURE ...
... THAT'S ...
VWEE
...A PAPER SHRED-DER!!!
VWEEE

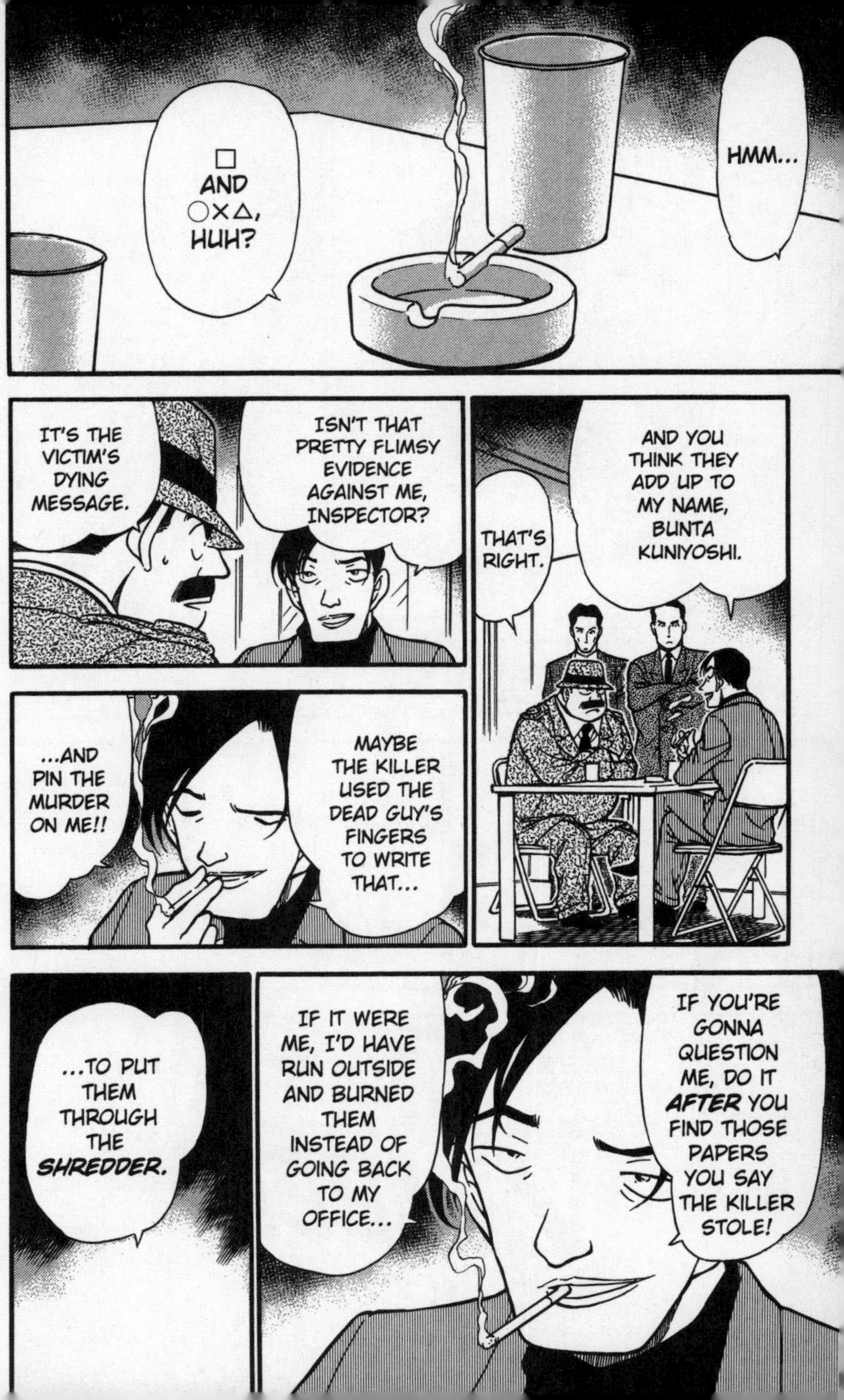
HMM...
□ AND ○×△, HUH?
AND YOU THINK THEY ADD UP TO MY NAME, BUNTA KUNIYOSHI.
THAT'S RIGHT.
ISN'T THAT PRETTY FLIMSY EVIDENCE AGAINST ME, INSPECTOR?
IT'S THE VICTIM'S DYING MESSAGE.
MAYBE THE KILLER USED THE DEAD GUY'S FINGERS TO WRITE THAT...
...AND PIN THE MURDER ON ME!!
IF YOU'RE GONNA QUESTION ME, DO IT ***AFTER*** YOU FIND THOSE PAPERS YOU SAY THE KILLER STOLE!
IF IT WERE ME, I'D HAVE RUN OUTSIDE AND BURNED THEM INSTEAD OF GOING BACK TO MY OFFICE...
...TO PUT THEM THROUGH THE ***SHREDDER.***

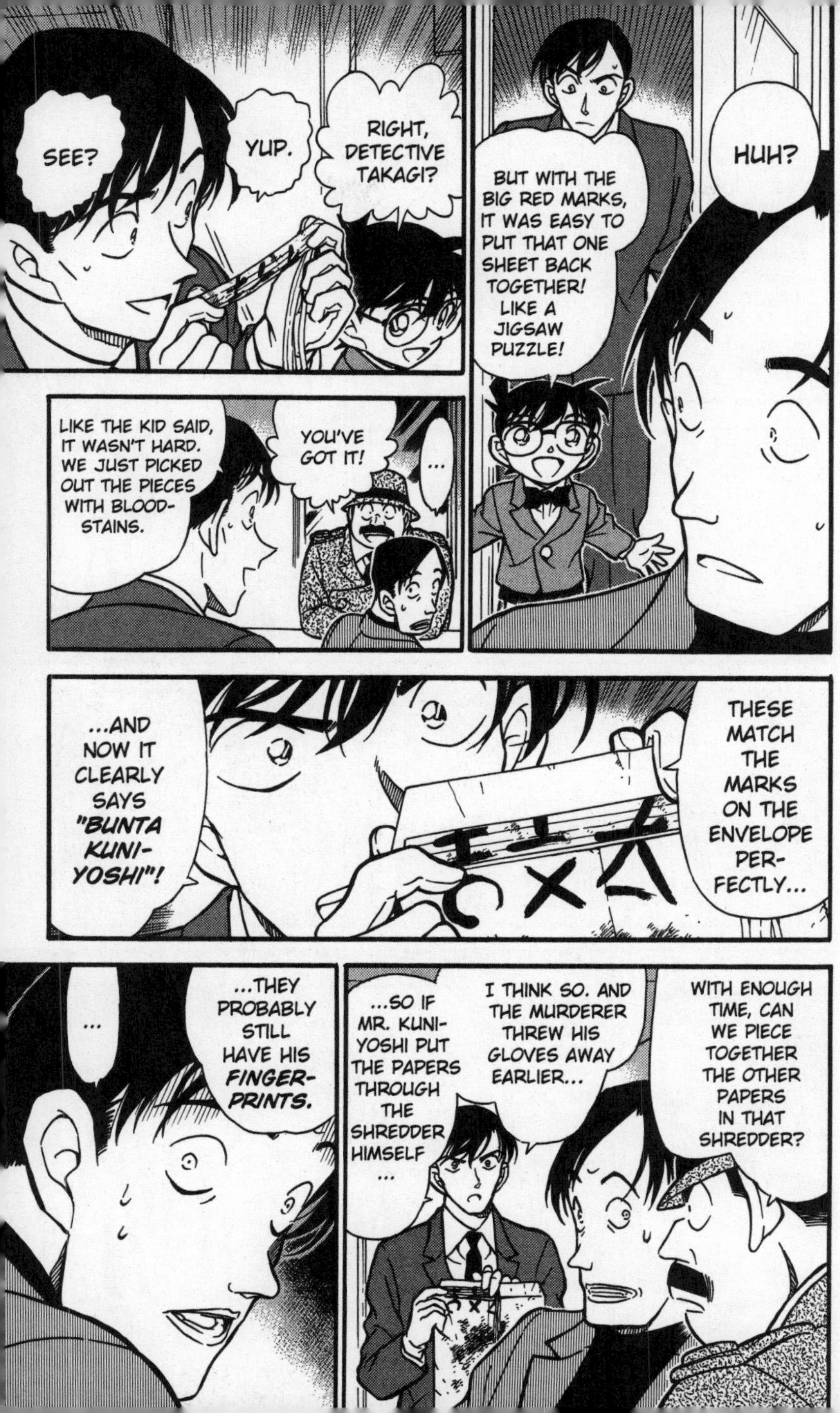
HUH?
BUT WITH THE BIG RED MARKS, IT WAS EASY TO PUT THAT ONE SHEET BACK TOGETHER! LIKE A JIGSAW PUZZLE!
RIGHT, DETECTIVE TAKAGI?
YUP.
SEE?
...
YOU'VE GOT IT!
LIKE THE KID SAID, IT WASN'T HARD. WE JUST PICKED OUT THE PIECES WITH BLOOD-STAINS.
THESE MATCH THE MARKS ON THE ENVELOPE PER-FECTLY...
...AND NOW IT CLEARLY SAYS *"BUNTA KUNI-YOSHI"*!
WITH ENOUGH TIME, CAN WE PIECE TOGETHER THE OTHER PAPERS IN THAT SHREDDER?
I THINK SO. AND THE MURDERER THREW HIS GLOVES AWAY EARLIER...
...SO IF MR. KUNI-YOSHI PUT THE PAPERS THROUGH THE SHREDDER HIMSELF ...
...THEY PROBABLY STILL HAVE HIS *FINGER-PRINTS.*
...

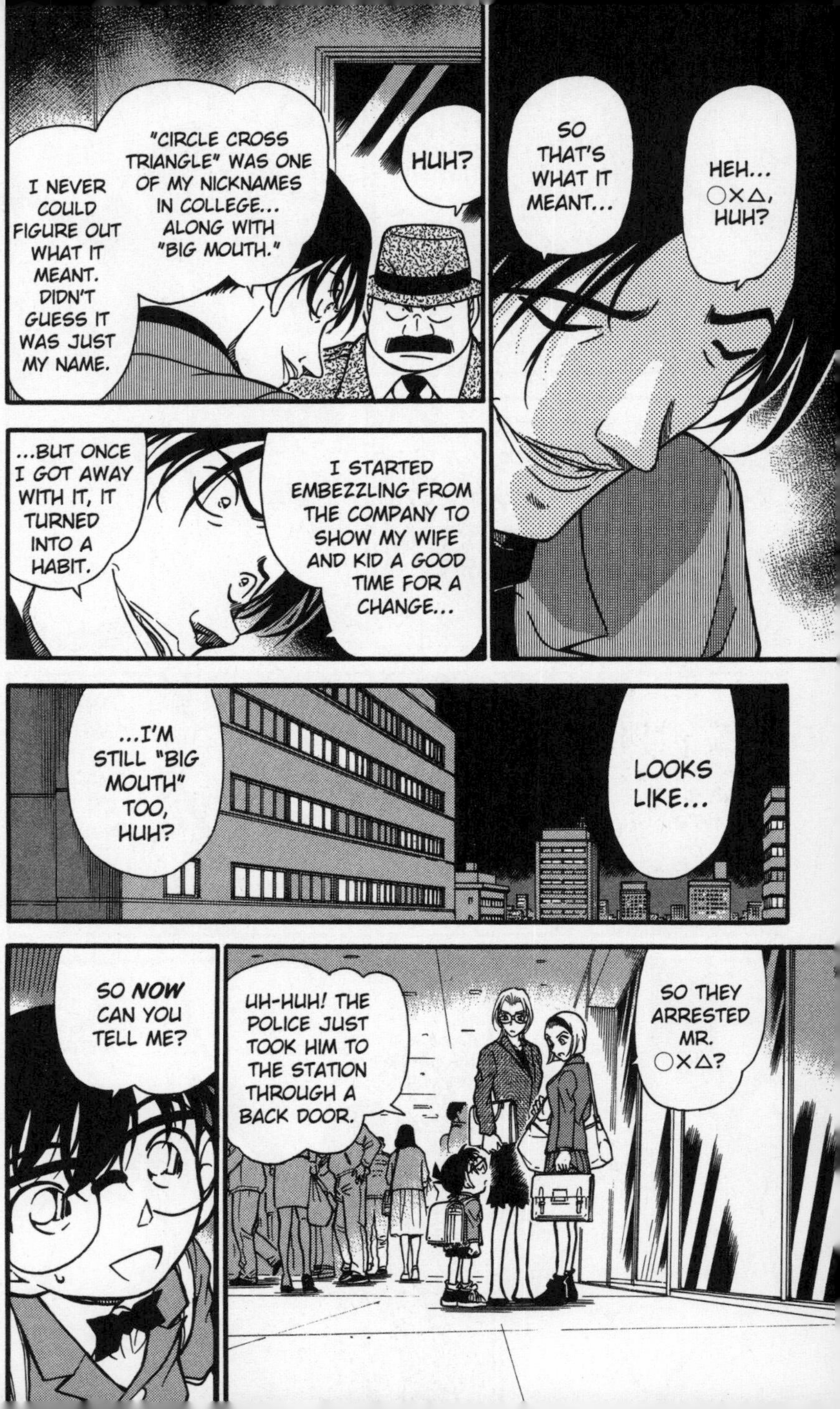
HEH... ○×△, HUH?
SO THAT'S WHAT IT MEANT...
HUH?
"CIRCLE CROSS TRIANGLE" WAS ONE OF MY NICKNAMES IN COLLEGE... ALONG WITH "BIG MOUTH."
I NEVER COULD FIGURE OUT WHAT IT MEANT. DIDN'T GUESS IT WAS JUST MY NAME.
I STARTED EMBEZZLING FROM THE COMPANY TO SHOW MY WIFE AND KID A GOOD TIME FOR A CHANGE...
...BUT ONCE I GOT AWAY WITH IT, IT TURNED INTO A HABIT.
LOOKS LIKE...
...I'M STILL "BIG MOUTH" TOO, HUH?
SO THEY ARRESTED MR. ○×△?
UH-HUH! THE POLICE JUST TOOK HIM TO THE STATION THROUGH A BACK DOOR.
SO *NOW* CAN YOU TELL ME?

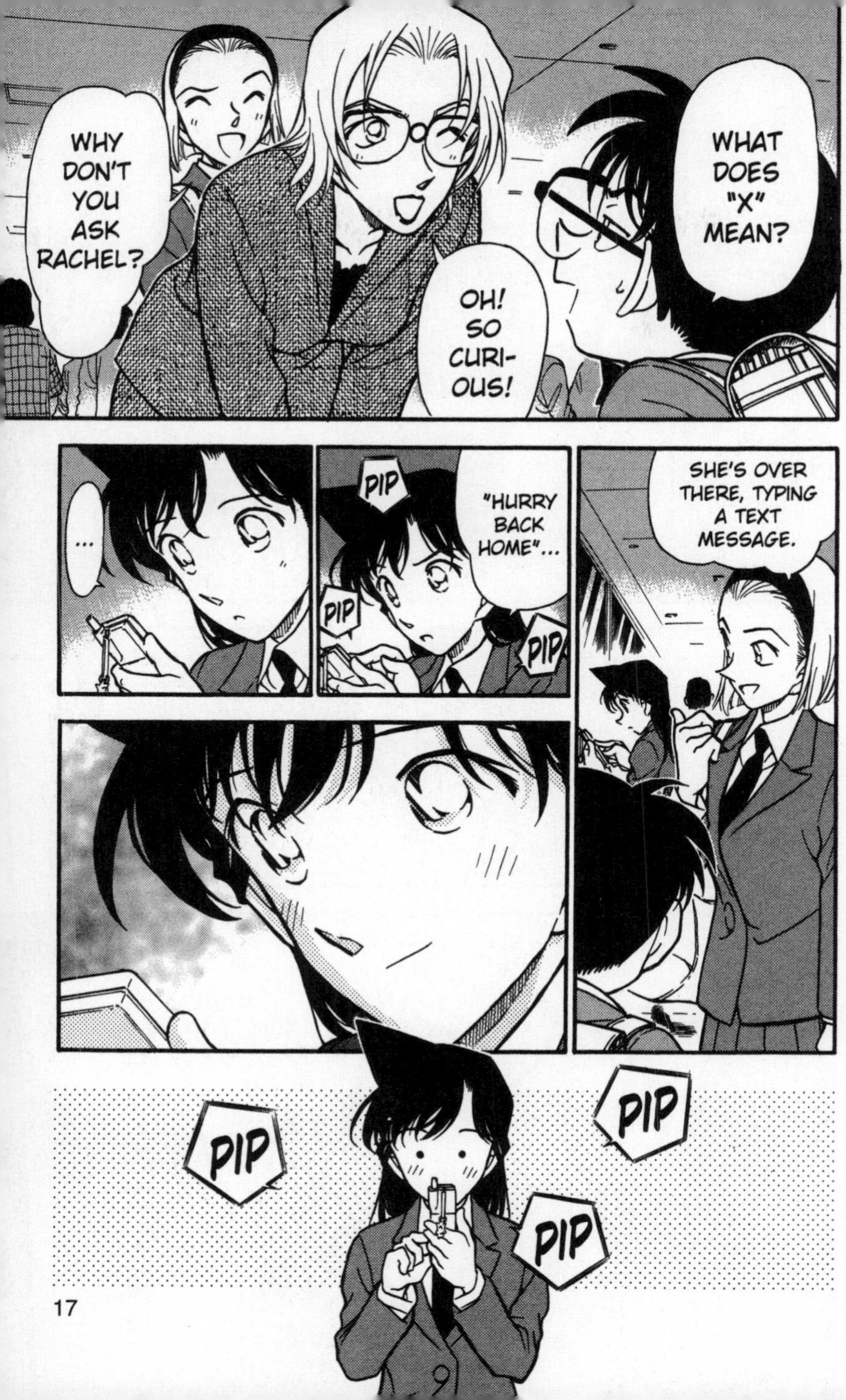
WHAT DOES "X" MEAN?
OH! SO CURI-OUS!
WHY DON'T YOU ASK RACHEL?
SHE'S OVER THERE, TYPING A TEXT MESSAGE.
PIP
"HURRY BACK HOME"...
PIP
PIP
...
PIP
PIP
PIP

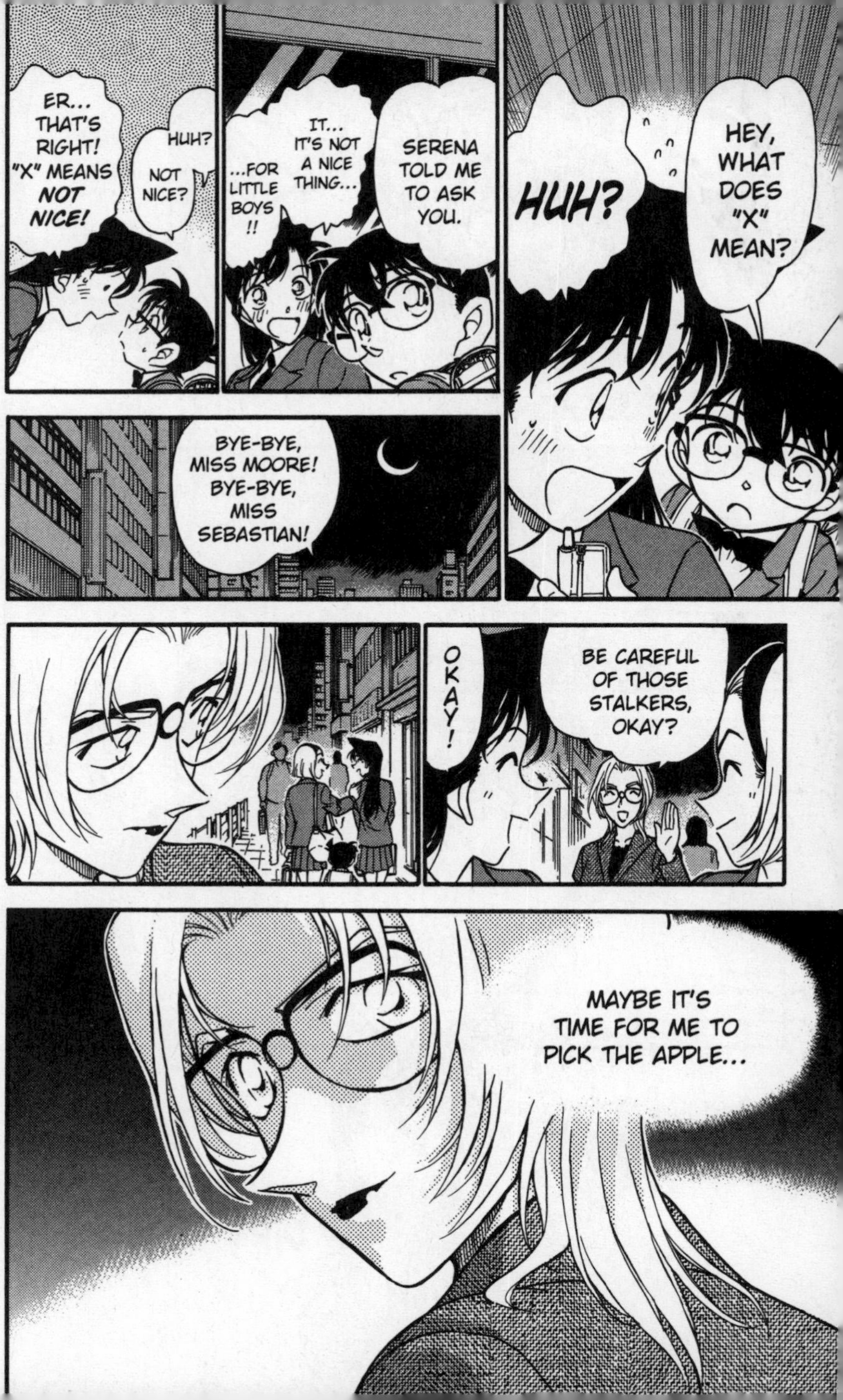
HEY, WHAT DOES "X" MEAN?
HUH?
SERENA TOLD ME TO ASK YOU.
IT... IT'S NOT A NICE THING...
...FOR LITTLE BOYS !!
HUH? NOT NICE?
ER... THAT'S RIGHT! "X" MEANS NOT NICE!
BYE-BYE, MISS MOORE! BYE-BYE, MISS SEBASTIAN!
BE CAREFUL OF THOSE STALKERS, OKAY?
OKAY!
MAYBE IT'S TIME FOR ME TO PICK THE APPLE...

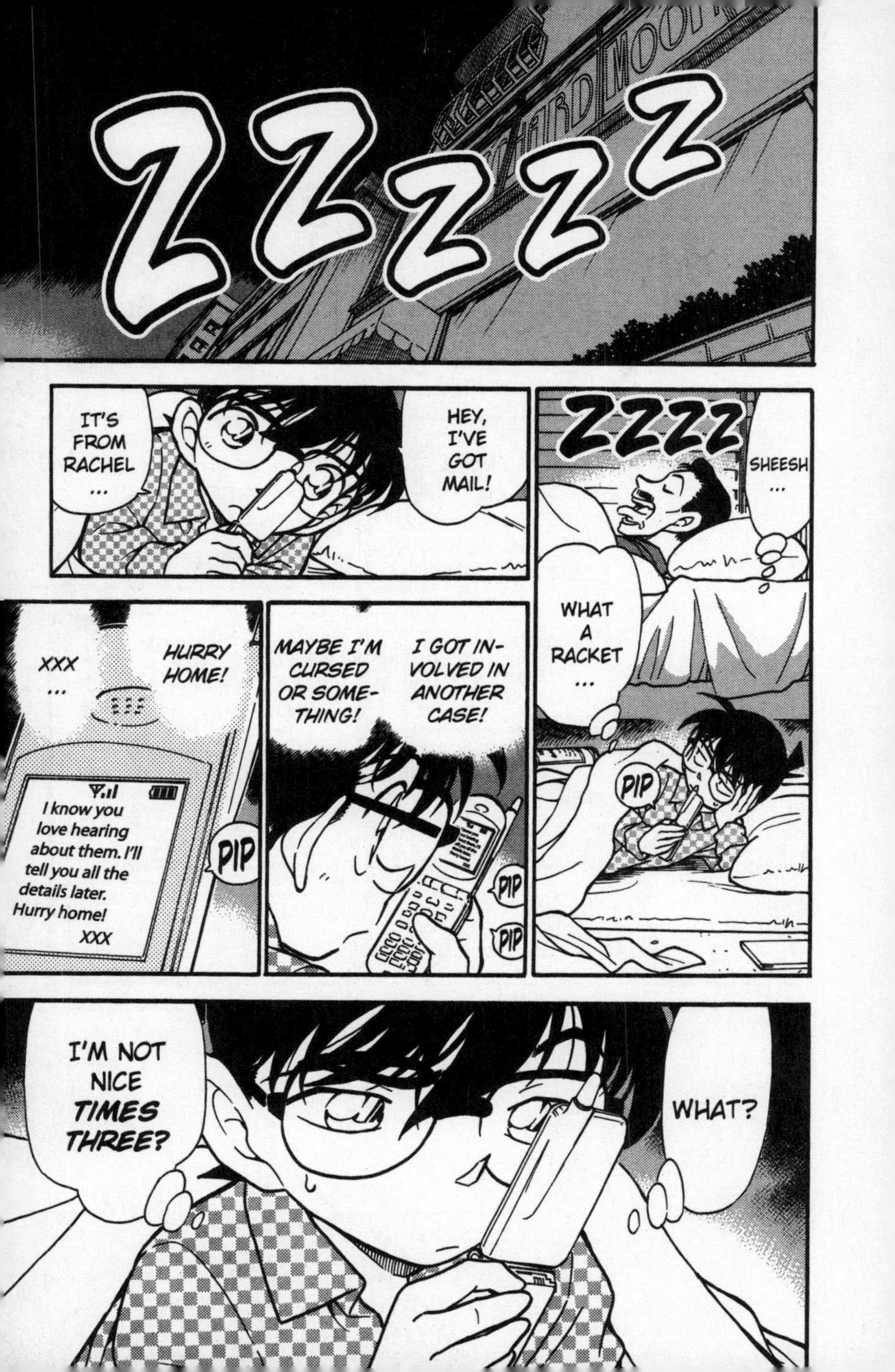
ZZZZZ
ZZZZ
SHEESH ...
WHAT A RACKET ...
PIP
HEY, I'VE GOT MAIL!
IT'S FROM RACHEL ...
I GOT IN-VOLVED IN ANOTHER CASE!
MAYBE I'M CURSED OR SOME-THING!
PIP
PIP
HURRY HOME!
XXX ...
I know you love hearing about them. I'll tell you all the details later. Hurry home!
XXX
PIP
WHAT?
I'M NOT NICE *TIMES THREE?*

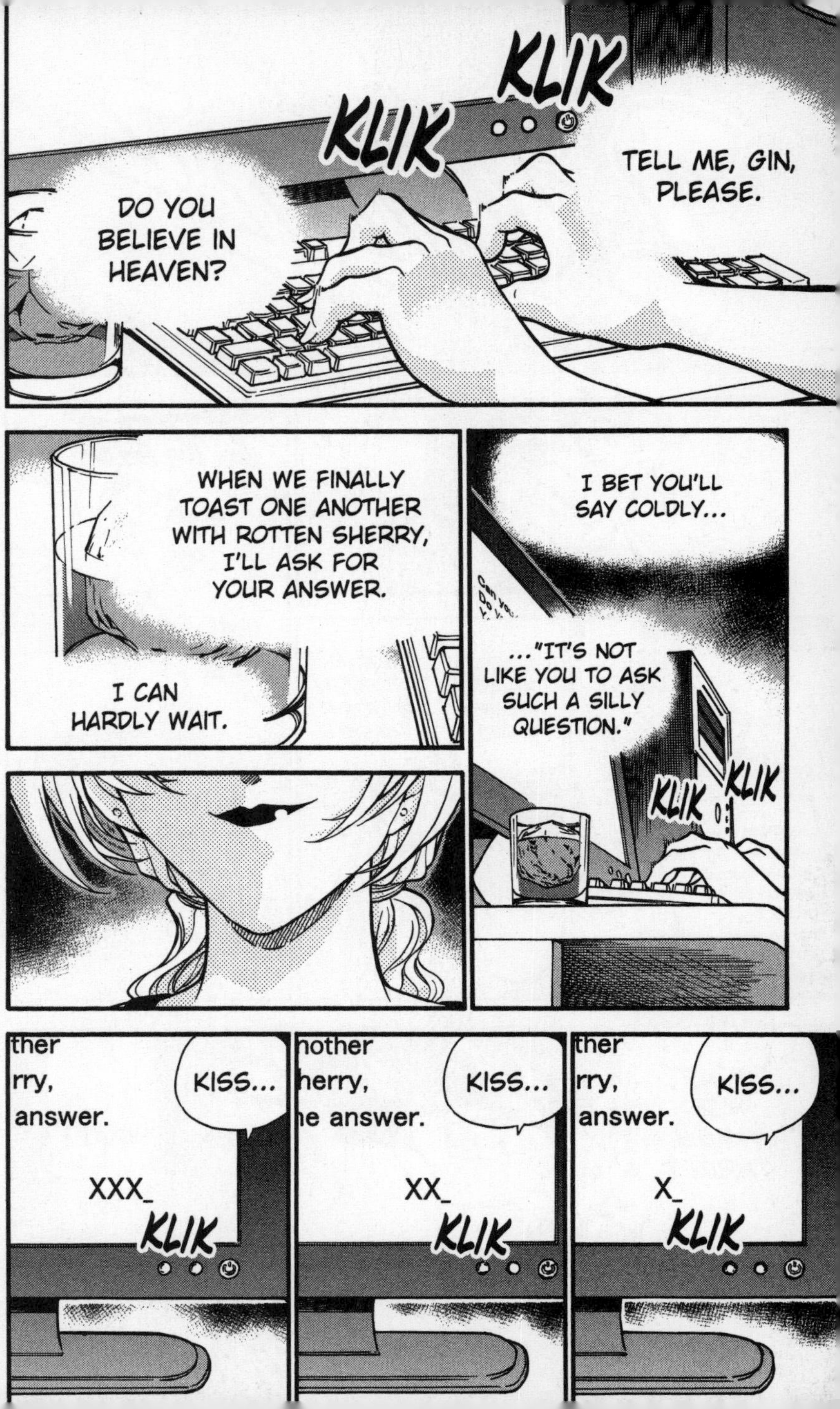
KLIK
KLIK
TELL ME, GIN, PLEASE.
DO YOU BELIEVE IN HEAVEN?
I BET YOU'LL SAY COLDLY...
..."IT'S NOT LIKE YOU TO ASK SUCH A SILLY QUESTION."
KLIK
KLIK
WHEN WE FINALLY TOAST ONE ANOTHER WITH ROTTEN SHERRY, I'LL ASK FOR YOUR ANSWER.
I CAN HARDLY WAIT.
KISS...
ther
rry,
answer.
X_
KLIK
KISS...
nother
herry,
he answer.
XX_
KLIK
KISS...
ther
rry,
answer.
XXX_
KLIK

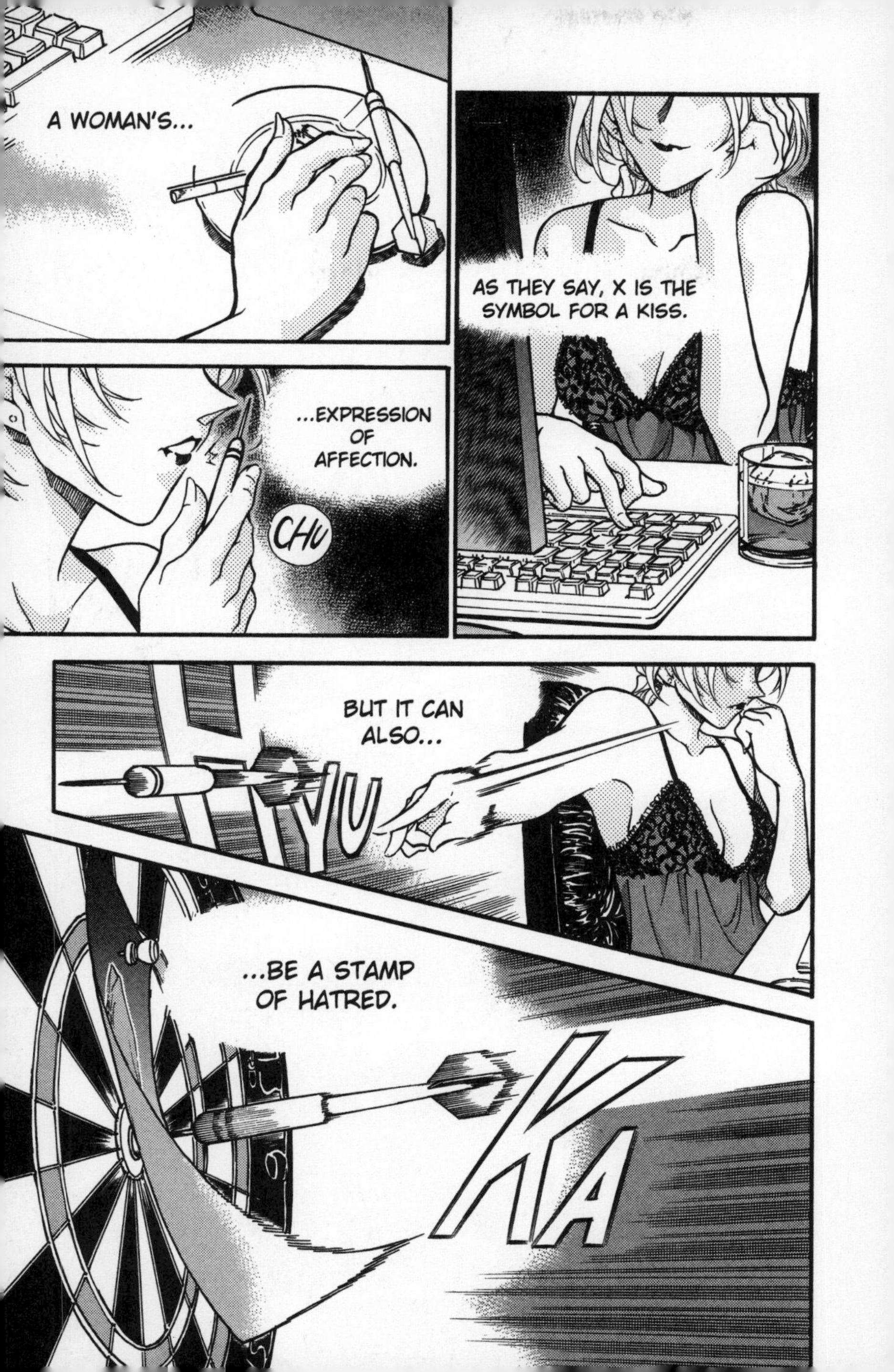
AS THEY SAY, X IS THE SYMBOL FOR A KISS.
A WOMAN'S...
...EXPRESSION OF AFFECTION.
CHU
BUT IT CAN ALSO...
YU
...BE A STAMP OF HATRED.
KA

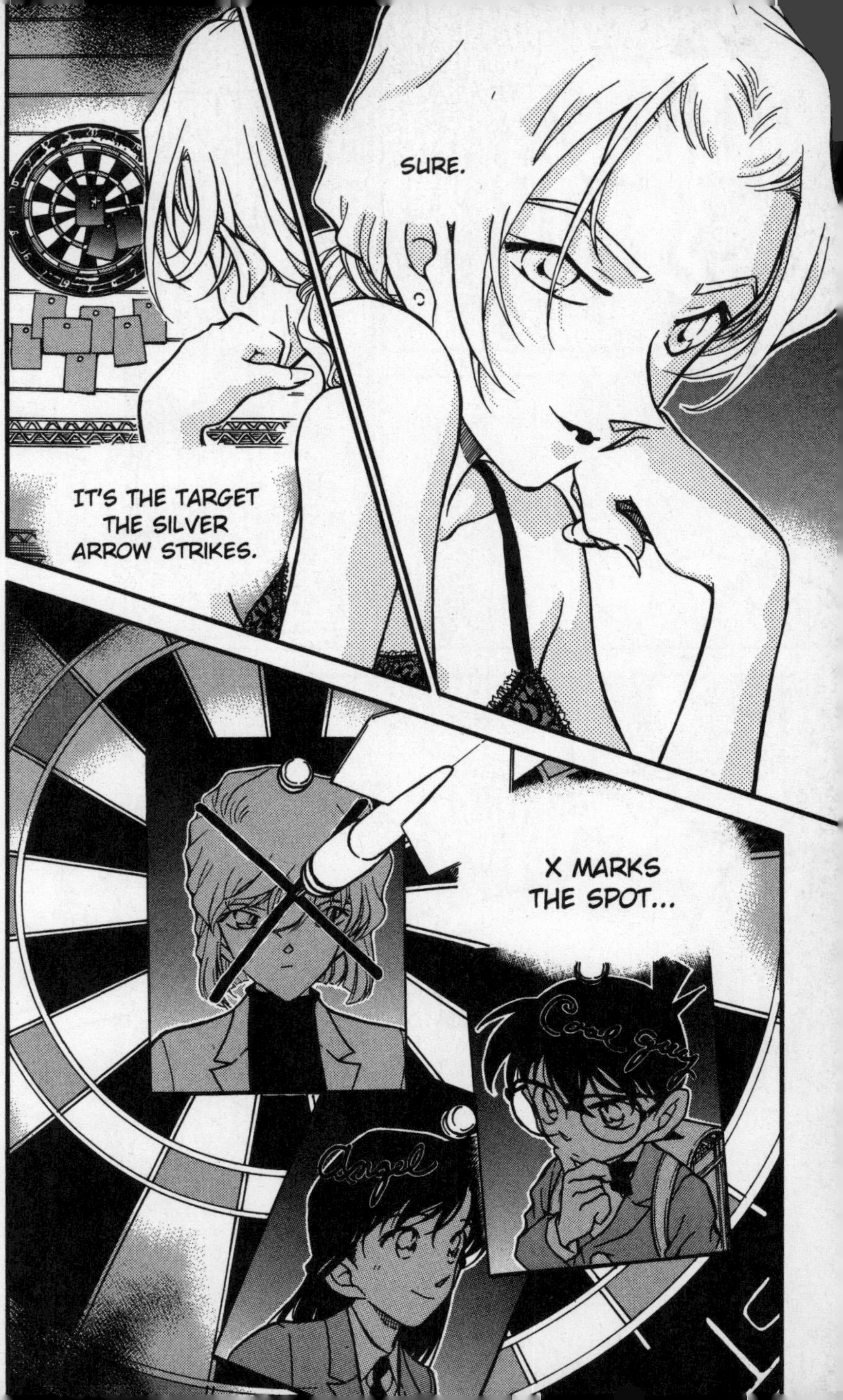
SURE.
IT'S THE TARGET THE SILVER ARROW STRIKES.
X MARKS THE SPOT...
Cool guy
Angel

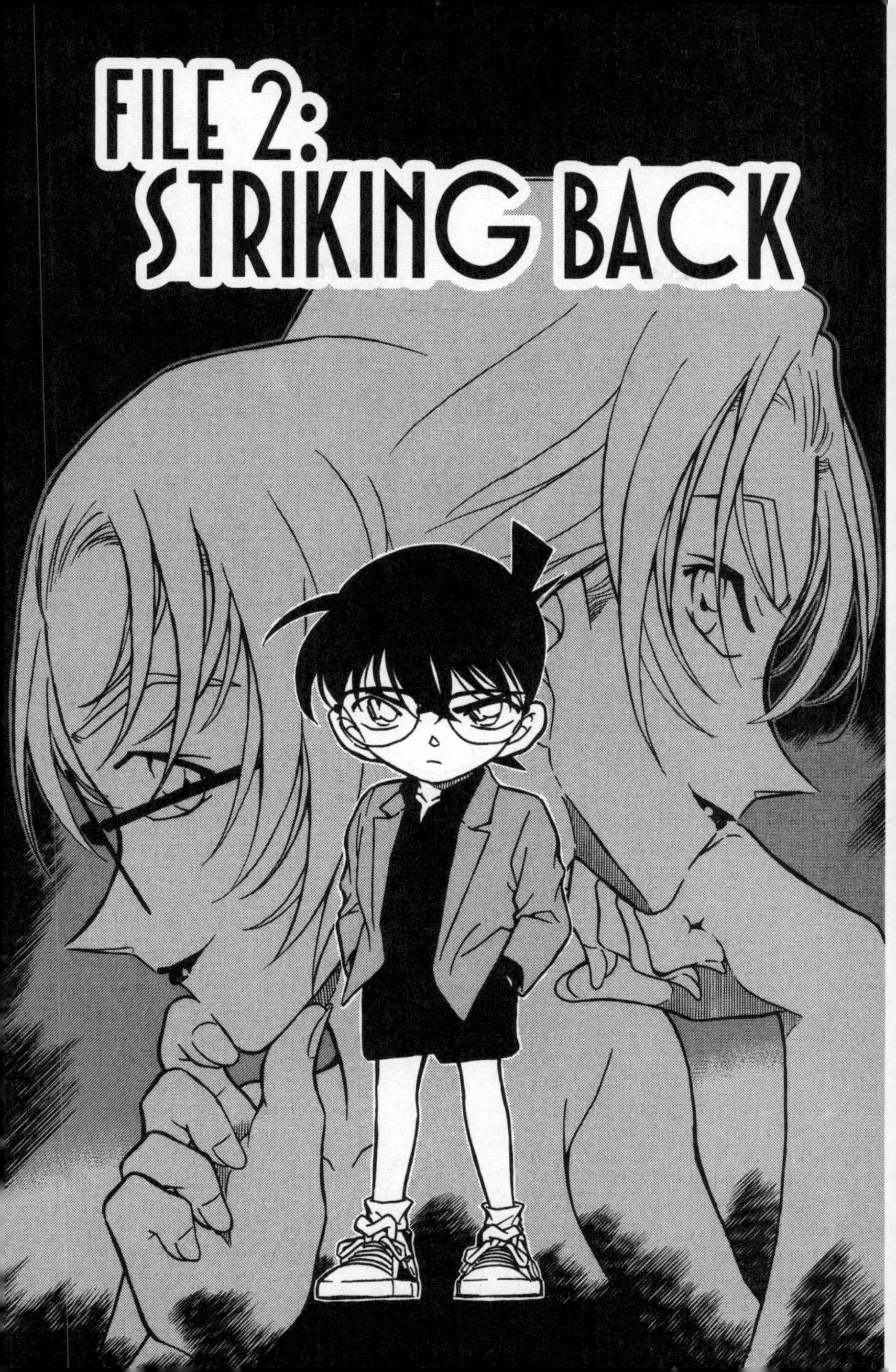
FILE 2:
STRIKING BACK

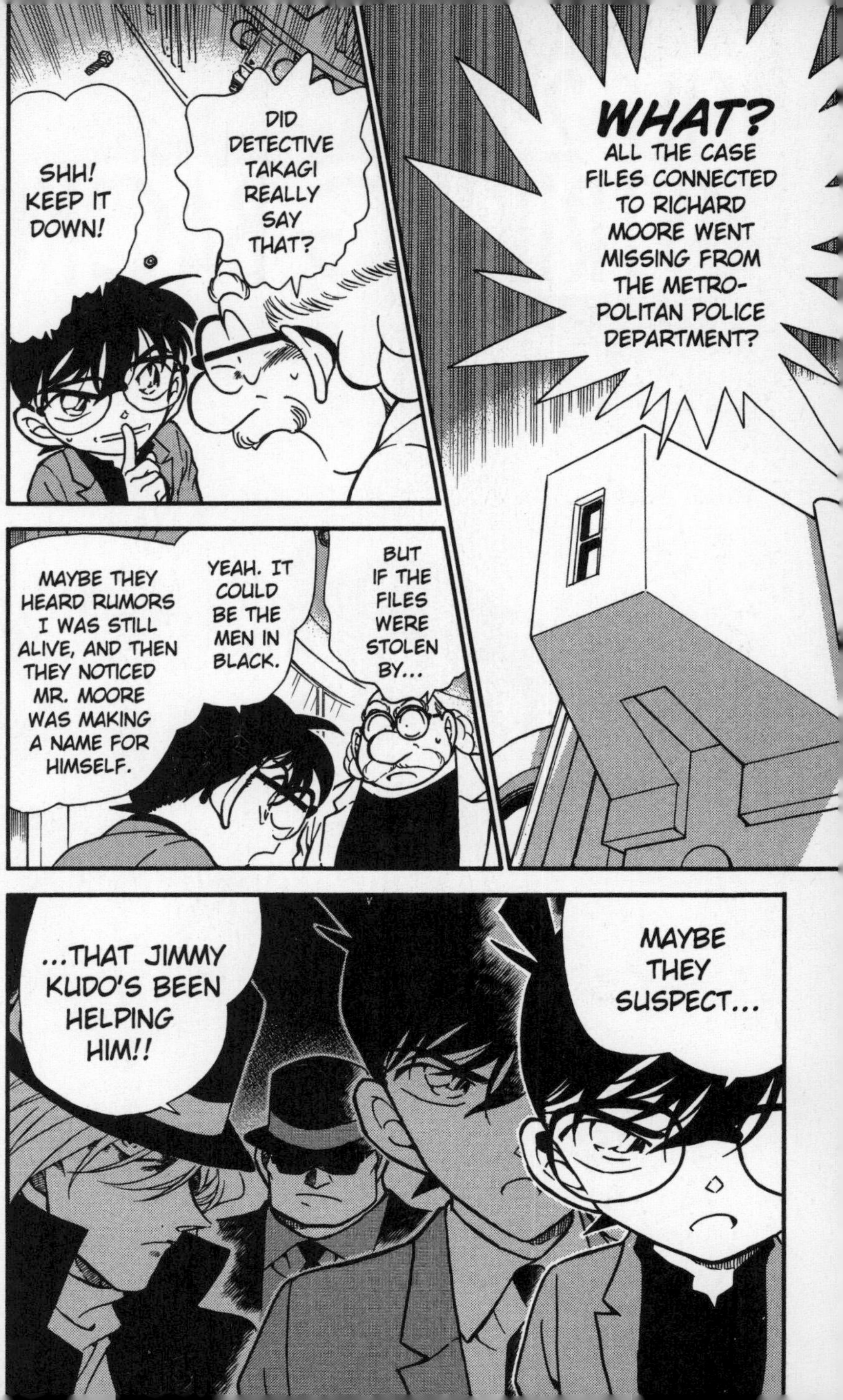
WHAT? ALL THE CASE FILES CONNECTED TO RICHARD MOORE WENT MISSING FROM THE METRO-POLITAN POLICE DEPARTMENT?
DID DETECTIVE TAKAGI REALLY SAY THAT?
SHH! KEEP IT DOWN!
BUT IF THE FILES WERE STOLEN BY...
YEAH. IT COULD BE THE MEN IN BLACK.
MAYBE THEY HEARD RUMORS I WAS STILL ALIVE, AND THEN THEY NOTICED MR. MOORE WAS MAKING A NAME FOR HIMSELF.
MAYBE THEY SUSPECT...
...THAT JIMMY KUDO'S BEEN HELPING HIM!!

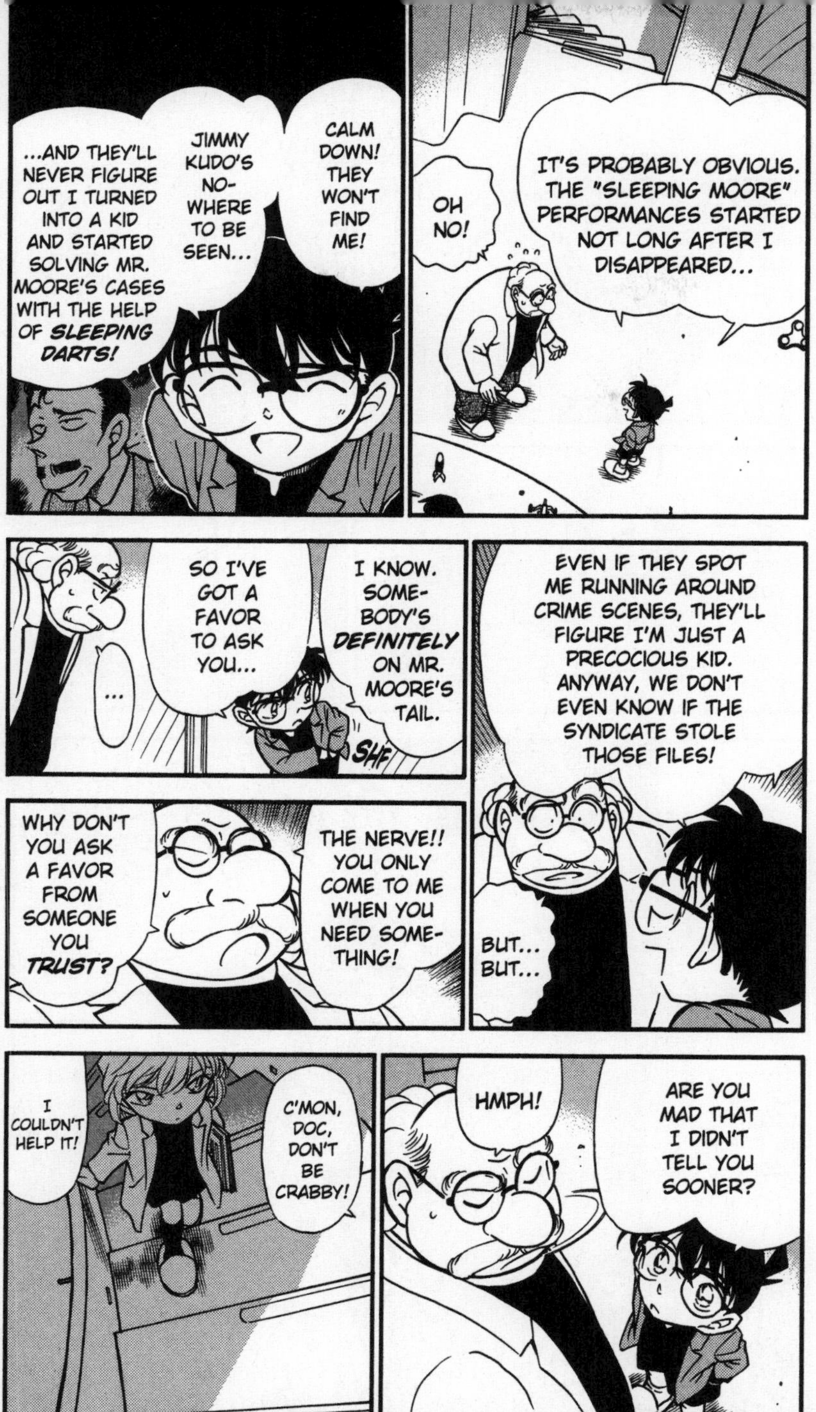
IT'S PROBABLY OBVIOUS. THE "SLEEPING MOORE" PERFORMANCES STARTED NOT LONG AFTER I DISAPPEARED...
OH NO!
CALM DOWN! THEY WON'T FIND ME!
JIMMY KUDO'S NO-WHERE TO BE SEEN...
...AND THEY'LL NEVER FIGURE OUT I TURNED INTO A KID AND STARTED SOLVING MR. MOORE'S CASES WITH THE HELP OF SLEEPING DARTS!
EVEN IF THEY SPOT ME RUNNING AROUND CRIME SCENES, THEY'LL FIGURE I'M JUST A PRECOCIOUS KID. ANYWAY, WE DON'T EVEN KNOW IF THE SYNDICATE STOLE THOSE FILES!
BUT... BUT...
I KNOW. SOME-BODY'S DEFINITELY ON MR. MOORE'S TAIL.
SHF
SO I'VE GOT A FAVOR TO ASK YOU...
...
THE NERVE!! YOU ONLY COME TO ME WHEN YOU NEED SOME-THING!
WHY DON'T YOU ASK A FAVOR FROM SOMEONE YOU TRUST?
ARE YOU MAD THAT I DIDN'T TELL YOU SOONER?
HMPH!
C'MON, DOC, DON'T BE CRABBY!
I COULDN'T HELP IT!

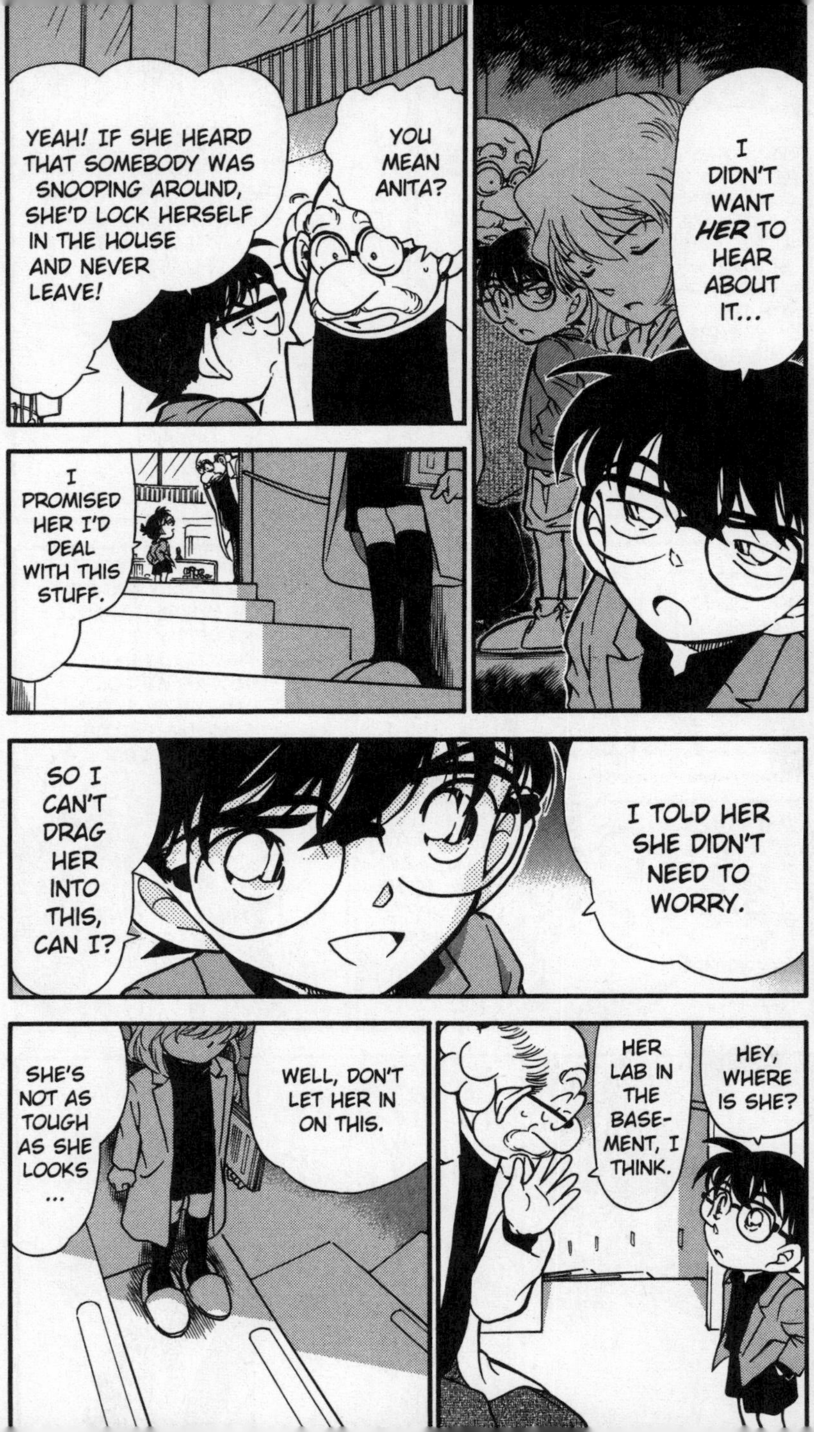
I DIDN'T WANT HER TO HEAR ABOUT IT...
YOU MEAN ANITA?
YEAH! IF SHE HEARD THAT SOMEBODY WAS SNOOPING AROUND, SHE'D LOCK HERSELF IN THE HOUSE AND NEVER LEAVE!
I PROMISED HER I'D DEAL WITH THIS STUFF.
I TOLD HER SHE DIDN'T NEED TO WORRY.
SO I CAN'T DRAG HER INTO THIS, CAN I?
HEY, WHERE IS SHE?
HER LAB IN THE BASEMENT, I THINK.
WELL, DON'T LET HER IN ON THIS.
SHE'S NOT AS TOUGH AS SHE LOOKS...

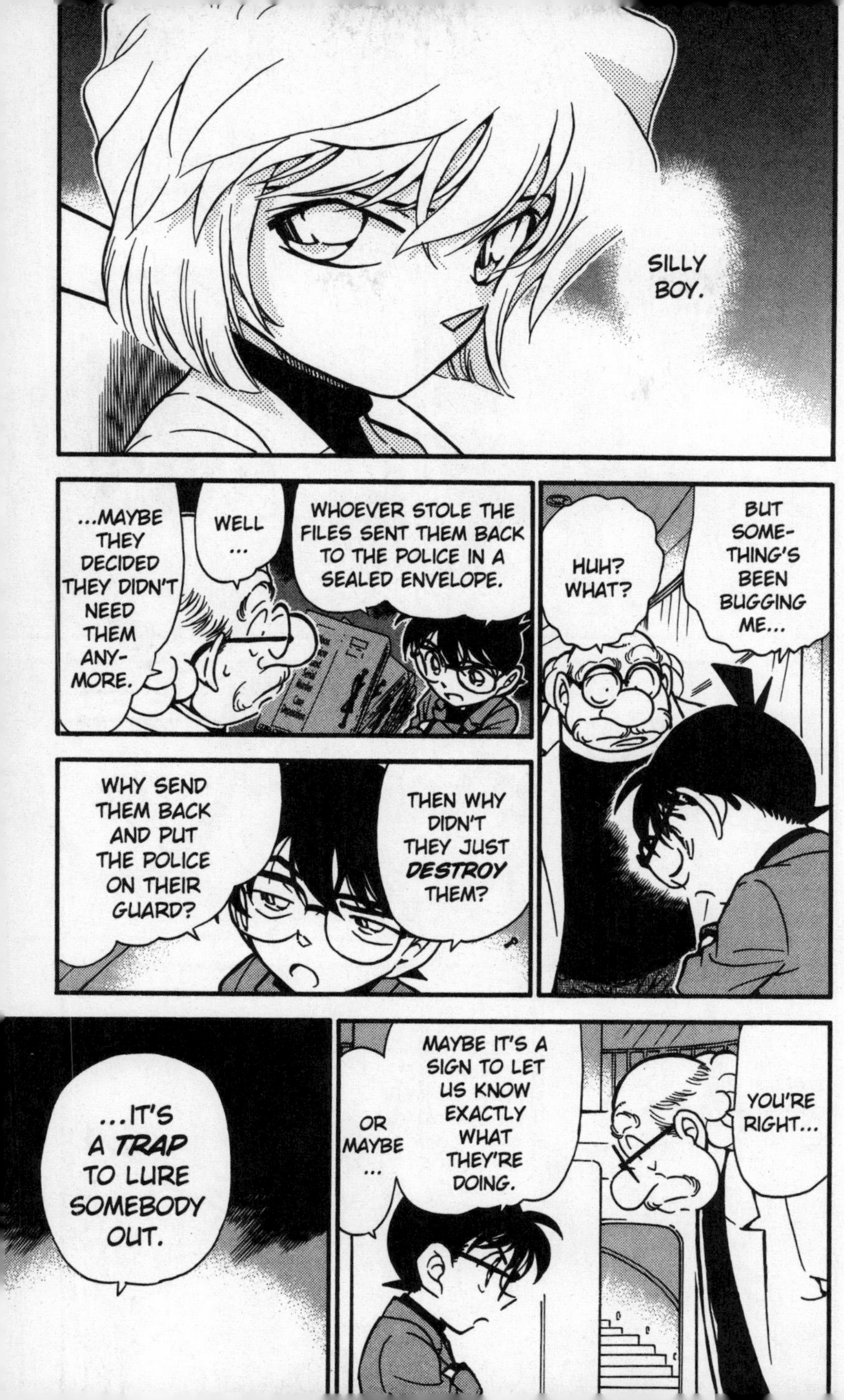
SILLY BOY.
BUT SOMETHING'S BEEN BUGGING ME...
HUH? WHAT?
WHOEVER STOLE THE FILES SENT THEM BACK TO THE POLICE IN A SEALED ENVELOPE.
WELL ...
...MAYBE THEY DECIDED THEY DIDN'T NEED THEM ANYMORE.
THEN WHY DIDN'T THEY JUST *DESTROY* THEM?
WHY SEND THEM BACK AND PUT THE POLICE ON THEIR GUARD?
YOU'RE RIGHT...
MAYBE IT'S A SIGN TO LET US KNOW EXACTLY WHAT THEY'RE DOING.
OR MAYBE ...
...IT'S A *TRAP* TO LURE SOMEBODY OUT.

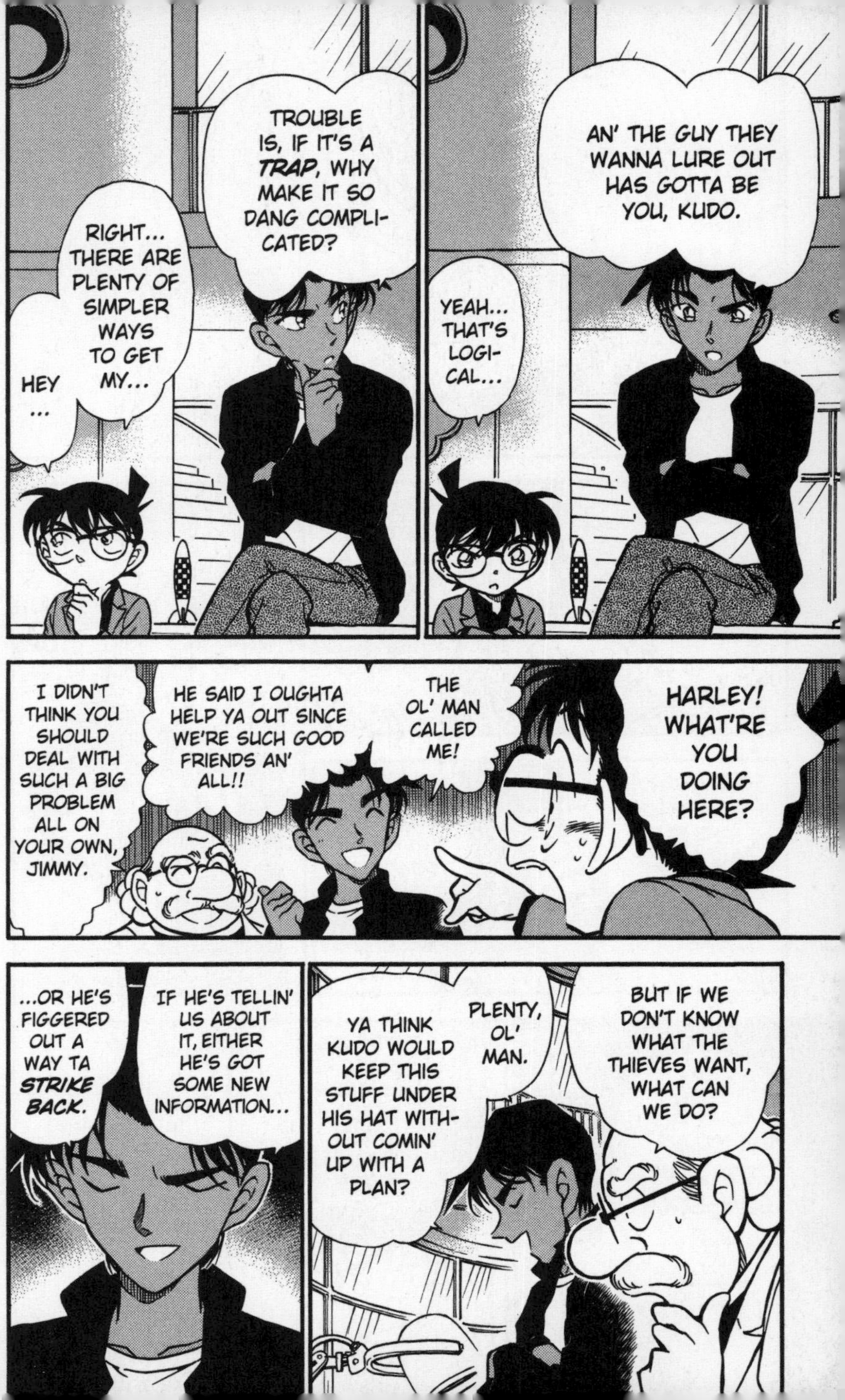
AN' THE GUY THEY WANNA LURE OUT HAS GOTTA BE YOU, KUDO.
YEAH... THAT'S LOGI-CAL...
TROUBLE IS, IF IT'S A *TRAP*, WHY MAKE IT SO DANG COMPLI-CATED?
RIGHT... THERE ARE PLENTY OF SIMPLER WAYS TO GET MY...
HEY ...
HARLEY! WHAT'RE YOU DOING HERE?
THE OL' MAN CALLED ME!
HE SAID I OUGHTA HELP YA OUT SINCE WE'RE SUCH GOOD FRIENDS AN' ALL!!
I DIDN'T THINK YOU SHOULD DEAL WITH SUCH A BIG PROBLEM ALL ON YOUR OWN, JIMMY.
BUT IF WE DON'T KNOW WHAT THE THIEVES WANT, WHAT CAN WE DO?
PLENTY, OL' MAN.
YA THINK KUDO WOULD KEEP THIS STUFF UNDER HIS HAT WITH-OUT COMIN' UP WITH A PLAN?
IF HE'S TELLIN' US ABOUT IT, EITHER HE'S GOT SOME NEW INFORMATION...
...OR HE'S FIGGERED OUT A WAY TA *STRIKE BACK*.

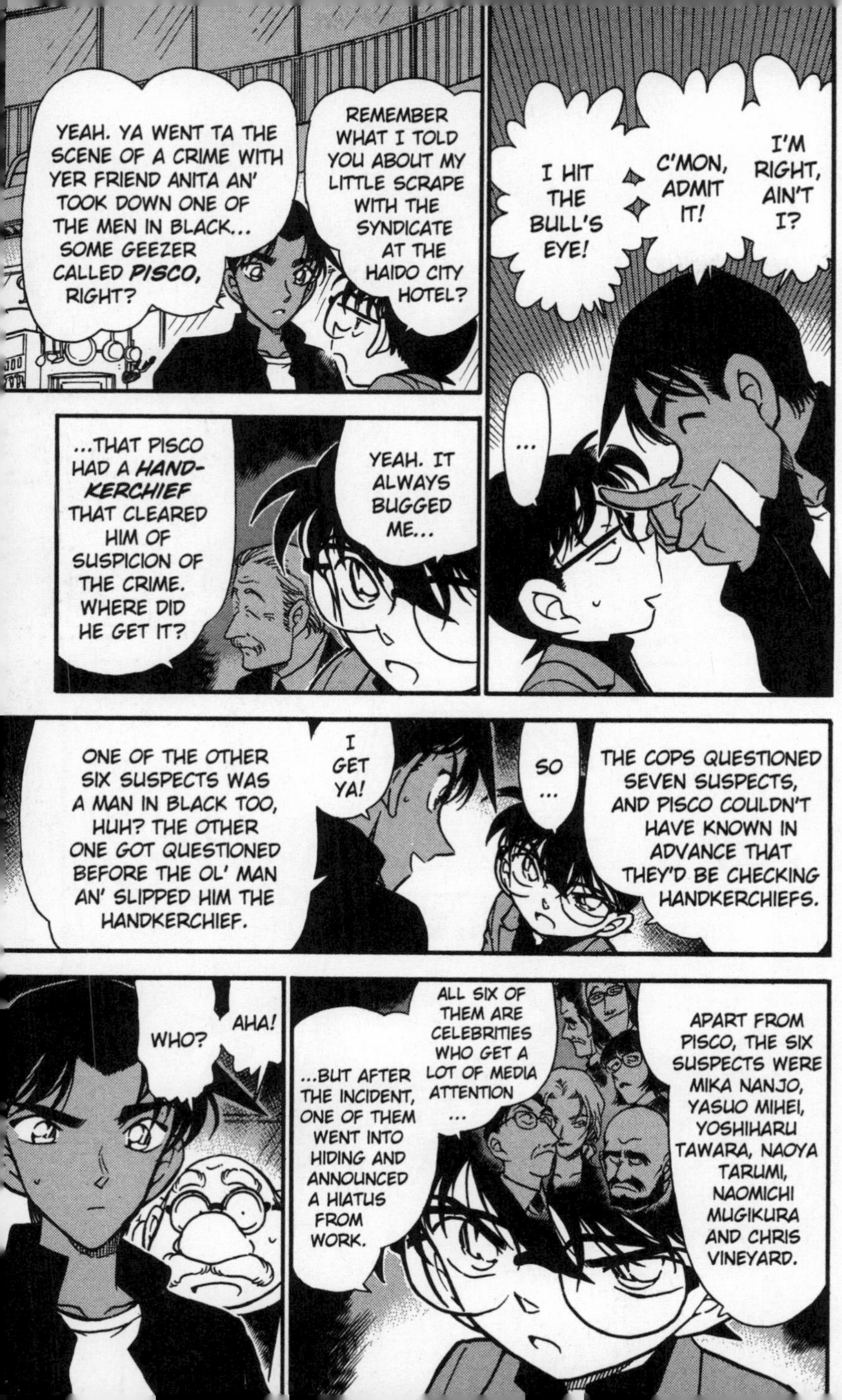
I'M RIGHT, AIN'T I?
C'MON, ADMIT IT!
I HIT THE BULL'S EYE!
...
REMEMBER WHAT I TOLD YOU ABOUT MY LITTLE SCRAPE WITH THE SYNDICATE AT THE HAIDO CITY HOTEL?
YEAH. YA WENT TA THE SCENE OF A CRIME WITH YER FRIEND ANITA AN' TOOK DOWN ONE OF THE MEN IN BLACK... SOME GEEZER CALLED PISCO, RIGHT?
YEAH. IT ALWAYS BUGGED ME...
...THAT PISCO HAD A HANDKERCHIEF THAT CLEARED HIM OF SUSPICION OF THE CRIME. WHERE DID HE GET IT?
THE COPS QUESTIONED SEVEN SUSPECTS, AND PISCO COULDN'T HAVE KNOWN IN ADVANCE THAT THEY'D BE CHECKING HANDKERCHIEFS.
SO ...
I GET YA!
ONE OF THE OTHER SIX SUSPECTS WAS A MAN IN BLACK TOO, HUH? THE OTHER ONE GOT QUESTIONED BEFORE THE OL' MAN AN' SLIPPED HIM THE HANDKERCHIEF.
APART FROM PISCO, THE SIX SUSPECTS WERE MIKA NANJO, YASUO MIHEI, YOSHIHARU TAWARA, NAOYA TARUMI, NAOMICHI MUGIKURA AND CHRIS VINEYARD.
ALL SIX OF THEM ARE CELEBRITIES WHO GET A LOT OF MEDIA ATTENTION ...
...BUT AFTER THE INCIDENT, ONE OF THEM WENT INTO HIDING AND ANNOUNCED A HIATUS FROM WORK.
AHA!
WHO?

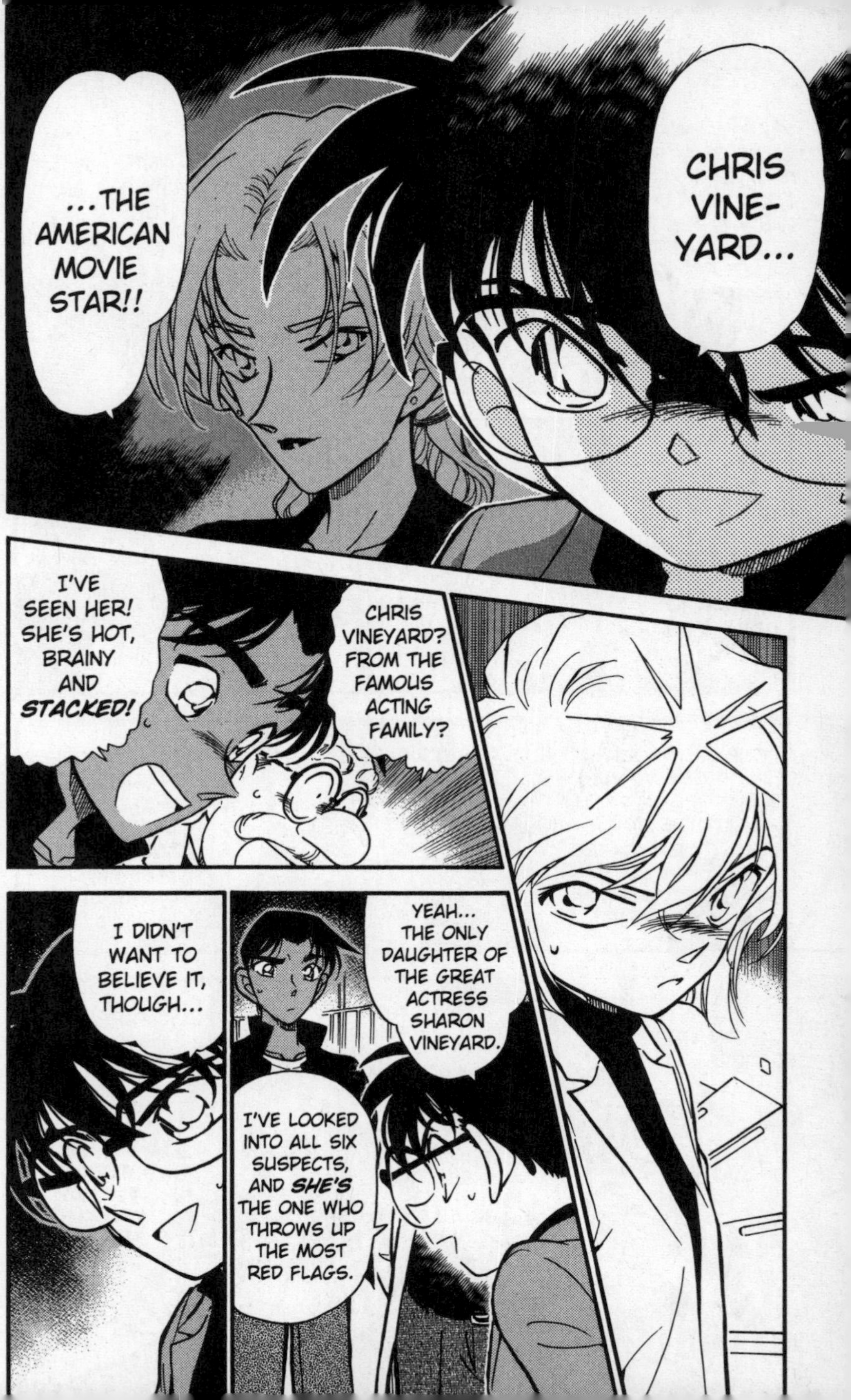
CHRIS VINE-YARD...
...THE AMERICAN MOVIE STAR!!
CHRIS VINEYARD? FROM THE FAMOUS ACTING FAMILY?
I'VE SEEN HER! SHE'S HOT, BRAINY AND *STACKED!*
YEAH... THE ONLY DAUGHTER OF THE GREAT ACTRESS SHARON VINEYARD.
I'VE LOOKED INTO ALL SIX SUSPECTS, AND *SHE'S* THE ONE WHO THROWS UP THE MOST RED FLAGS.
I DIDN'T WANT TO BELIEVE IT, THOUGH...

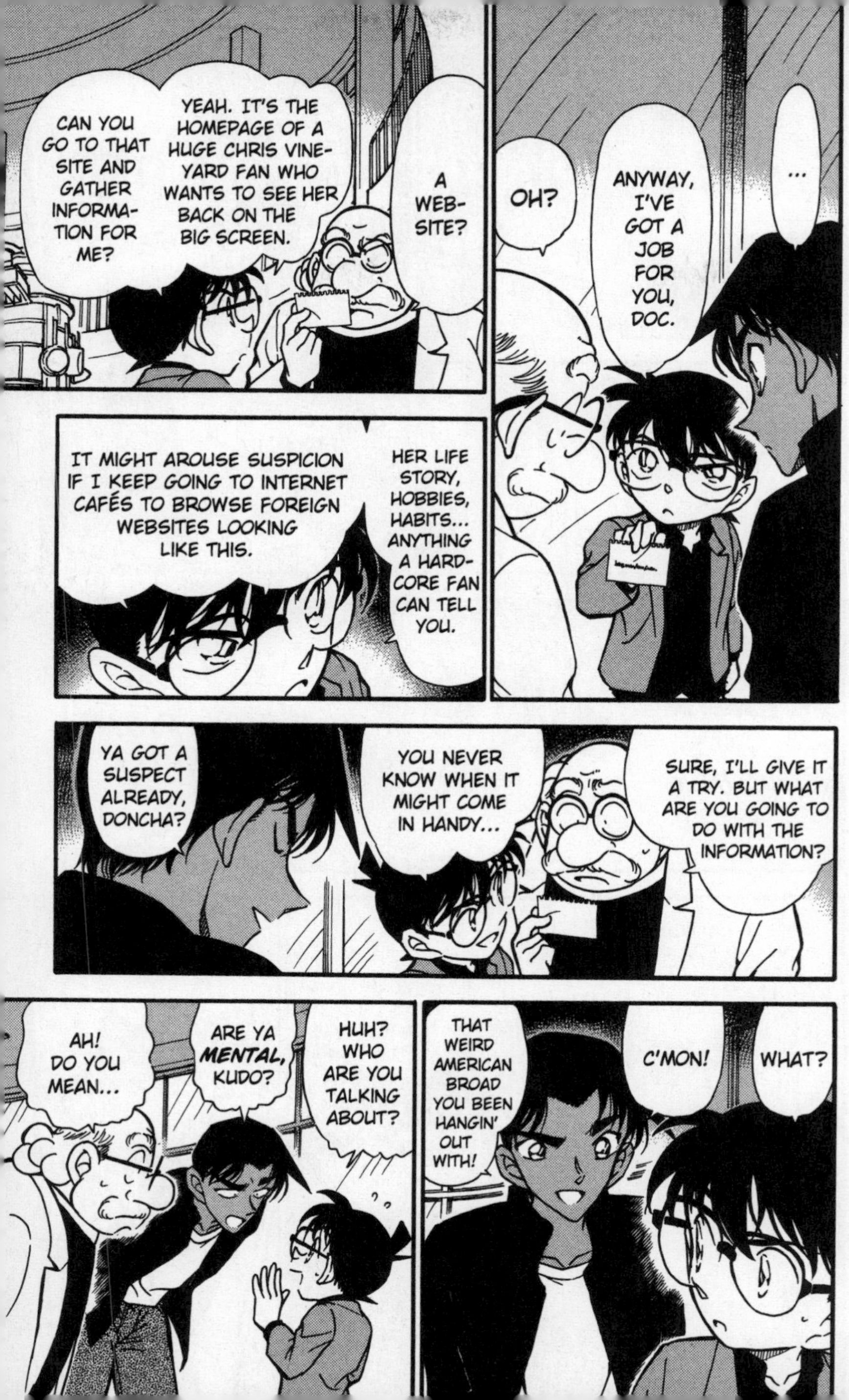
...
ANYWAY, I'VE GOT A JOB FOR YOU, DOC.
OH?
A WEB-SITE?
YEAH. IT'S THE HOMEPAGE OF A HUGE CHRIS VINE-YARD FAN WHO WANTS TO SEE HER BACK ON THE BIG SCREEN.
CAN YOU GO TO THAT SITE AND GATHER INFORMA-TION FOR ME?
HER LIFE STORY, HOBBIES, HABITS... ANYTHING A HARD-CORE FAN CAN TELL YOU.
IT MIGHT AROUSE SUSPICION IF I KEEP GOING TO INTERNET CAFÉS TO BROWSE FOREIGN WEBSITES LOOKING LIKE THIS.
SURE, I'LL GIVE IT A TRY. BUT WHAT ARE YOU GOING TO DO WITH THE INFORMATION?
YOU NEVER KNOW WHEN IT MIGHT COME IN HANDY...
YA GOT A SUSPECT ALREADY, DONCHA?
WHAT?
C'MON!
THAT WEIRD AMERICAN BROAD YOU BEEN HANGIN' OUT WITH!
HUH? WHO ARE YOU TALKING ABOUT?
ARE YA *MENTAL,* KUDO?
AH! DO YOU MEAN...

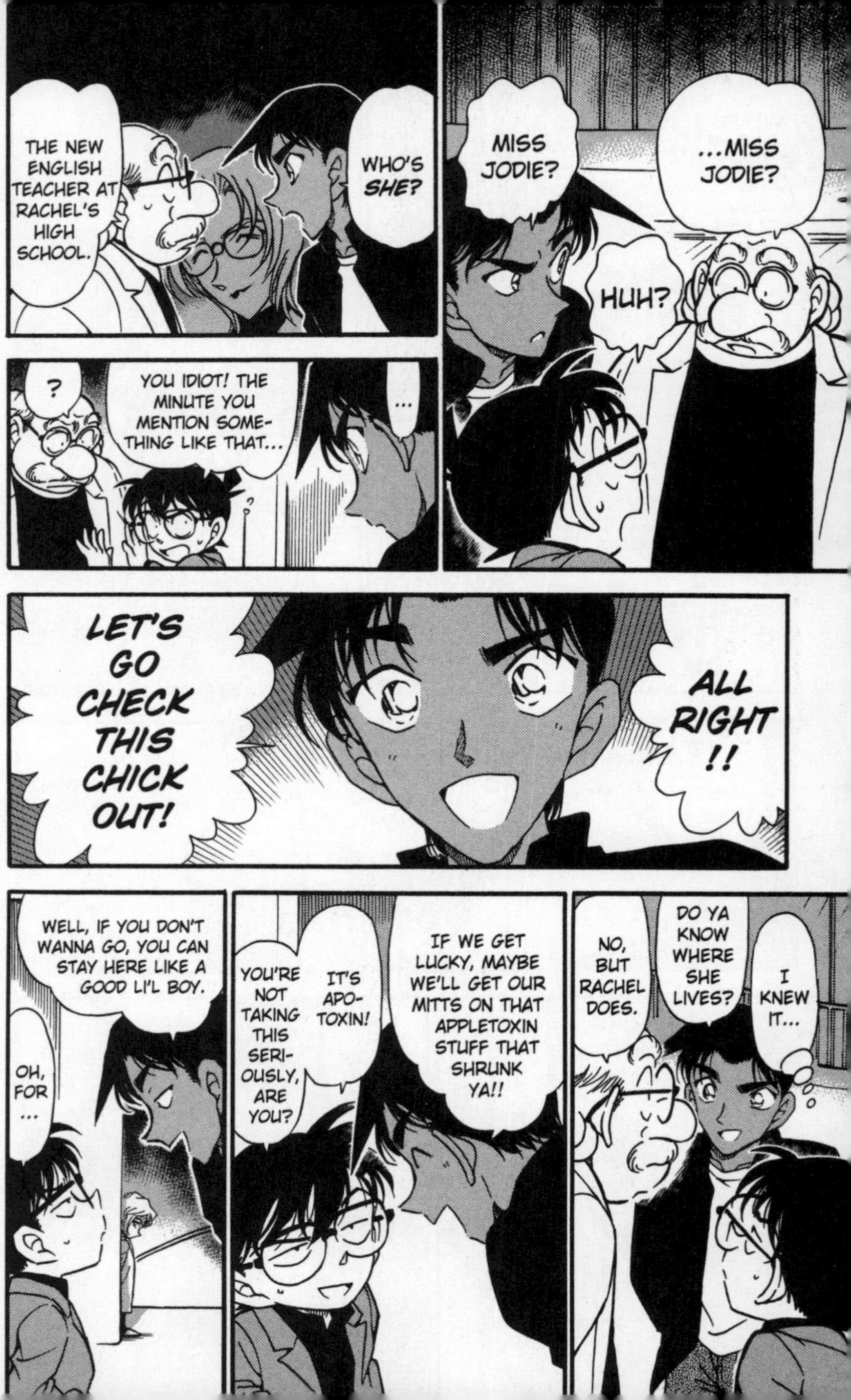
...MISS JODIE?
MISS JODIE?
HUH?
WHO'S SHE?
THE NEW ENGLISH TEACHER AT RACHEL'S HIGH SCHOOL.
...
YOU IDIOT! THE MINUTE YOU MENTION SOMETHING LIKE THAT...
?
ALL RIGHT!!
LET'S GO CHECK THIS CHICK OUT!
I KNEW IT...
DO YA KNOW WHERE SHE LIVES?
NO, BUT RACHEL DOES.
IF WE GET LUCKY, MAYBE WE'LL GET OUR MITTS ON THAT APPLETOXIN STUFF THAT SHRUNK YA!!
IT'S APOTOXIN!
YOU'RE NOT TAKING THIS SERIOUSLY, ARE YOU?
WELL, IF YOU DON'T WANNA GO, YOU CAN STAY HERE LIKE A GOOD LI'L BOY.
OH, FOR ...

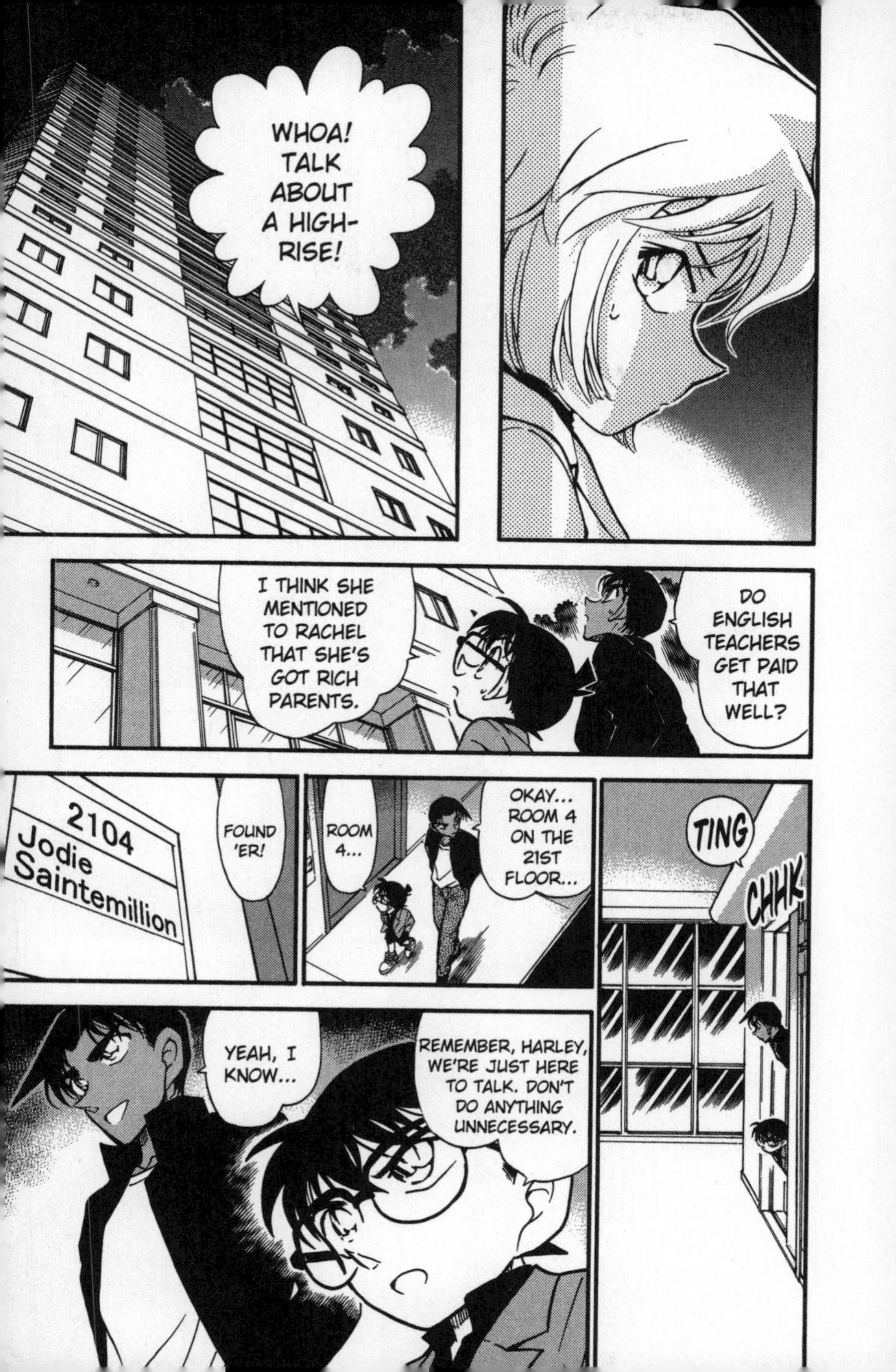
WHOA! TALK ABOUT A HIGH-RISE!
DO ENGLISH TEACHERS GET PAID THAT WELL?
I THINK SHE MENTIONED TO RACHEL THAT SHE'S GOT RICH PARENTS.
TING
CHHK
OKAY... ROOM 4 ON THE 21ST FLOOR...
ROOM 4...
FOUND 'ER!
2104
Jodie Saintemillion
REMEMBER, HARLEY, WE'RE JUST HERE TO TALK. DON'T DO ANYTHING UNNECESSARY.
YEAH, I KNOW...

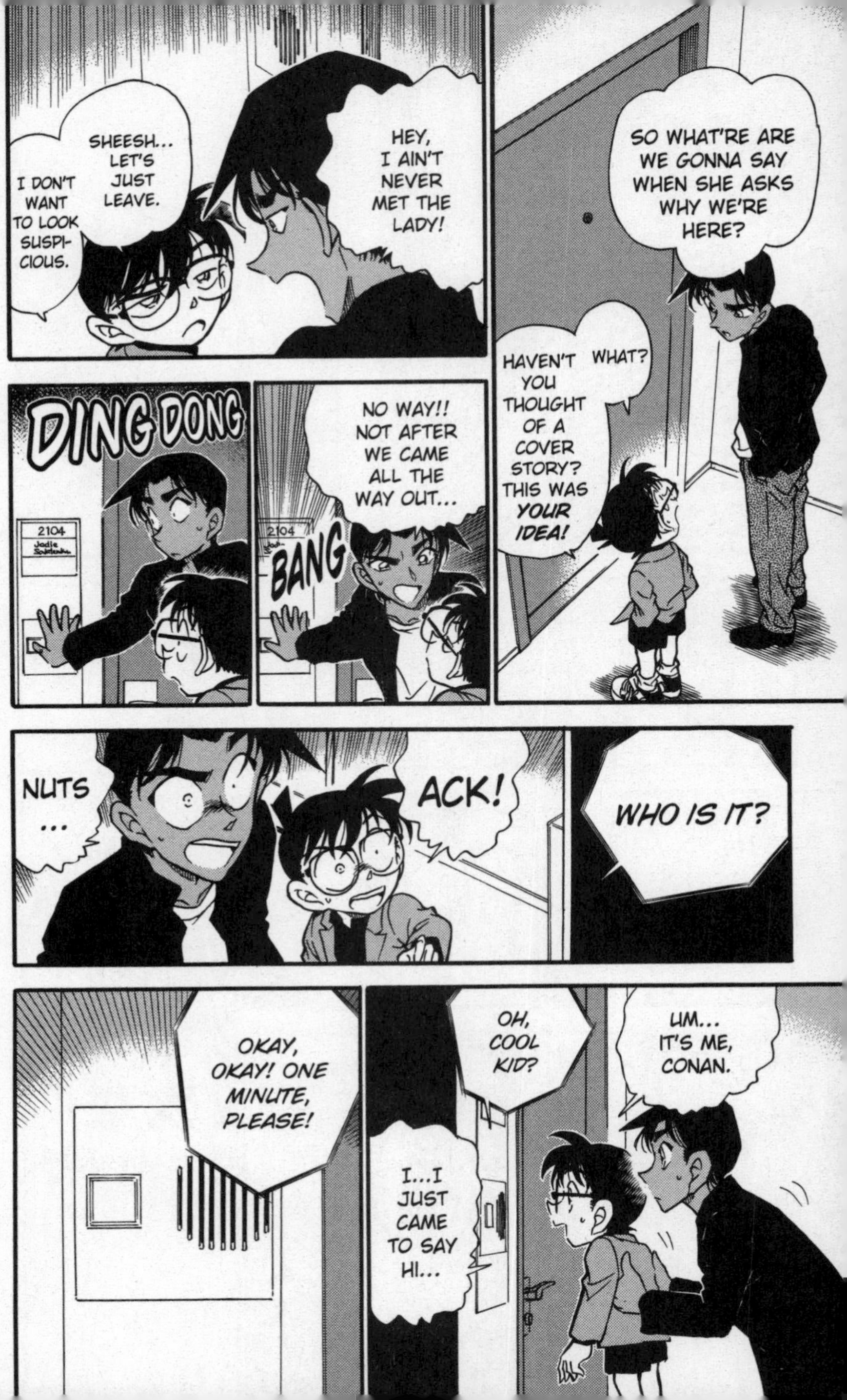
SO WHAT'RE ARE WE GONNA SAY WHEN SHE ASKS WHY WE'RE HERE?
WHAT?
HAVEN'T YOU THOUGHT OF A COVER STORY? THIS WAS *YOUR IDEA!*
HEY, I AIN'T NEVER MET THE LADY!
SHEESH... LET'S JUST LEAVE.
I DON'T WANT TO LOOK SUSPICIOUS.
NO WAY!! NOT AFTER WE CAME ALL THE WAY OUT...
2104
BANG
DING DONG
2104
WHO IS IT?
ACK!
NUTS...
UM... IT'S ME, CONAN.
OH, COOL KID?
I...I JUST CAME TO SAY HI...
OKAY, OKAY! ONE MINUTE, PLEASE!

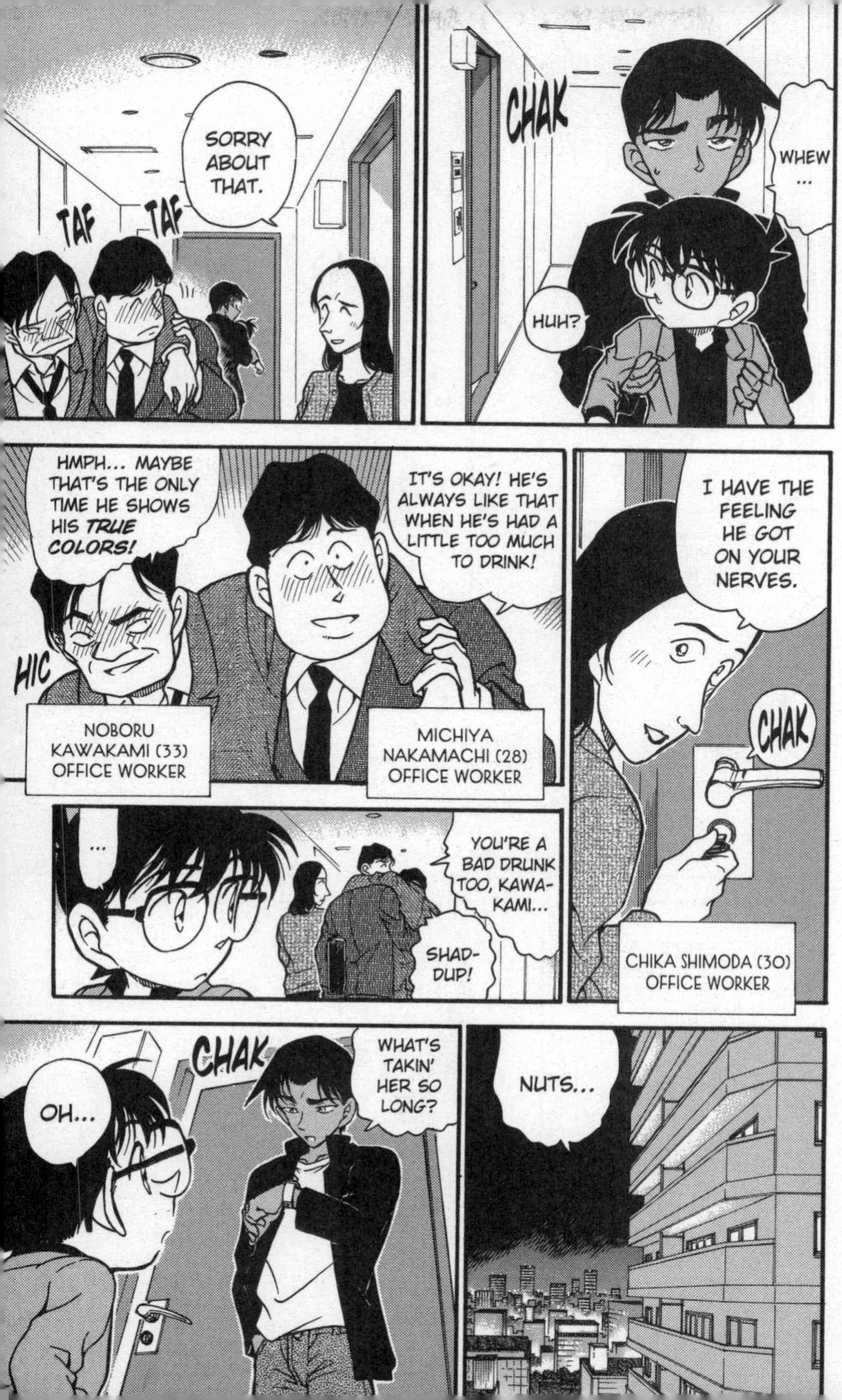
CHAK
WHEW ...
HUH?
SORRY ABOUT THAT.
TAF TAF
I HAVE THE FEELING HE GOT ON YOUR NERVES.
CHAK
CHIKA SHIMODA (30) OFFICE WORKER
IT'S OKAY! HE'S ALWAYS LIKE THAT WHEN HE'S HAD A LITTLE TOO MUCH TO DRINK!
MICHIYA NAKAMACHI (28) OFFICE WORKER
HMPH... MAYBE THAT'S THE ONLY TIME HE SHOWS HIS *TRUE COLORS!*
HIC
NOBORU KAWAKAMI (33) OFFICE WORKER
YOU'RE A BAD DRUNK TOO, KAWA-KAMI...
SHAD-DUP!
...
NUTS...
WHAT'S TAKIN' HER SO LONG?
CHAK
OH...

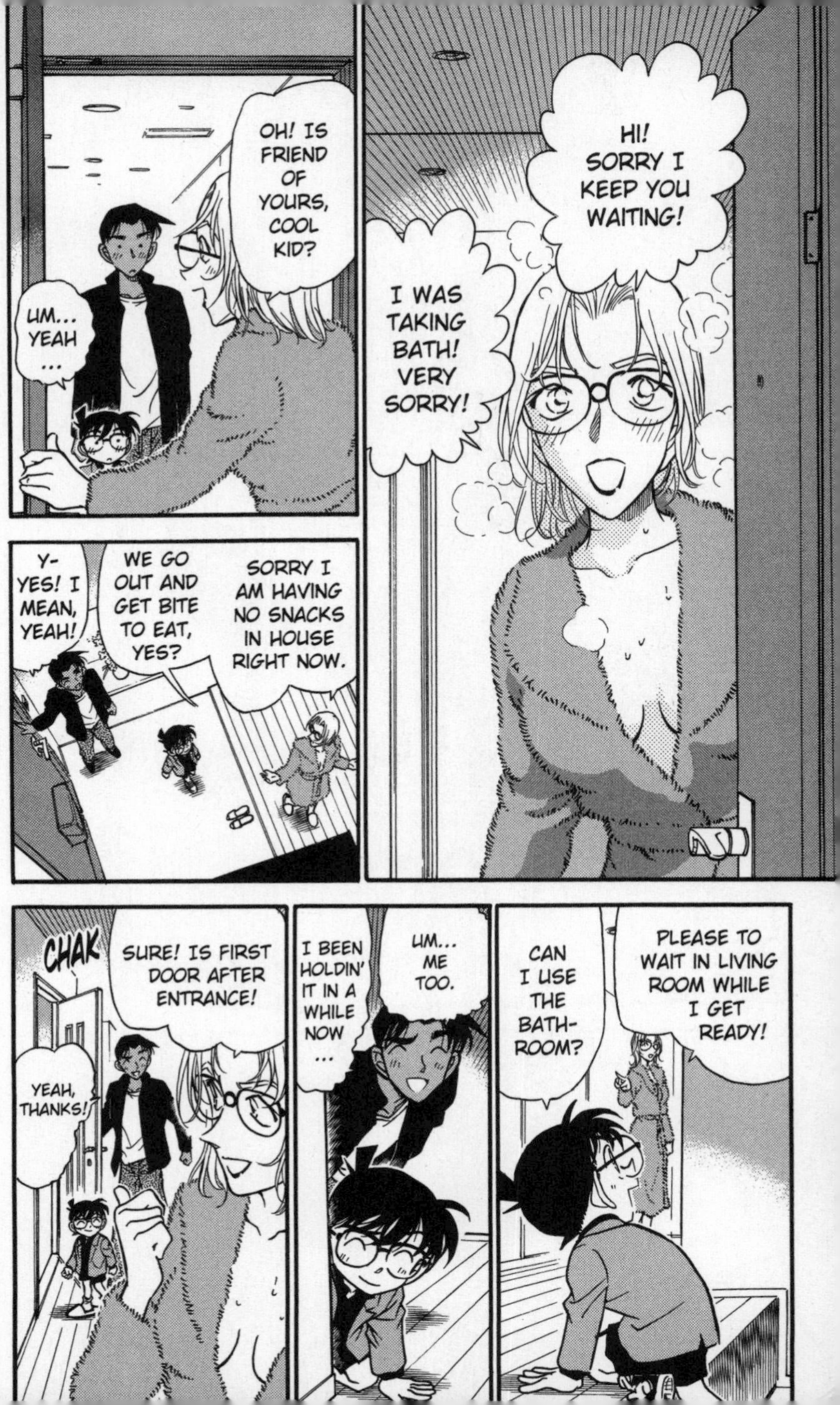
HI! SORRY I KEEP YOU WAITING!
I WAS TAKING BATH! VERY SORRY!
OH! IS FRIEND OF YOURS, COOL KID?
UM... YEAH ...
SORRY I AM HAVING NO SNACKS IN HOUSE RIGHT NOW.
WE GO OUT AND GET BITE TO EAT, YES?
Y-YES! I MEAN, YEAH!
PLEASE TO WAIT IN LIVING ROOM WHILE I GET READY!
CAN I USE THE BATH-ROOM?
UM... ME TOO.
I BEEN HOLDIN' IT IN A WHILE NOW ...
SURE! IS FIRST DOOR AFTER ENTRANCE!
CHAK
YEAH, THANKS!

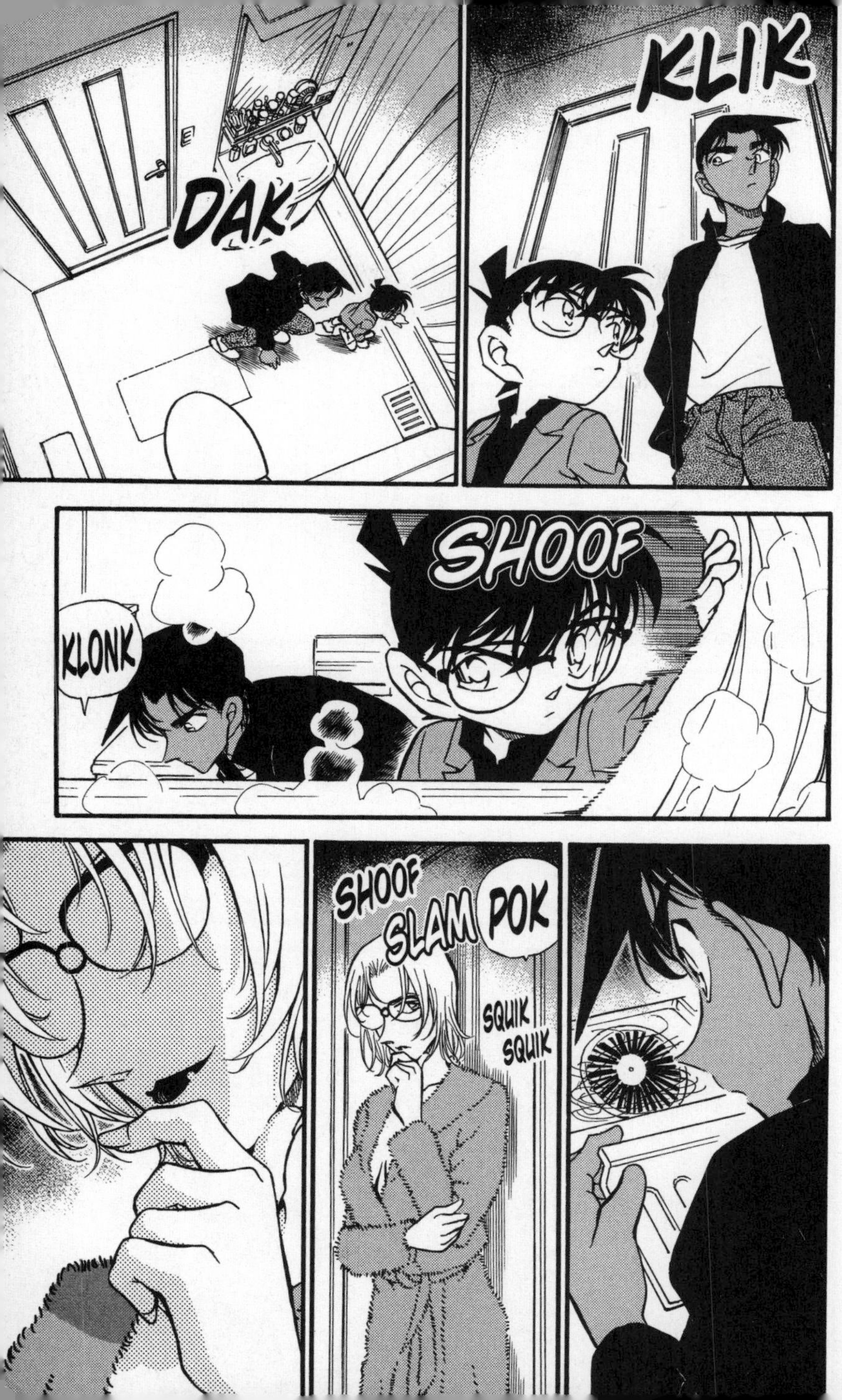
KLIK
DAK
SHOOF
KLONK
SHOOF
SLAM
POK
SQUIK
SQUIK

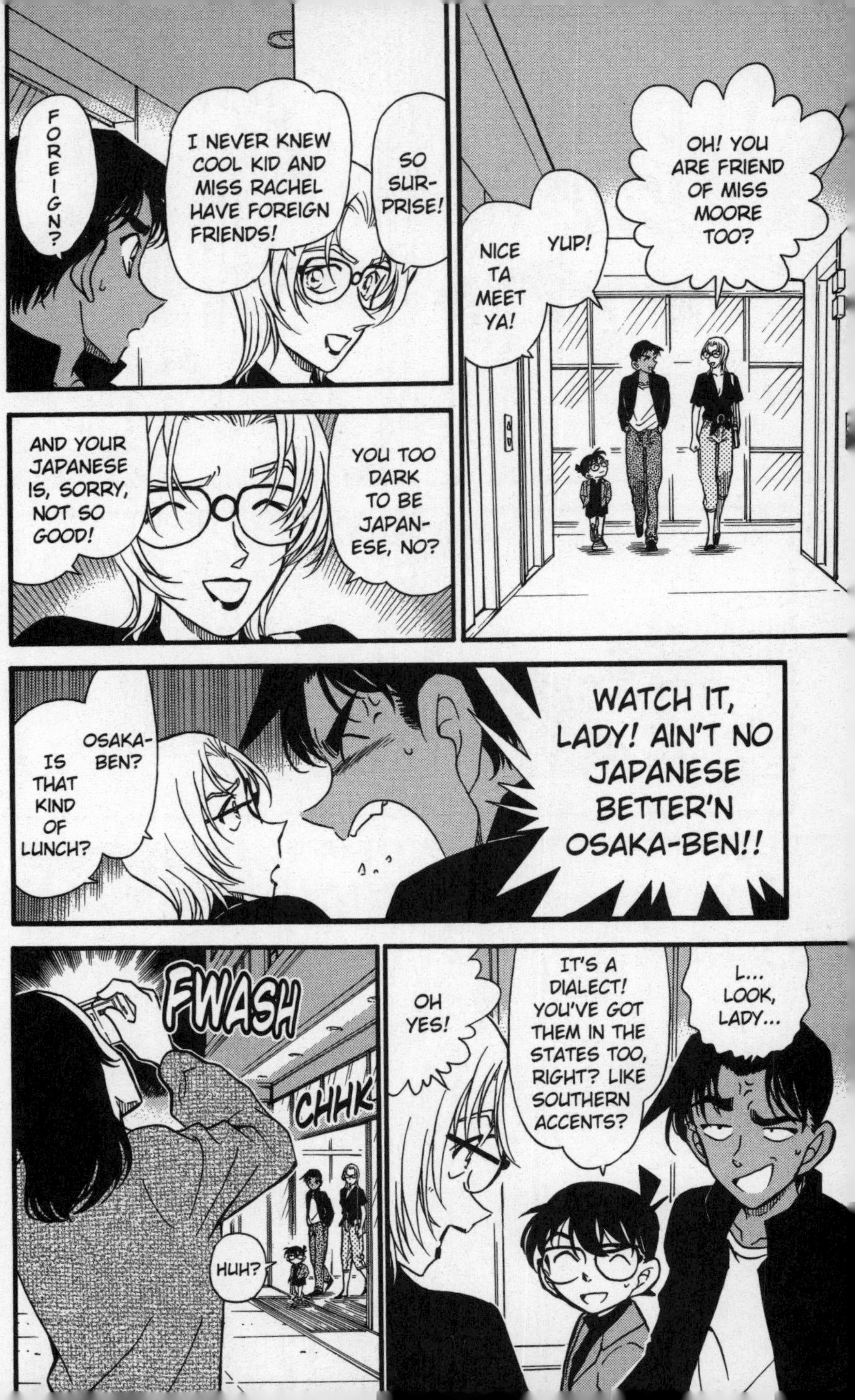
OH! YOU ARE FRIEND OF MISS MOORE TOO?
YUP!
NICE TA MEET YA!
SO SUR-PRISE!
I NEVER KNEW COOL KID AND MISS RACHEL HAVE FOREIGN FRIENDS!
FOREIGN?
YOU TOO DARK TO BE JAPAN-ESE, NO?
AND YOUR JAPANESE IS, SORRY, NOT SO GOOD!
WATCH IT, LADY! AIN'T NO JAPANESE BETTER'N OSAKA-BEN!!
OSAKA-BEN? IS THAT KIND OF LUNCH?
L... LOOK, LADY...
IT'S A DIALECT! YOU'VE GOT THEM IN THE STATES TOO, RIGHT? LIKE SOUTHERN ACCENTS?
OH YES!
FWASH
CHHK
HUH?

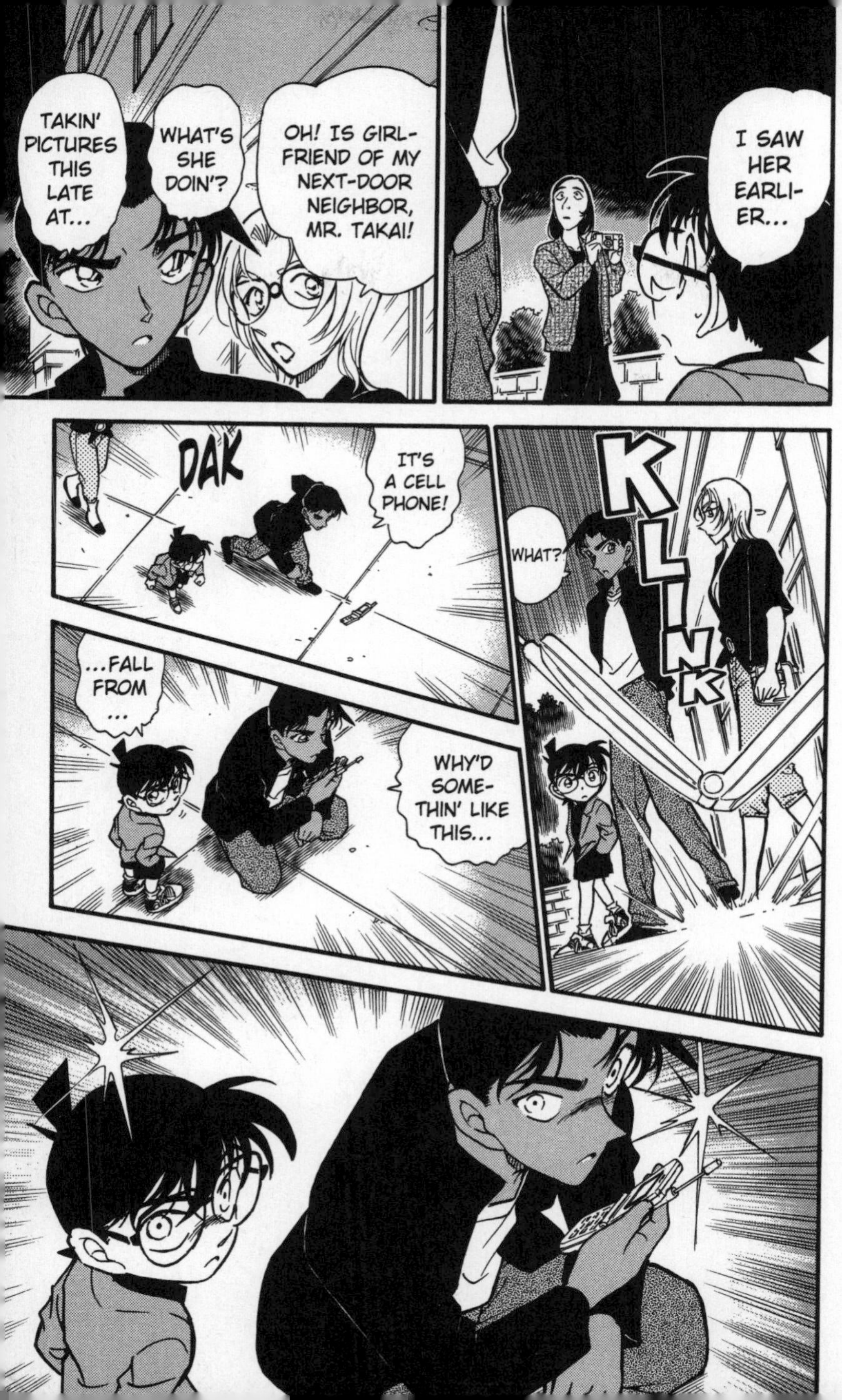
I SAW HER EARLI-ER...
OH! IS GIRL-FRIEND OF MY NEXT-DOOR NEIGHBOR, MR. TAKAI!
WHAT'S SHE DOIN'?
TAKIN' PICTURES THIS LATE AT...
KLINK
WHAT?
DAK
IT'S A CELL PHONE!
WHY'D SOME-THIN' LIKE THIS...
...FALL FROM ...

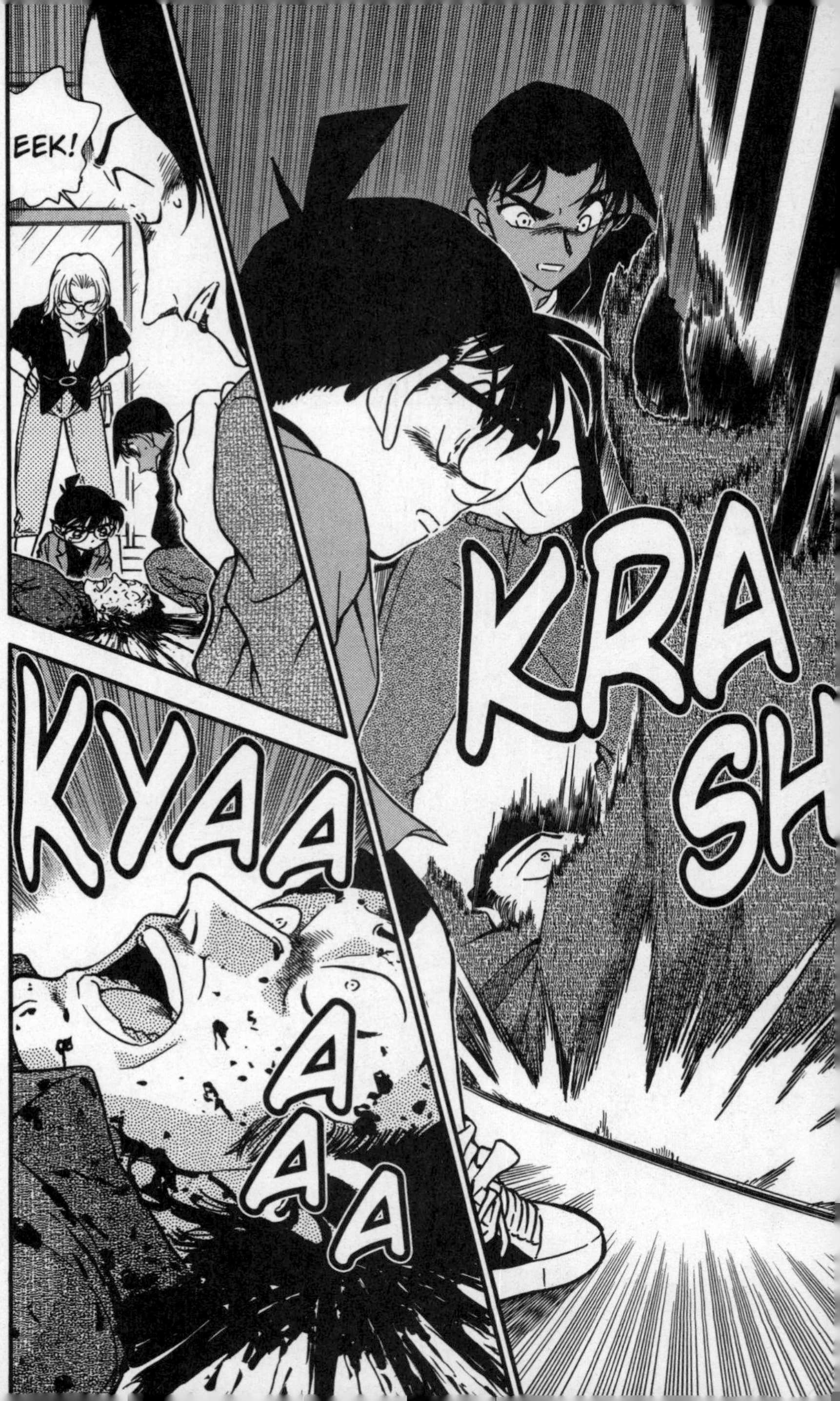
KRA
SH
EEK!
KYAAAAA

THE FLYING NEIGHBOR

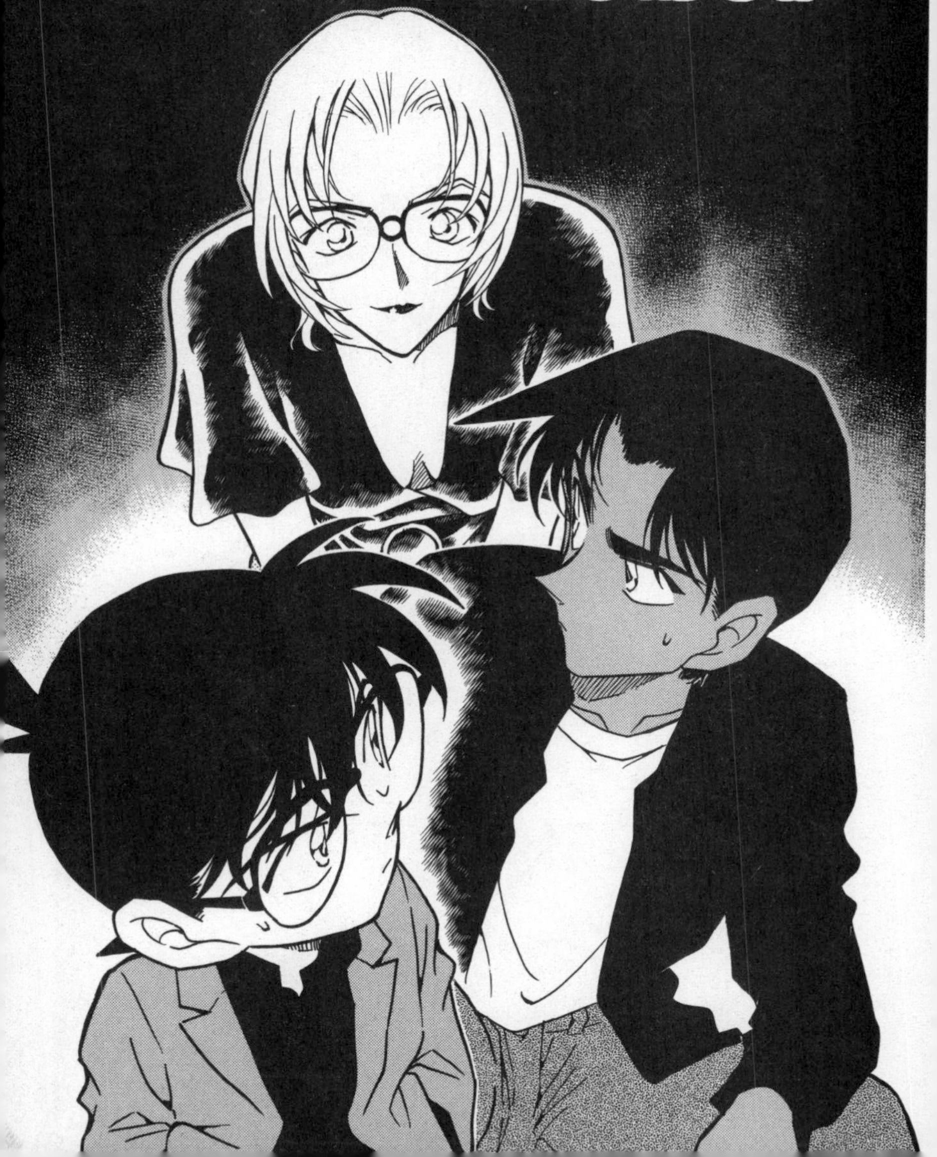

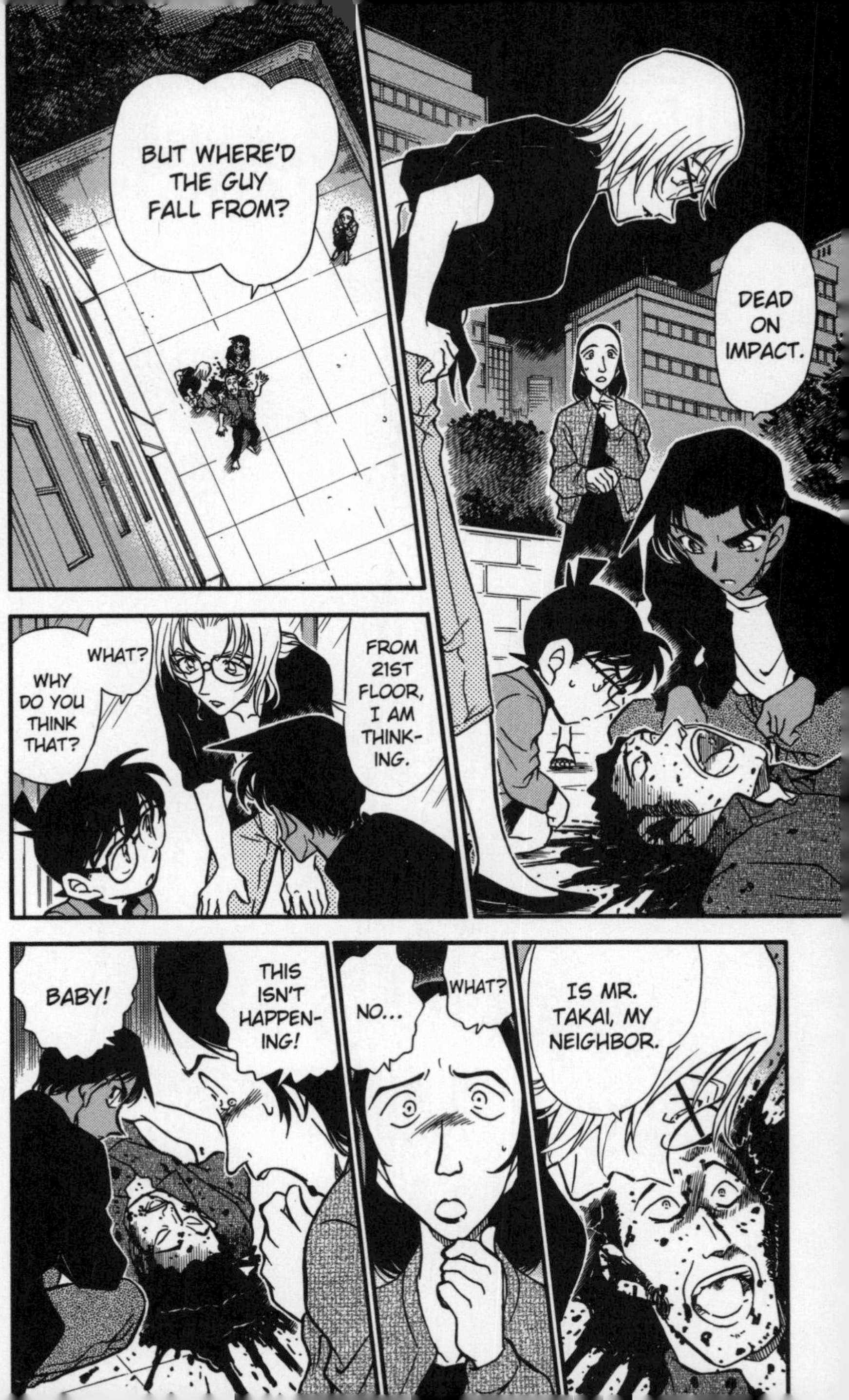
DEAD ON IMPACT.
BUT WHERE'D THE GUY FALL FROM?
FROM 21ST FLOOR, I AM THINK-ING.
WHAT?
WHY DO YOU THINK THAT?
IS MR. TAKAI, MY NEIGHBOR.
WHAT?
NO...
THIS ISN'T HAPPEN-ING!
BABY!

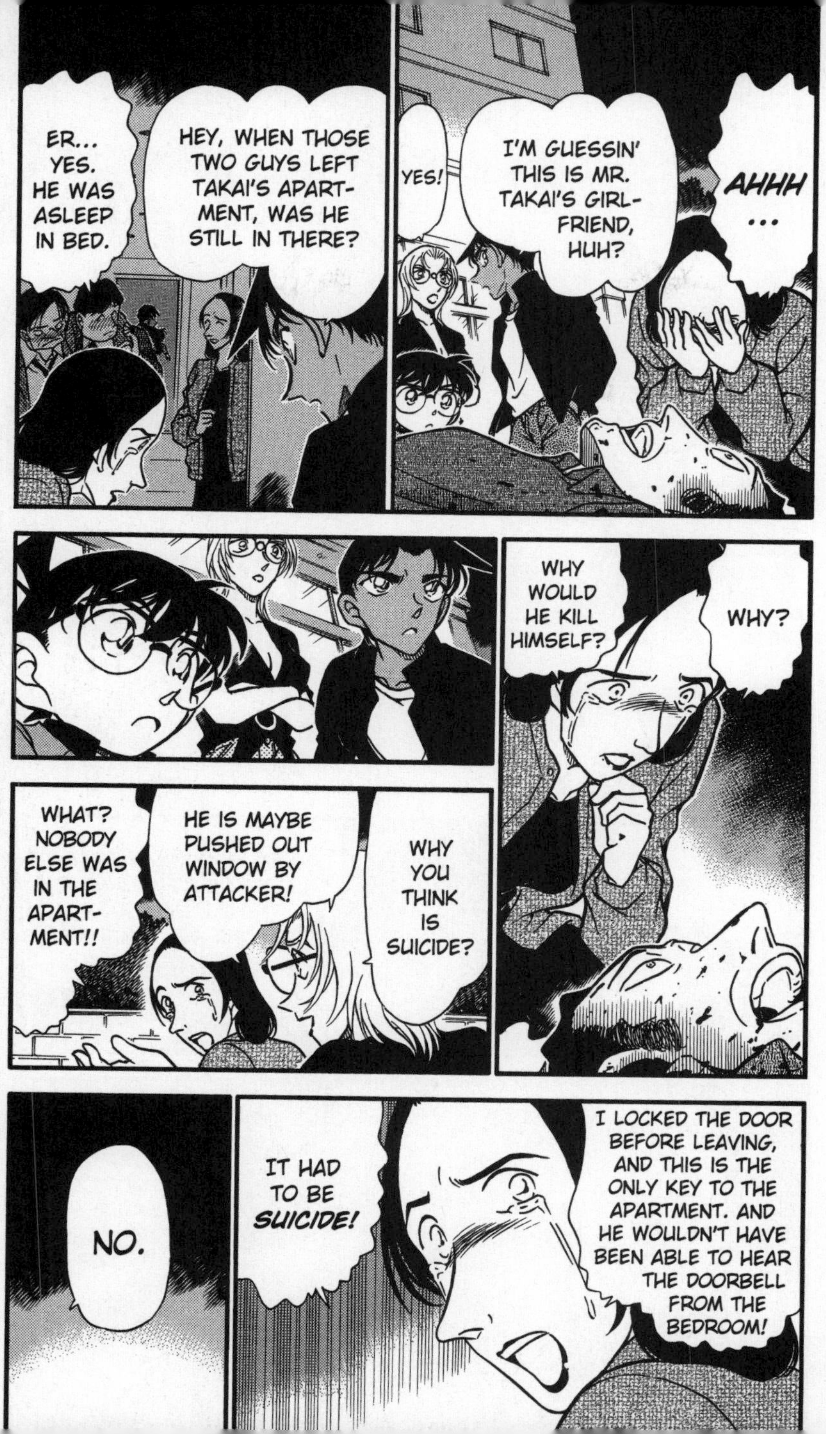
AHHH ...
I'M GUESSIN' THIS IS MR. TAKAI'S GIRL-FRIEND, HUH?
YES!
HEY, WHEN THOSE TWO GUYS LEFT TAKAI'S APART-MENT, WAS HE STILL IN THERE?
ER... YES. HE WAS ASLEEP IN BED.
WHY?
WHY WOULD HE KILL HIMSELF?
WHY YOU THINK IS SUICIDE?
HE IS MAYBE PUSHED OUT WINDOW BY ATTACKER!
WHAT? NOBODY ELSE WAS IN THE APART-MENT!!
I LOCKED THE DOOR BEFORE LEAVING, AND THIS IS THE ONLY KEY TO THE APARTMENT. AND HE WOULDN'T HAVE BEEN ABLE TO HEAR THE DOORBELL FROM THE BEDROOM!
IT HAD TO BE *SUICIDE!*
NO.

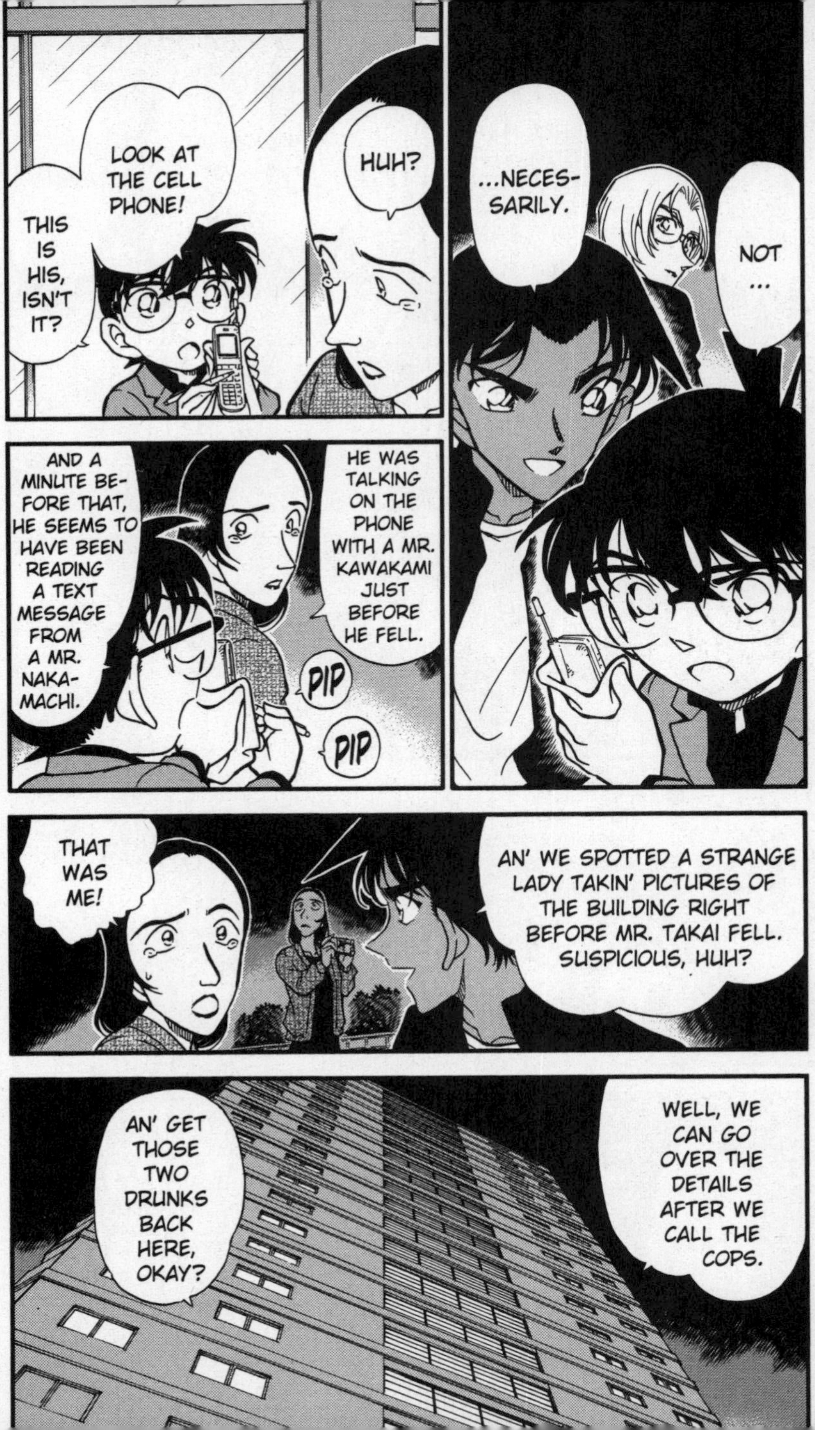
NOT ...
...NECES-SARILY.
HUH?
LOOK AT THE CELL PHONE!
THIS IS HIS, ISN'T IT?
HE WAS TALKING ON THE PHONE WITH A MR. KAWAKAMI JUST BEFORE HE FELL.
PIP
PIP
AND A MINUTE BEFORE THAT, HE SEEMS TO HAVE BEEN READING A TEXT MESSAGE FROM A MR. NAKA-MACHI.
AN' WE SPOTTED A STRANGE LADY TAKIN' PICTURES OF THE BUILDING RIGHT BEFORE MR. TAKAI FELL. SUSPICIOUS, HUH?
THAT WAS ME!
WELL, WE CAN GO OVER THE DETAILS AFTER WE CALL THE COPS.
AN' GET THOSE TWO DRUNKS BACK HERE, OKAY?

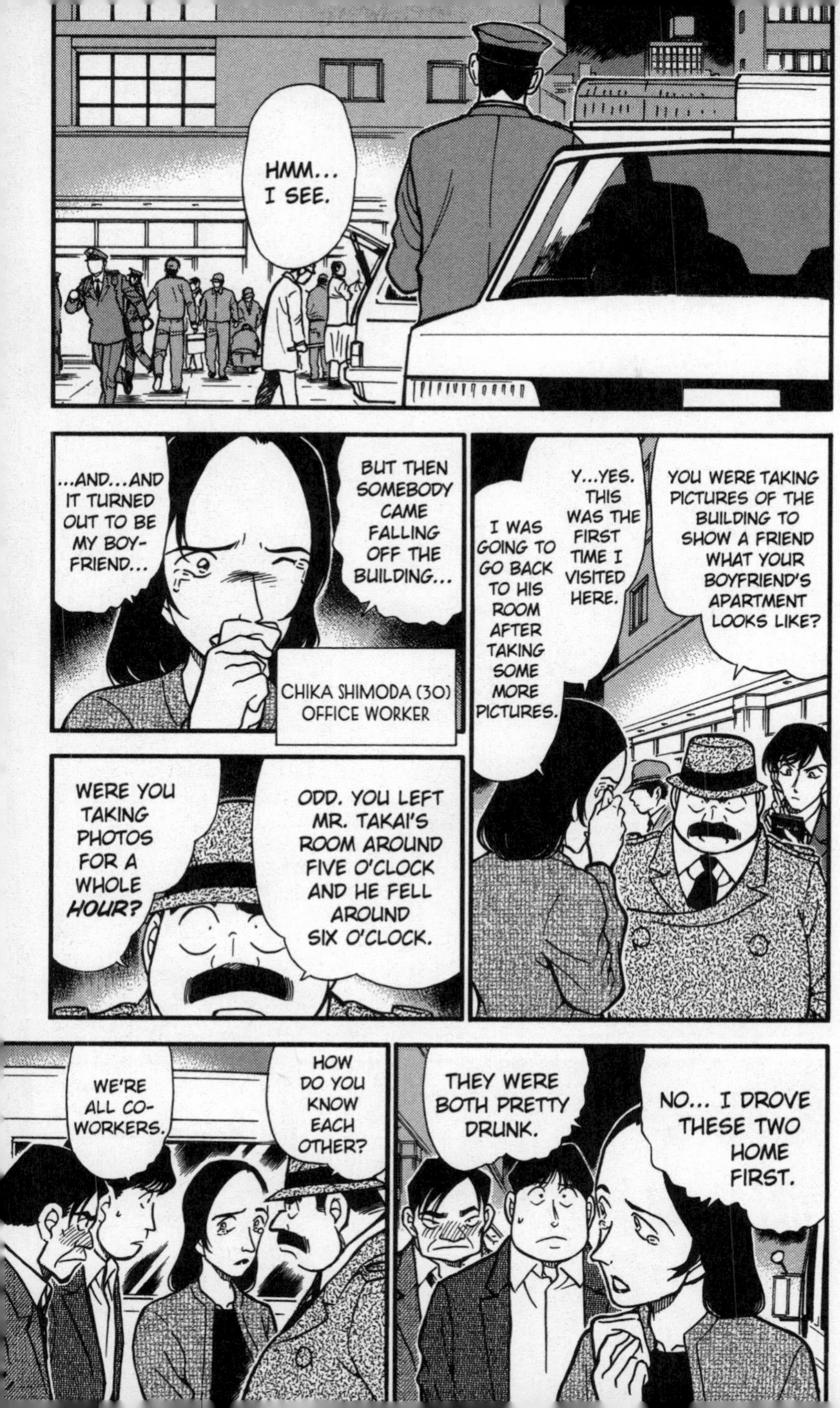
HMM... I SEE.
YOU WERE TAKING PICTURES OF THE BUILDING TO SHOW A FRIEND WHAT YOUR BOYFRIEND'S APARTMENT LOOKS LIKE?
Y...YES. THIS WAS THE FIRST TIME I VISITED HERE.
I WAS GOING TO GO BACK TO HIS ROOM AFTER TAKING SOME MORE PICTURES.
BUT THEN SOMEBODY CAME FALLING OFF THE BUILDING...
...AND...AND IT TURNED OUT TO BE MY BOY-FRIEND...
CHIKA SHIMODA (30) OFFICE WORKER
ODD. YOU LEFT MR. TAKAI'S ROOM AROUND FIVE O'CLOCK AND HE FELL AROUND SIX O'CLOCK.
WERE YOU TAKING PHOTOS FOR A WHOLE *HOUR?*
NO... I DROVE THESE TWO HOME FIRST.
THEY WERE BOTH PRETTY DRUNK.
HOW DO YOU KNOW EACH OTHER?
WE'RE ALL CO-WORKERS.

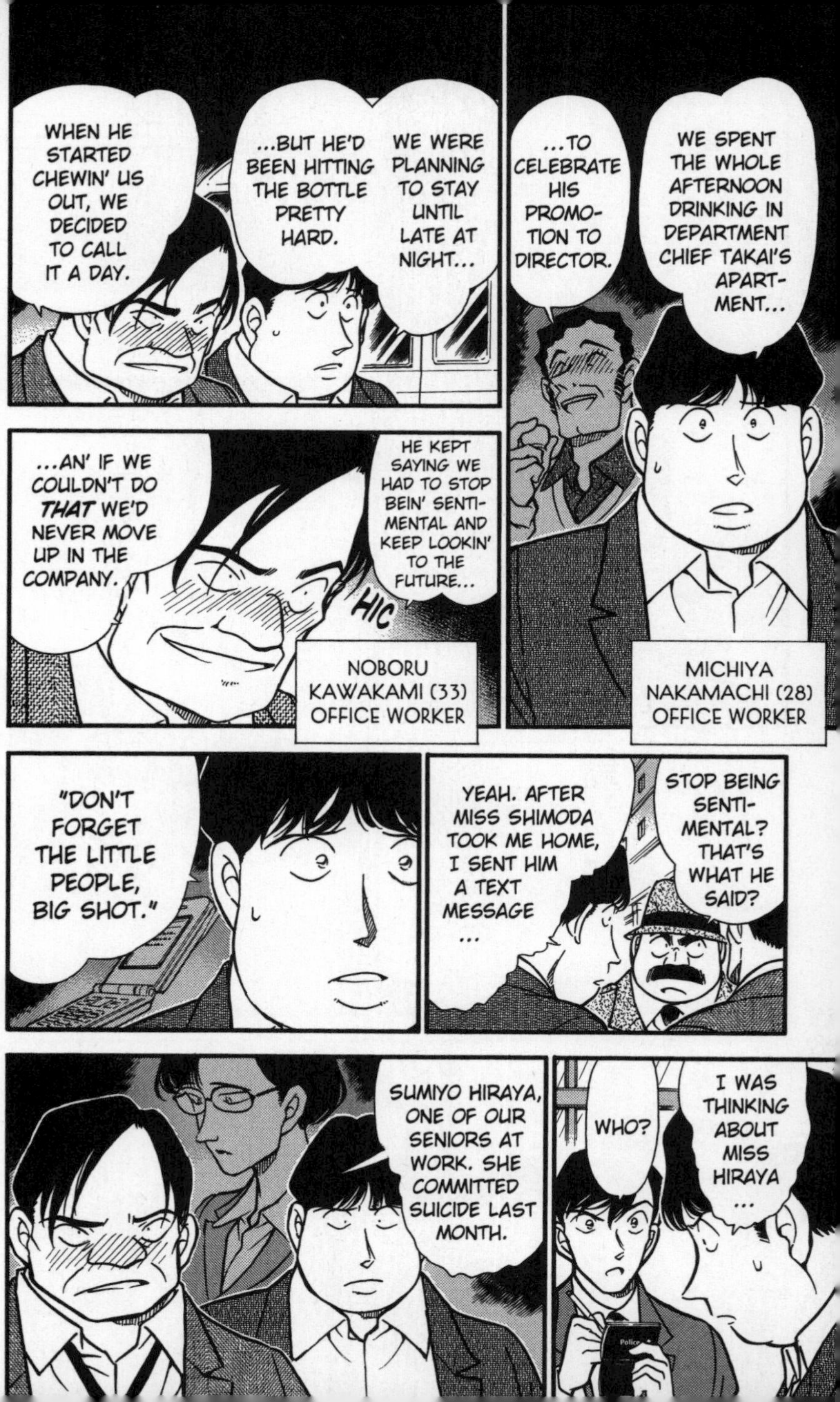
WE SPENT THE WHOLE AFTERNOON DRINKING IN DEPARTMENT CHIEF TAKAI'S APARTMENT...
...TO CELEBRATE HIS PROMOTION TO DIRECTOR.
MICHIYA NAKAMACHI (28) OFFICE WORKER
WE WERE PLANNING TO STAY UNTIL LATE AT NIGHT...
...BUT HE'D BEEN HITTING THE BOTTLE PRETTY HARD.
WHEN HE STARTED CHEWIN' US OUT, WE DECIDED TO CALL IT A DAY.
HE KEPT SAYING WE HAD TO STOP BEIN' SENTIMENTAL AND KEEP LOOKIN' TO THE FUTURE...
HIC
...AN' IF WE COULDN'T DO *THAT* WE'D NEVER MOVE UP IN THE COMPANY.
NOBORU KAWAKAMI (33) OFFICE WORKER
STOP BEING SENTIMENTAL? THAT'S WHAT HE SAID?
YEAH. AFTER MISS SHIMODA TOOK ME HOME, I SENT HIM A TEXT MESSAGE ...
"DON'T FORGET THE LITTLE PEOPLE, BIG SHOT."
I WAS THINKING ABOUT MISS HIRAYA ...
WHO?
SUMIYO HIRAYA, ONE OF OUR SENIORS AT WORK. SHE COMMITTED SUICIDE LAST MONTH.

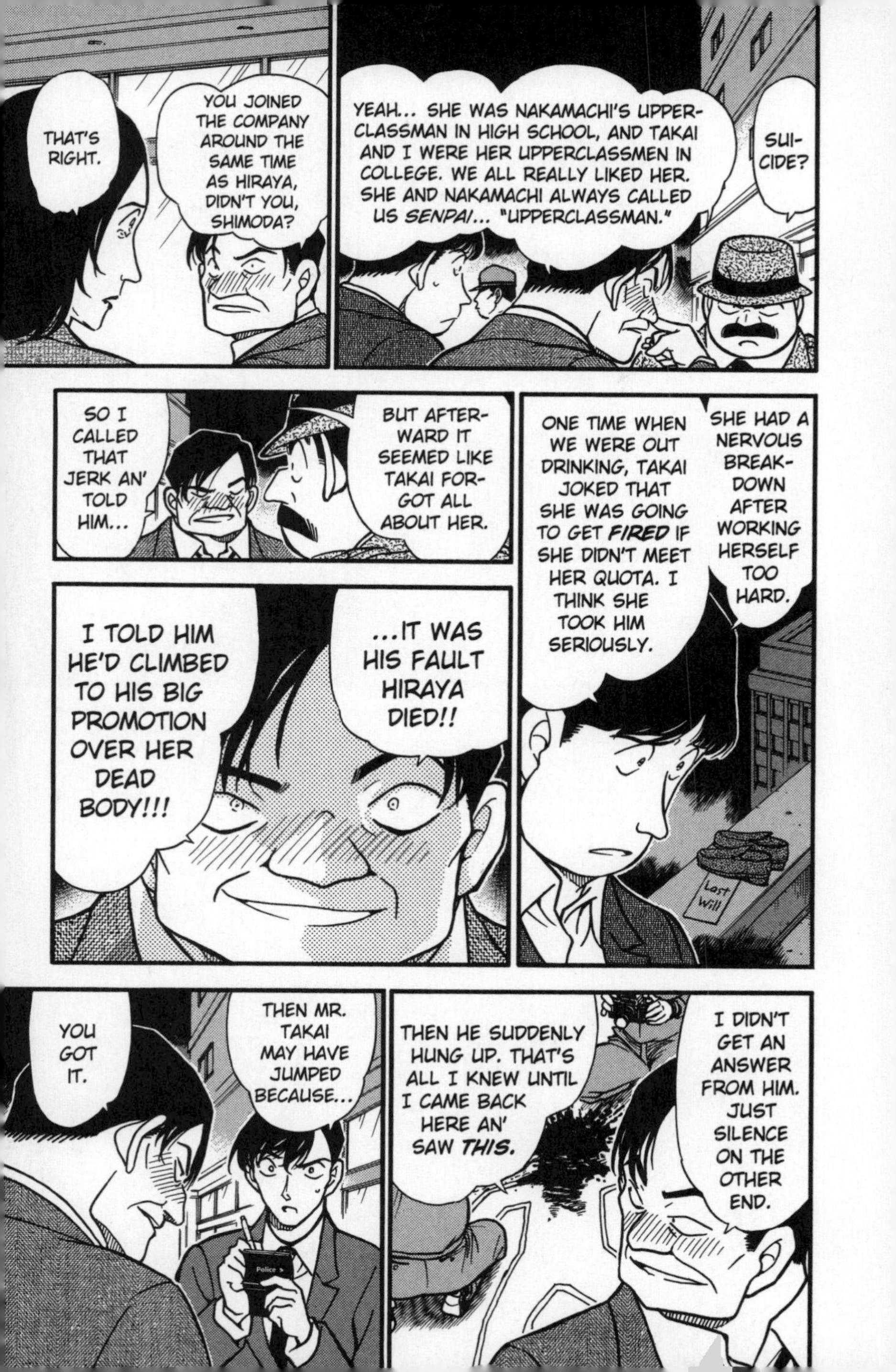
SUI-CIDE?
YEAH... SHE WAS NAKAMACHI'S UPPER-CLASSMAN IN HIGH SCHOOL, AND TAKAI AND I WERE HER UPPERCLASSMEN IN COLLEGE. WE ALL REALLY LIKED HER. SHE AND NAKAMACHI ALWAYS CALLED US *SENPAI*... "UPPERCLASSMAN."
YOU JOINED THE COMPANY AROUND THE SAME TIME AS HIRAYA, DIDN'T YOU, SHIMODA?
THAT'S RIGHT.
SHE HAD A NERVOUS BREAK-DOWN AFTER WORKING HERSELF TOO HARD.
ONE TIME WHEN WE WERE OUT DRINKING, TAKAI JOKED THAT SHE WAS GOING TO GET ***FIRED*** IF SHE DIDN'T MEET HER QUOTA. I THINK SHE TOOK HIM SERIOUSLY.
Last Will
BUT AFTER-WARD IT SEEMED LIKE TAKAI FOR-GOT ALL ABOUT HER.
SO I CALLED THAT JERK AN' TOLD HIM...
I TOLD HIM HE'D CLIMBED TO HIS BIG PROMOTION OVER HER DEAD BODY!!!
...IT WAS HIS FAULT HIRAYA DIED!!
I DIDN'T GET AN ANSWER FROM HIM. JUST SILENCE ON THE OTHER END.
THEN HE SUDDENLY HUNG UP. THAT'S ALL I KNEW UNTIL I CAME BACK HERE AN' SAW ***THIS.***
THEN MR. TAKAI MAY HAVE JUMPED BECAUSE...
YOU GOT IT.
Police

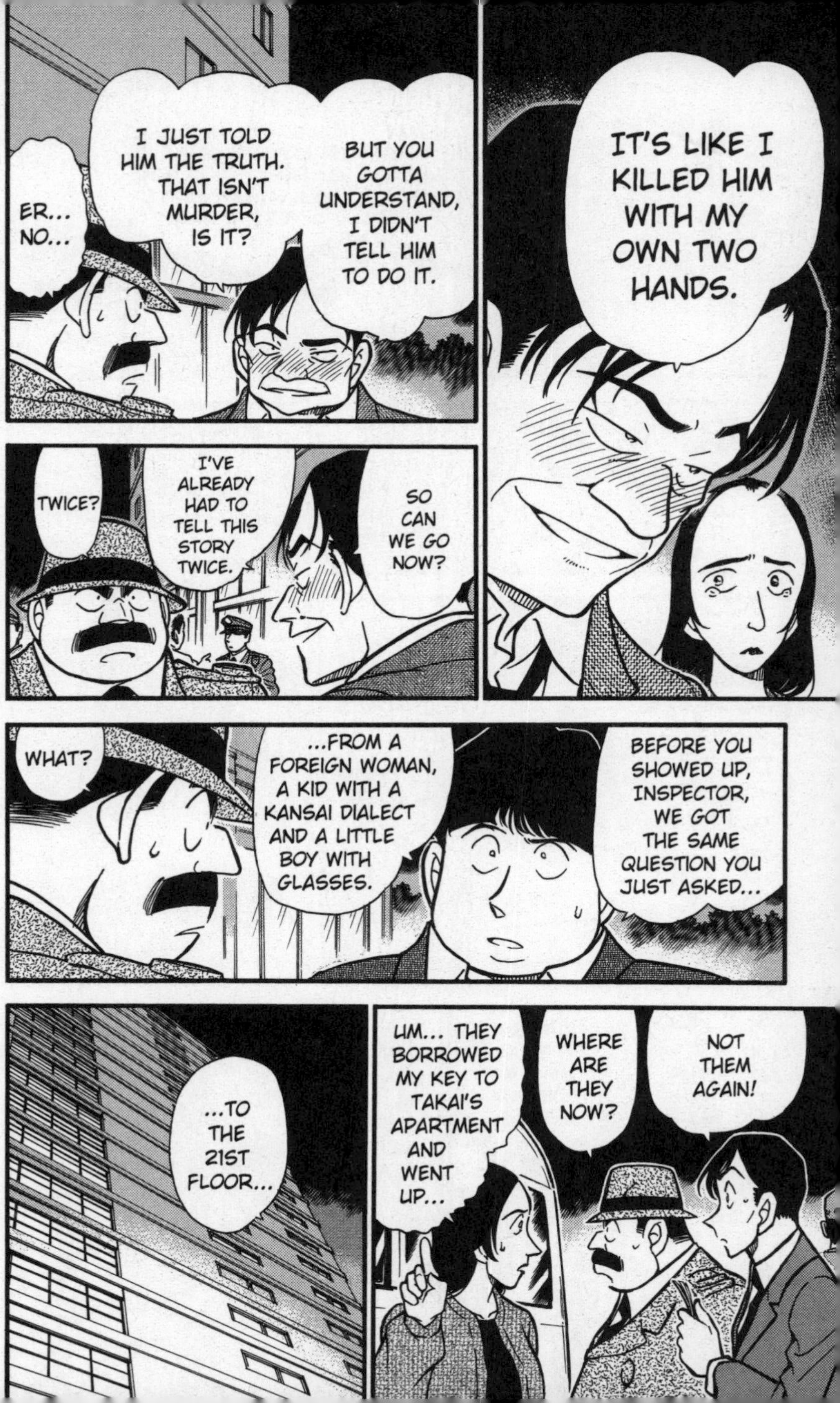
IT'S LIKE I KILLED HIM WITH MY OWN TWO HANDS.
BUT YOU GOTTA UNDERSTAND, I DIDN'T TELL HIM TO DO IT.
I JUST TOLD HIM THE TRUTH. THAT ISN'T MURDER, IS IT?
ER... NO...
SO CAN WE GO NOW?
I'VE ALREADY HAD TO TELL THIS STORY TWICE.
TWICE?
BEFORE YOU SHOWED UP, INSPECTOR, WE GOT THE SAME QUESTION YOU JUST ASKED...
...FROM A FOREIGN WOMAN, A KID WITH A KANSAI DIALECT AND A LITTLE BOY WITH GLASSES.
WHAT?
NOT THEM AGAIN!
WHERE ARE THEY NOW?
UM... THEY BORROWED MY KEY TO TAKAI'S APARTMENT AND WENT UP...
...TO THE 21ST FLOOR...

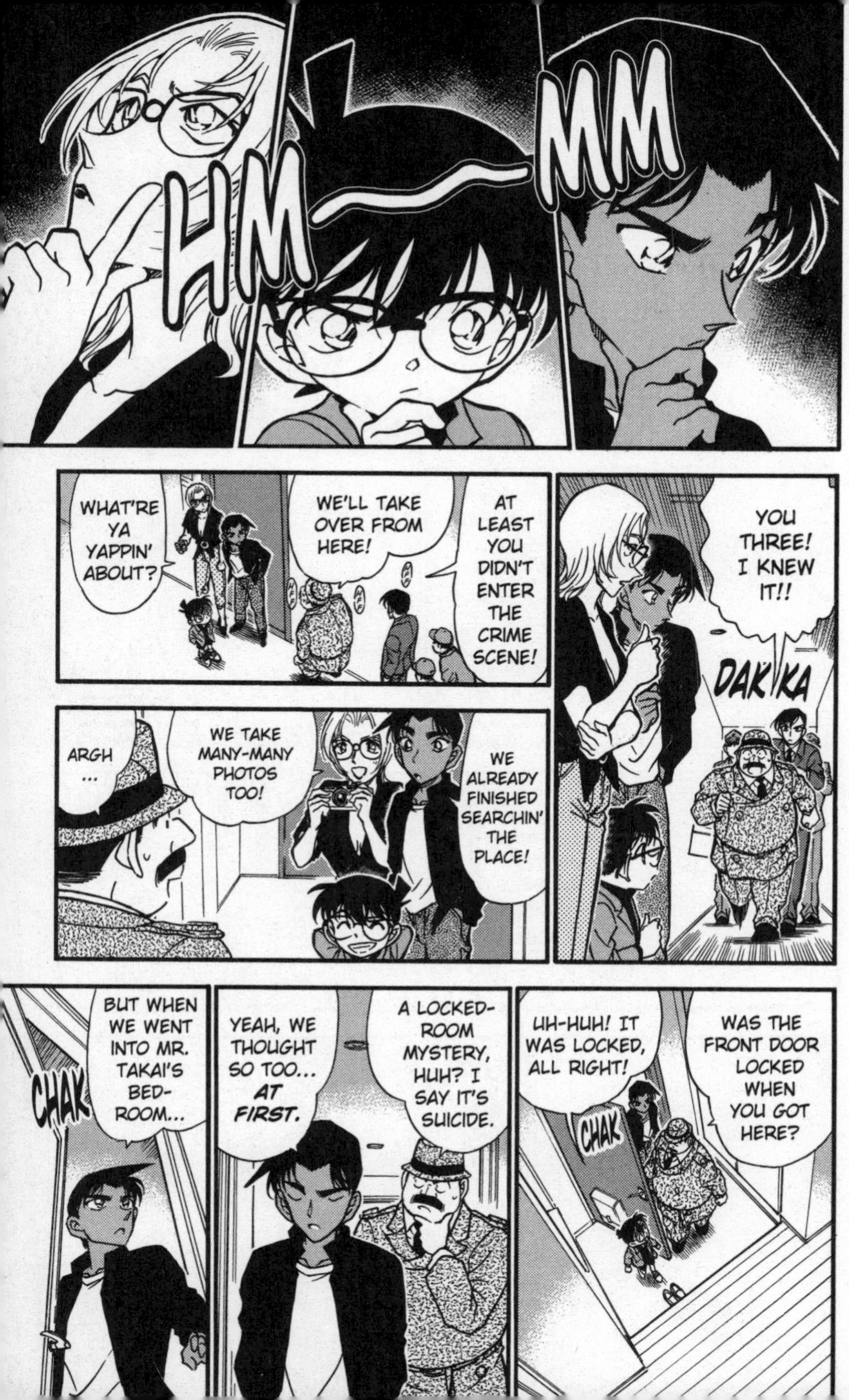
HM~MM
YOU THREE! I KNEW IT!!
DAK KA
AT LEAST YOU DIDN'T ENTER THE CRIME SCENE!
WE'LL TAKE OVER FROM HERE!
WHAT'RE YA YAPPIN' ABOUT?
WE ALREADY FINISHED SEARCHIN' THE PLACE!
WE TAKE MANY-MANY PHOTOS TOO!
ARGH ...
WAS THE FRONT DOOR LOCKED WHEN YOU GOT HERE?
UH-HUH! IT WAS LOCKED, ALL RIGHT!
CHAK
A LOCKED-ROOM MYSTERY, HUH? I SAY IT'S SUICIDE.
YEAH, WE THOUGHT SO TOO... **AT FIRST.**
BUT WHEN WE WENT INTO MR. TAKAI'S BED-ROOM...
CHAK

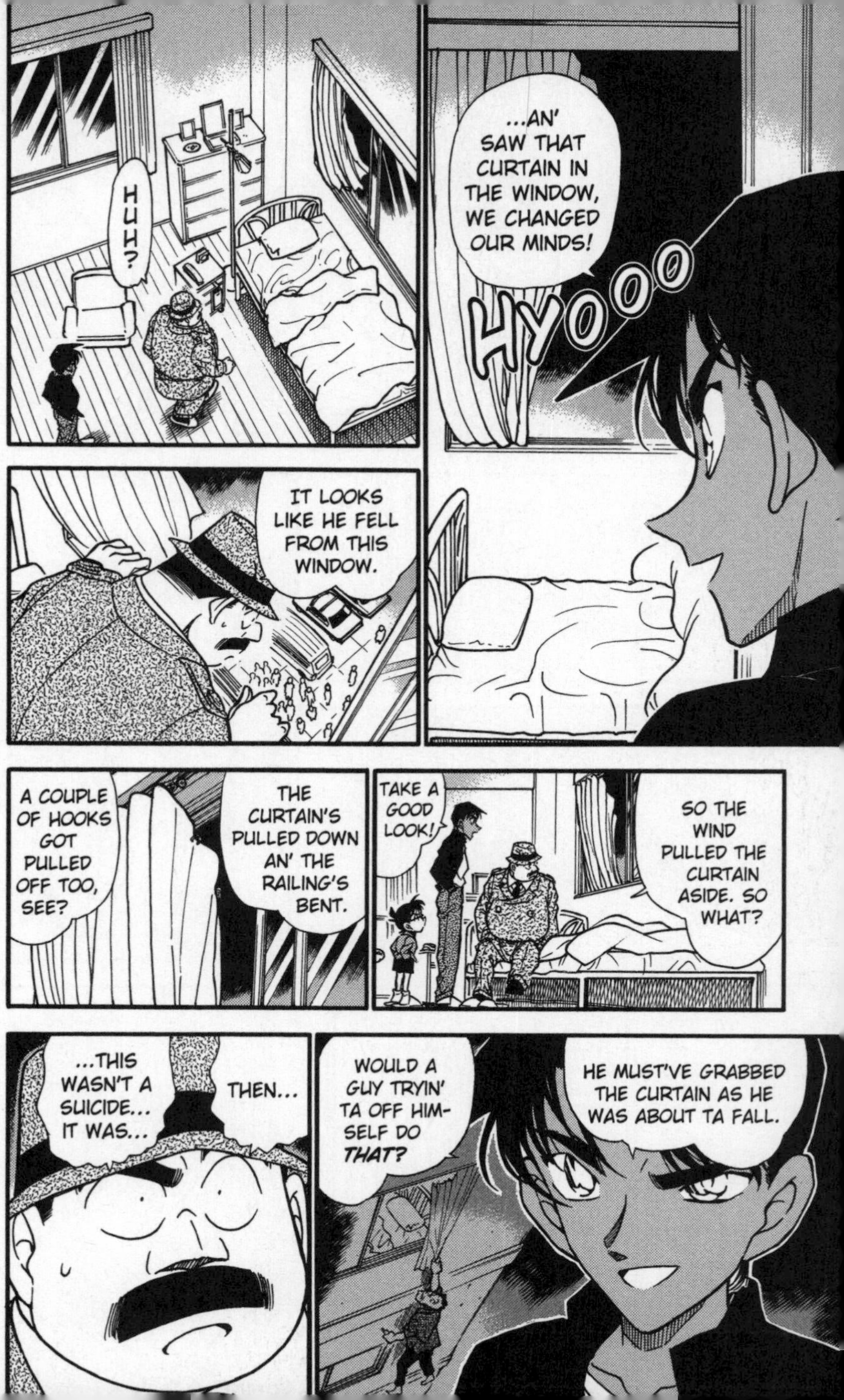
...AN' SAW THAT CURTAIN IN THE WINDOW, WE CHANGED OUR MINDS!
HYOOO
HUH?
IT LOOKS LIKE HE FELL FROM THIS WINDOW.
SO THE WIND PULLED THE CURTAIN ASIDE. SO WHAT?
TAKE A GOOD LOOK!
THE CURTAIN'S PULLED DOWN AN' THE RAILING'S BENT.
A COUPLE OF HOOKS GOT PULLED OFF TOO, SEE?
HE MUST'VE GRABBED THE CURTAIN AS HE WAS ABOUT TA FALL.
WOULD A GUY TRYIN' TA OFF HIM-SELF DO *THAT*?
THEN...
...THIS WASN'T A SUICIDE... IT WAS...

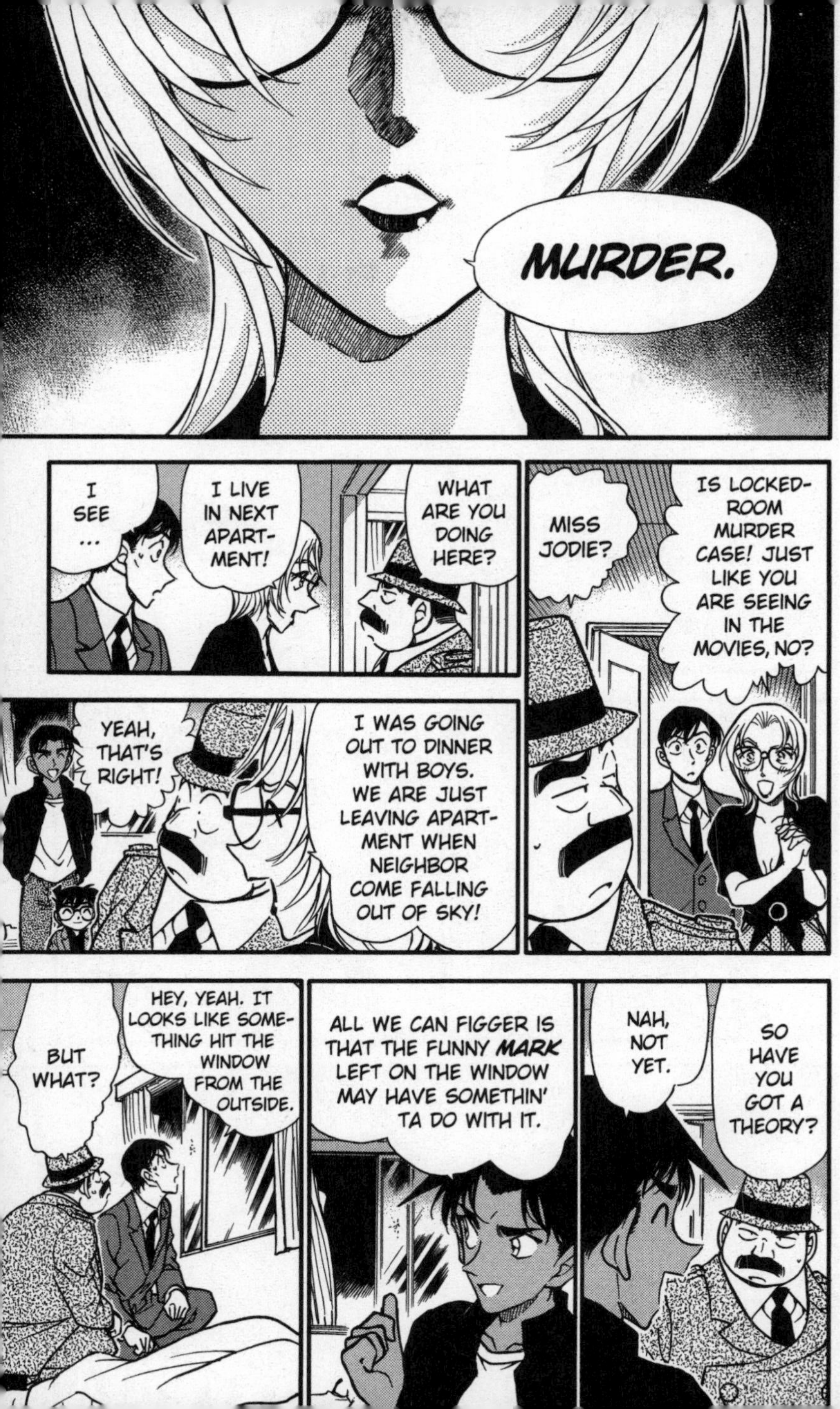
MURDER.
IS LOCKED-ROOM MURDER CASE! JUST LIKE YOU ARE SEEING IN THE MOVIES, NO?
MISS JODIE?
WHAT ARE YOU DOING HERE?
I LIVE IN NEXT APARTMENT!
I SEE ...
I WAS GOING OUT TO DINNER WITH BOYS. WE ARE JUST LEAVING APARTMENT WHEN NEIGHBOR COME FALLING OUT OF SKY!
YEAH, THAT'S RIGHT!
SO HAVE YOU GOT A THEORY?
NAH, NOT YET.
ALL WE CAN FIGGER IS THAT THE FUNNY MARK LEFT ON THE WINDOW MAY HAVE SOMETHIN' TA DO WITH IT.
HEY, YEAH. IT LOOKS LIKE SOMETHING HIT THE WINDOW FROM THE OUTSIDE.
BUT WHAT?

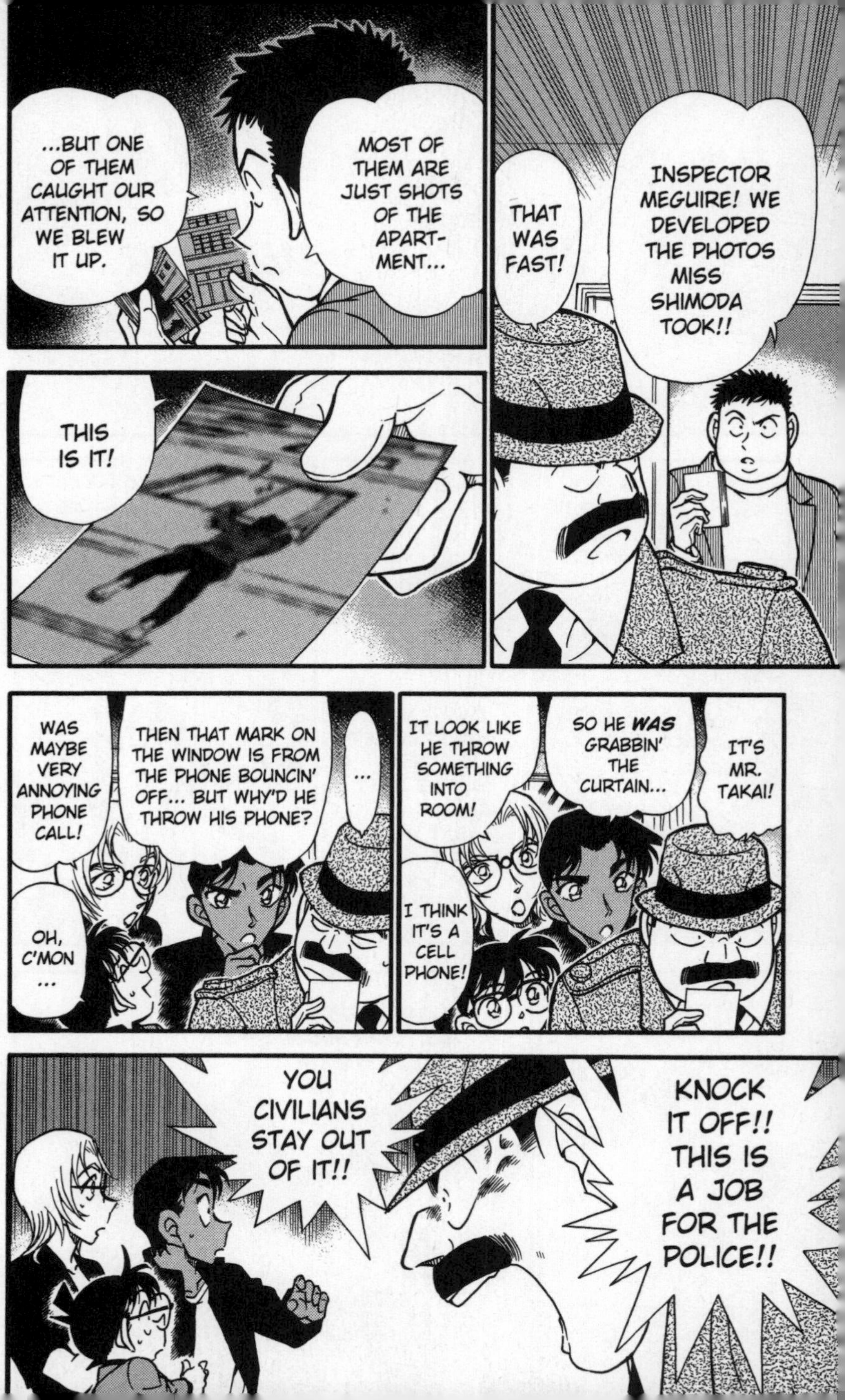
INSPECTOR MEGUIRE! WE DEVELOPED THE PHOTOS MISS SHIMODA TOOK!!
THAT WAS FAST!
MOST OF THEM ARE JUST SHOTS OF THE APART-MENT...
...BUT ONE OF THEM CAUGHT OUR ATTENTION, SO WE BLEW IT UP.
THIS IS IT!
IT'S MR. TAKAI!
SO HE *WAS* GRABBIN' THE CURTAIN...
IT LOOK LIKE HE THROW SOMETHING INTO ROOM!
I THINK IT'S A CELL PHONE!
...
THEN THAT MARK ON THE WINDOW IS FROM THE PHONE BOUNCIN' OFF... BUT WHY'D HE THROW HIS PHONE?
WAS MAYBE VERY ANNOYING PHONE CALL!
OH, C'MON ...
KNOCK IT OFF!! THIS IS A JOB FOR THE POLICE!!
YOU CIVILIANS STAY OUT OF IT!!

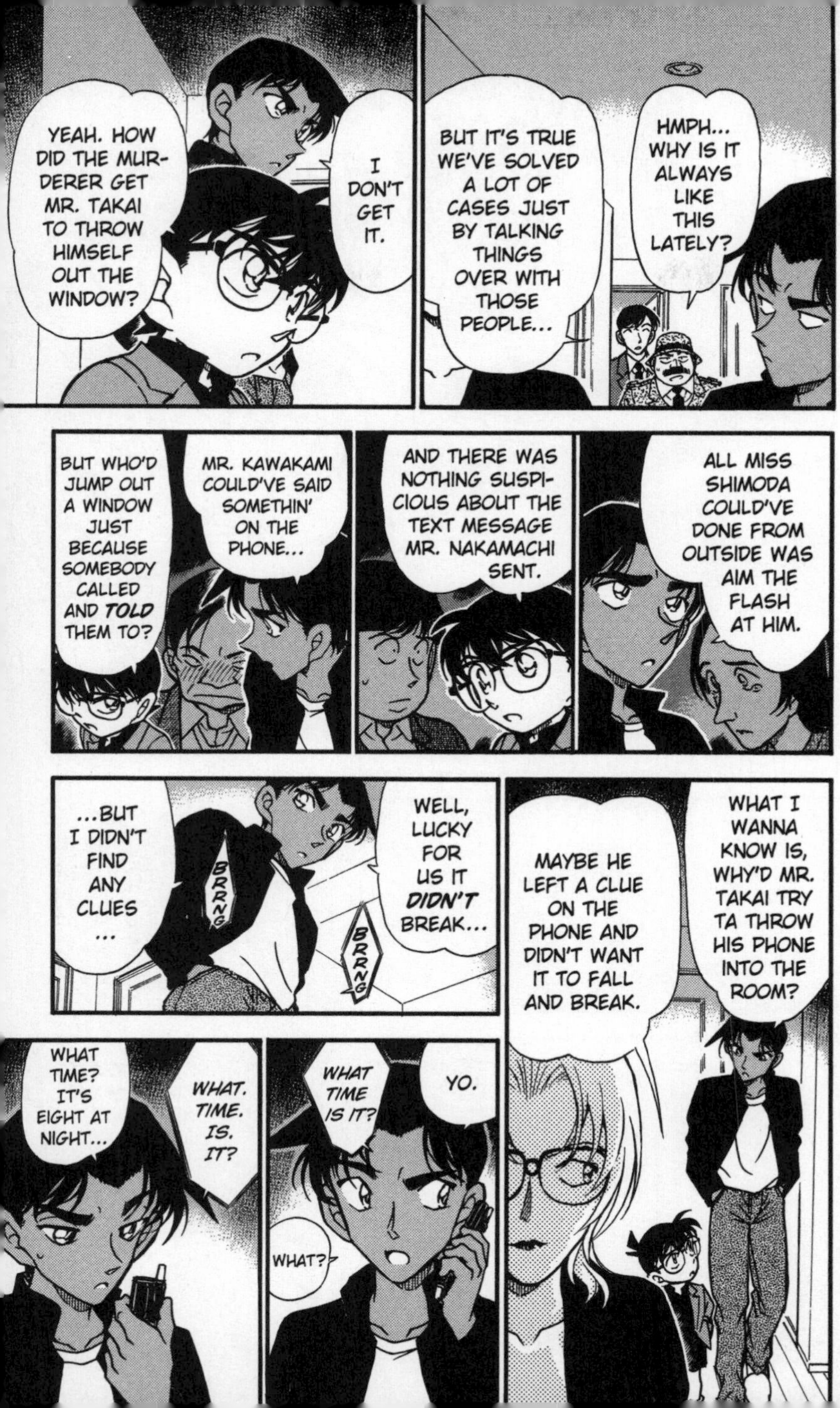
HMPH... WHY IS IT ALWAYS LIKE THIS LATELY?
BUT IT'S TRUE WE'VE SOLVED A LOT OF CASES JUST BY TALKING THINGS OVER WITH THOSE PEOPLE...
I DON'T GET IT.
YEAH. HOW DID THE MURDERER GET MR. TAKAI TO THROW HIMSELF OUT THE WINDOW?
ALL MISS SHIMODA COULD'VE DONE FROM OUTSIDE WAS AIM THE FLASH AT HIM.
AND THERE WAS NOTHING SUSPICIOUS ABOUT THE TEXT MESSAGE MR. NAKAMACHI SENT.
MR. KAWAKAMI COULD'VE SAID SOMETHIN' ON THE PHONE...
BUT WHO'D JUMP OUT A WINDOW JUST BECAUSE SOMEBODY CALLED AND *TOLD* THEM TO?
WHAT I WANNA KNOW IS, WHY'D MR. TAKAI TRY TA THROW HIS PHONE INTO THE ROOM?
MAYBE HE LEFT A CLUE ON THE PHONE AND DIDN'T WANT IT TO FALL AND BREAK.
WELL, LUCKY FOR US IT *DIDN'T* BREAK...
BRRNG
BRRNG
...BUT I DIDN'T FIND ANY CLUES...
YO.
WHAT TIME IS IT?
WHAT?
WHAT. TIME. IS. IT?
WHAT TIME? IT'S EIGHT AT NIGHT...

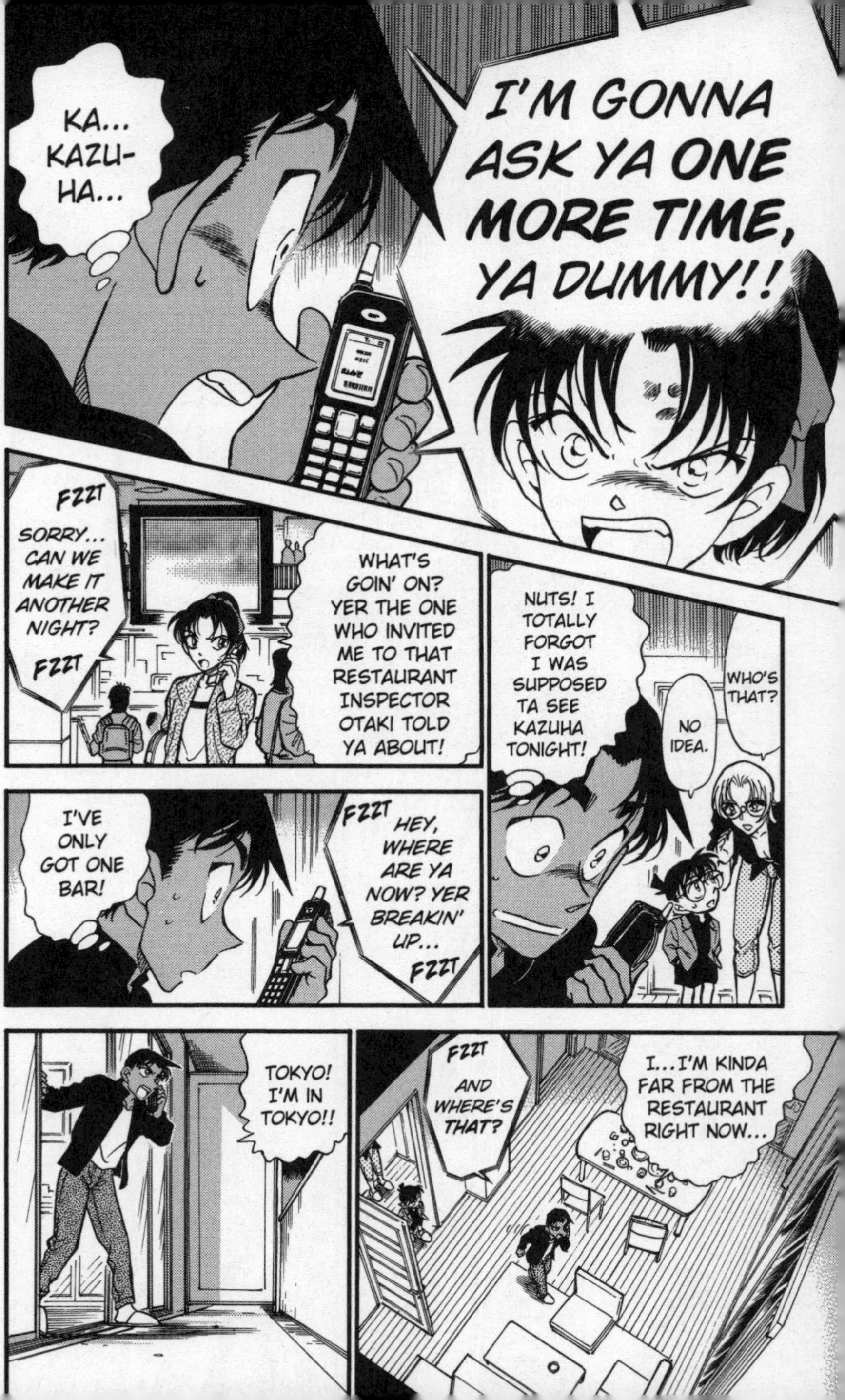
I'M GONNA ASK YA ONE MORE TIME, YA DUMMY!!
KA... KAZUHA...
NUTS! I TOTALLY FORGOT I WAS SUPPOSED TA SEE KAZUHA TONIGHT!
WHO'S THAT?
NO IDEA.
WHAT'S GOIN' ON? YER THE ONE WHO INVITED ME TO THAT RESTAURANT INSPECTOR OTAKI TOLD YA ABOUT!
FZZT
SORRY... CAN WE MAKE IT ANOTHER NIGHT?
FZZT
FZZT
HEY, WHERE ARE YA NOW? YER BREAKIN' UP...
FZZT
I'VE ONLY GOT ONE BAR!
I...I'M KINDA FAR FROM THE RESTAURANT RIGHT NOW...
FZZT
AND WHERE'S THAT?
TOKYO! I'M IN TOKYO!!

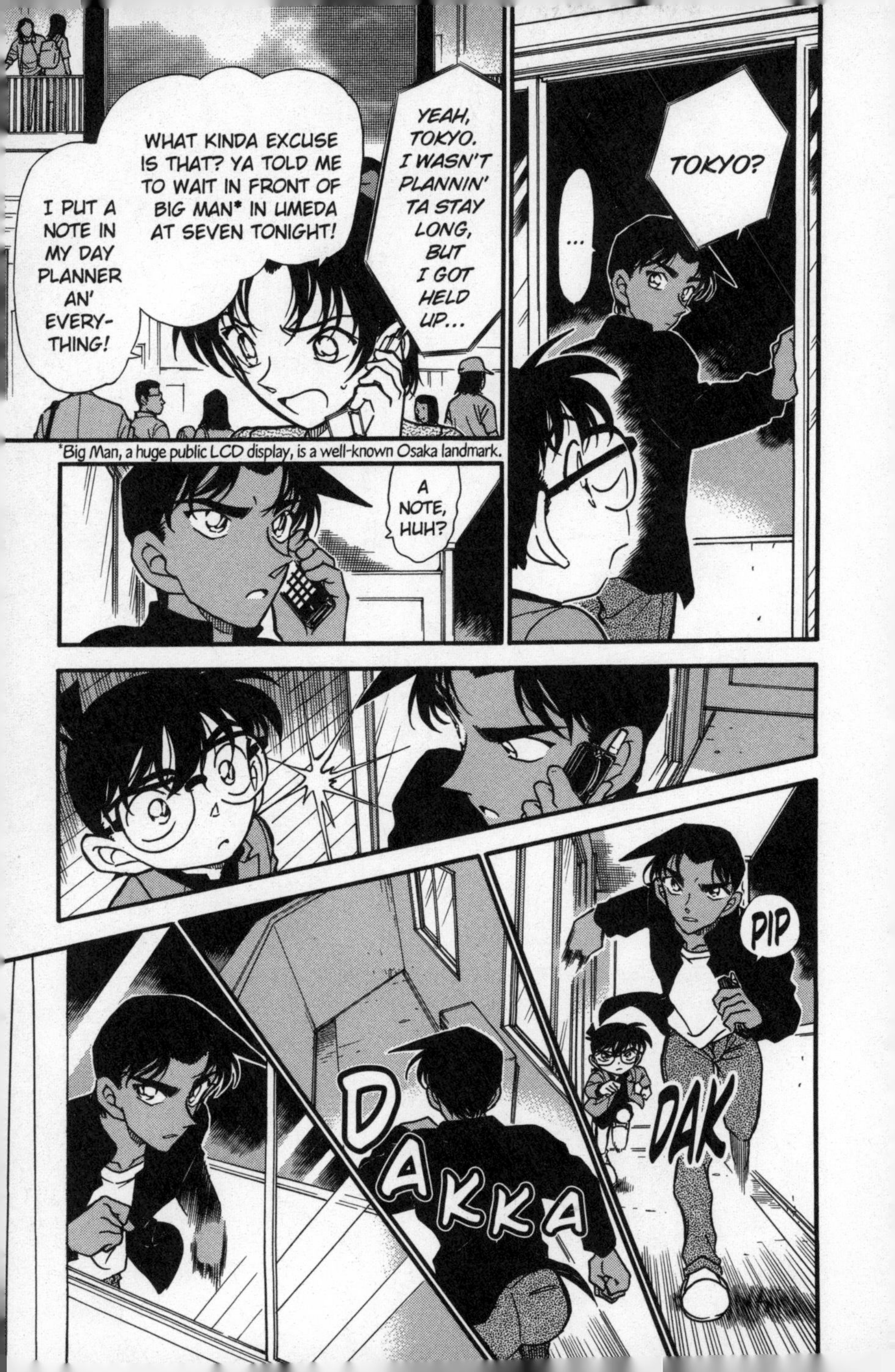
TOKYO?
...
YEAH, TOKYO. I WASN'T PLANNIN' TA STAY LONG, BUT I GOT HELD UP...
WHAT KINDA EXCUSE IS THAT? YA TOLD ME TO WAIT IN FRONT OF BIG MAN* IN UMEDA AT SEVEN TONIGHT!
I PUT A NOTE IN MY DAY PLANNER AN' EVERY-THING!
A NOTE, HUH?
PIP
DAK
DAKKA

*Big Man, a huge public LCD display, is a well-known Osaka landmark.

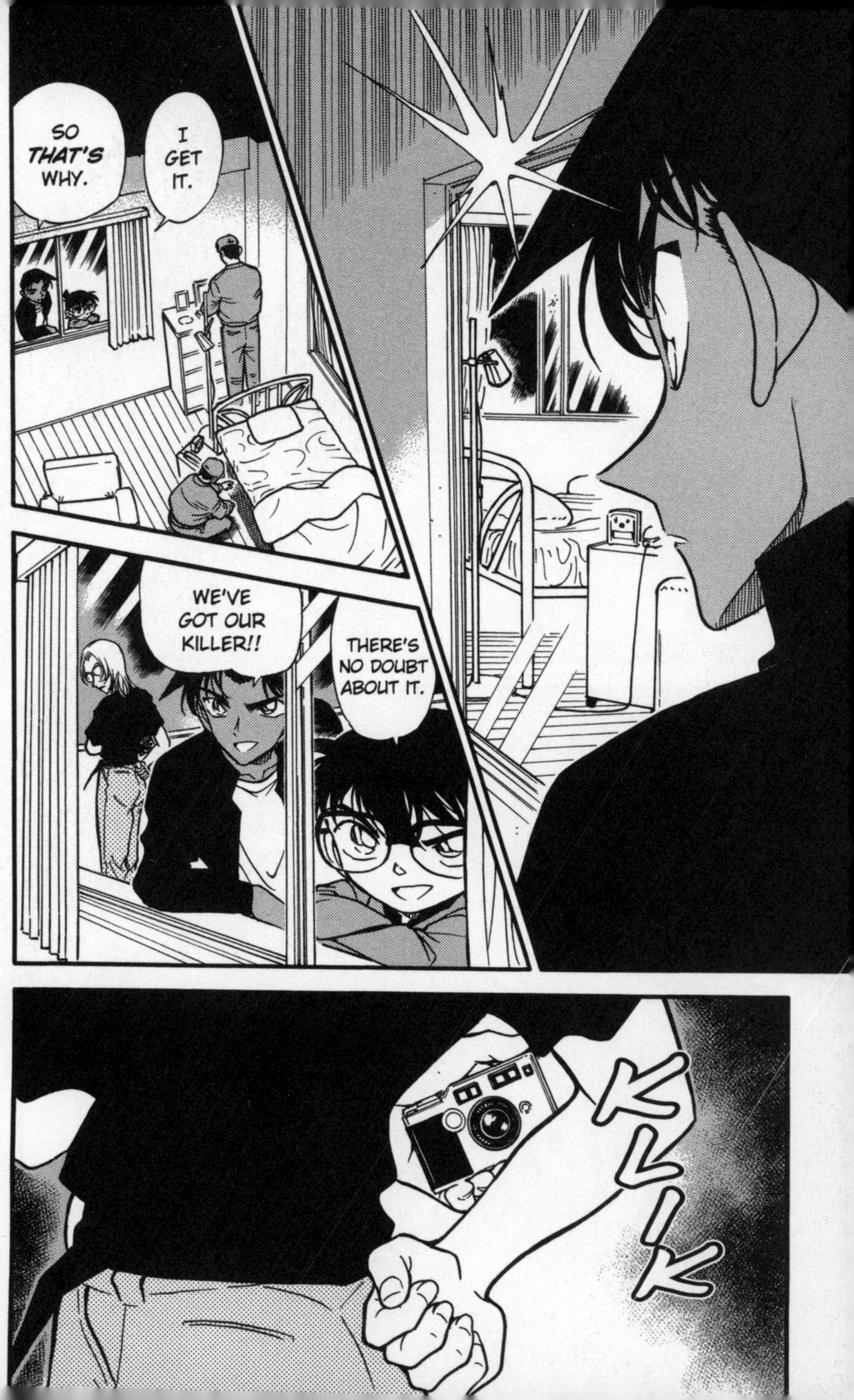
I GET IT.
SO *THAT'S* WHY.
THERE'S NO DOUBT ABOUT IT.
WE'VE GOT OUR KILLER!!

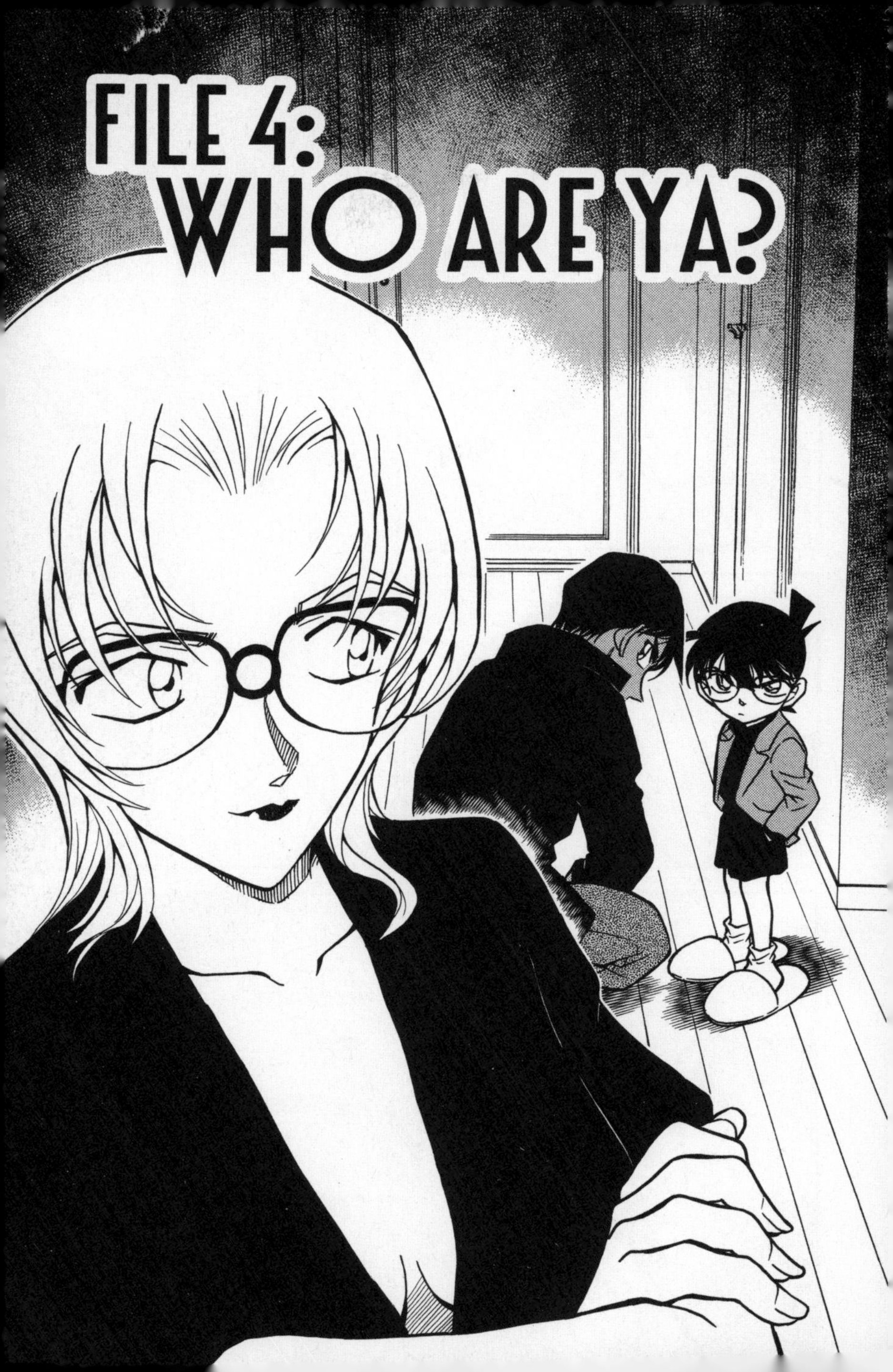
FILE 4:
WHO ARE YA?

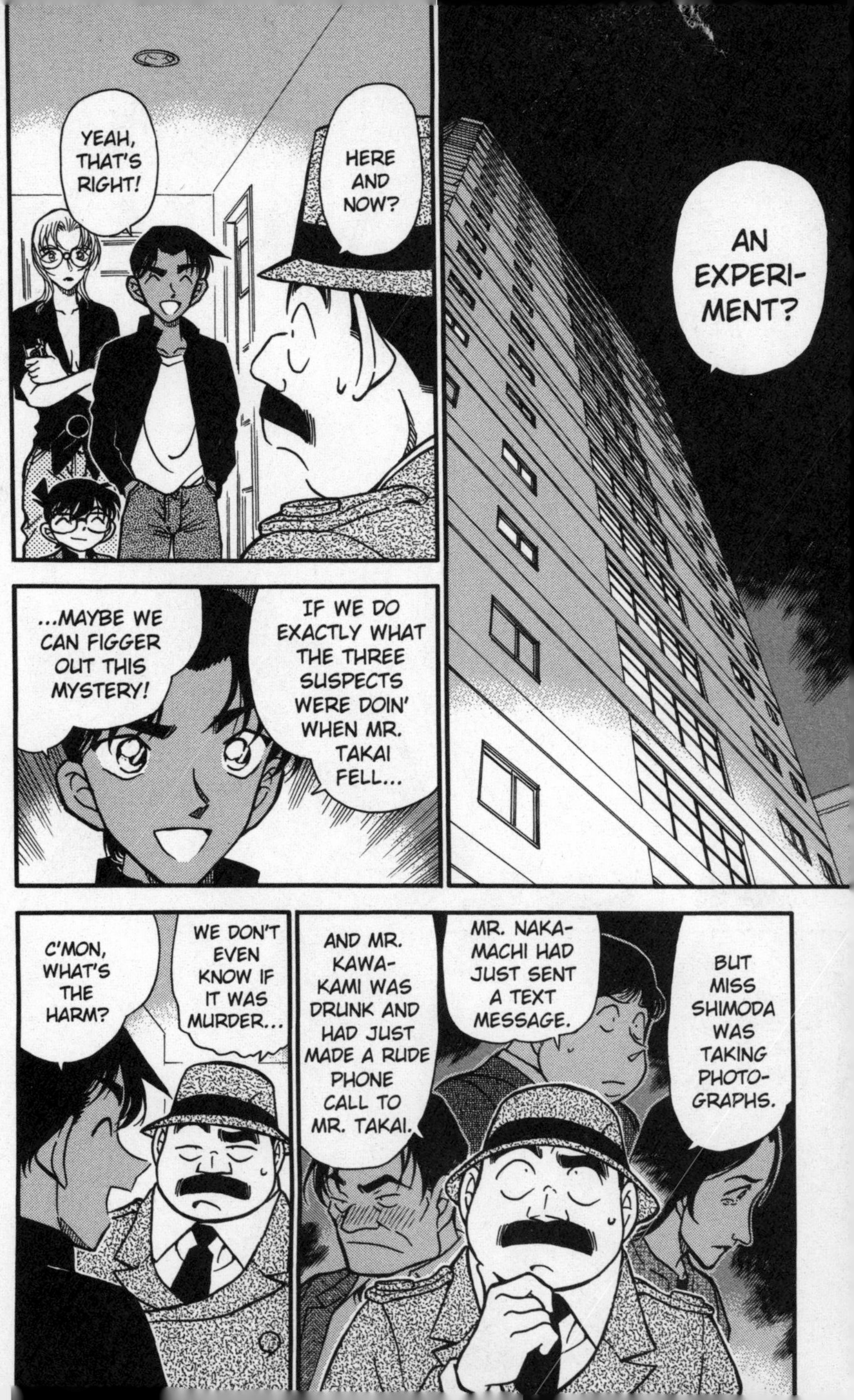
AN EXPERI-MENT?
HERE AND NOW?
YEAH, THAT'S RIGHT!
IF WE DO EXACTLY WHAT THE THREE SUSPECTS WERE DOIN' WHEN MR. TAKAI FELL...
...MAYBE WE CAN FIGGER OUT THIS MYSTERY!
BUT MISS SHIMODA WAS TAKING PHOTO-GRAPHS.
MR. NAKA-MACHI HAD JUST SENT A TEXT MESSAGE.
AND MR. KAWA-KAMI WAS DRUNK AND HAD JUST MADE A RUDE PHONE CALL TO MR. TAKAI.
WE DON'T EVEN KNOW IF IT WAS MURDER...
C'MON, WHAT'S THE HARM?

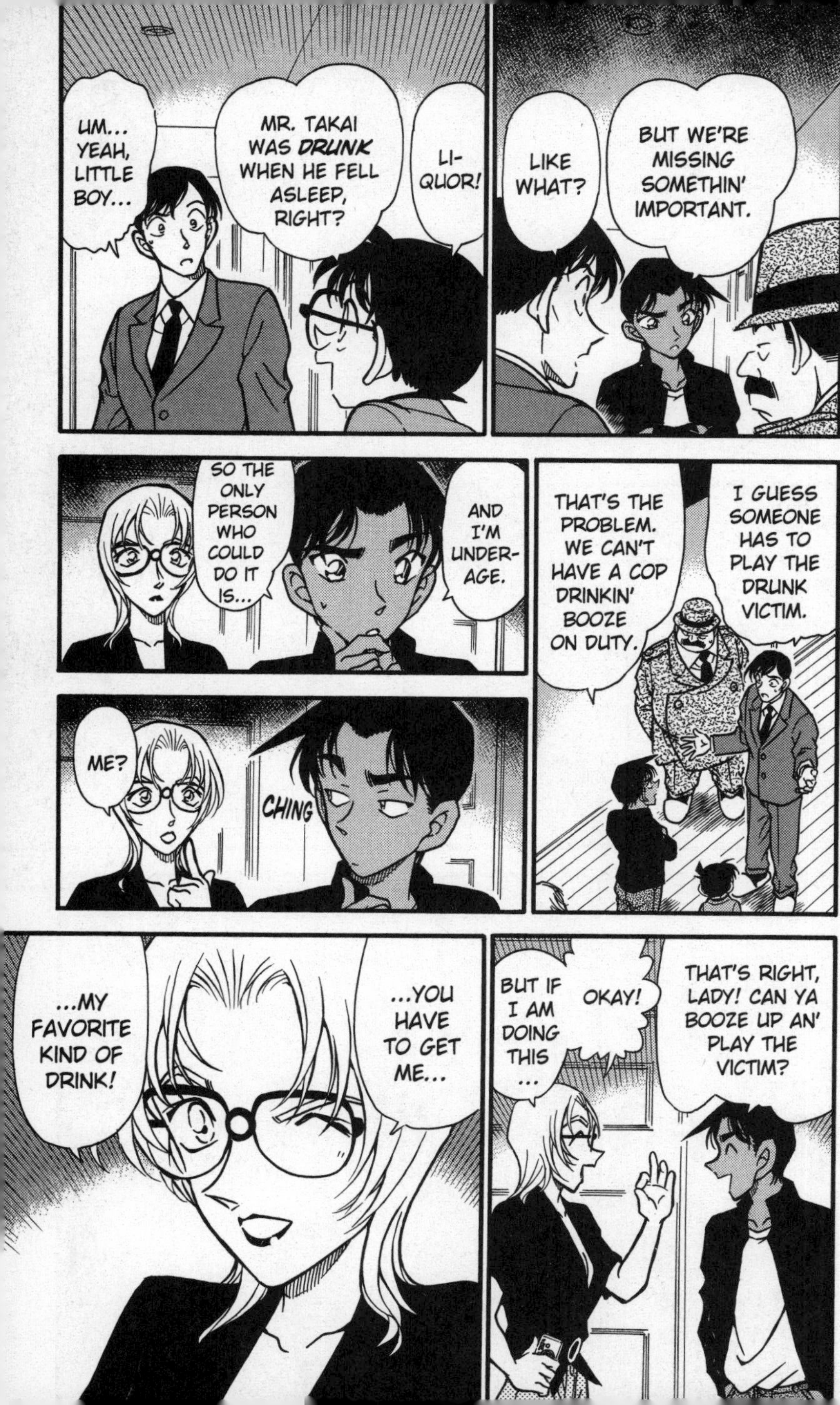
BUT WE'RE MISSING SOMETHIN' IMPORTANT.
LIKE WHAT?
LI-QUOR!
MR. TAKAI WAS DRUNK WHEN HE FELL ASLEEP, RIGHT?
UM... YEAH, LITTLE BOY...
I GUESS SOMEONE HAS TO PLAY THE DRUNK VICTIM.
THAT'S THE PROBLEM. WE CAN'T HAVE A COP DRINKIN' BOOZE ON DUTY.
AND I'M UNDER-AGE.
SO THE ONLY PERSON WHO COULD DO IT IS...
CHING
ME?
THAT'S RIGHT, LADY! CAN YA BOOZE UP AN' PLAY THE VICTIM?
OKAY!
BUT IF I AM DOING THIS ...
...YOU HAVE TO GET ME...
...MY FAVORITE KIND OF DRINK!

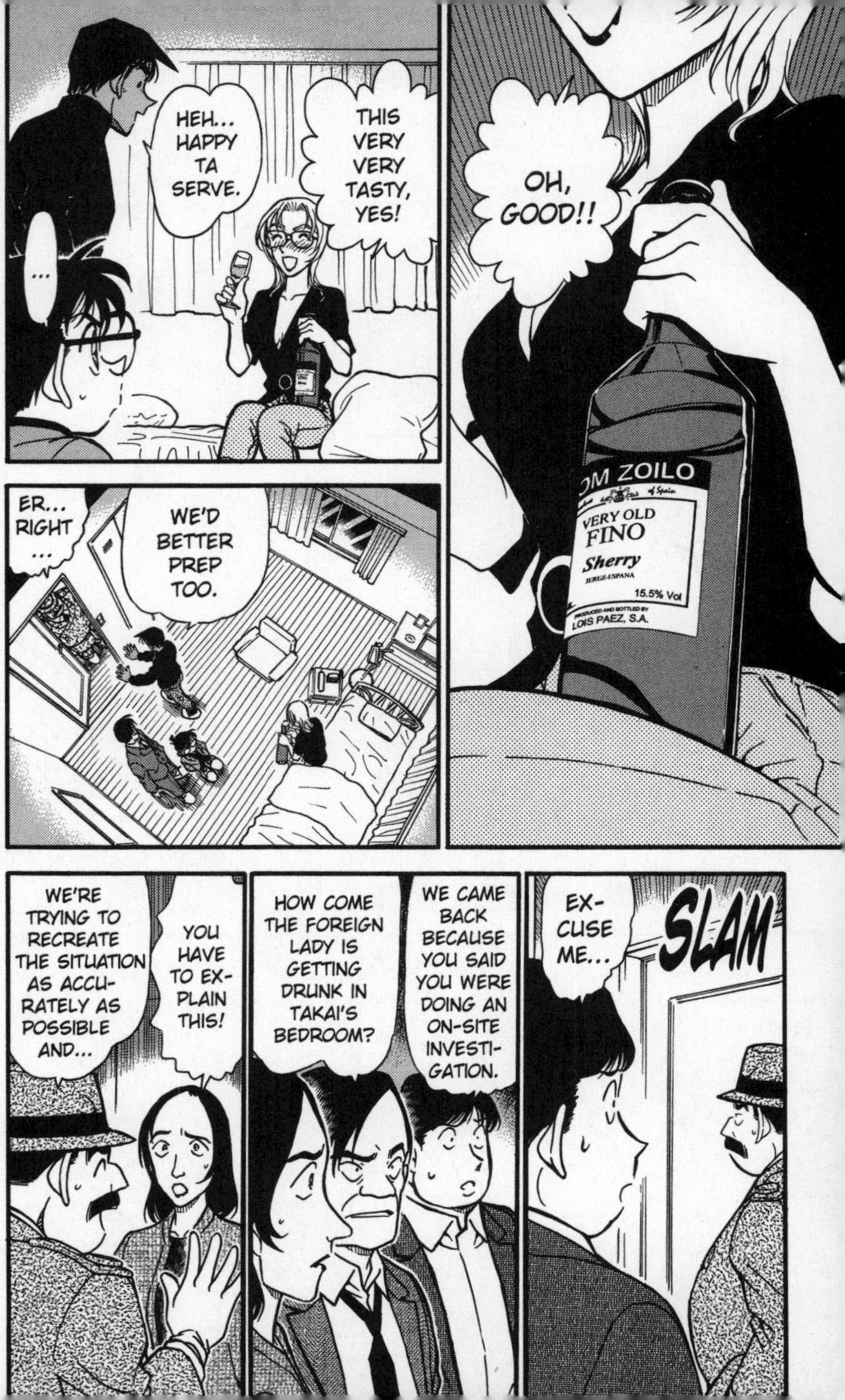
OH, GOOD!!
OM ZOILO
VERY OLD FINO
Sherry
JEREZ-ESPANA
15.5% Vol
PRODUCED AND BOTTLED BY
LOIS PAEZ, S.A.
THIS VERY VERY TASTY, YES!
HEH... HAPPY TA SERVE.
...
WE'D BETTER PREP TOO.
ER... RIGHT ...
SLAM
EX-CUSE ME...
WE CAME BACK BECAUSE YOU SAID YOU WERE DOING AN ON-SITE INVESTI-GATION.
HOW COME THE FOREIGN LADY IS GETTING DRUNK IN TAKAI'S BEDROOM?
YOU HAVE TO EX-PLAIN THIS!
WE'RE TRYING TO RECREATE THE SITUATION AS ACCU-RATELY AS POSSIBLE AND...

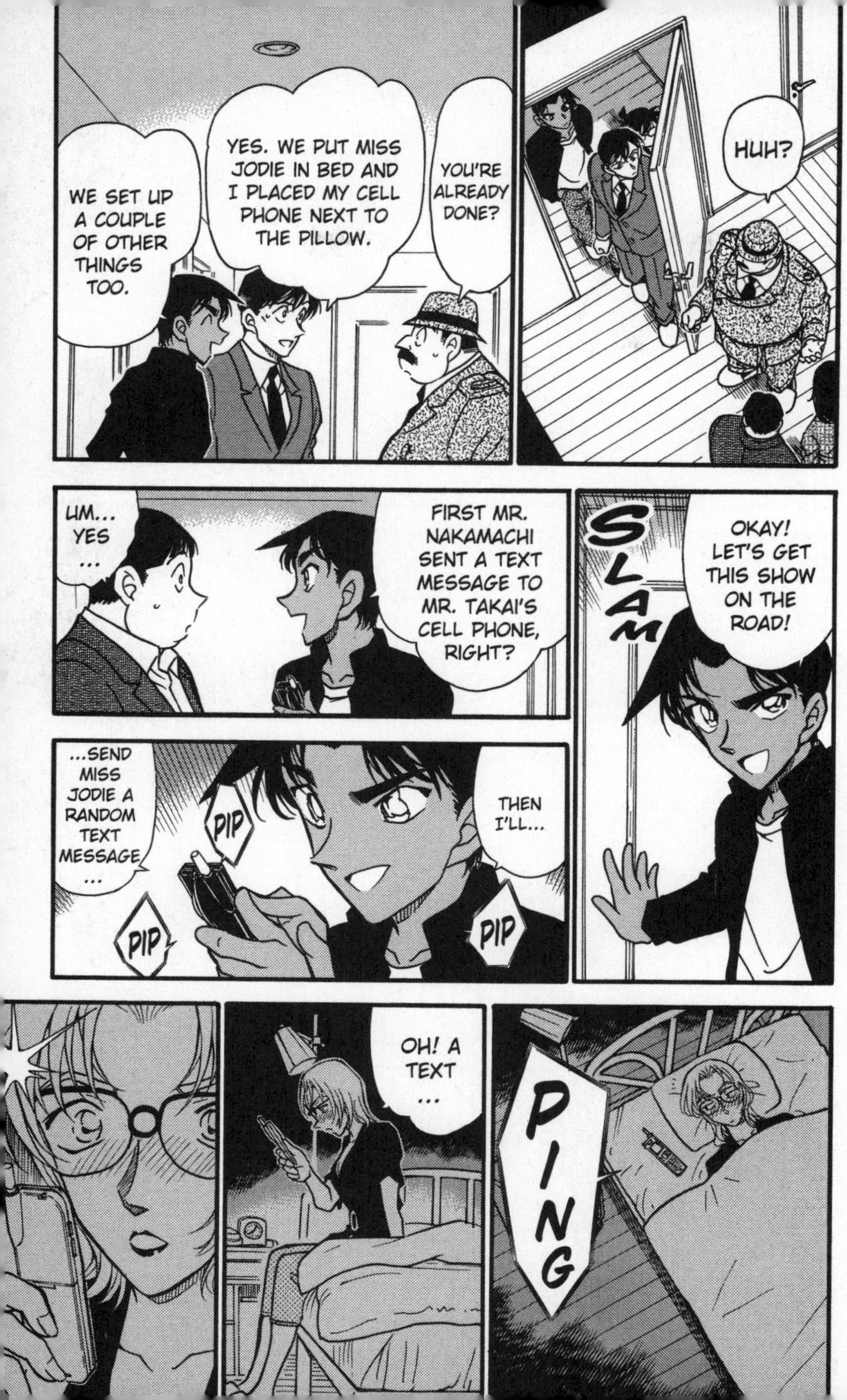
HUH?
YOU'RE ALREADY DONE?
YES. WE PUT MISS JODIE IN BED AND I PLACED MY CELL PHONE NEXT TO THE PILLOW.
WE SET UP A COUPLE OF OTHER THINGS TOO.
SLAM
OKAY! LET'S GET THIS SHOW ON THE ROAD!
FIRST MR. NAKAMACHI SENT A TEXT MESSAGE TO MR. TAKAI'S CELL PHONE, RIGHT?
UM... YES ...
THEN I'LL...
PIP
PIP
...SEND MISS JODIE A RANDOM TEXT MESSAGE ...
PIP
PING
OH! A TEXT ...

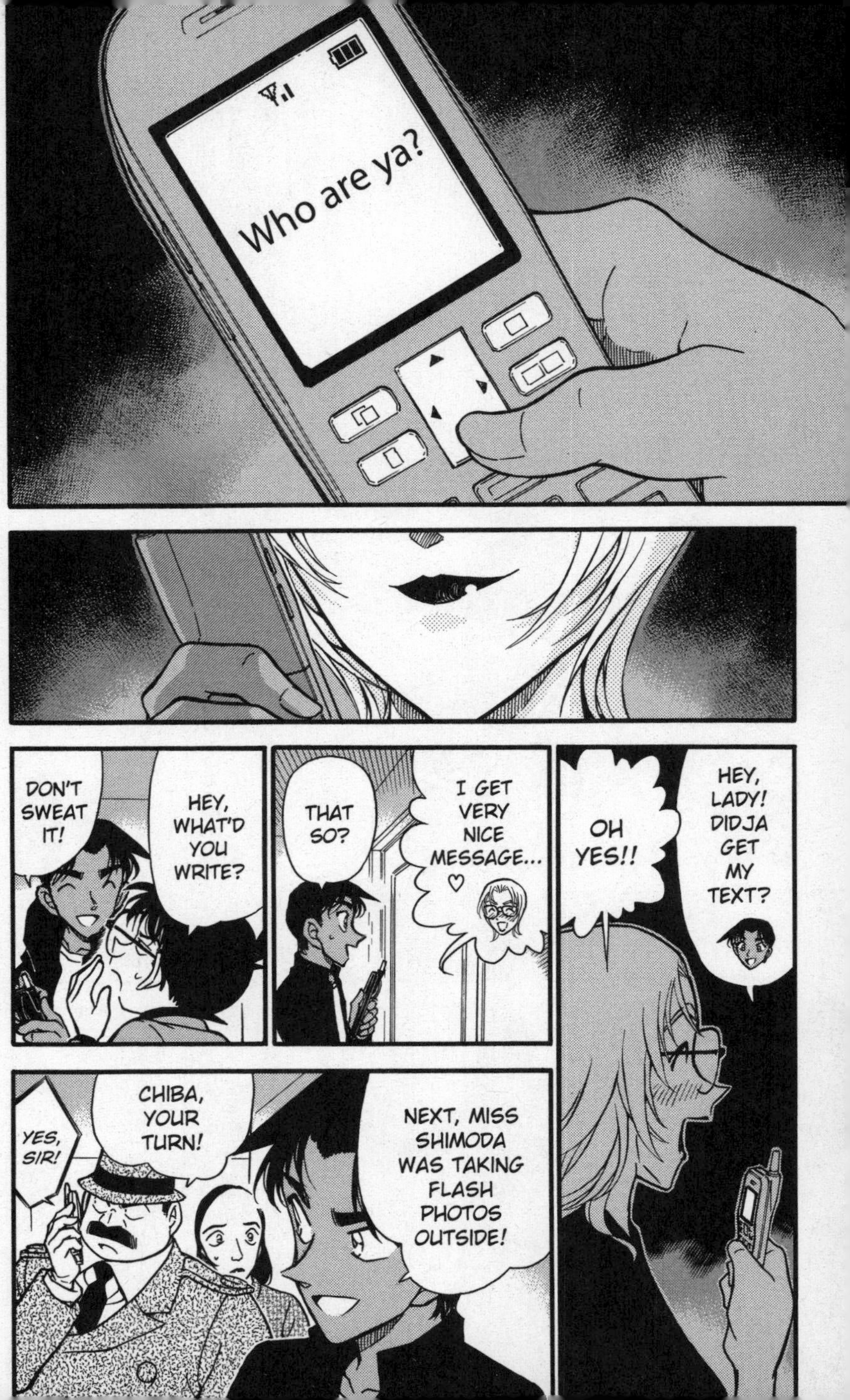
Who are ya?
HEY, LADY! DIDJA GET MY TEXT?
OH YES!!
I GET VERY NICE MESSAGE... ♡
THAT SO?
HEY, WHAT'D YOU WRITE?
DON'T SWEAT IT!
NEXT, MISS SHIMODA WAS TAKING FLASH PHOTOS OUTSIDE!
CHIBA, YOUR TURN!
YES, SIR!

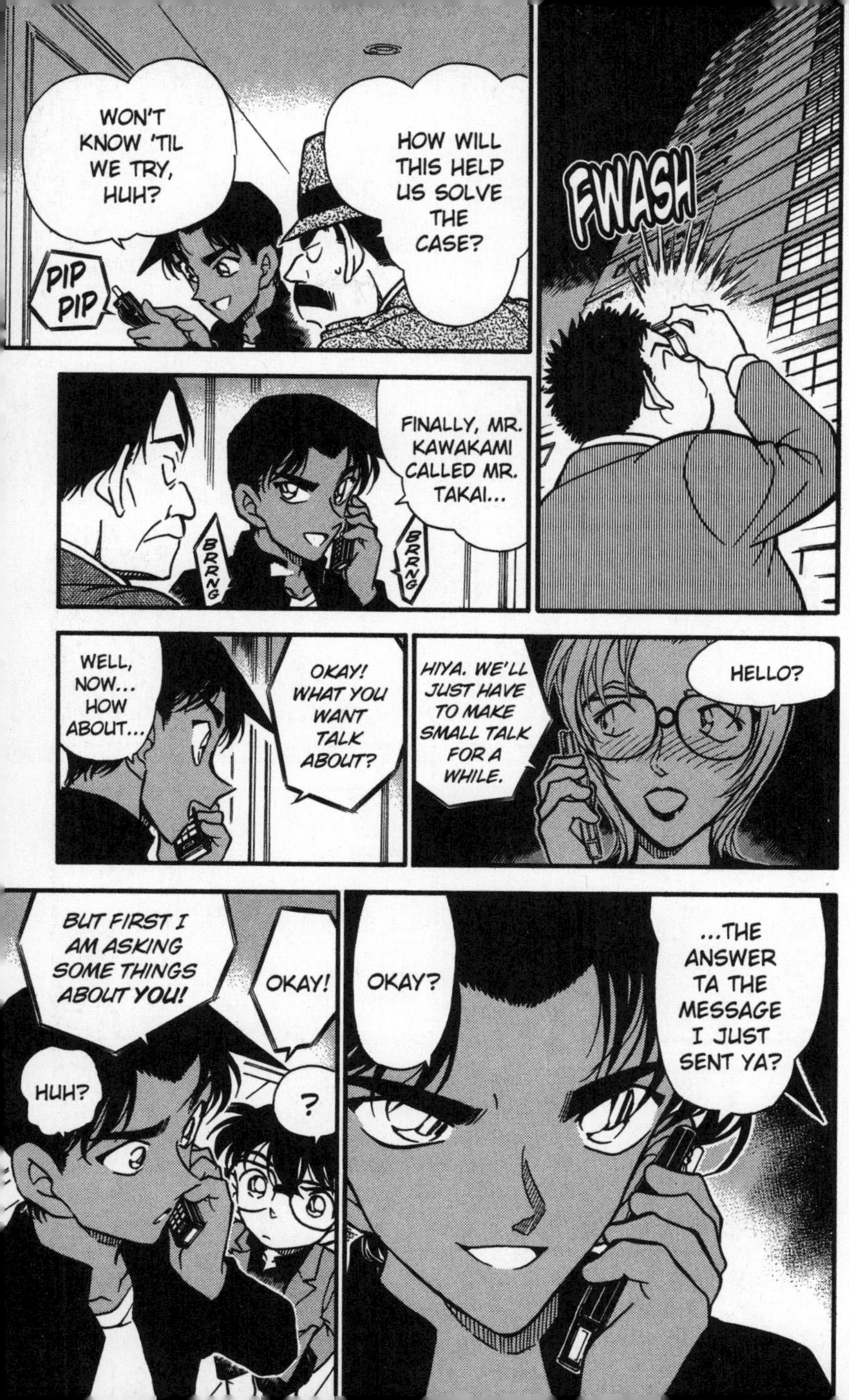
FWASH
HOW WILL THIS HELP US SOLVE THE CASE?
WON'T KNOW 'TIL WE TRY, HUH?
PIP PIP
FINALLY, MR. KAWAKAMI CALLED MR. TAKAI...
BRRNG
BRRNG
HELLO?
HIYA. WE'LL JUST HAVE TO MAKE SMALL TALK FOR A WHILE.
OKAY! WHAT YOU WANT TALK ABOUT?
WELL, NOW... HOW ABOUT...
...THE ANSWER TA THE MESSAGE I JUST SENT YA?
OKAY?
OKAY!
BUT FIRST I AM ASKING SOME THINGS ABOUT YOU!
?
HUH?

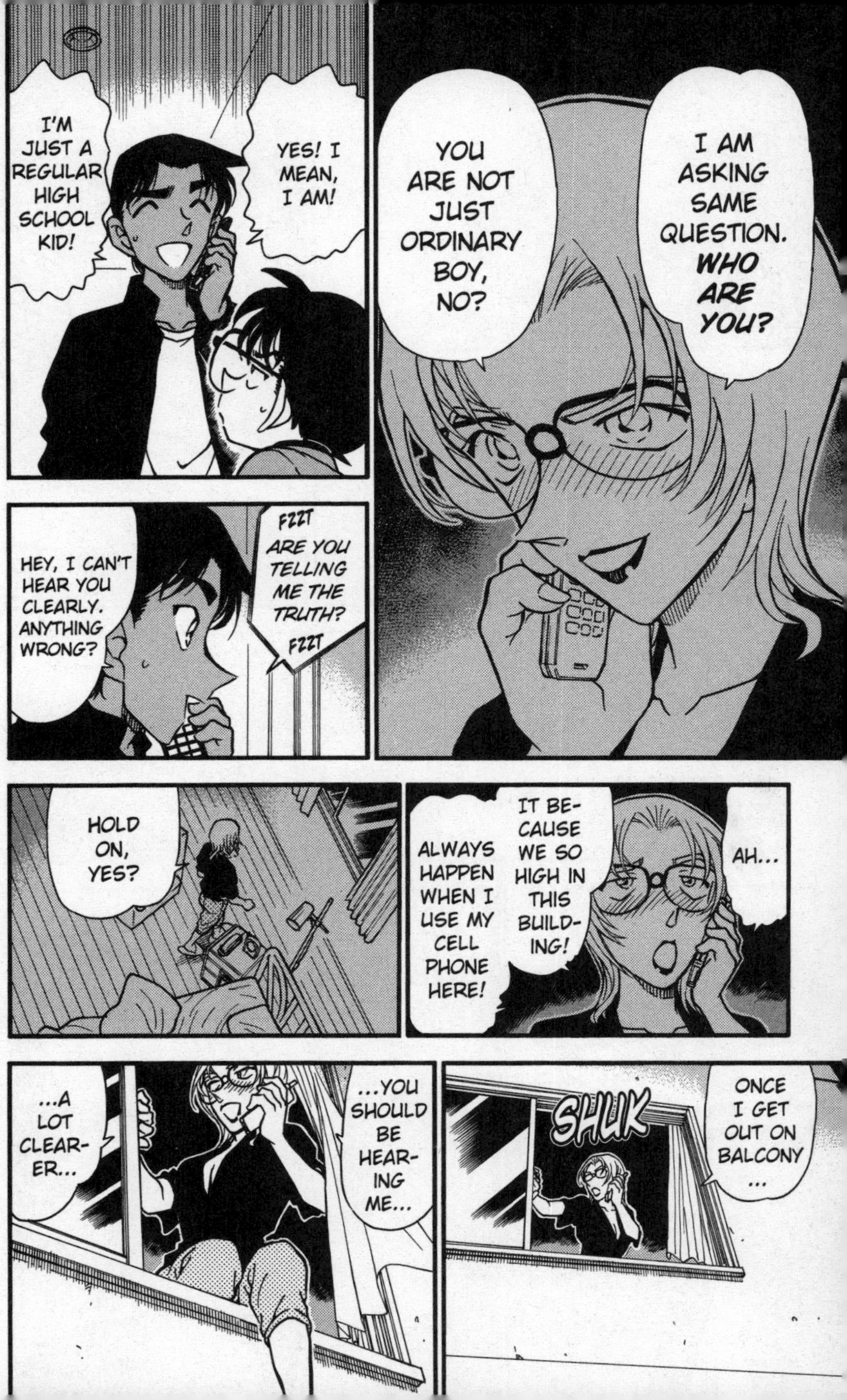
I AM ASKING SAME QUESTION. WHO ARE YOU?
YOU ARE NOT JUST ORDINARY BOY, NO?
YES! I MEAN, I AM!
I'M JUST A REGULAR HIGH SCHOOL KID!
FZZT ARE YOU TELLING ME THE TRUTH? FZZT
HEY, I CAN'T HEAR YOU CLEARLY. ANYTHING WRONG?
AH...
IT BE-CAUSE WE SO HIGH IN THIS BUILD-ING!
ALWAYS HAPPEN WHEN I USE MY CELL PHONE HERE!
HOLD ON, YES?
SHUK
ONCE I GET OUT ON BALCONY ...
...YOU SHOULD BE HEAR-ING ME...
...A LOT CLEAR-ER...

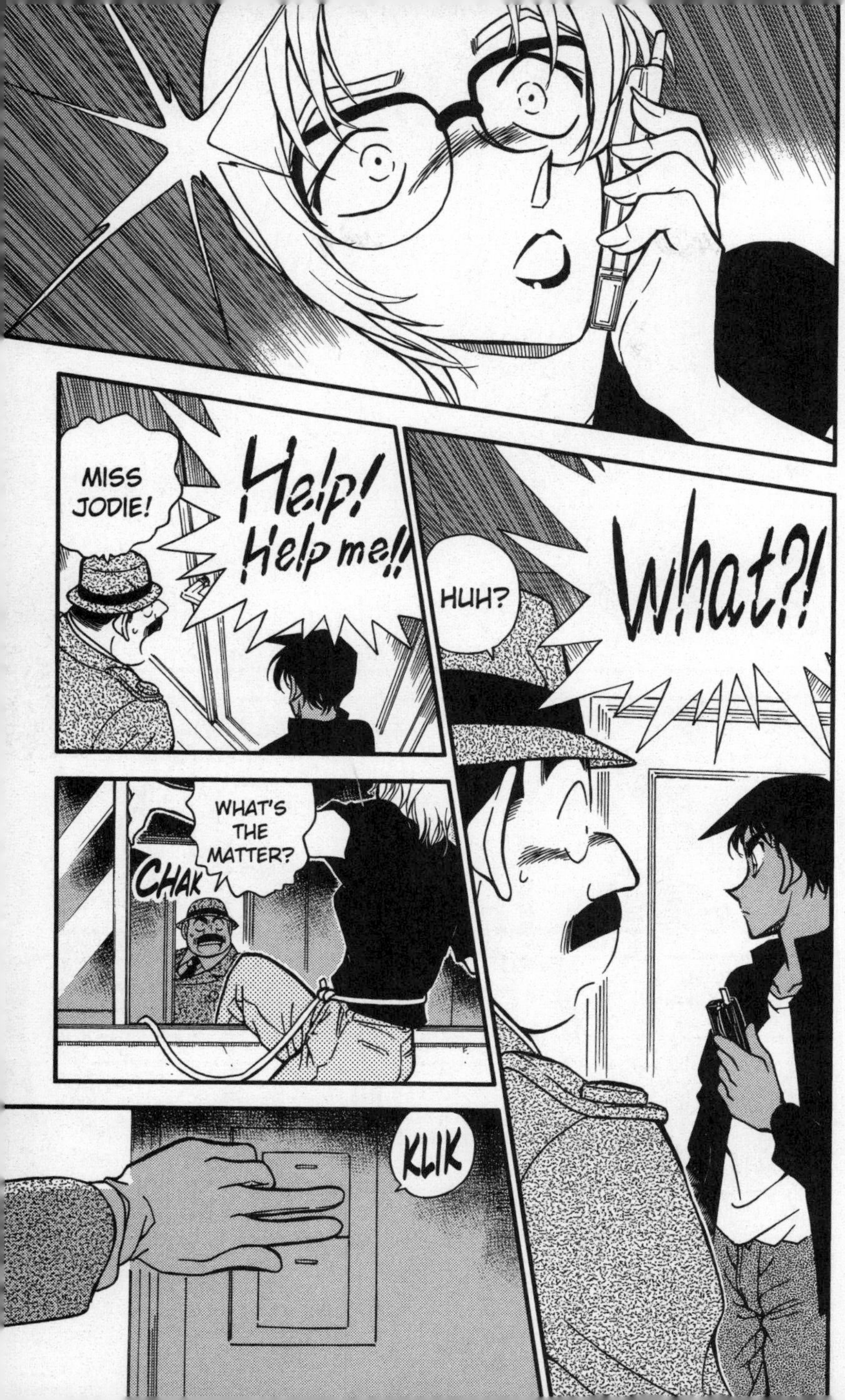
What?!
HUH?
Help! Help me!!
MISS JODIE!
WHAT'S THE MATTER?
CHAK
KLIK

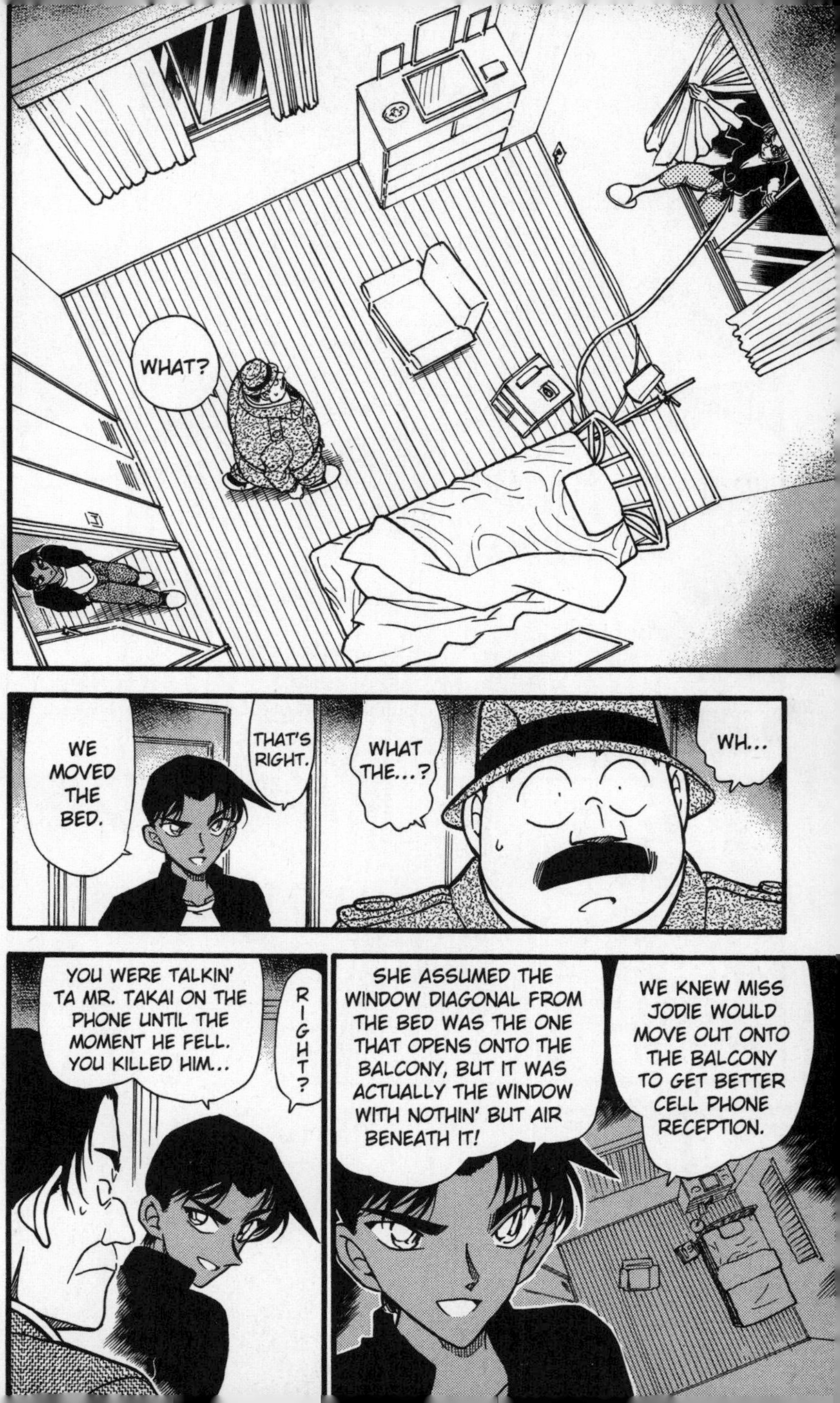
WHAT?
WH...
WHAT THE...?
THAT'S RIGHT.
WE MOVED THE BED.
WE KNEW MISS JODIE WOULD MOVE OUT ONTO THE BALCONY TO GET BETTER CELL PHONE RECEPTION.
SHE ASSUMED THE WINDOW DIAGONAL FROM THE BED WAS THE ONE THAT OPENS ONTO THE BALCONY, BUT IT WAS ACTUALLY THE WINDOW WITH NOTHIN' BUT AIR BENEATH IT!
YOU WERE TALKIN' TA MR. TAKAI ON THE PHONE UNTIL THE MOMENT HE FELL. YOU KILLED HIM...
RIGHT?

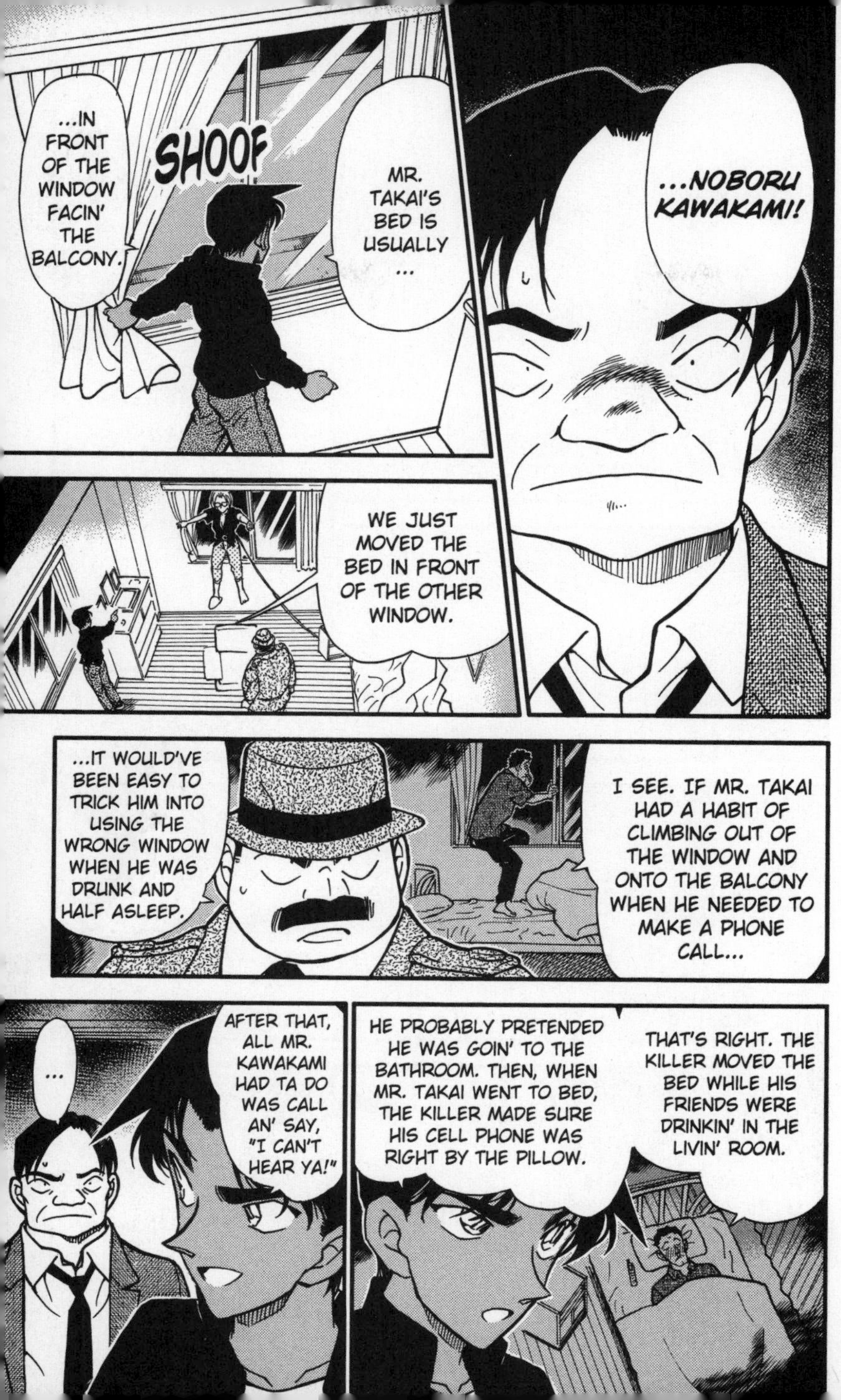
...NOBORU KAWAKAMI!
MR. TAKAI'S BED IS USUALLY ...
SHOOF
...IN FRONT OF THE WINDOW FACIN' THE BALCONY.
WE JUST MOVED THE BED IN FRONT OF THE OTHER WINDOW.
I SEE. IF MR. TAKAI HAD A HABIT OF CLIMBING OUT OF THE WINDOW AND ONTO THE BALCONY WHEN HE NEEDED TO MAKE A PHONE CALL...
...IT WOULD'VE BEEN EASY TO TRICK HIM INTO USING THE WRONG WINDOW WHEN HE WAS DRUNK AND HALF ASLEEP.
THAT'S RIGHT. THE KILLER MOVED THE BED WHILE HIS FRIENDS WERE DRINKIN' IN THE LIVIN' ROOM.
HE PROBABLY PRETENDED HE WAS GOIN' TO THE BATHROOM. THEN, WHEN MR. TAKAI WENT TO BED, THE KILLER MADE SURE HIS CELL PHONE WAS RIGHT BY THE PILLOW.
AFTER THAT, ALL MR. KAWAKAMI HAD TA DO WAS CALL AN' SAY, "I CAN'T HEAR YA!"
...

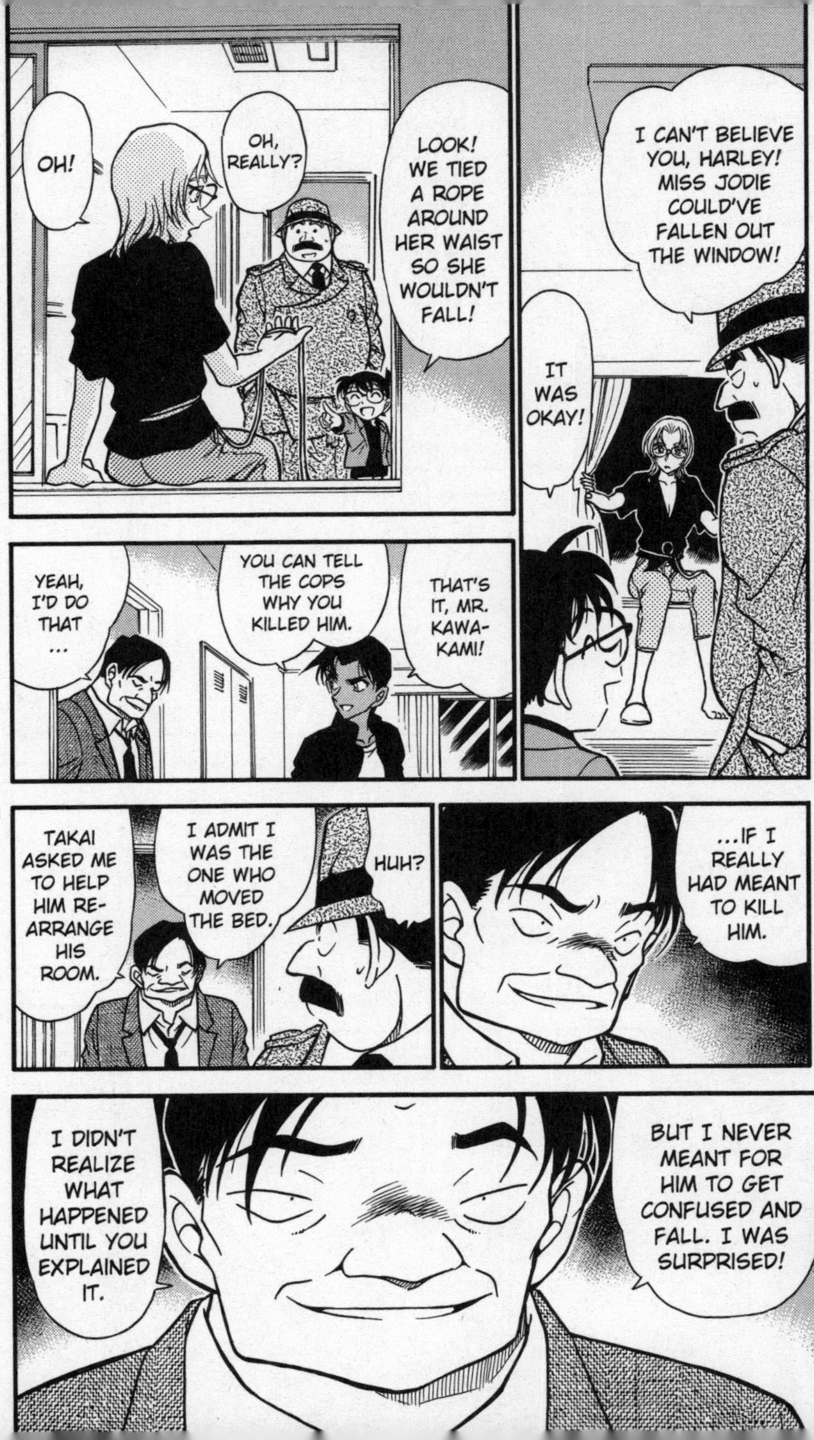
I CAN'T BELIEVE YOU, HARLEY! MISS JODIE COULD'VE FALLEN OUT THE WINDOW!
IT WAS OKAY!
LOOK! WE TIED A ROPE AROUND HER WAIST SO SHE WOULDN'T FALL!
OH, REALLY?
OH!
THAT'S IT, MR. KAWA-KAMI!
YOU CAN TELL THE COPS WHY YOU KILLED HIM.
YEAH, I'D DO THAT ...
...IF I REALLY HAD MEANT TO KILL HIM.
HUH?
I ADMIT I WAS THE ONE WHO MOVED THE BED.
TAKAI ASKED ME TO HELP HIM RE-ARRANGE HIS ROOM.
BUT I NEVER MEANT FOR HIM TO GET CONFUSED AND FALL. I WAS SURPRISED!
I DIDN'T REALIZE WHAT HAPPENED UNTIL YOU EXPLAINED IT.

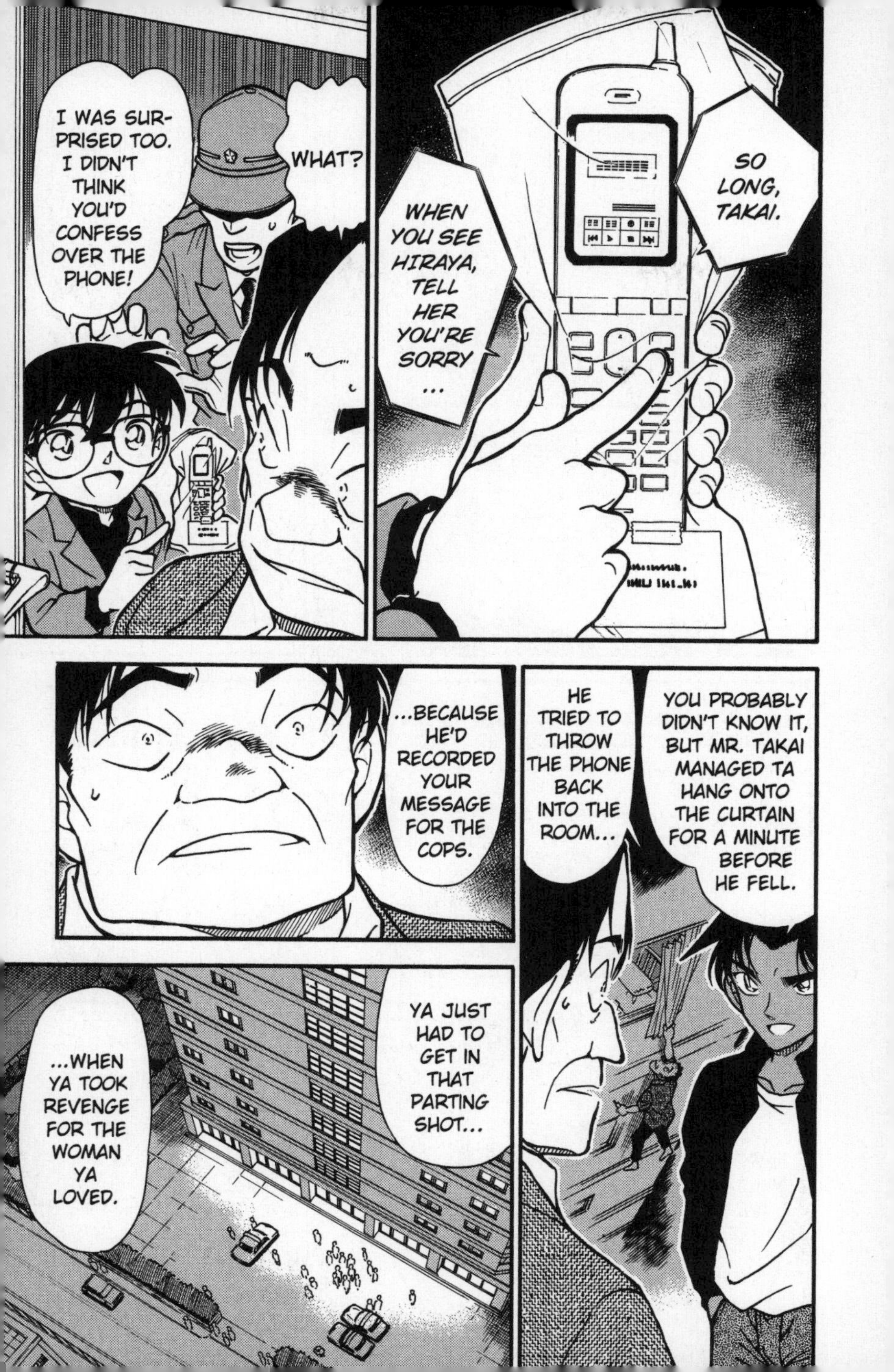
SO LONG, TAKAI.
WHEN YOU SEE HIRAYA, TELL HER YOU'RE SORRY...
WHAT?
I WAS SURPRISED TOO. I DIDN'T THINK YOU'D CONFESS OVER THE PHONE!
YOU PROBABLY DIDN'T KNOW IT, BUT MR. TAKAI MANAGED TA HANG ONTO THE CURTAIN FOR A MINUTE BEFORE HE FELL.
HE TRIED TO THROW THE PHONE BACK INTO THE ROOM...
...BECAUSE HE'D RECORDED YOUR MESSAGE FOR THE COPS.
YA JUST HAD TO GET IN THAT PARTING SHOT...
...WHEN YA TOOK REVENGE FOR THE WOMAN YA LOVED.

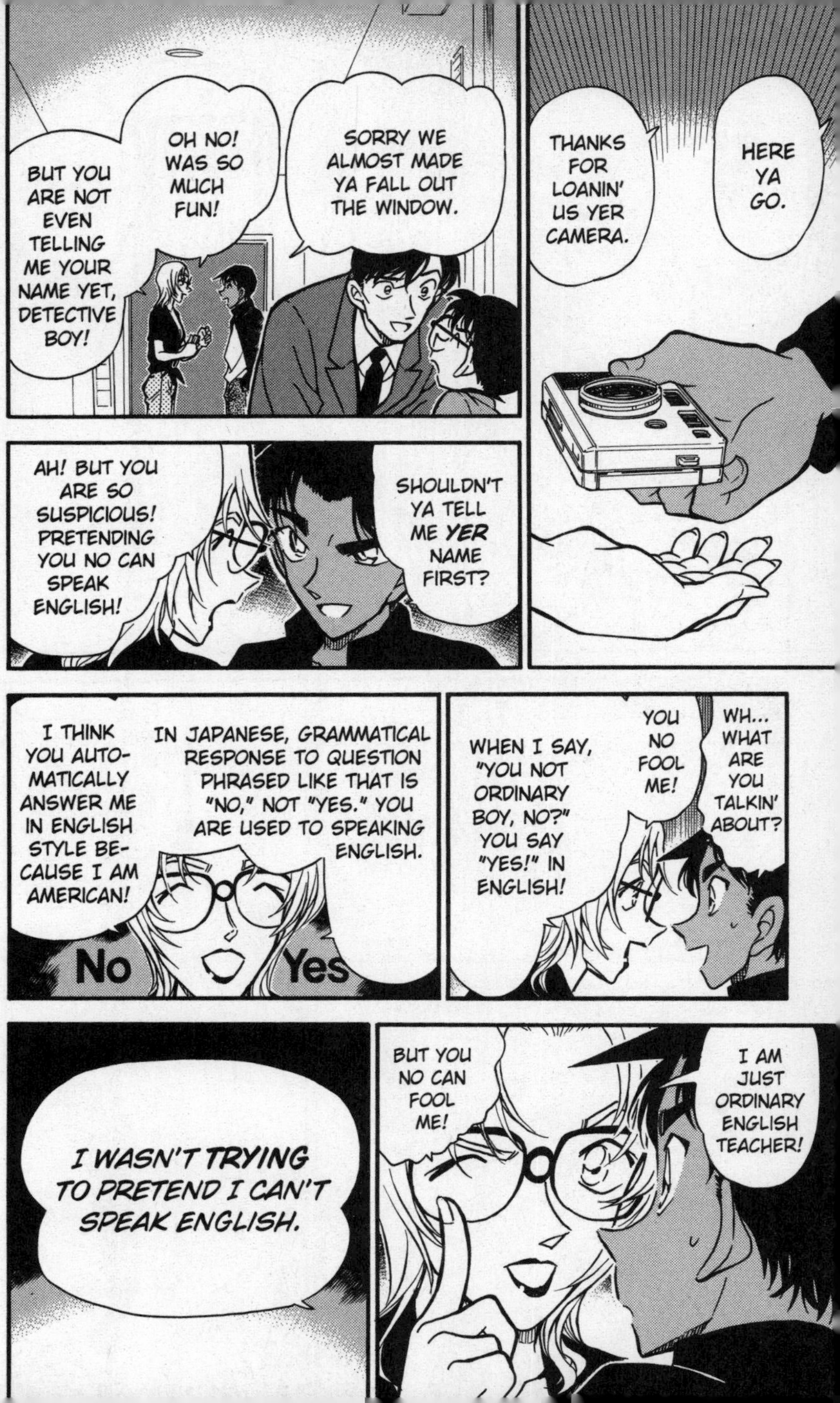
HERE YA GO.
THANKS FOR LOANIN' US YER CAMERA.
SORRY WE ALMOST MADE YA FALL OUT THE WINDOW.
OH NO! WAS SO MUCH FUN!
BUT YOU ARE NOT EVEN TELLING ME YOUR NAME YET, DETECTIVE BOY!
SHOULDN'T YA TELL ME *YER* NAME FIRST?
AH! BUT YOU ARE SO SUSPICIOUS! PRETENDING YOU NO CAN SPEAK ENGLISH!
WH... WHAT ARE YOU TALKIN' ABOUT?
YOU NO FOOL ME!
WHEN I SAY, "YOU NOT ORDINARY BOY, NO?" YOU SAY "YES!" IN ENGLISH!
IN JAPANESE, GRAMMATICAL RESPONSE TO QUESTION PHRASED LIKE THAT IS "NO," NOT "YES." YOU ARE USED TO SPEAKING ENGLISH.
I THINK YOU AUTO-MATICALLY ANSWER ME IN ENGLISH STYLE BE-CAUSE I AM AMERICAN!
No
Yes
I AM JUST ORDINARY ENGLISH TEACHER!
BUT YOU NO CAN FOOL ME!
I WASN'T TRYING TO PRETEND I CAN'T SPEAK ENGLISH.

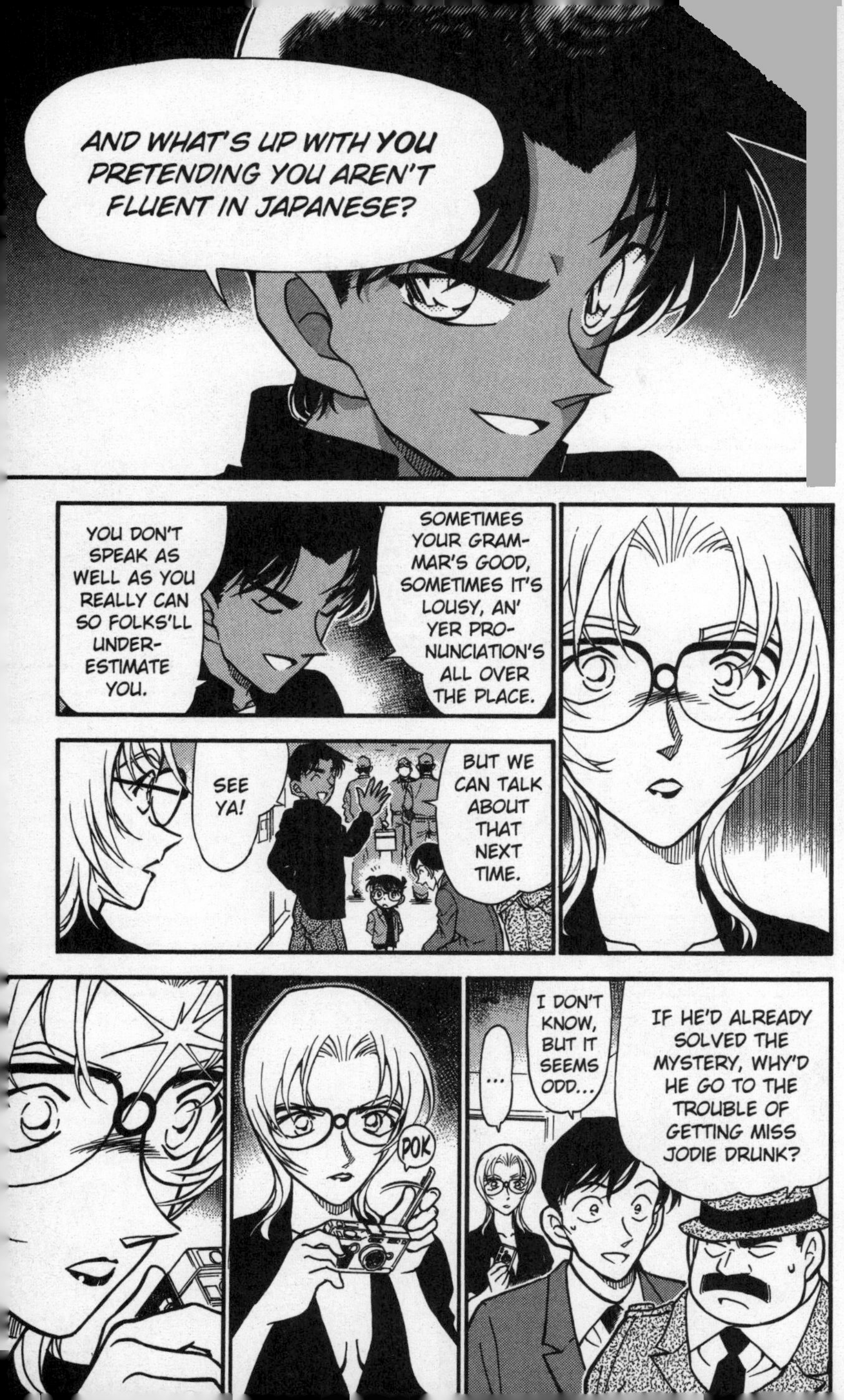
AND WHAT'S UP WITH YOU PRETENDING YOU AREN'T FLUENT IN JAPANESE?
SOMETIMES YOUR GRAM-MAR'S GOOD, SOMETIMES IT'S LOUSY, AN' YER PRO-NUNCIATION'S ALL OVER THE PLACE.
YOU DON'T SPEAK AS WELL AS YOU REALLY CAN SO FOLKS'LL UNDER-ESTIMATE YOU.
BUT WE CAN TALK ABOUT THAT NEXT TIME.
SEE YA!
IF HE'D ALREADY SOLVED THE MYSTERY, WHY'D HE GO TO THE TROUBLE OF GETTING MISS JODIE DRUNK?
I DON'T KNOW, BUT IT SEEMS ODD...
...
POK

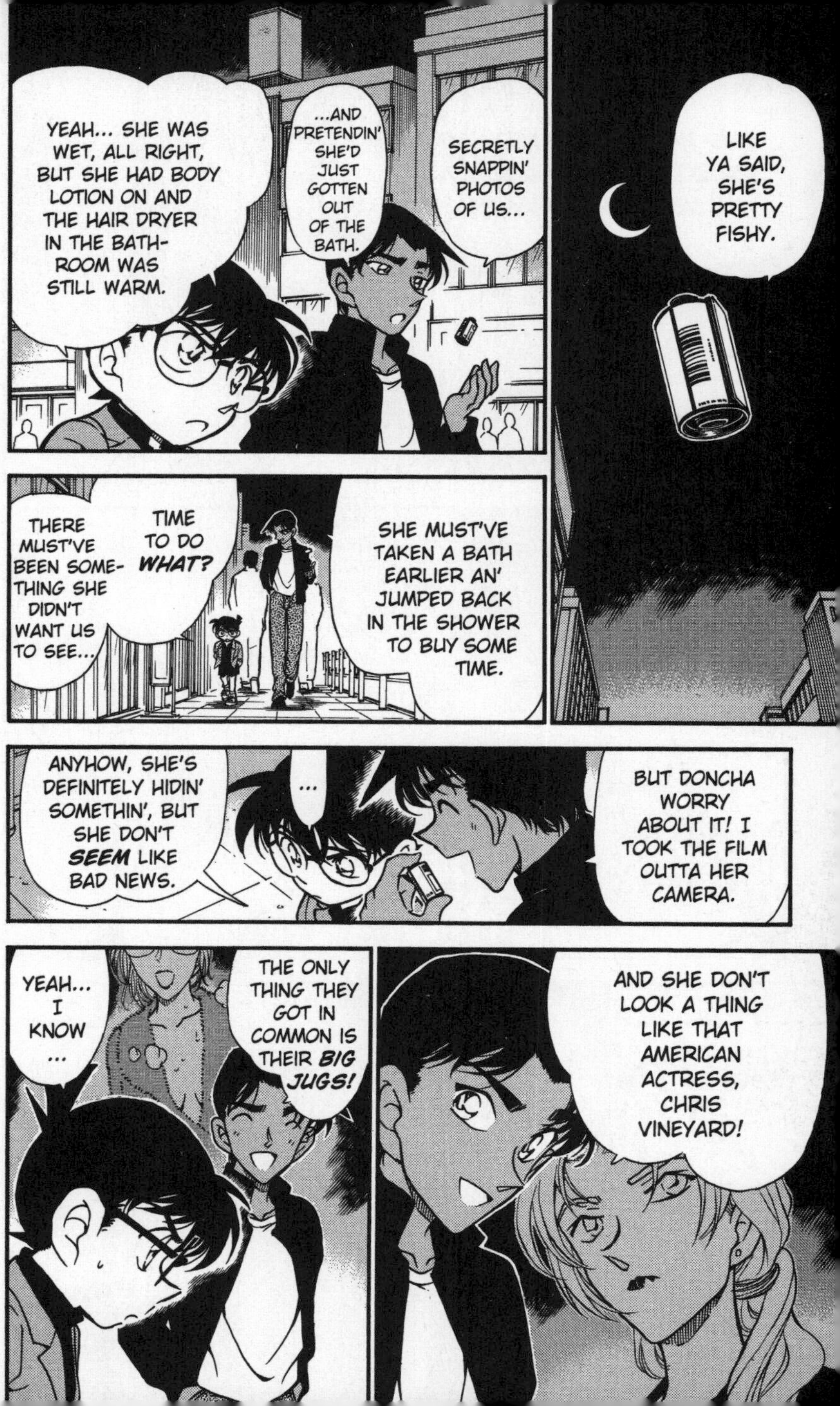
LIKE YA SAID, SHE'S PRETTY FISHY.
SECRETLY SNAPPIN' PHOTOS OF US...
...AND PRETENDIN' SHE'D JUST GOTTEN OUT OF THE BATH.
YEAH... SHE WAS WET, ALL RIGHT, BUT SHE HAD BODY LOTION ON AND THE HAIR DRYER IN THE BATH-ROOM WAS STILL WARM.
SHE MUST'VE TAKEN A BATH EARLIER AN' JUMPED BACK IN THE SHOWER TO BUY SOME TIME.
TIME TO DO WHAT?
THERE MUST'VE BEEN SOME-THING SHE DIDN'T WANT US TO SEE...
BUT DONCHA WORRY ABOUT IT! I TOOK THE FILM OUTTA HER CAMERA.
...
ANYHOW, SHE'S DEFINITELY HIDIN' SOMETHIN', BUT SHE DON'T SEEM LIKE BAD NEWS.
AND SHE DON'T LOOK A THING LIKE THAT AMERICAN ACTRESS, CHRIS VINEYARD!
THE ONLY THING THEY GOT IN COMMON IS THEIR BIG JUGS!
YEAH... I KNOW ...

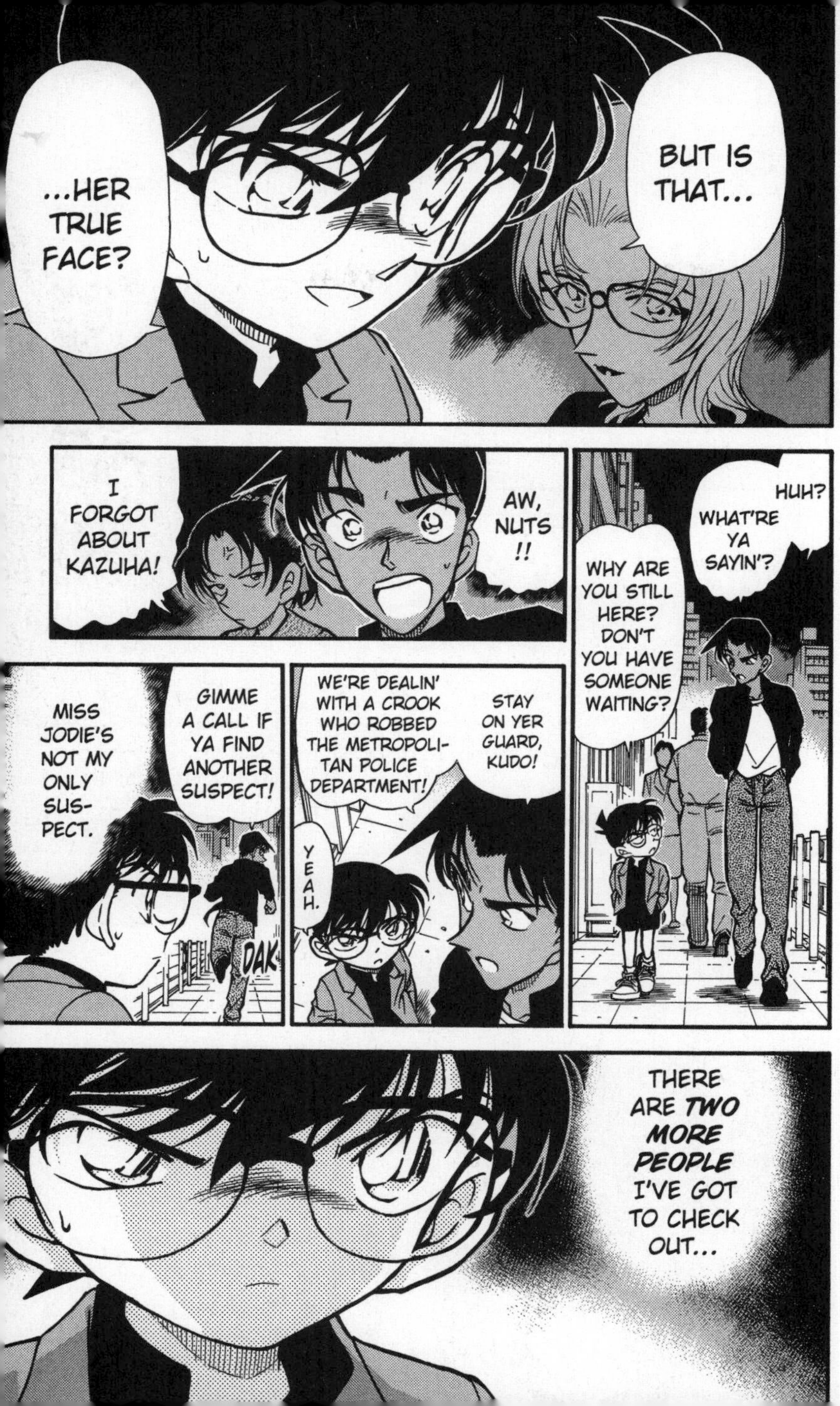
BUT IS THAT...
...HER TRUE FACE?
HUH?
WHAT'RE YA SAYIN'?
WHY ARE YOU STILL HERE? DON'T YOU HAVE SOMEONE WAITING?
AW, NUTS!!
I FORGOT ABOUT KAZUHA!
STAY ON YER GUARD, KUDO!
WE'RE DEALIN' WITH A CROOK WHO ROBBED THE METROPOLITAN POLICE DEPARTMENT!
YEAH.
GIMME A CALL IF YA FIND ANOTHER SUSPECT!
DAK
MISS JODIE'S NOT MY ONLY SUSPECT.
THERE ARE ***TWO MORE PEOPLE*** I'VE GOT TO CHECK OUT...

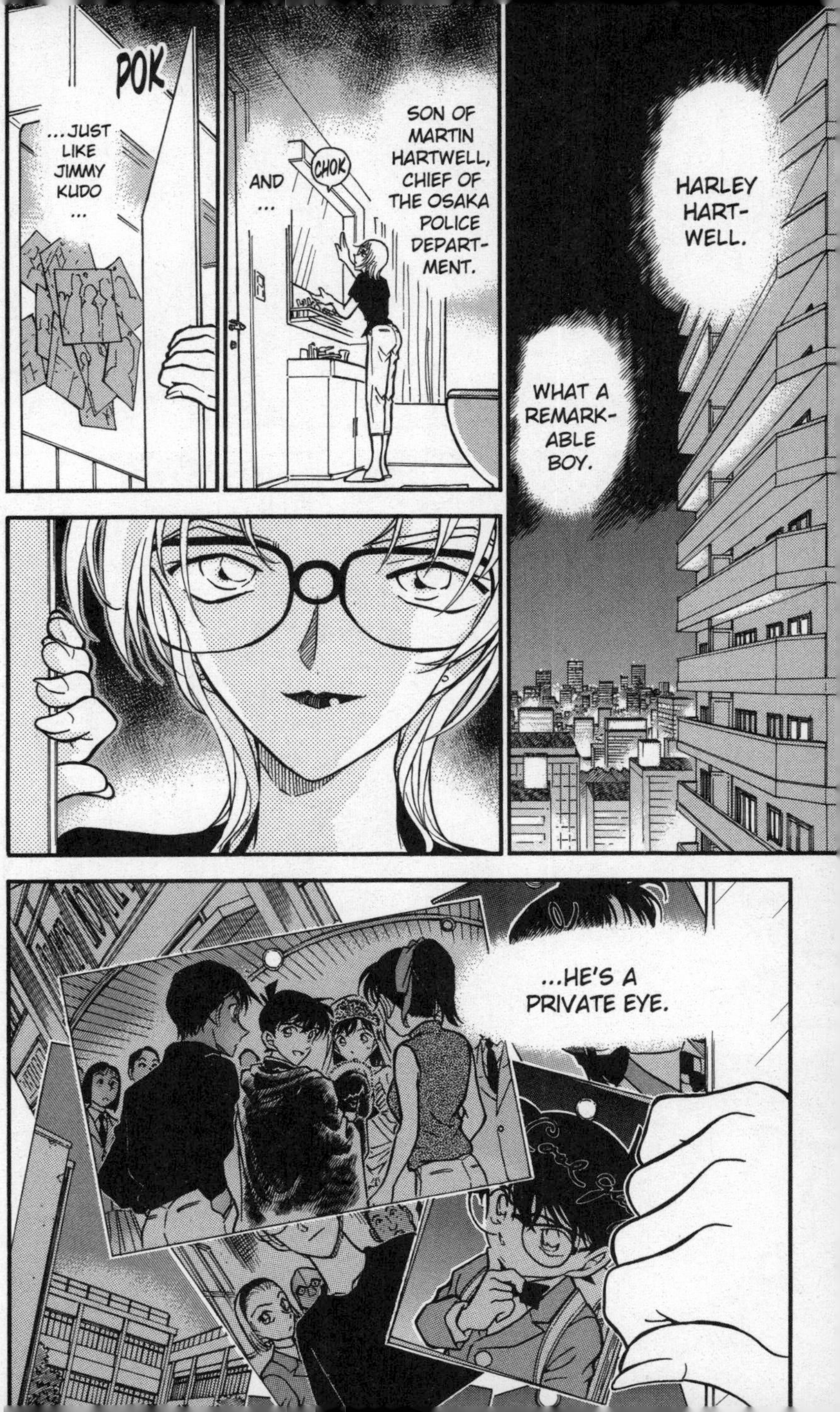
HARLEY HART-WELL.
WHAT A REMARK-ABLE BOY.
SON OF MARTIN HARTWELL, CHIEF OF THE OSAKA POLICE DEPART-MENT.
CHOK
AND ...
POK
...JUST LIKE JIMMY KUDO ...
...HE'S A PRIVATE EYE.

FILE 5: BOOING UP A STORM

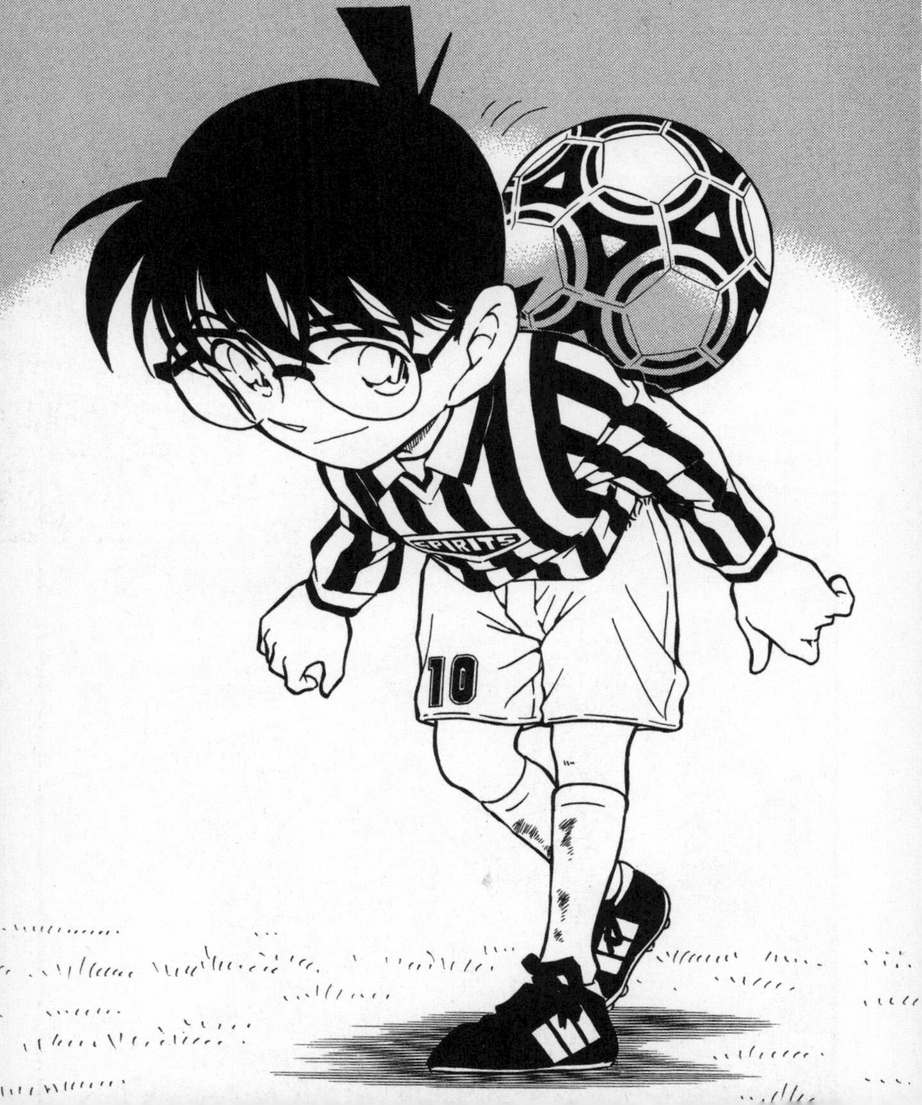
SPIRITS
10

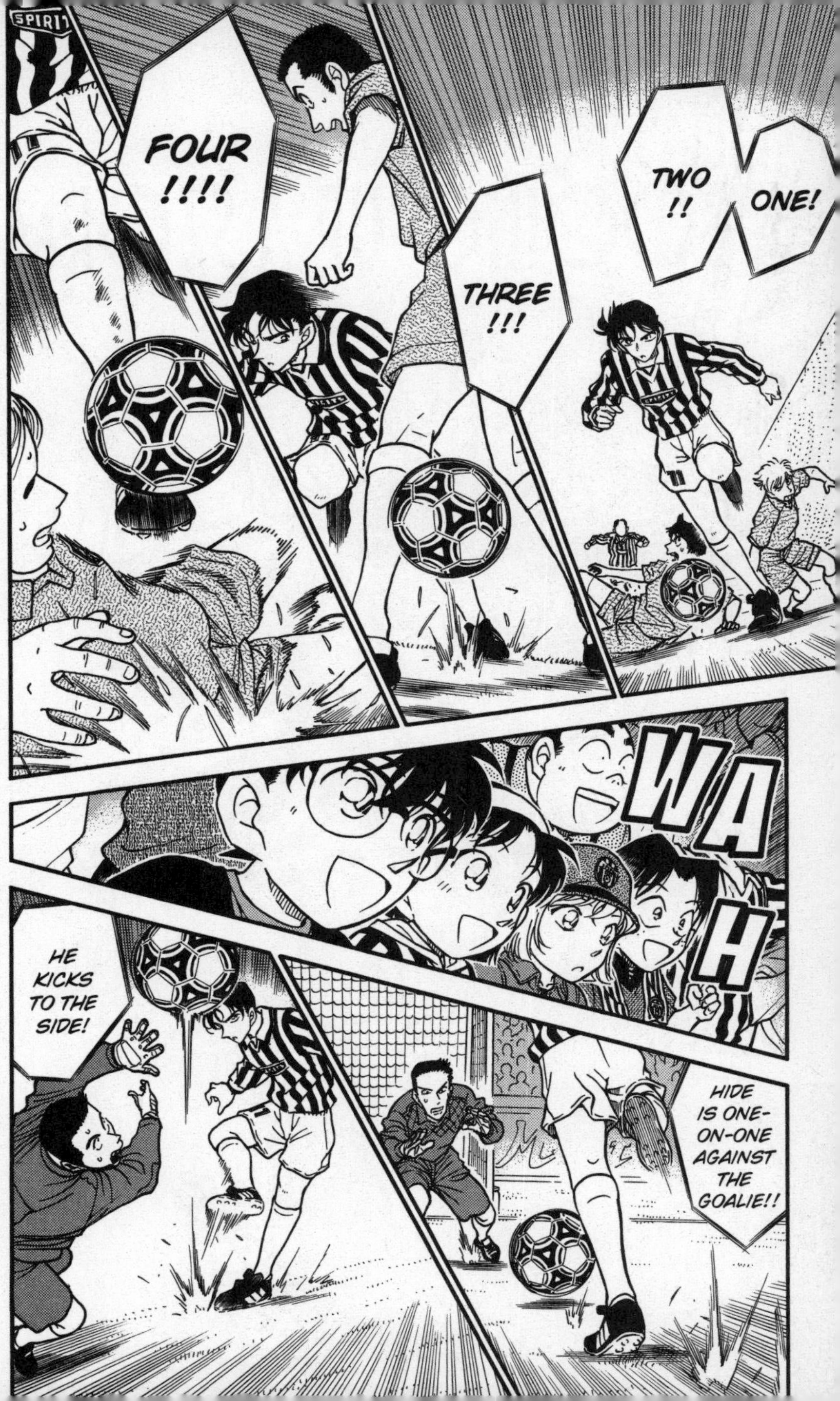
ONE!
TWO !!
THREE !!!
FOUR !!!!
WAAH
HIDE IS ONE-ON-ONE AGAINST THE GOALIE!!
HE KICKS TO THE SIDE!

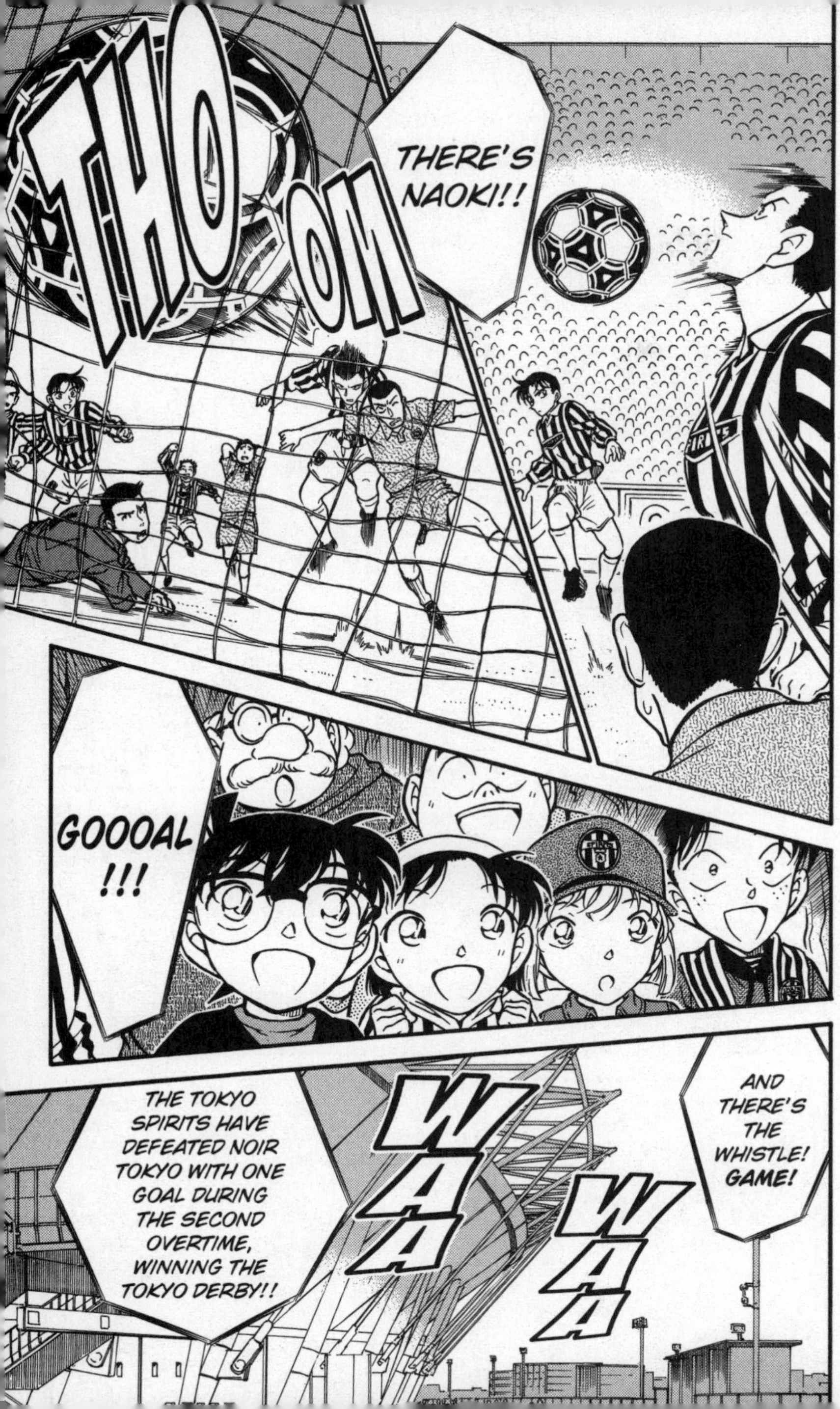
THERE'S NAOKI!!
THOOM
GOOOAL!!!
AND THERE'S THE WHISTLE! GAME!
WAA
WAA
THE TOKYO SPIRITS HAVE DEFEATED NOIR TOKYO WITH ONE GOAL DURING THE SECOND OVERTIME, WINNING THE TOKYO DERBY!!

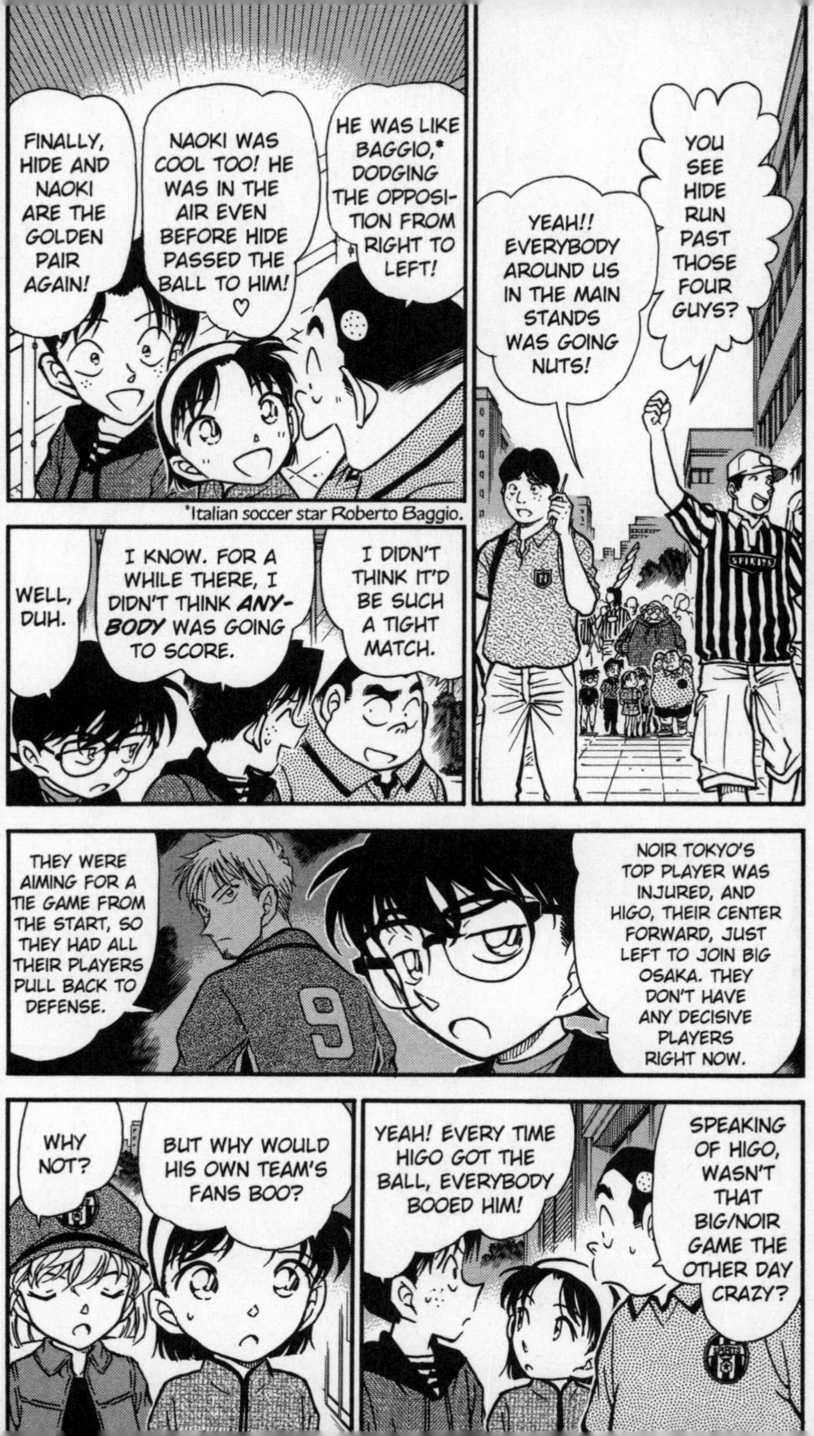
YOU SEE HIDE RUN PAST THOSE FOUR GUYS?
YEAH!! EVERYBODY AROUND US IN THE MAIN STANDS WAS GOING NUTS!
HE WAS LIKE BAGGIO,* DODGING THE OPPOSITION FROM RIGHT TO LEFT!
NAOKI WAS COOL TOO! HE WAS IN THE AIR EVEN BEFORE HIDE PASSED THE BALL TO HIM! ♡
FINALLY, HIDE AND NAOKI ARE THE GOLDEN PAIR AGAIN!
I DIDN'T THINK IT'D BE SUCH A TIGHT MATCH.
I KNOW. FOR A WHILE THERE, I DIDN'T THINK *ANYBODY* WAS GOING TO SCORE.
WELL, DUH.
NOIR TOKYO'S TOP PLAYER WAS INJURED, AND HIGO, THEIR CENTER FORWARD, JUST LEFT TO JOIN BIG OSAKA. THEY DON'T HAVE ANY DECISIVE PLAYERS RIGHT NOW.
THEY WERE AIMING FOR A TIE GAME FROM THE START, SO THEY HAD ALL THEIR PLAYERS PULL BACK TO DEFENSE.
SPEAKING OF HIGO, WASN'T THAT BIG/NOIR GAME THE OTHER DAY CRAZY?
YEAH! EVERY TIME HIGO GOT THE BALL, EVERYBODY BOOED HIM!
BUT WHY WOULD HIS OWN TEAM'S FANS BOO?
WHY NOT?

*Italian soccer star Roberto Baggio.

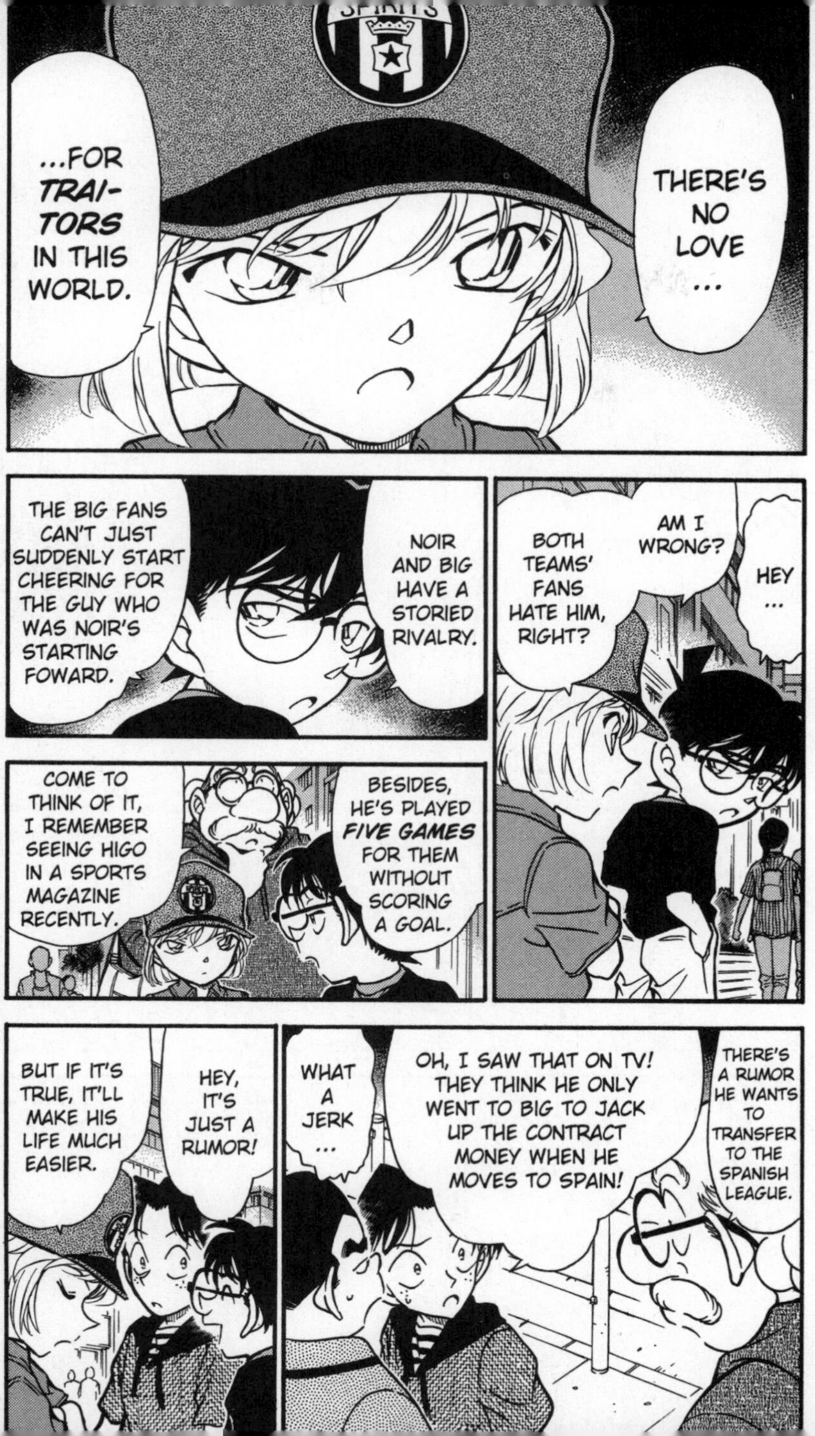
THERE'S NO LOVE ...
...FOR TRAITORS IN THIS WORLD.
HEY ...
AM I WRONG?
BOTH TEAMS' FANS HATE HIM, RIGHT?
NOIR AND BIG HAVE A STORIED RIVALRY.
THE BIG FANS CAN'T JUST SUDDENLY START CHEERING FOR THE GUY WHO WAS NOIR'S STARTING FOWARD.
BESIDES, HE'S PLAYED FIVE GAMES FOR THEM WITHOUT SCORING A GOAL.
COME TO THINK OF IT, I REMEMBER SEEING HIGO IN A SPORTS MAGAZINE RECENTLY.
THERE'S A RUMOR HE WANTS TO TRANSFER TO THE SPANISH LEAGUE.
OH, I SAW THAT ON TV! THEY THINK HE ONLY WENT TO BIG TO JACK UP THE CONTRACT MONEY WHEN HE MOVES TO SPAIN!
WHAT A JERK ...
HEY, IT'S JUST A RUMOR!
BUT IF IT'S TRUE, IT'LL MAKE HIS LIFE MUCH EASIER.

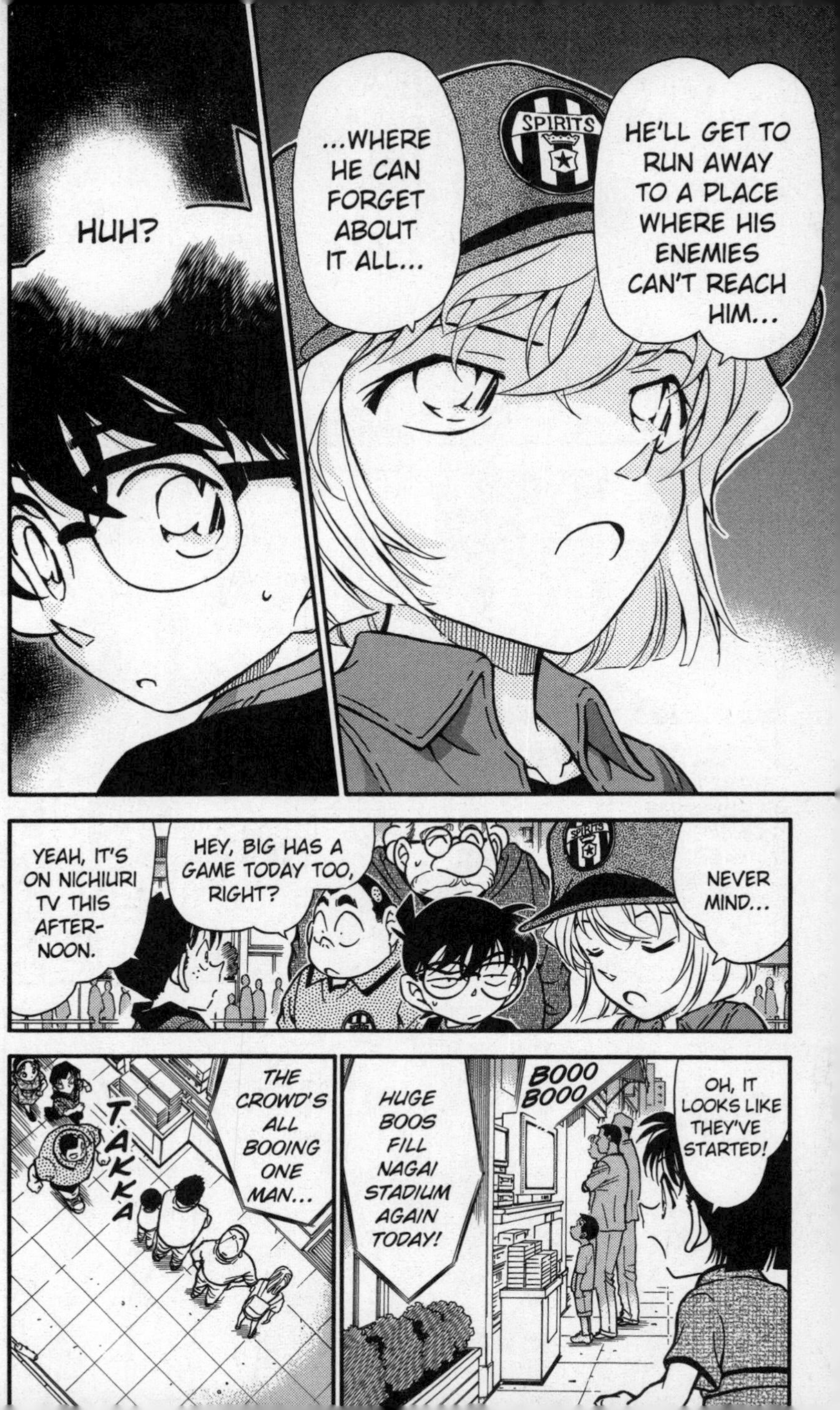
HE'LL GET TO RUN AWAY TO A PLACE WHERE HIS ENEMIES CAN'T REACH HIM...
...WHERE HE CAN FORGET ABOUT IT ALL...
HUH?
NEVER MIND...
HEY, BIG HAS A GAME TODAY TOO, RIGHT?
YEAH, IT'S ON NICHIURI TV THIS AFTER-NOON.
OH, IT LOOKS LIKE THEY'VE STARTED!
BOOO BOOO
HUGE BOOS FILL NAGAI STADIUM AGAIN TODAY!
THE CROWD'S ALL BOOING ONE MAN...
TAKKA
SPIRITS

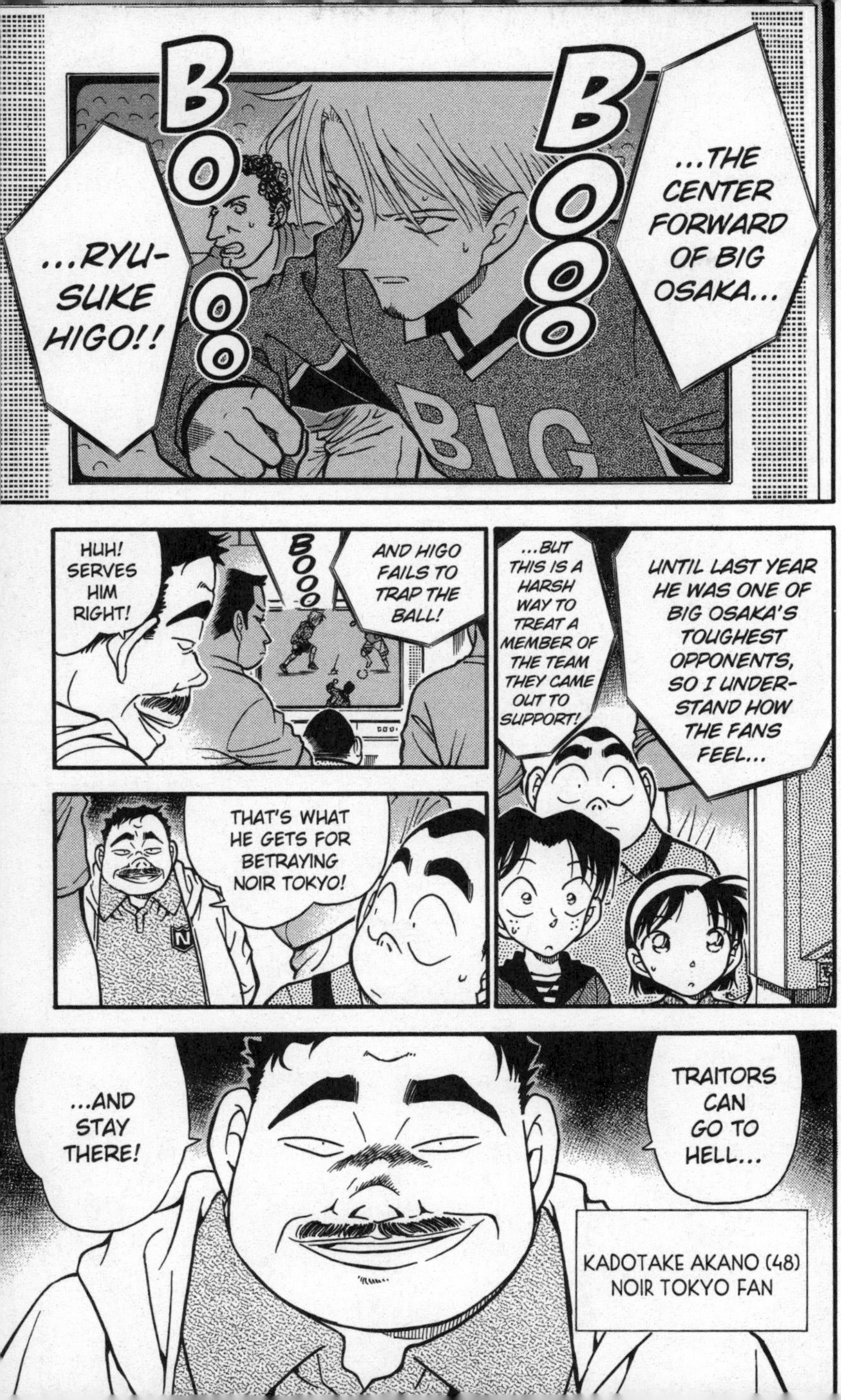
...THE CENTER FORWARD OF BIG OSAKA...
BOOOOO
BOOOO
...RYU-SUKE HIGO!!
BIG
UNTIL LAST YEAR HE WAS ONE OF BIG OSAKA'S TOUGHEST OPPONENTS, SO I UNDER-STAND HOW THE FANS FEEL...
...BUT THIS IS A HARSH WAY TO TREAT A MEMBER OF THE TEAM THEY CAME OUT TO SUPPORT!
AND HIGO FAILS TO TRAP THE BALL!
BOOO
HUH! SERVES HIM RIGHT!
THAT'S WHAT HE GETS FOR BETRAYING NOIR TOKYO!
TRAITORS CAN GO TO HELL...
...AND STAY THERE!
KADOTAKE AKANO (48)
NOIR TOKYO FAN

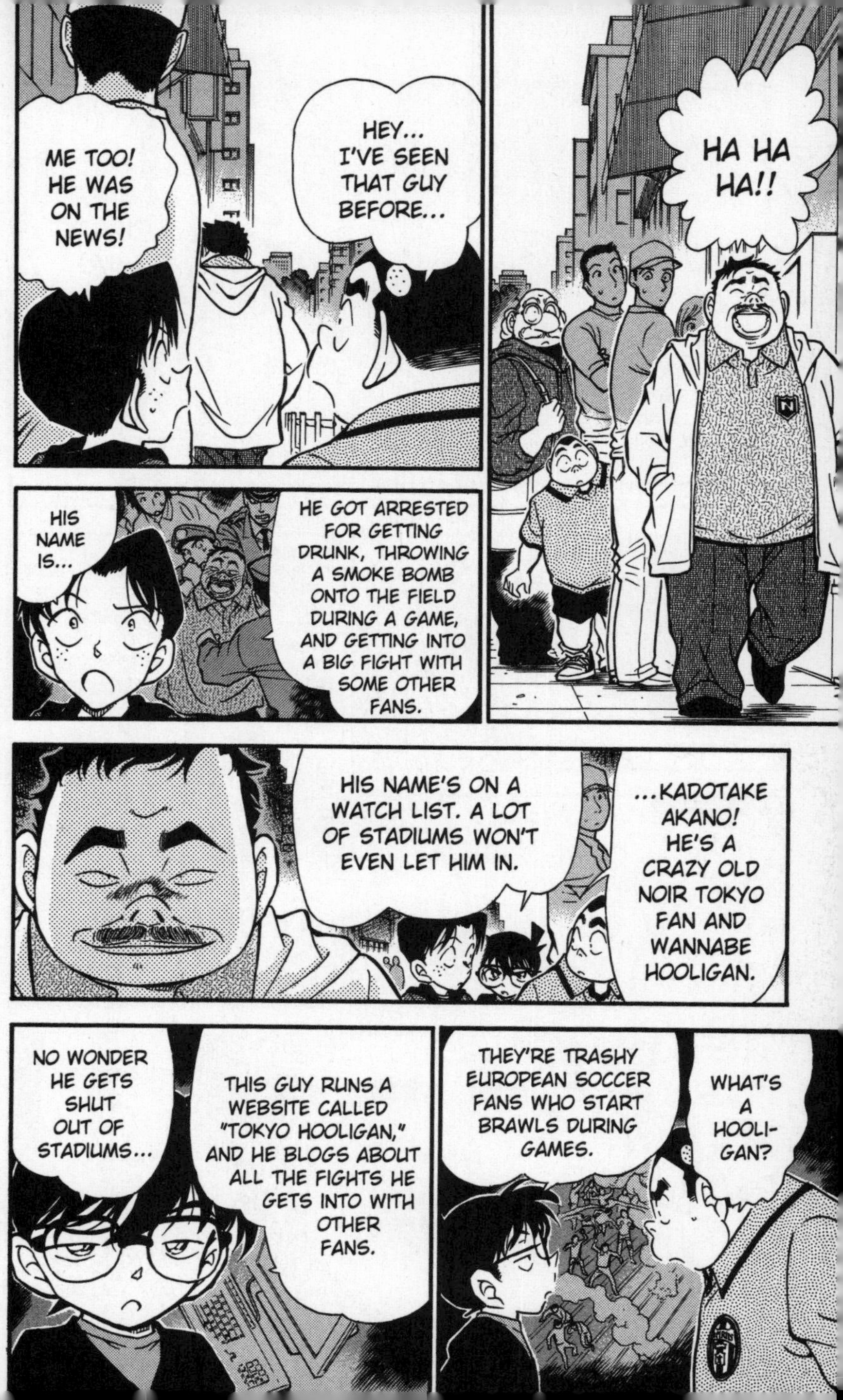
HA HA HA!!
HEY... I'VE SEEN THAT GUY BEFORE...
ME TOO! HE WAS ON THE NEWS!
HE GOT ARRESTED FOR GETTING DRUNK, THROWING A SMOKE BOMB ONTO THE FIELD DURING A GAME, AND GETTING INTO A BIG FIGHT WITH SOME OTHER FANS.
HIS NAME IS...
...KADOTAKE AKANO! HE'S A CRAZY OLD NOIR TOKYO FAN AND WANNABE HOOLIGAN.
HIS NAME'S ON A WATCH LIST. A LOT OF STADIUMS WON'T EVEN LET HIM IN.
WHAT'S A HOOLI-GAN?
THEY'RE TRASHY EUROPEAN SOCCER FANS WHO START BRAWLS DURING GAMES.
THIS GUY RUNS A WEBSITE CALLED "TOKYO HOOLIGAN," AND HE BLOGS ABOUT ALL THE FIGHTS HE GETS INTO WITH OTHER FANS.
NO WONDER HE GETS SHUT OUT OF STADIUMS...

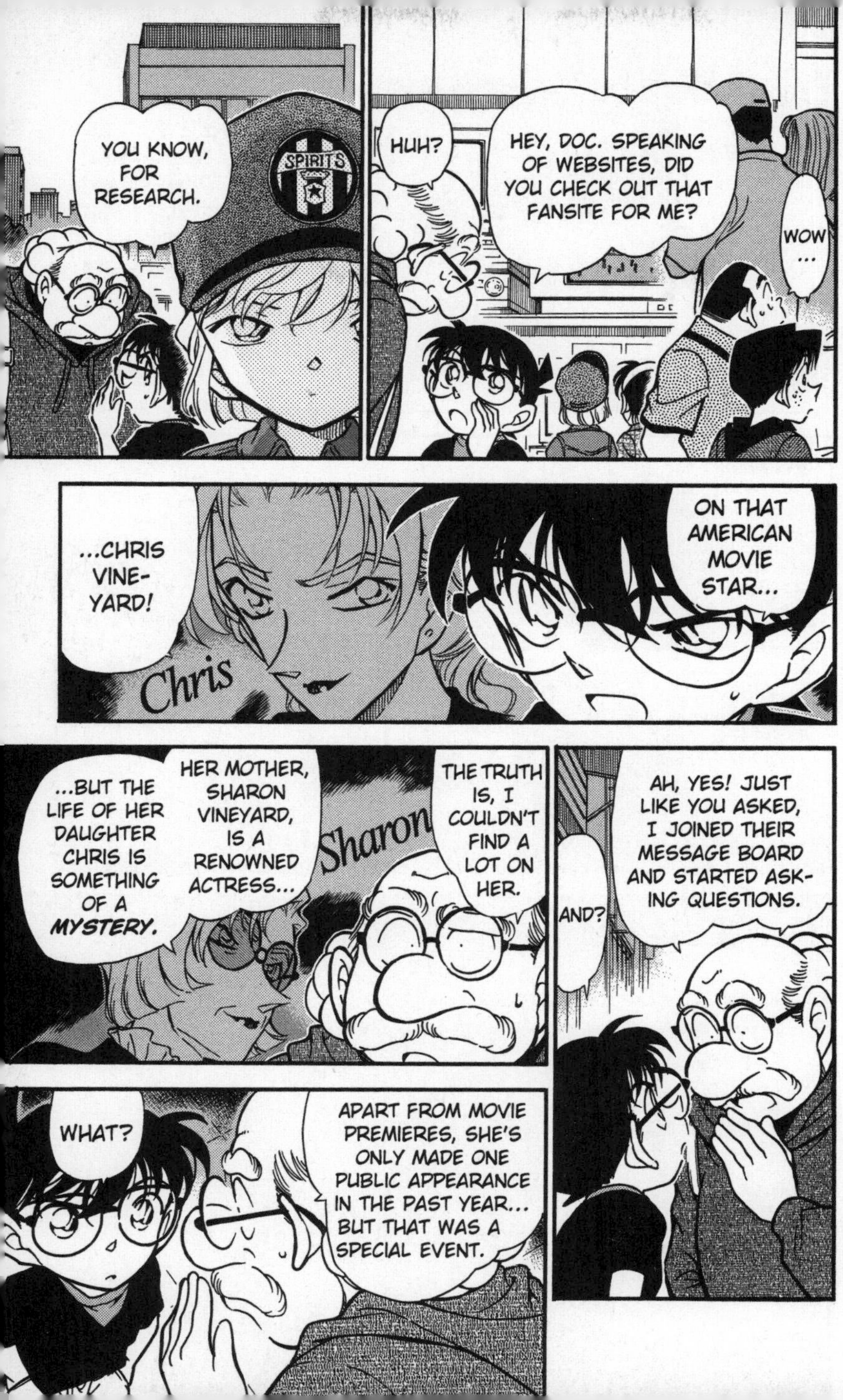
WOW...
HEY, DOC. SPEAKING OF WEBSITES, DID YOU CHECK OUT THAT FANSITE FOR ME?
HUH?
YOU KNOW, FOR RESEARCH.
SPIRITS
ON THAT AMERICAN MOVIE STAR...
...CHRIS VINEYARD!
Chris
AH, YES! JUST LIKE YOU ASKED, I JOINED THEIR MESSAGE BOARD AND STARTED ASKING QUESTIONS.
AND?
THE TRUTH IS, I COULDN'T FIND A LOT ON HER.
Sharon
HER MOTHER, SHARON VINEYARD, IS A RENOWNED ACTRESS...
...BUT THE LIFE OF HER DAUGHTER CHRIS IS SOMETHING OF A *MYSTERY*.
APART FROM MOVIE PREMIERES, SHE'S ONLY MADE ONE PUBLIC APPEARANCE IN THE PAST YEAR... BUT THAT WAS A SPECIAL EVENT.
WHAT?

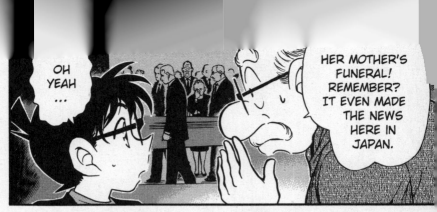

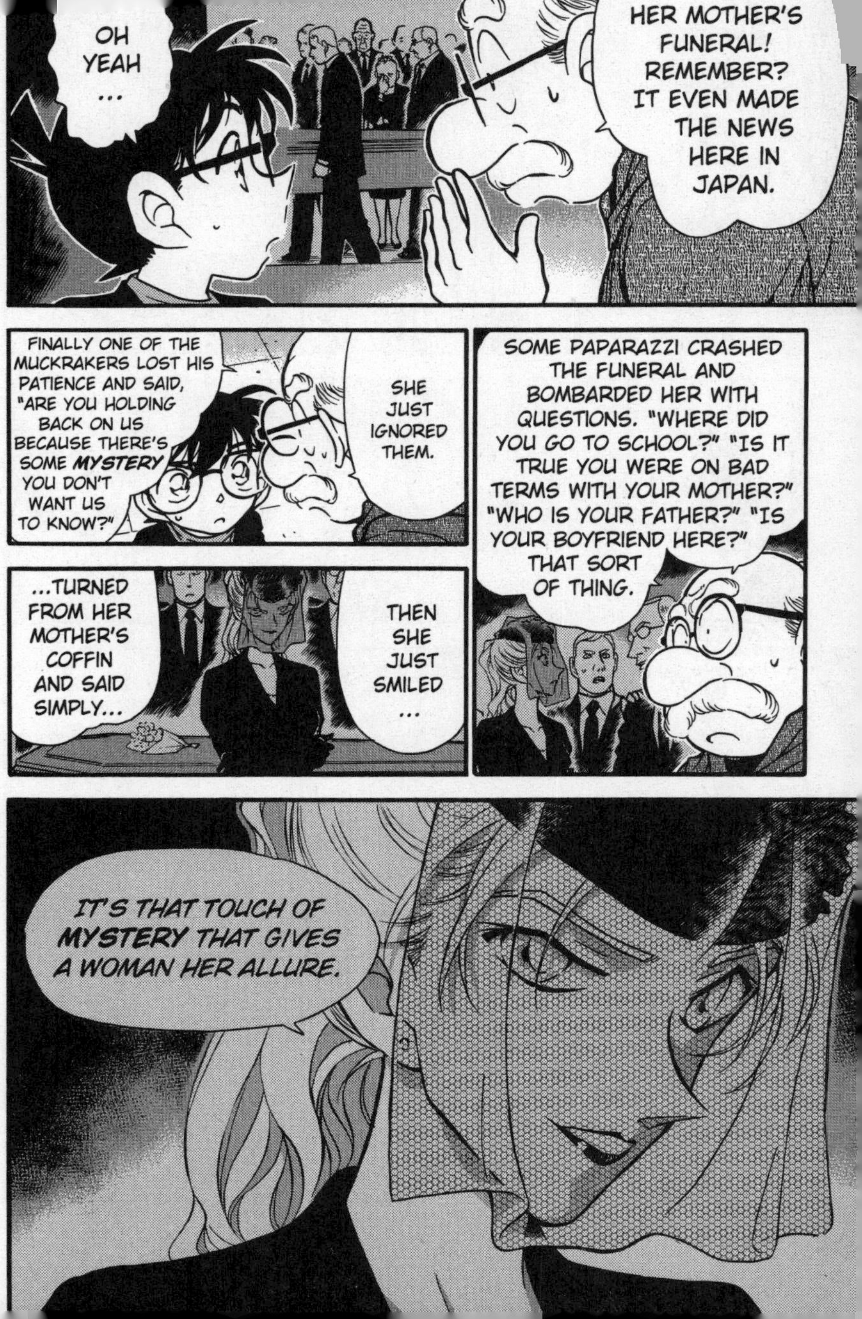
HER MOTHER'S FUNERAL! REMEMBER? IT EVEN MADE THE NEWS HERE IN JAPAN.
OH YEAH ...
SOME PAPARAZZI CRASHED THE FUNERAL AND BOMBARDED HER WITH QUESTIONS. "WHERE DID YOU GO TO SCHOOL?" "IS IT TRUE YOU WERE ON BAD TERMS WITH YOUR MOTHER?" "WHO IS YOUR FATHER?" "IS YOUR BOYFRIEND HERE?" THAT SORT OF THING.
SHE JUST IGNORED THEM.
FINALLY ONE OF THE MUCKRAKERS LOST HIS PATIENCE AND SAID, "ARE YOU HOLDING BACK ON US BECAUSE THERE'S SOME MYSTERY YOU DON'T WANT US TO KNOW?"
THEN SHE JUST SMILED ...
...TURNED FROM HER MOTHER'S COFFIN AND SAID SIMPLY...
IT'S THAT TOUCH OF MYSTERY THAT GIVES A WOMAN HER ALLURE.

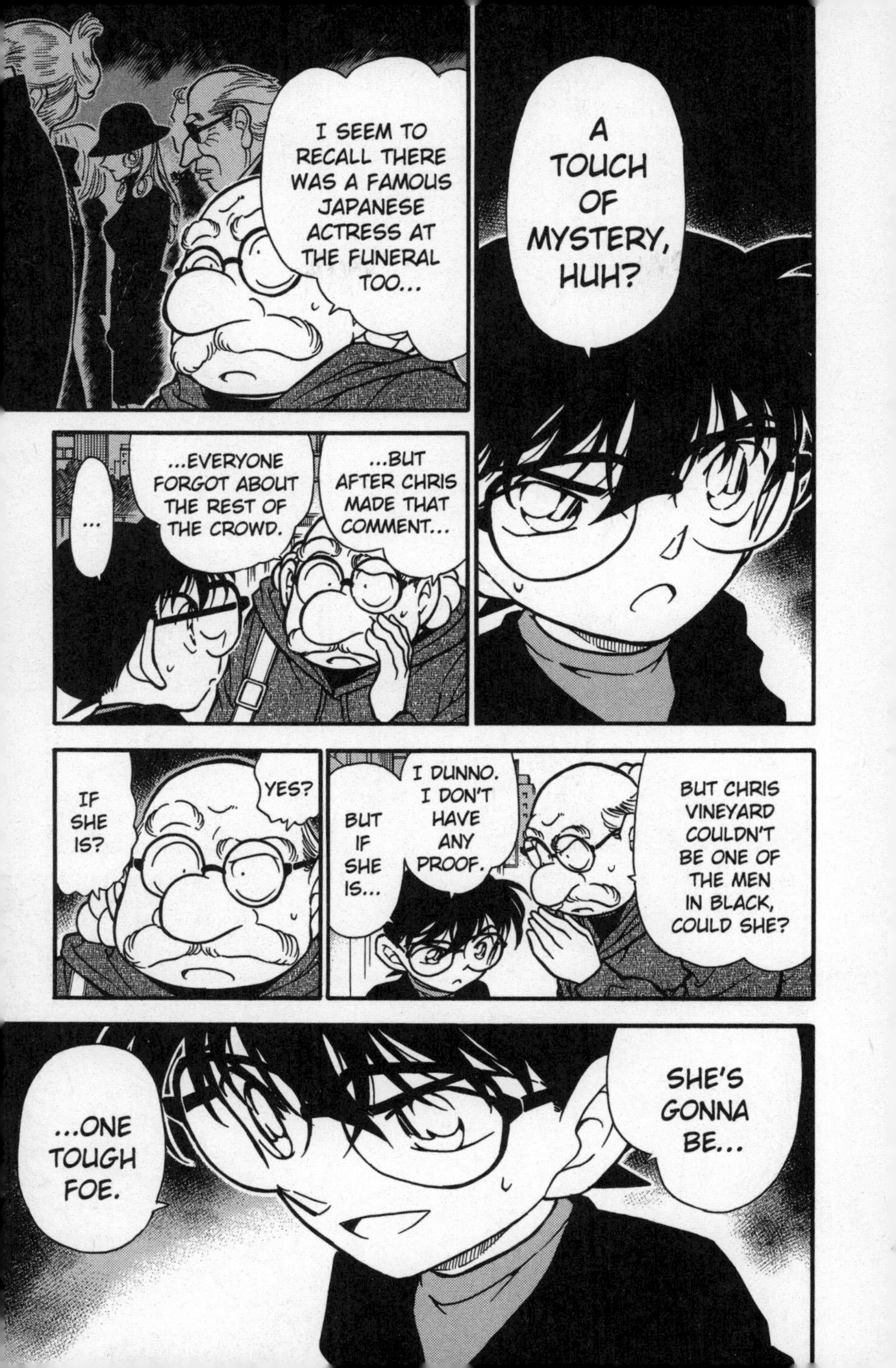
A TOUCH OF MYSTERY, HUH?
I SEEM TO RECALL THERE WAS A FAMOUS JAPANESE ACTRESS AT THE FUNERAL TOO...
...BUT AFTER CHRIS MADE THAT COMMENT...
...EVERYONE FORGOT ABOUT THE REST OF THE CROWD.
...
BUT CHRIS VINEYARD COULDN'T BE ONE OF THE MEN IN BLACK, COULD SHE?
I DUNNO. I DON'T HAVE ANY PROOF.
BUT IF SHE IS...
YES?
IF SHE IS?
SHE'S GONNA BE...
...ONE TOUGH FOE.

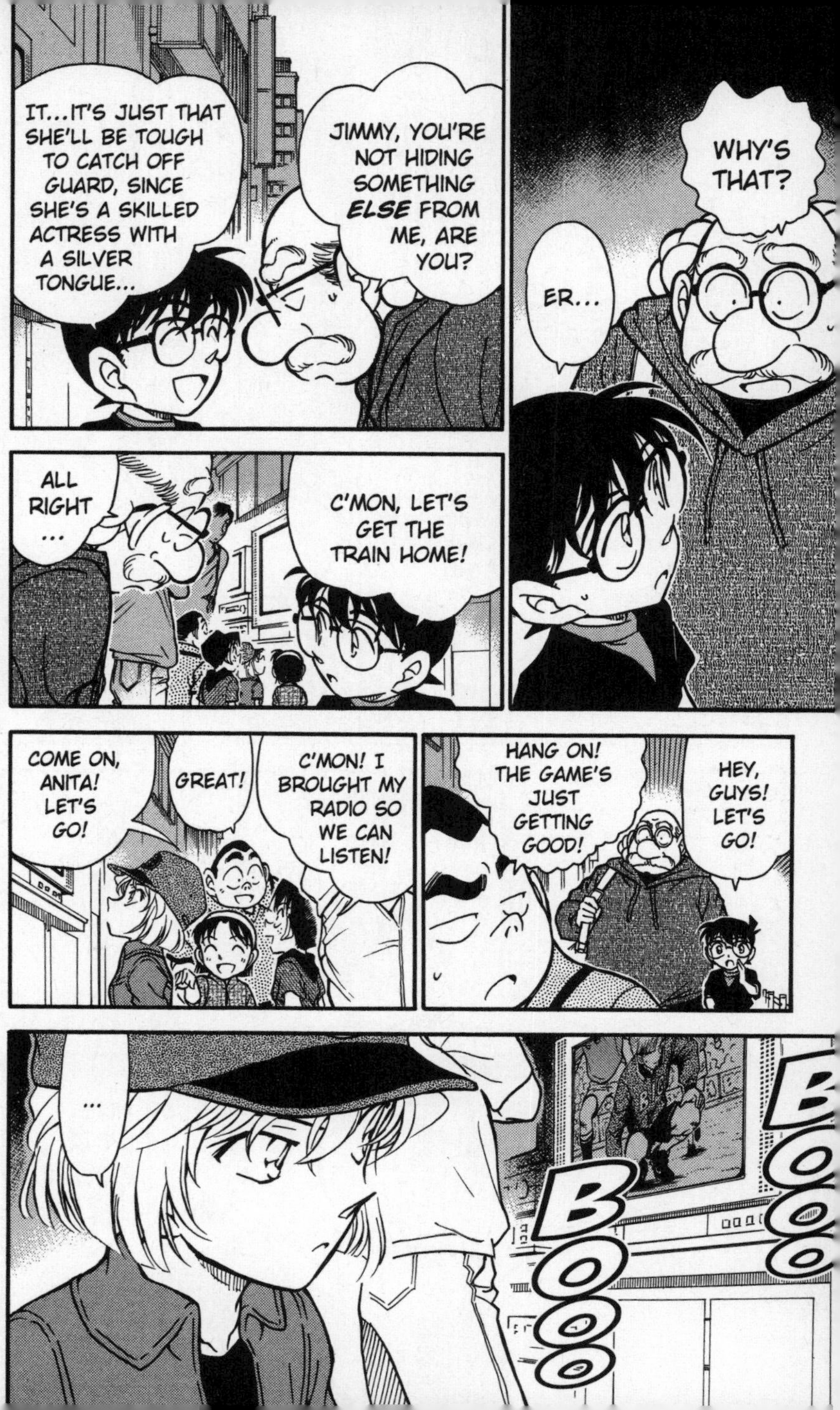
WHY'S THAT?
ER...
JIMMY, YOU'RE NOT HIDING SOMETHING *ELSE* FROM ME, ARE YOU?
IT...IT'S JUST THAT SHE'LL BE TOUGH TO CATCH OFF GUARD, SINCE SHE'S A SKILLED ACTRESS WITH A SILVER TONGUE...
C'MON, LET'S GET THE TRAIN HOME!
ALL RIGHT ...
HEY, GUYS! LET'S GO!
HANG ON! THE GAME'S JUST GETTING GOOD!
C'MON! I BROUGHT MY RADIO SO WE CAN LISTEN!
GREAT!
COME ON, ANITA! LET'S GO!
BOOOO
BOOOO
...

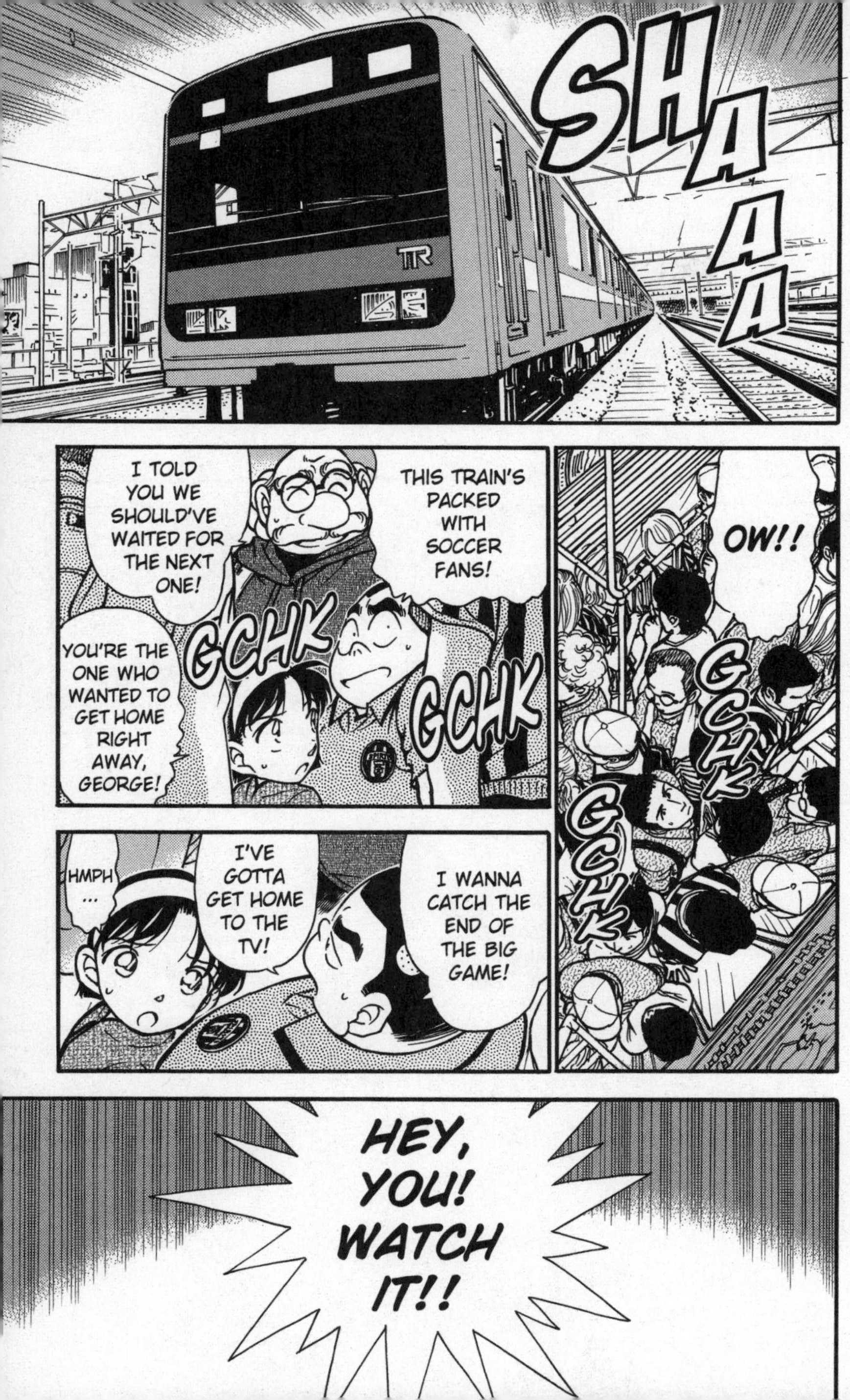
SHAAAA
OW!!
GCHK
GCHK
THIS TRAIN'S PACKED WITH SOCCER FANS!
I TOLD YOU WE SHOULD'VE WAITED FOR THE NEXT ONE!
GCHK
GCHK
YOU'RE THE ONE WHO WANTED TO GET HOME RIGHT AWAY, GEORGE!
I WANNA CATCH THE END OF THE BIG GAME!
I'VE GOTTA GET HOME TO THE TV!
HMPH …
HEY, YOU! WATCH IT!!

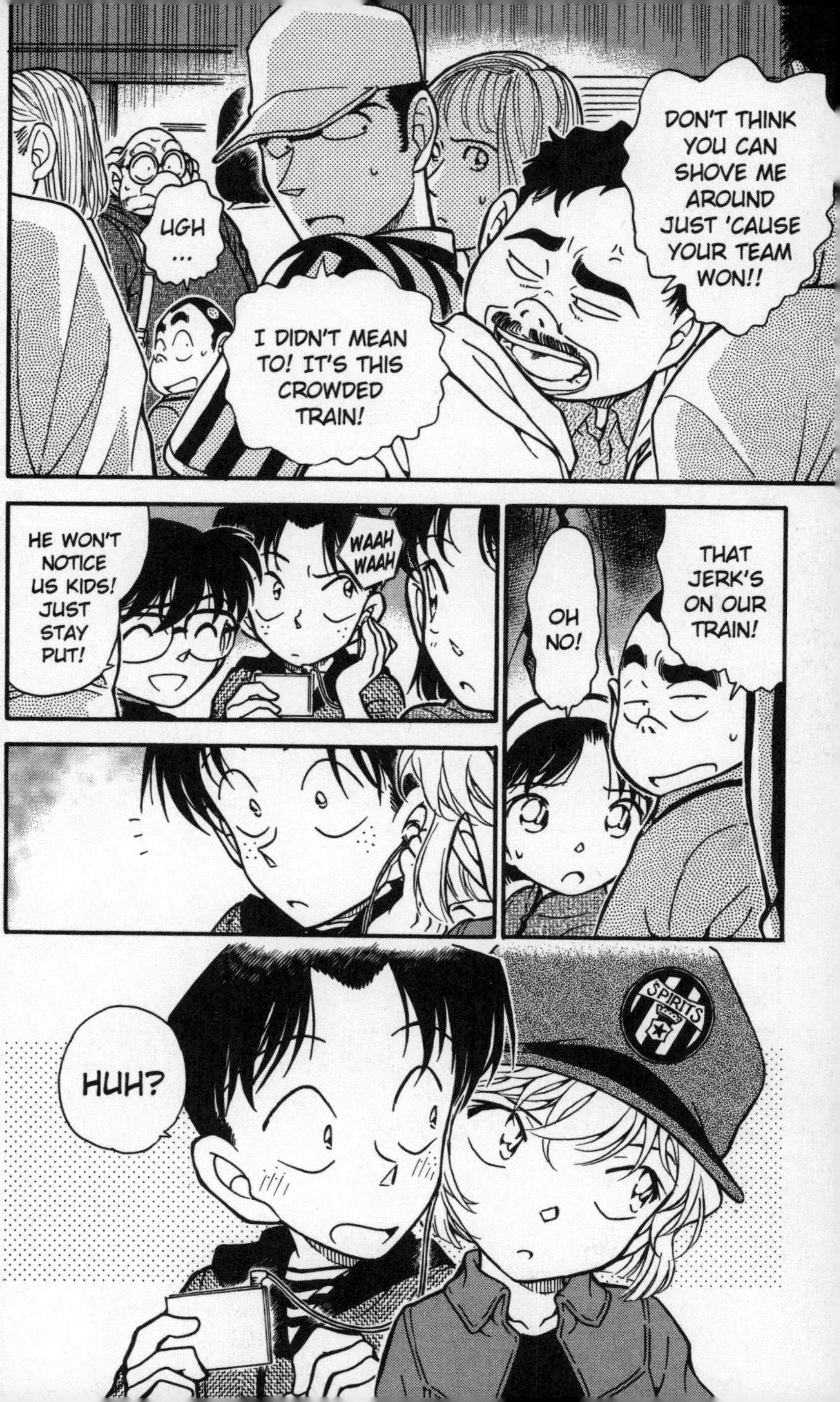
DON'T THINK YOU CAN SHOVE ME AROUND JUST 'CAUSE YOUR TEAM WON!!
I DIDN'T MEAN TO! IT'S THIS CROWDED TRAIN!
UGH ...
THAT JERK'S ON OUR TRAIN!
OH NO!
WAAH WAAH
HE WON'T NOTICE US KIDS! JUST STAY PUT!
SPIRITS
HUH?

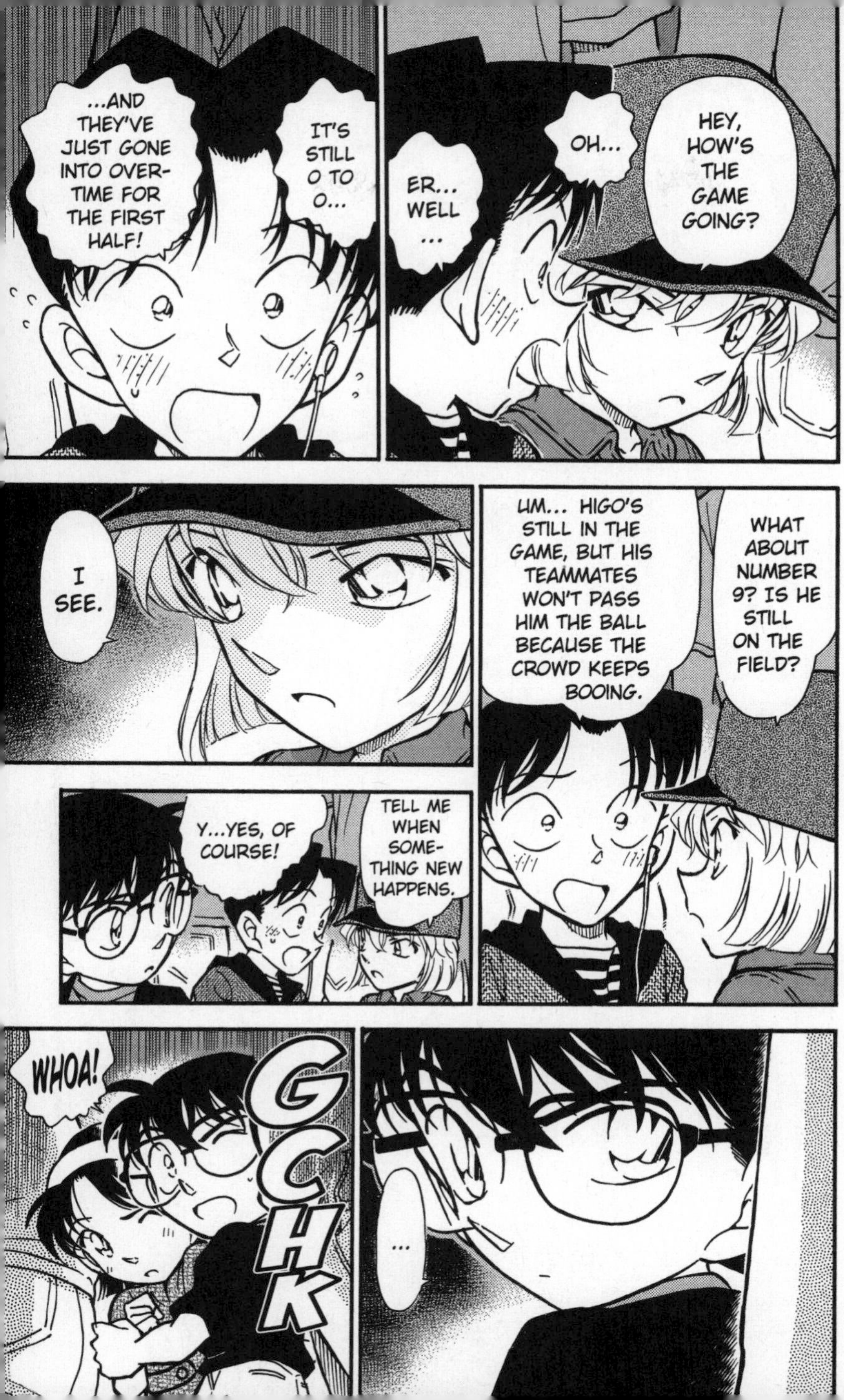
HEY, HOW'S THE GAME GOING?
OH...
ER... WELL ...
IT'S STILL 0 TO 0...
...AND THEY'VE JUST GONE INTO OVER-TIME FOR THE FIRST HALF!
WHAT ABOUT NUMBER 9? IS HE STILL ON THE FIELD?
UM... HIGO'S STILL IN THE GAME, BUT HIS TEAMMATES WON'T PASS HIM THE BALL BECAUSE THE CROWD KEEPS BOOING.
I SEE.
TELL ME WHEN SOME-THING NEW HAPPENS.
Y...YES, OF COURSE!
...
GCHK
WHOA!

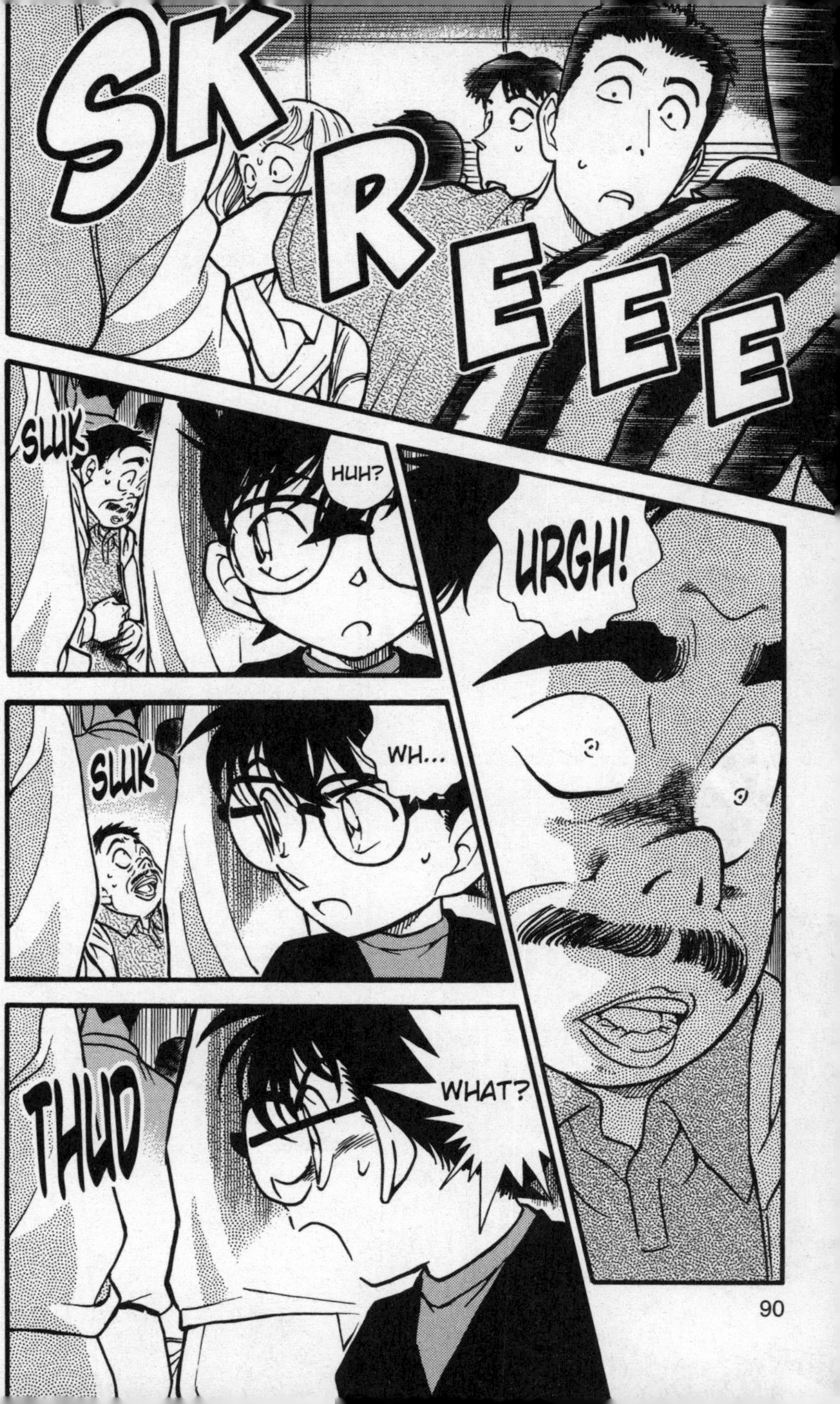
SKREEEE
URGH!
HUH?
SLUK
WH...
SLUK
WHAT?
THUD

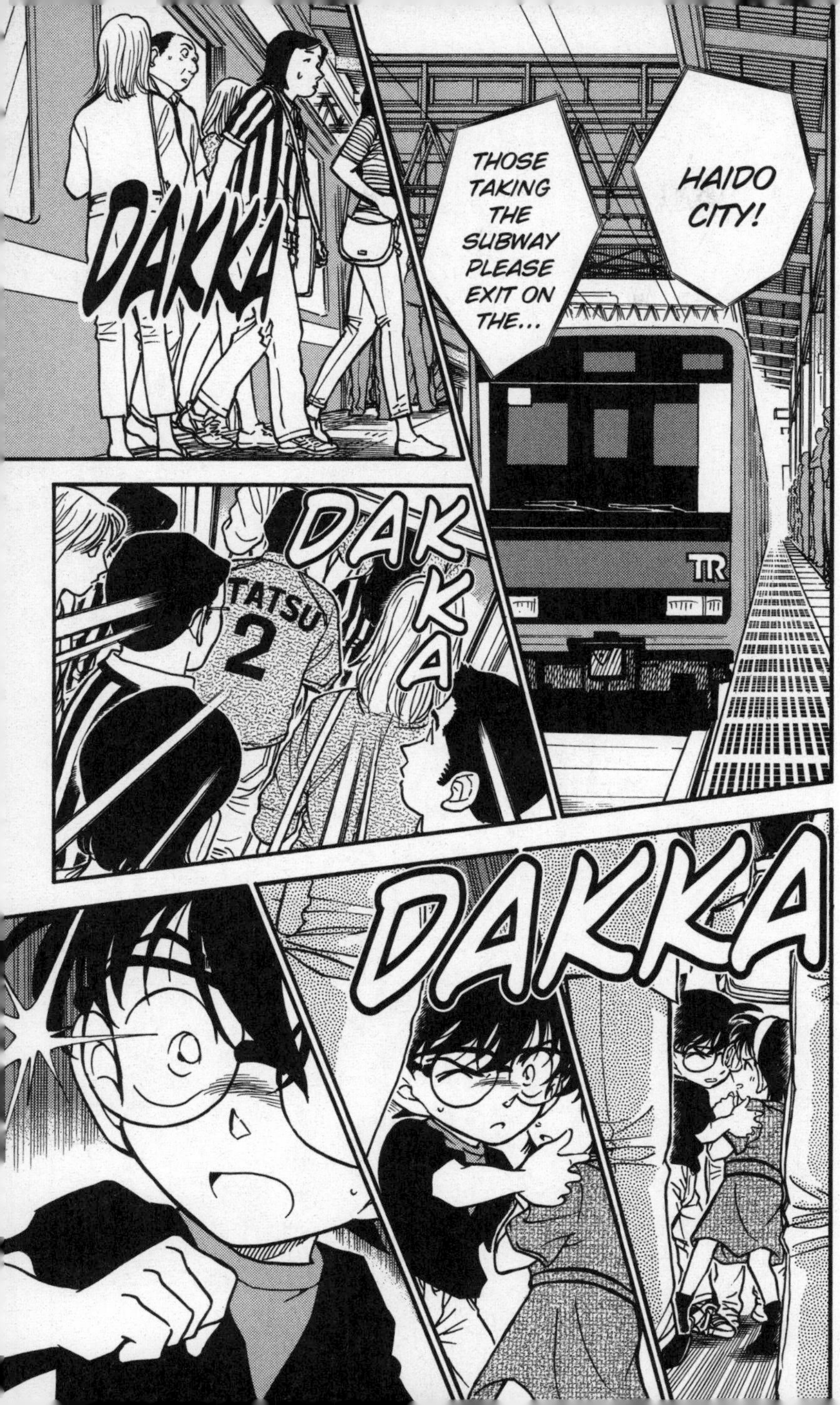
HAIDO CITY!
THOSE TAKING THE SUBWAY PLEASE EXIT ON THE...
TR
DAKKA
DAKKA
TATSU
2
DAKKA

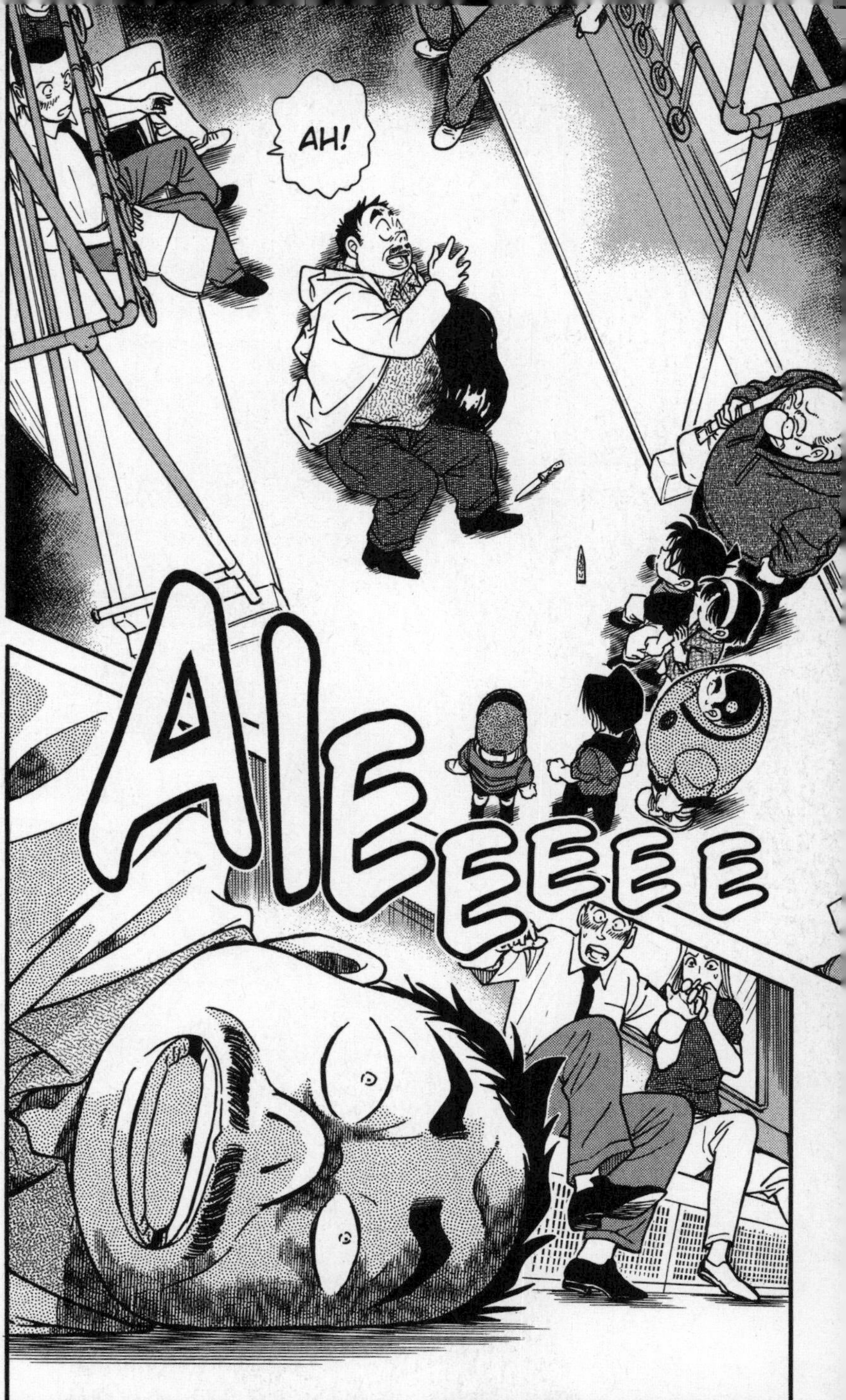
AH!
AIEEEEE

THE SUSPICIOUS FAN

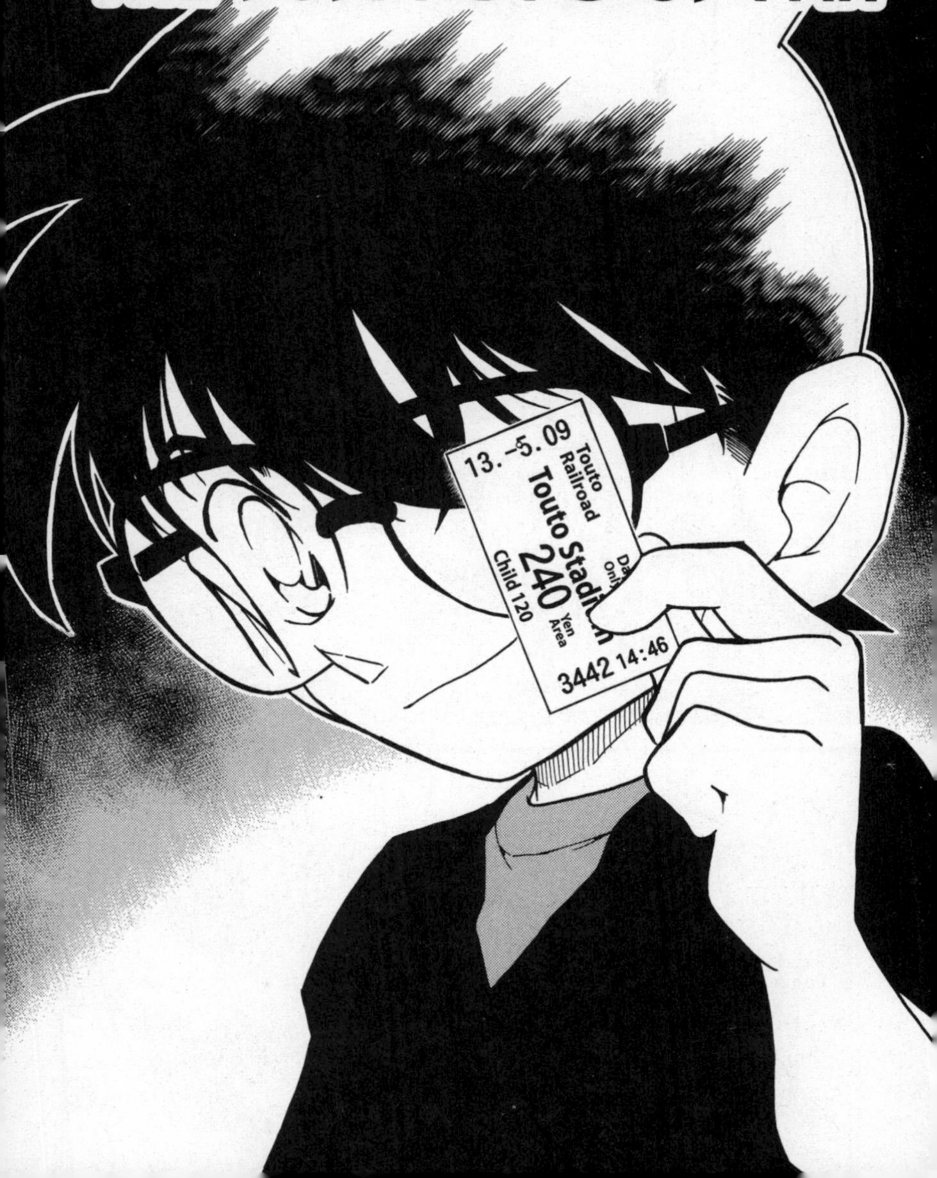
Touto Railroad
13.-5.09
240 Yen Area
Child 120
3442 14:46

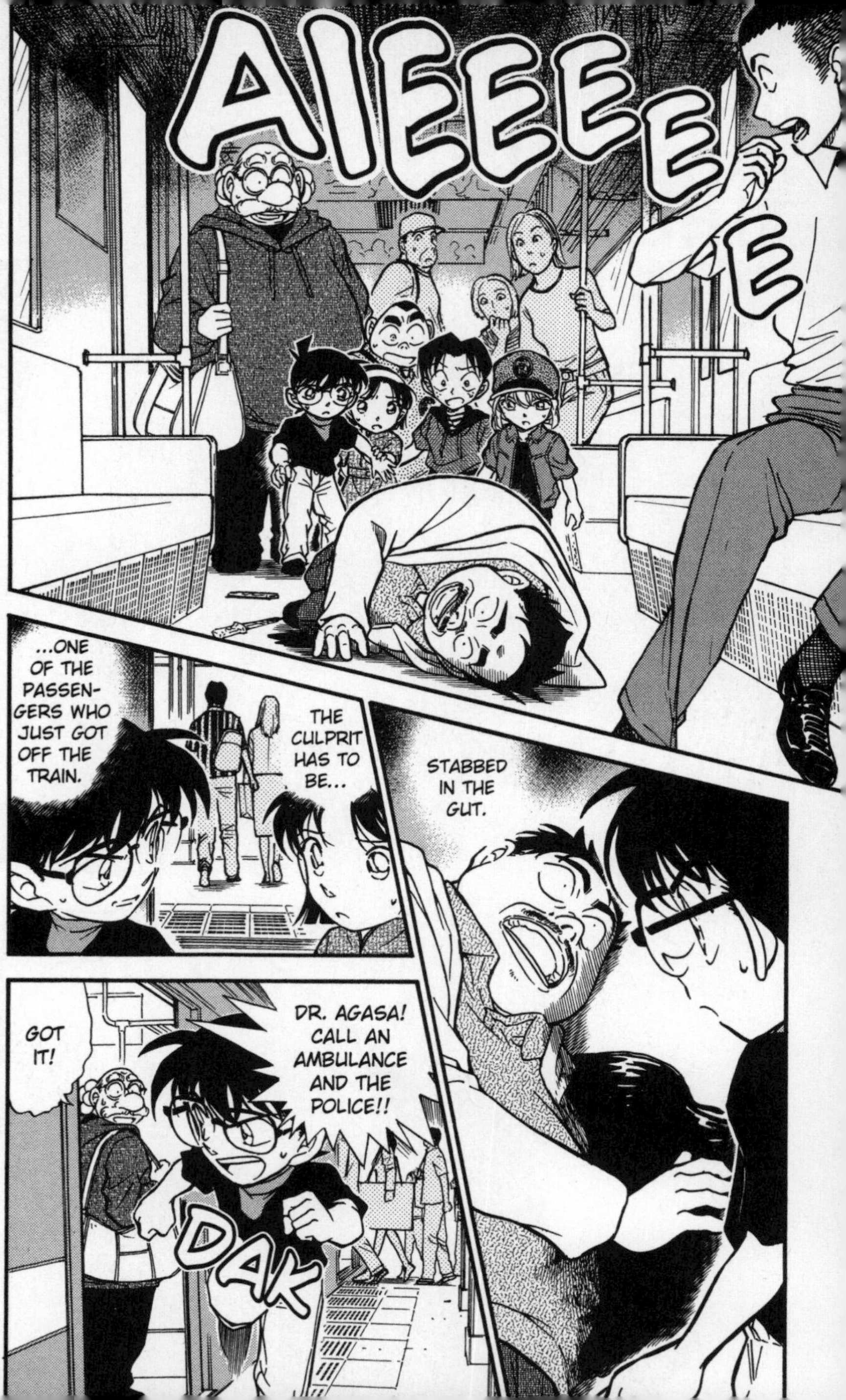
AIEEEEE
STABBED IN THE GUT.
THE CULPRIT HAS TO BE...
...ONE OF THE PASSENGERS WHO JUST GOT OFF THE TRAIN.
DR. AGASA! CALL AN AMBULANCE AND THE POLICE!!
GOT IT!
DAK

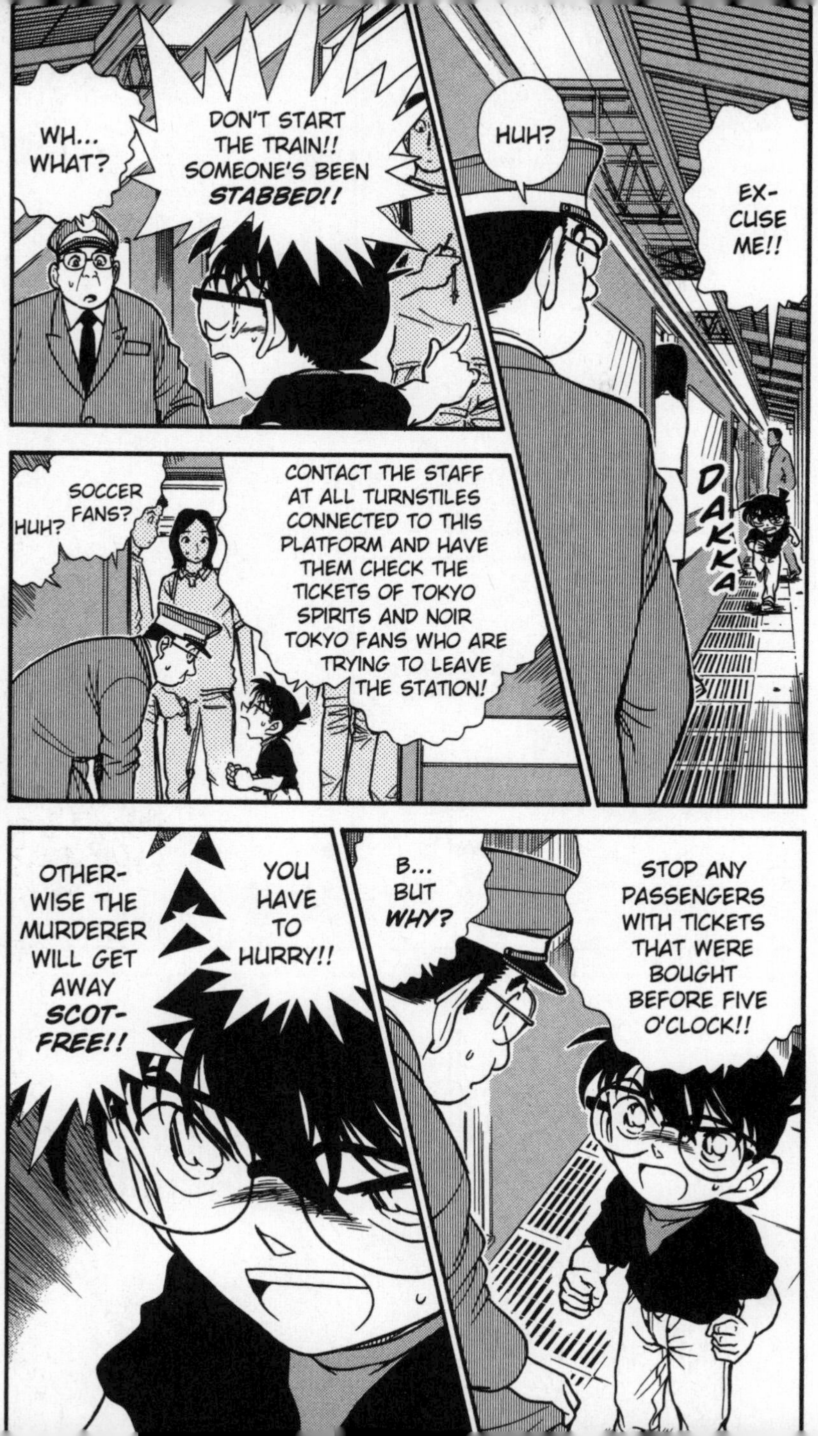
EX-CUSE ME!!
HUH?
DAKKA
DON'T START THE TRAIN!! SOMEONE'S BEEN STABBED!!
WH... WHAT?
CONTACT THE STAFF AT ALL TURNSTILES CONNECTED TO THIS PLATFORM AND HAVE THEM CHECK THE TICKETS OF TOKYO SPIRITS AND NOIR TOKYO FANS WHO ARE TRYING TO LEAVE THE STATION!
SOCCER FANS?
HUH?
STOP ANY PASSENGERS WITH TICKETS THAT WERE BOUGHT BEFORE FIVE O'CLOCK!!
B... BUT WHY?
YOU HAVE TO HURRY!!
OTHER-WISE THE MURDERER WILL GET AWAY SCOT-FREE!!

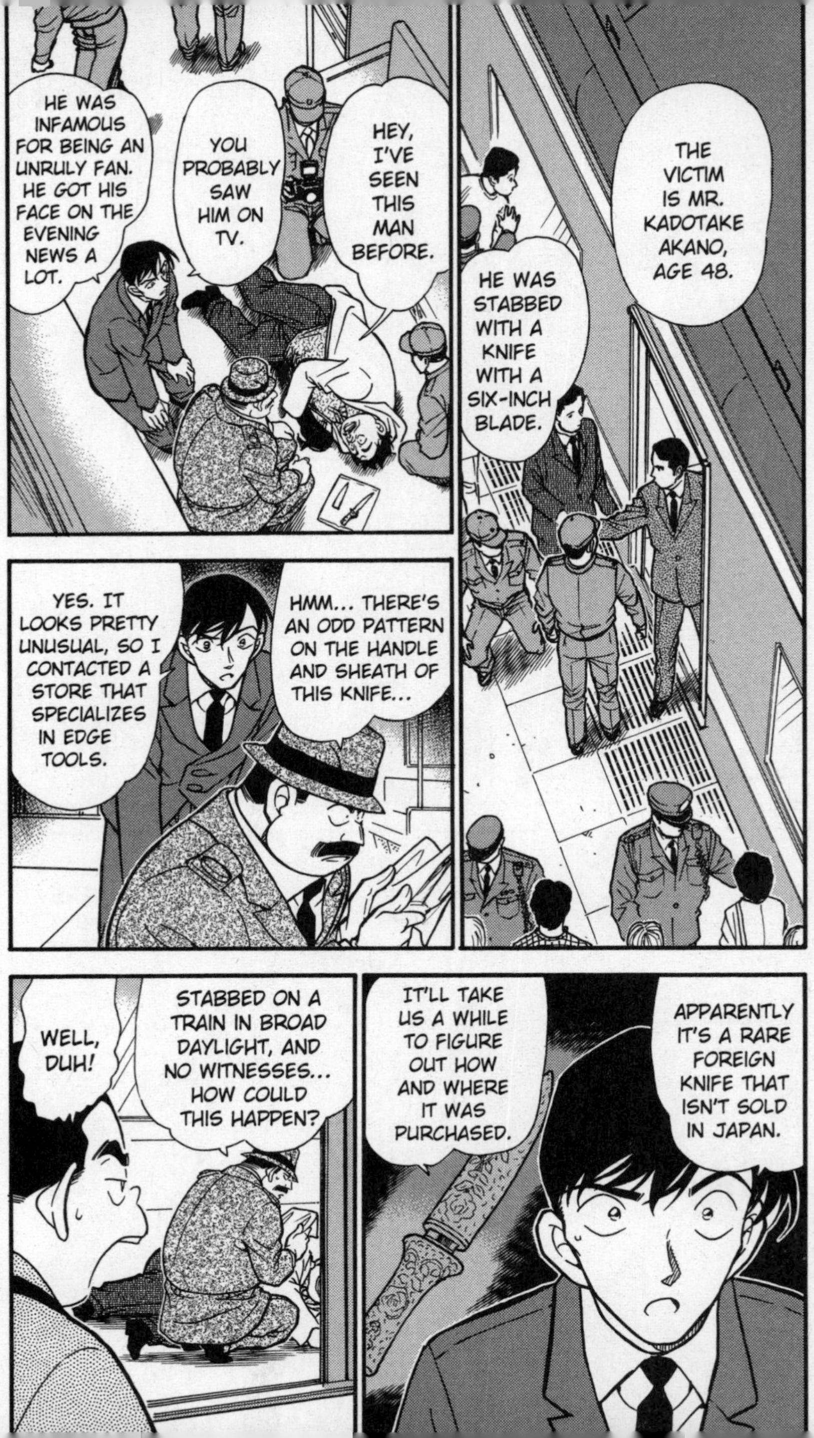
THE VICTIM IS MR. KADOTAKE AKANO, AGE 48.
HE WAS STABBED WITH A KNIFE WITH A SIX-INCH BLADE.
HEY, I'VE SEEN THIS MAN BEFORE.
YOU PROBABLY SAW HIM ON TV.
HE WAS INFAMOUS FOR BEING AN UNRULY FAN. HE GOT HIS FACE ON THE EVENING NEWS A LOT.
HMM... THERE'S AN ODD PATTERN ON THE HANDLE AND SHEATH OF THIS KNIFE...
YES. IT LOOKS PRETTY UNUSUAL, SO I CONTACTED A STORE THAT SPECIALIZES IN EDGE TOOLS.
APPARENTLY IT'S A RARE FOREIGN KNIFE THAT ISN'T SOLD IN JAPAN.
IT'LL TAKE US A WHILE TO FIGURE OUT HOW AND WHERE IT WAS PURCHASED.
STABBED ON A TRAIN IN BROAD DAYLIGHT, AND NO WITNESSES... HOW COULD THIS HAPPEN?
WELL, DUH!

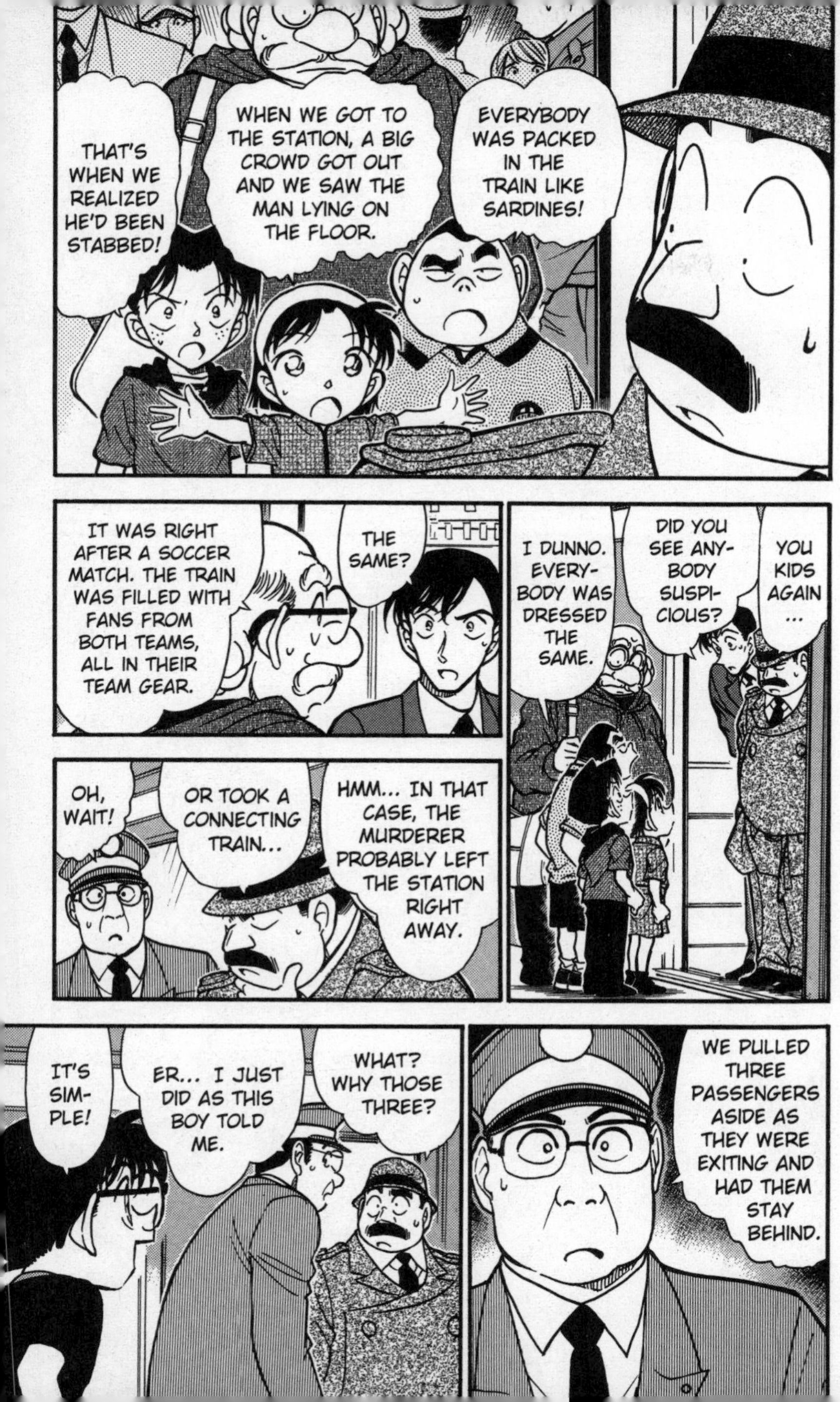
EVERYBODY WAS PACKED IN THE TRAIN LIKE SARDINES!
WHEN WE GOT TO THE STATION, A BIG CROWD GOT OUT AND WE SAW THE MAN LYING ON THE FLOOR.
THAT'S WHEN WE REALIZED HE'D BEEN STABBED!
YOU KIDS AGAIN...
DID YOU SEE ANYBODY SUSPICIOUS?
I DUNNO. EVERYBODY WAS DRESSED THE SAME.
THE SAME?
IT WAS RIGHT AFTER A SOCCER MATCH. THE TRAIN WAS FILLED WITH FANS FROM BOTH TEAMS, ALL IN THEIR TEAM GEAR.
HMM... IN THAT CASE, THE MURDERER PROBABLY LEFT THE STATION RIGHT AWAY.
OR TOOK A CONNECTING TRAIN...
OH, WAIT!
WE PULLED THREE PASSENGERS ASIDE AS THEY WERE EXITING AND HAD THEM STAY BEHIND.
WHAT? WHY THOSE THREE?
ER... I JUST DID AS THIS BOY TOLD ME.
IT'S SIMPLE!

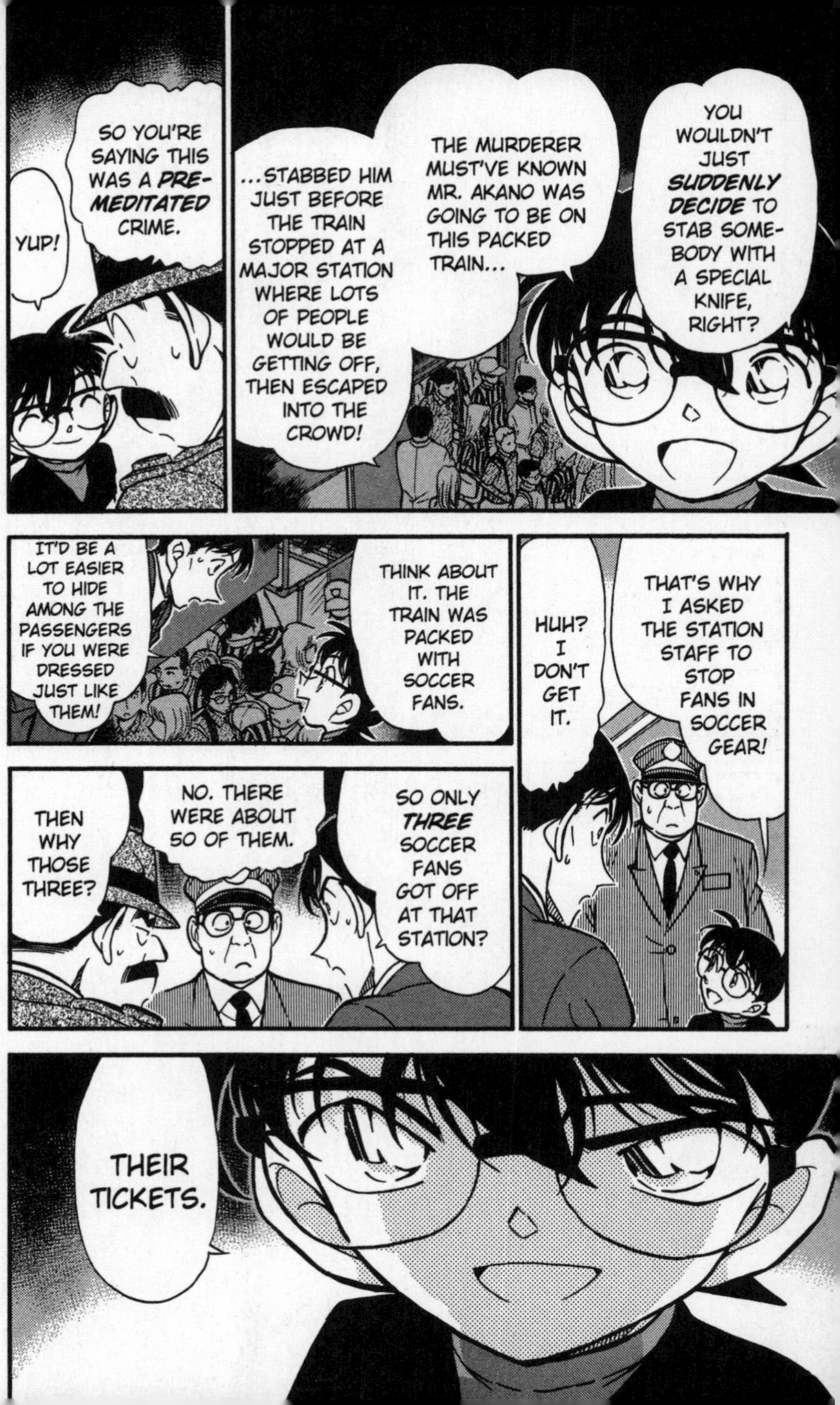
YOU WOULDN'T JUST SUDDENLY DECIDE TO STAB SOMEBODY WITH A SPECIAL KNIFE, RIGHT?
THE MURDERER MUST'VE KNOWN MR. AKANO WAS GOING TO BE ON THIS PACKED TRAIN...
...STABBED HIM JUST BEFORE THE TRAIN STOPPED AT A MAJOR STATION WHERE LOTS OF PEOPLE WOULD BE GETTING OFF, THEN ESCAPED INTO THE CROWD!
SO YOU'RE SAYING THIS WAS A PREMEDITATED CRIME.
YUP!
THAT'S WHY I ASKED THE STATION STAFF TO STOP FANS IN SOCCER GEAR!
HUH? I DON'T GET IT.
THINK ABOUT IT. THE TRAIN WAS PACKED WITH SOCCER FANS.
IT'D BE A LOT EASIER TO HIDE AMONG THE PASSENGERS IF YOU WERE DRESSED JUST LIKE THEM!
SO ONLY THREE SOCCER FANS GOT OFF AT THAT STATION?
NO. THERE WERE ABOUT 50 OF THEM.
THEN WHY THOSE THREE?
THEIR TICKETS.

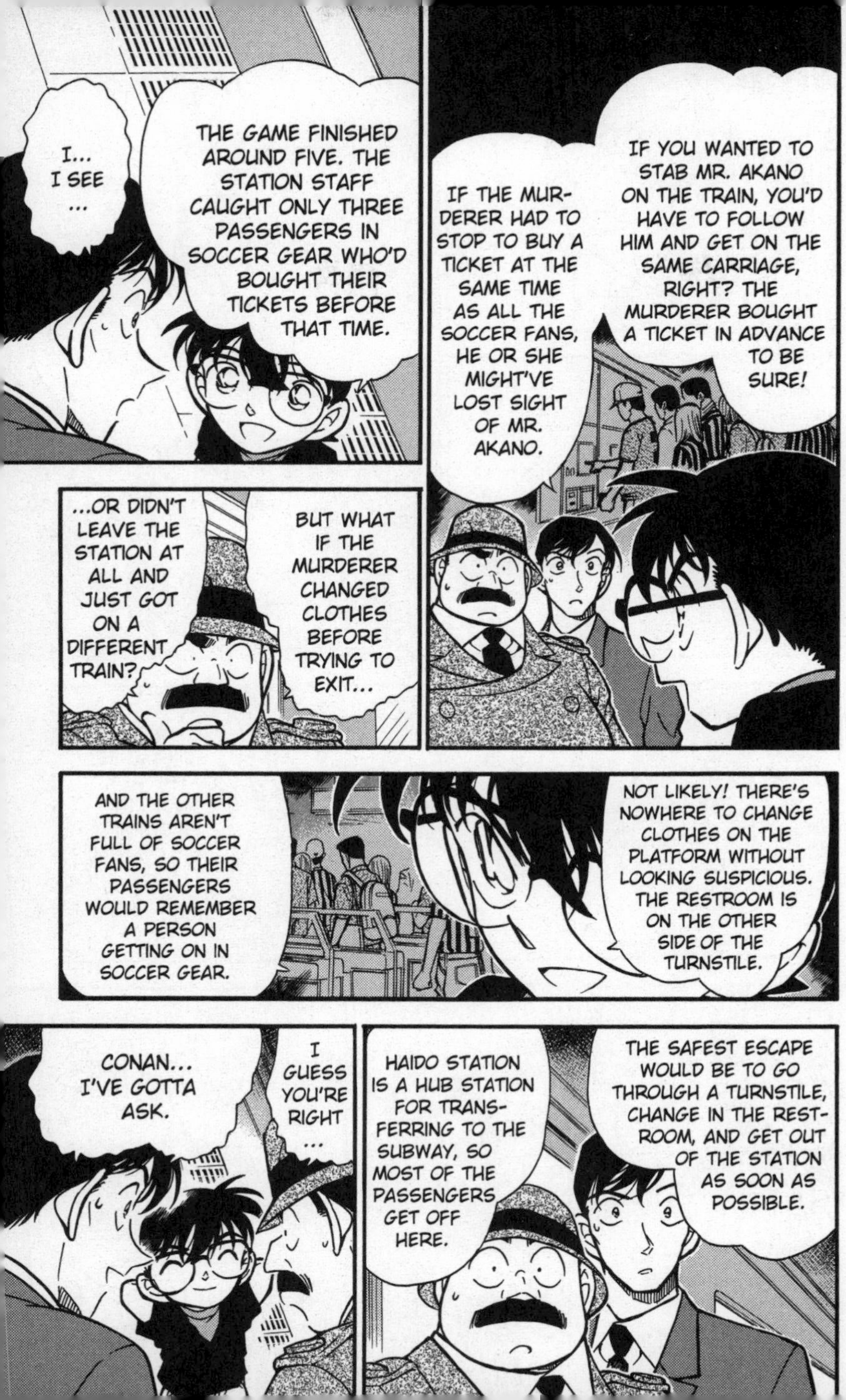
IF YOU WANTED TO STAB MR. AKANO ON THE TRAIN, YOU'D HAVE TO FOLLOW HIM AND GET ON THE SAME CARRIAGE, RIGHT? THE MURDERER BOUGHT A TICKET IN ADVANCE TO BE SURE!
IF THE MURDERER HAD TO STOP TO BUY A TICKET AT THE SAME TIME AS ALL THE SOCCER FANS, HE OR SHE MIGHT'VE LOST SIGHT OF MR. AKANO.
THE GAME FINISHED AROUND FIVE. THE STATION STAFF CAUGHT ONLY THREE PASSENGERS IN SOCCER GEAR WHO'D BOUGHT THEIR TICKETS BEFORE THAT TIME.
I... I SEE ...
BUT WHAT IF THE MURDERER CHANGED CLOTHES BEFORE TRYING TO EXIT...
...OR DIDN'T LEAVE THE STATION AT ALL AND JUST GOT ON A DIFFERENT TRAIN?
NOT LIKELY! THERE'S NOWHERE TO CHANGE CLOTHES ON THE PLATFORM WITHOUT LOOKING SUSPICIOUS. THE RESTROOM IS ON THE OTHER SIDE OF THE TURNSTILE.
AND THE OTHER TRAINS AREN'T FULL OF SOCCER FANS, SO THEIR PASSENGERS WOULD REMEMBER A PERSON GETTING ON IN SOCCER GEAR.
THE SAFEST ESCAPE WOULD BE TO GO THROUGH A TURNSTILE, CHANGE IN THE REST-ROOM, AND GET OUT OF THE STATION AS SOON AS POSSIBLE.
HAIDO STATION IS A HUB STATION FOR TRANS-FERRING TO THE SUBWAY, SO MOST OF THE PASSENGERS GET OFF HERE.
I GUESS YOU'RE RIGHT ...
CONAN... I'VE GOTTA ASK.

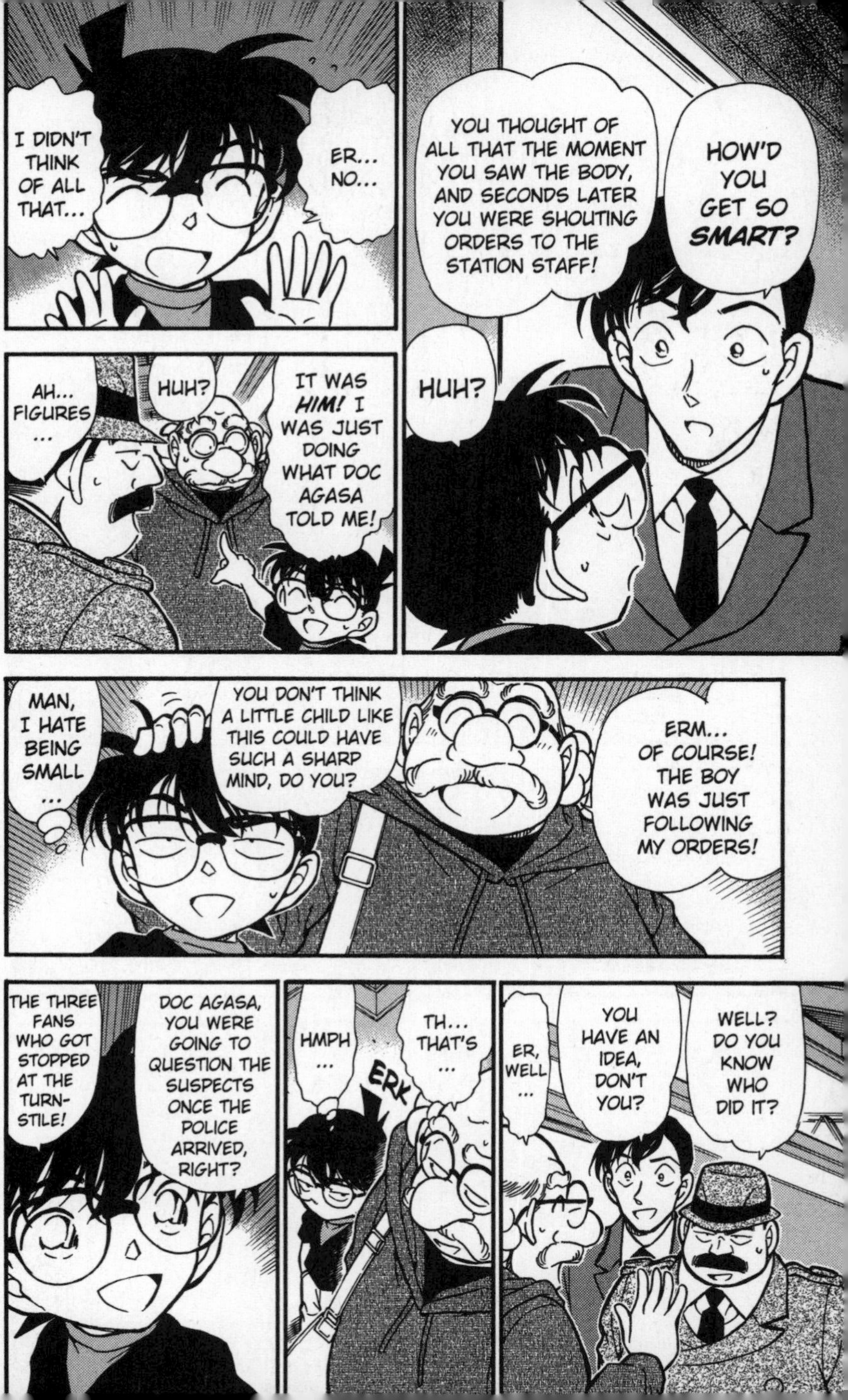
HOW'D YOU GET SO **SMART?**
YOU THOUGHT OF ALL THAT THE MOMENT YOU SAW THE BODY, AND SECONDS LATER YOU WERE SHOUTING ORDERS TO THE STATION STAFF!
HUH?
ER... NO...
I DIDN'T THINK OF ALL THAT...
IT WAS *HIM!* I WAS JUST DOING WHAT DOC AGASA TOLD ME!
HUH?
AH... FIGURES...
ERM... OF COURSE! THE BOY WAS JUST FOLLOWING MY ORDERS!
YOU DON'T THINK A LITTLE CHILD LIKE THIS COULD HAVE SUCH A SHARP MIND, DO YOU?
MAN, I HATE BEING SMALL...
WELL? DO YOU KNOW WHO DID IT?
YOU HAVE AN IDEA, DON'T YOU?
ER, WELL...
TH... THAT'S...
ERK
HMPH...
DOC AGASA, YOU WERE GOING TO QUESTION THE SUSPECTS ONCE THE POLICE ARRIVED, RIGHT?
THE THREE FANS WHO GOT STOPPED AT THE TURN-STILE!

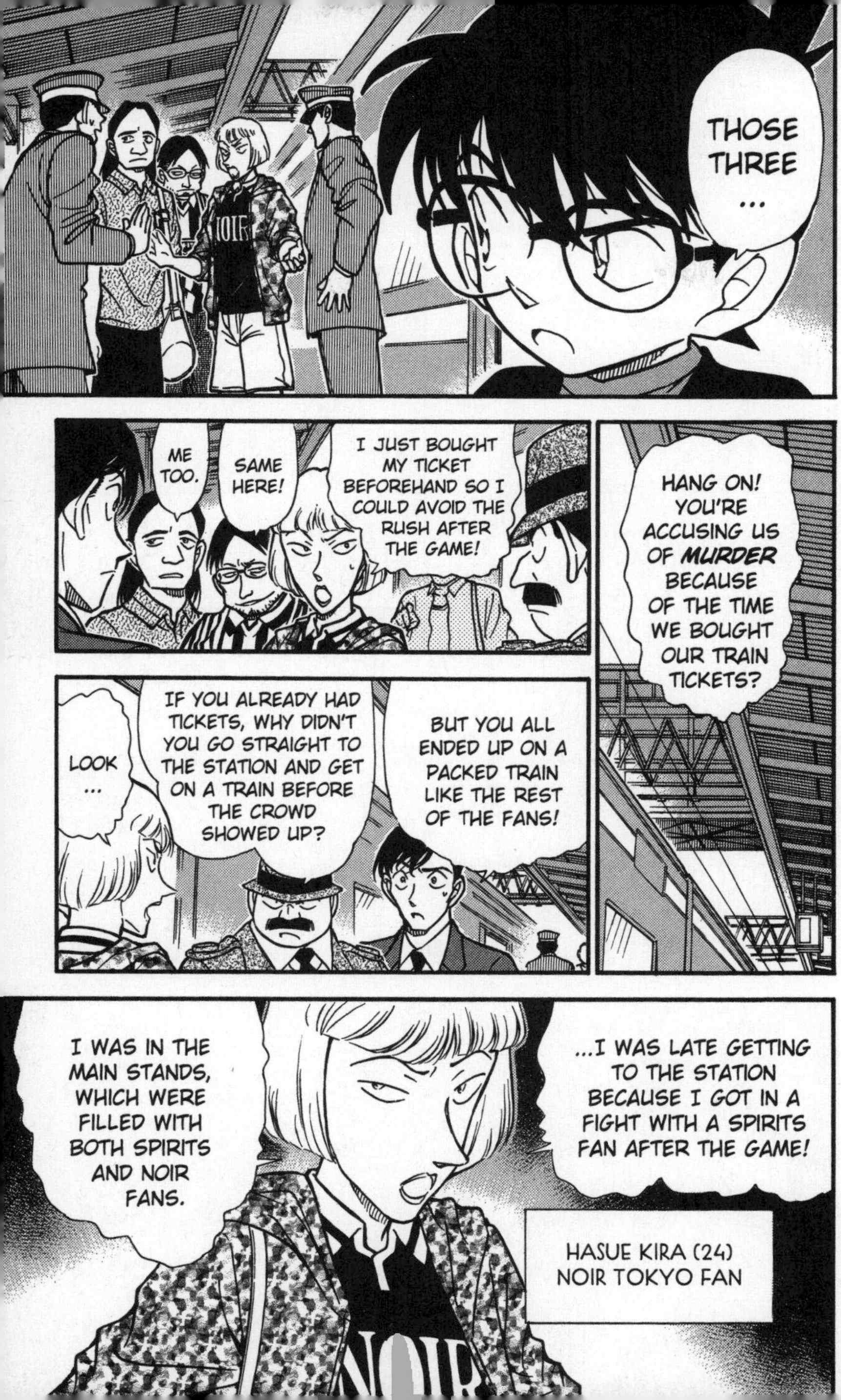
THOSE THREE ...
HANG ON! YOU'RE ACCUSING US OF *MURDER* BECAUSE OF THE TIME WE BOUGHT OUR TRAIN TICKETS?
I JUST BOUGHT MY TICKET BEFOREHAND SO I COULD AVOID THE RUSH AFTER THE GAME!
SAME HERE!
ME TOO.
BUT YOU ALL ENDED UP ON A PACKED TRAIN LIKE THE REST OF THE FANS!
IF YOU ALREADY HAD TICKETS, WHY DIDN'T YOU GO STRAIGHT TO THE STATION AND GET ON A TRAIN BEFORE THE CROWD SHOWED UP?
LOOK ...
...I WAS LATE GETTING TO THE STATION BECAUSE I GOT IN A FIGHT WITH A SPIRITS FAN AFTER THE GAME!
I WAS IN THE MAIN STANDS, WHICH WERE FILLED WITH BOTH SPIRITS AND NOIR FANS.
HASUE KIRA (24) NOIR TOKYO FAN

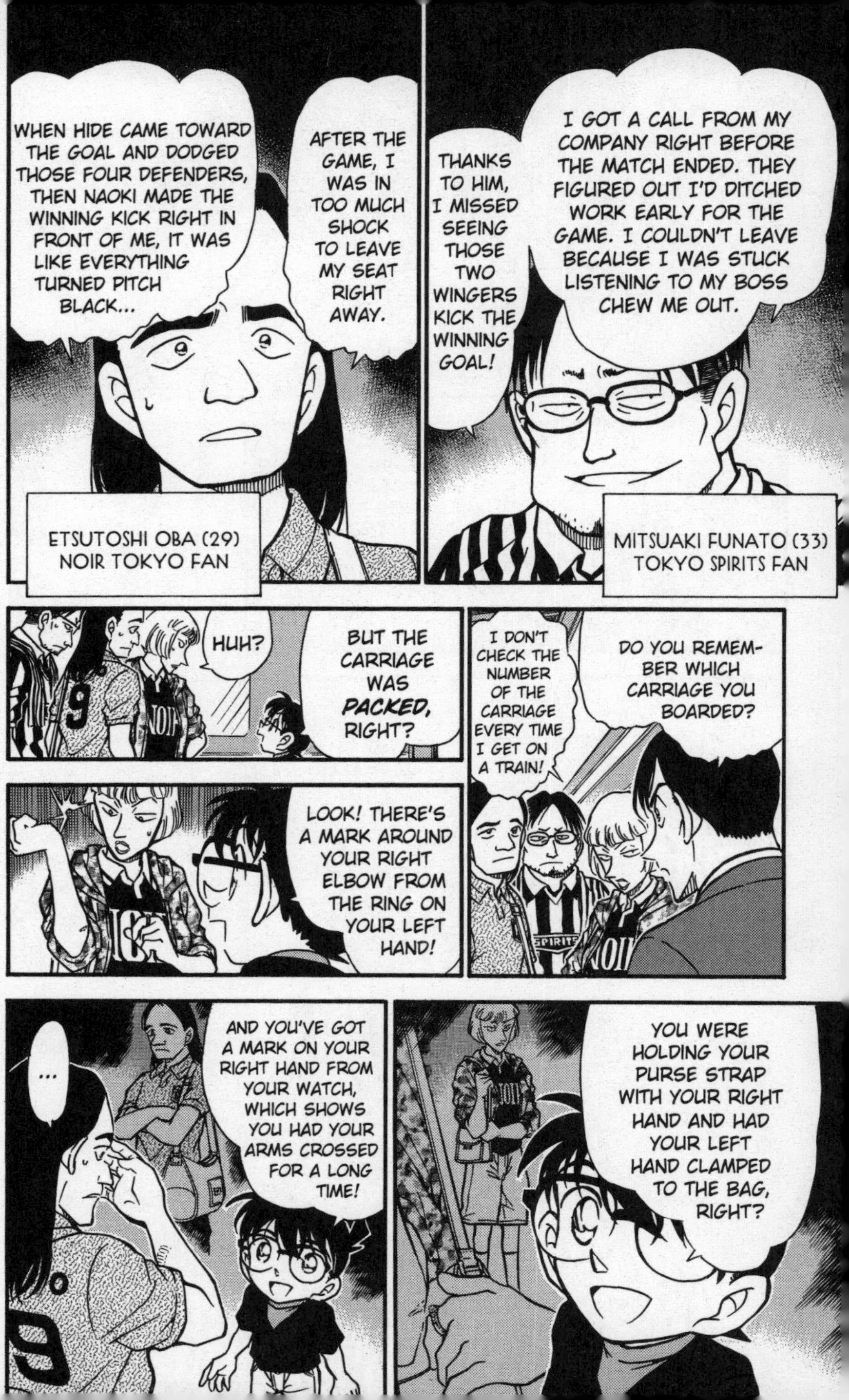
I GOT A CALL FROM MY COMPANY RIGHT BEFORE THE MATCH ENDED. THEY FIGURED OUT I'D DITCHED WORK EARLY FOR THE GAME. I COULDN'T LEAVE BECAUSE I WAS STUCK LISTENING TO MY BOSS CHEW ME OUT.
THANKS TO HIM, I MISSED SEEING THOSE TWO WINGERS KICK THE WINNING GOAL!
MITSUAKI FUNATO (33) TOKYO SPIRITS FAN
WHEN HIDE CAME TOWARD THE GOAL AND DODGED THOSE FOUR DEFENDERS, THEN NAOKI MADE THE WINNING KICK RIGHT IN FRONT OF ME, IT WAS LIKE EVERYTHING TURNED PITCH BLACK...
AFTER THE GAME, I WAS IN TOO MUCH SHOCK TO LEAVE MY SEAT RIGHT AWAY.
ETSUTOSHI OBA (29) NOIR TOKYO FAN
DO YOU REMEMBER WHICH CARRIAGE YOU BOARDED?
I DON'T CHECK THE NUMBER OF THE CARRIAGE EVERY TIME I GET ON A TRAIN!
BUT THE CARRIAGE WAS *PACKED,* RIGHT?
HUH?
LOOK! THERE'S A MARK AROUND YOUR RIGHT ELBOW FROM THE RING ON YOUR LEFT HAND!
YOU WERE HOLDING YOUR PURSE STRAP WITH YOUR RIGHT HAND AND HAD YOUR LEFT HAND CLAMPED TO THE BAG, RIGHT?
AND YOU'VE GOT A MARK ON YOUR RIGHT HAND FROM YOUR WATCH, WHICH SHOWS YOU HAD YOUR ARMS CROSSED FOR A LONG TIME!
...

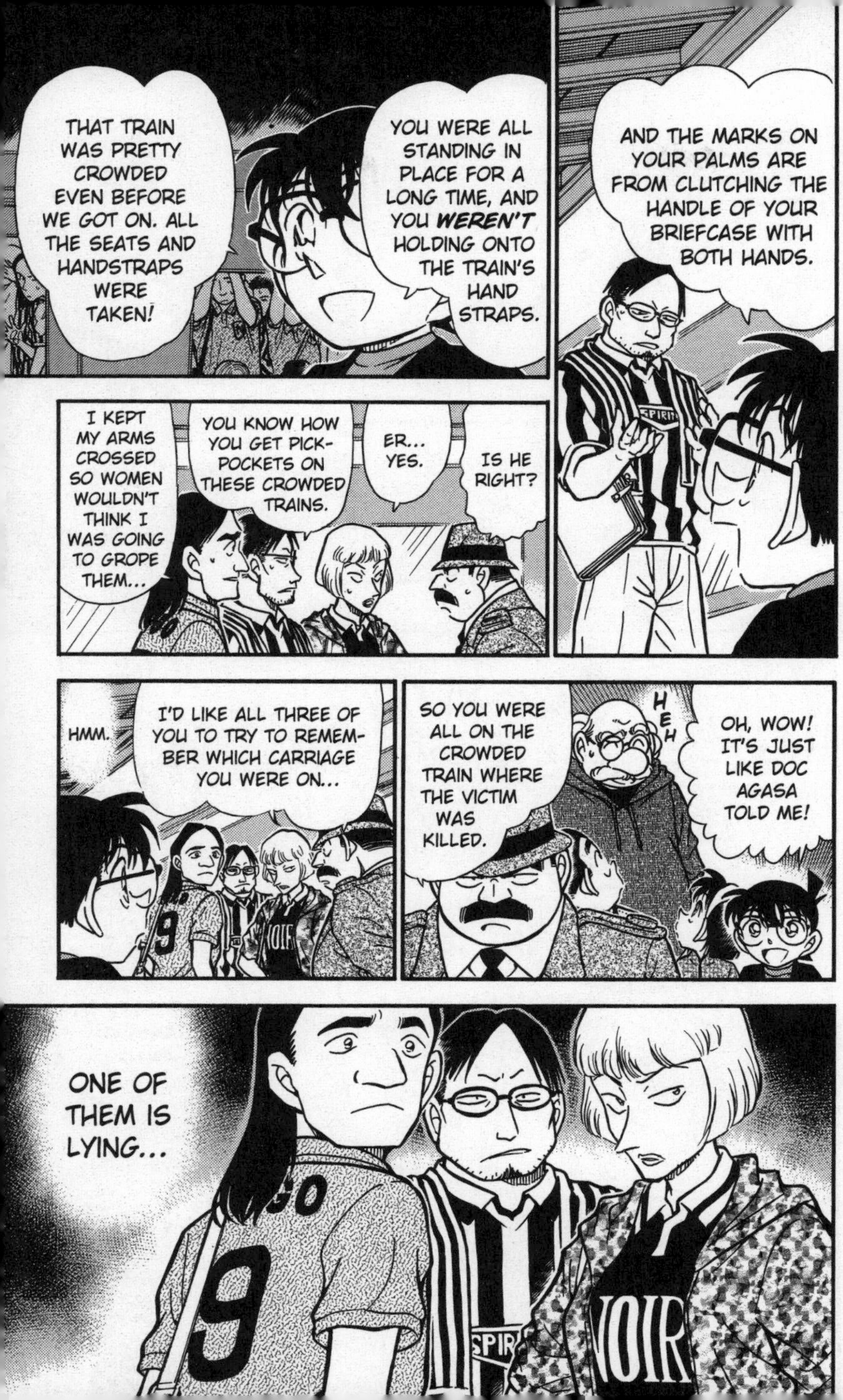
THAT TRAIN WAS PRETTY CROWDED EVEN BEFORE WE GOT ON. ALL THE SEATS AND HANDSTRAPS WERE TAKEN!
YOU WERE ALL STANDING IN PLACE FOR A LONG TIME, AND YOU ***WEREN'T*** HOLDING ONTO THE TRAIN'S HAND STRAPS.
AND THE MARKS ON YOUR PALMS ARE FROM CLUTCHING THE HANDLE OF YOUR BRIEFCASE WITH BOTH HANDS.
SPIRIT
I KEPT MY ARMS CROSSED SO WOMEN WOULDN'T THINK I WAS GOING TO GROPE THEM...
YOU KNOW HOW YOU GET PICK-POCKETS ON THESE CROWDED TRAINS.
ER... YES.
IS HE RIGHT?
HMM.
I'D LIKE ALL THREE OF YOU TO TRY TO REMEMBER WHICH CARRIAGE YOU WERE ON...
9
NOIR
SO YOU WERE ALL ON THE CROWDED TRAIN WHERE THE VICTIM WAS KILLED.
HEH
OH, WOW! IT'S JUST LIKE DOC AGASA TOLD ME!
ONE OF THEM IS LYING...
GO
9
SPIR
NOIR

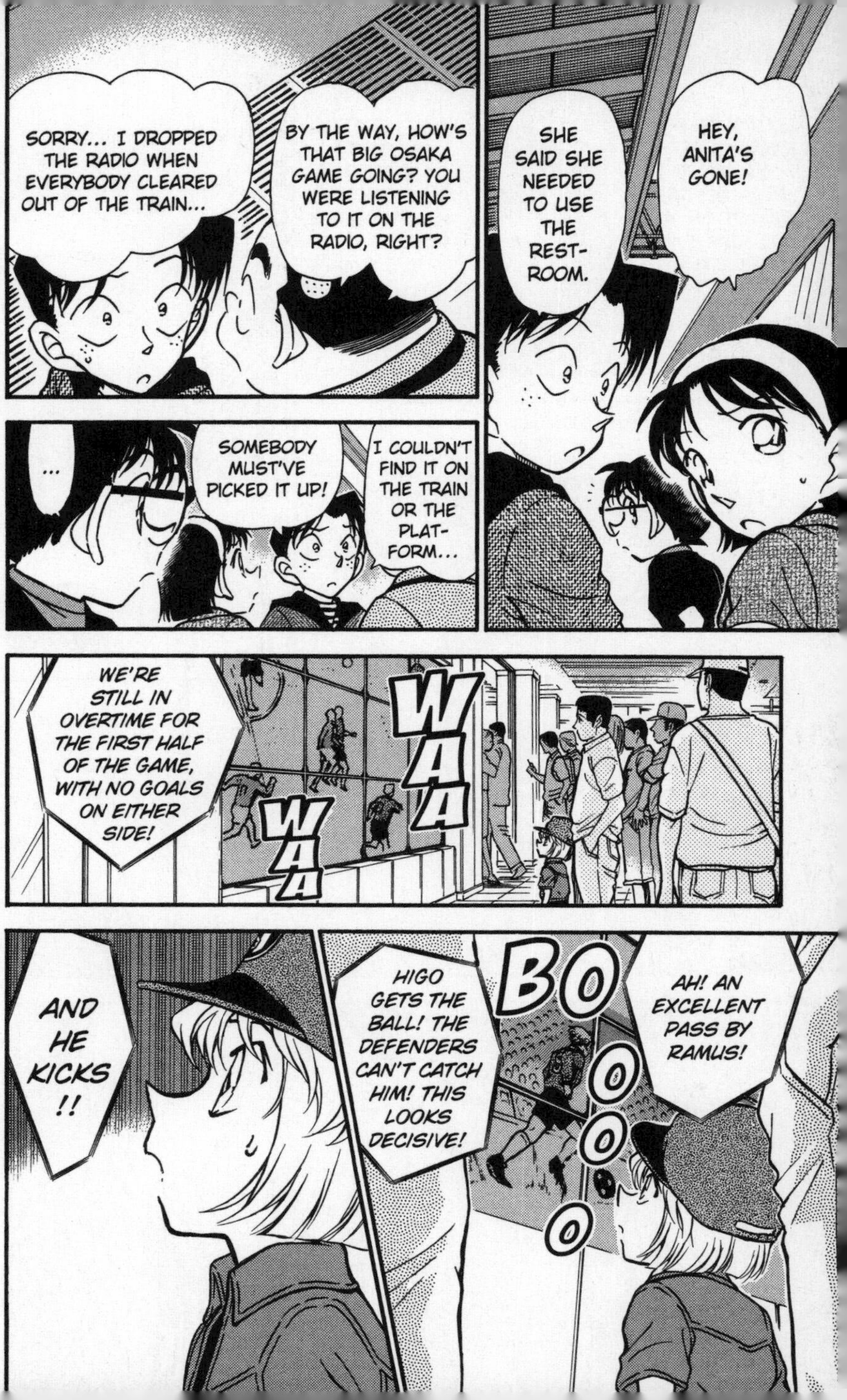
HEY, ANITA'S GONE!
SHE SAID SHE NEEDED TO USE THE REST-ROOM.
BY THE WAY, HOW'S THAT BIG OSAKA GAME GOING? YOU WERE LISTENING TO IT ON THE RADIO, RIGHT?
SORRY... I DROPPED THE RADIO WHEN EVERYBODY CLEARED OUT OF THE TRAIN...
I COULDN'T FIND IT ON THE TRAIN OR THE PLAT-FORM...
SOMEBODY MUST'VE PICKED IT UP!
...
WAA
WE'RE STILL IN OVERTIME FOR THE FIRST HALF OF THE GAME, WITH NO GOALS ON EITHER SIDE!
WAA
AH! AN EXCELLENT PASS BY RAMUS!
BOOOOOOO
HIGO GETS THE BALL! THE DEFENDERS CAN'T CATCH HIM! THIS LOOKS DECISIVE!
AND HE KICKS!!

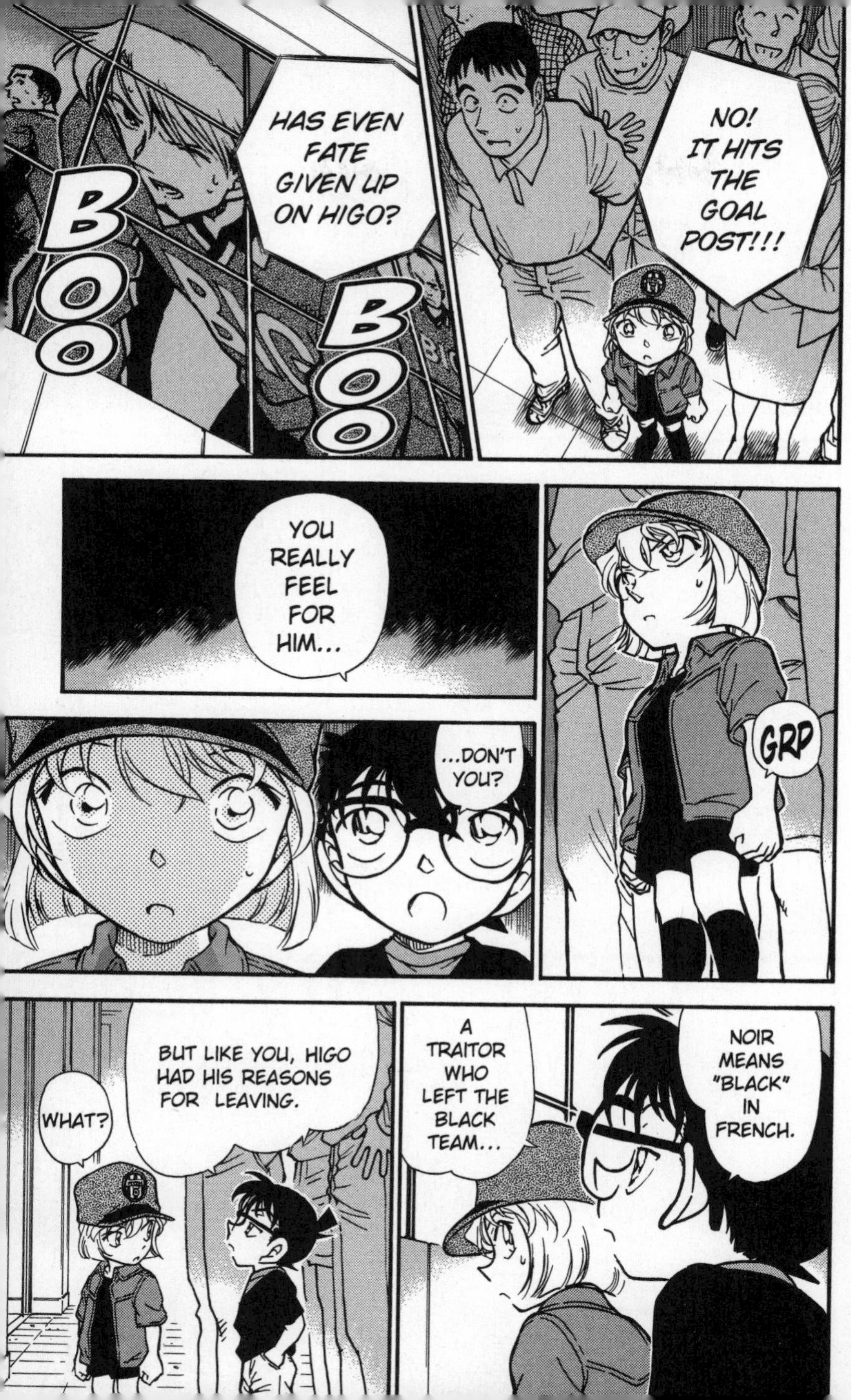
NO! IT HITS THE GOAL POST!!!
HAS EVEN FATE GIVEN UP ON HIGO?
BOO
BOO
GRP
YOU REALLY FEEL FOR HIM...
...DON'T YOU?
NOIR MEANS "BLACK" IN FRENCH.
A TRAITOR WHO LEFT THE BLACK TEAM...
BUT LIKE YOU, HIGO HAD HIS REASONS FOR LEAVING.
WHAT?

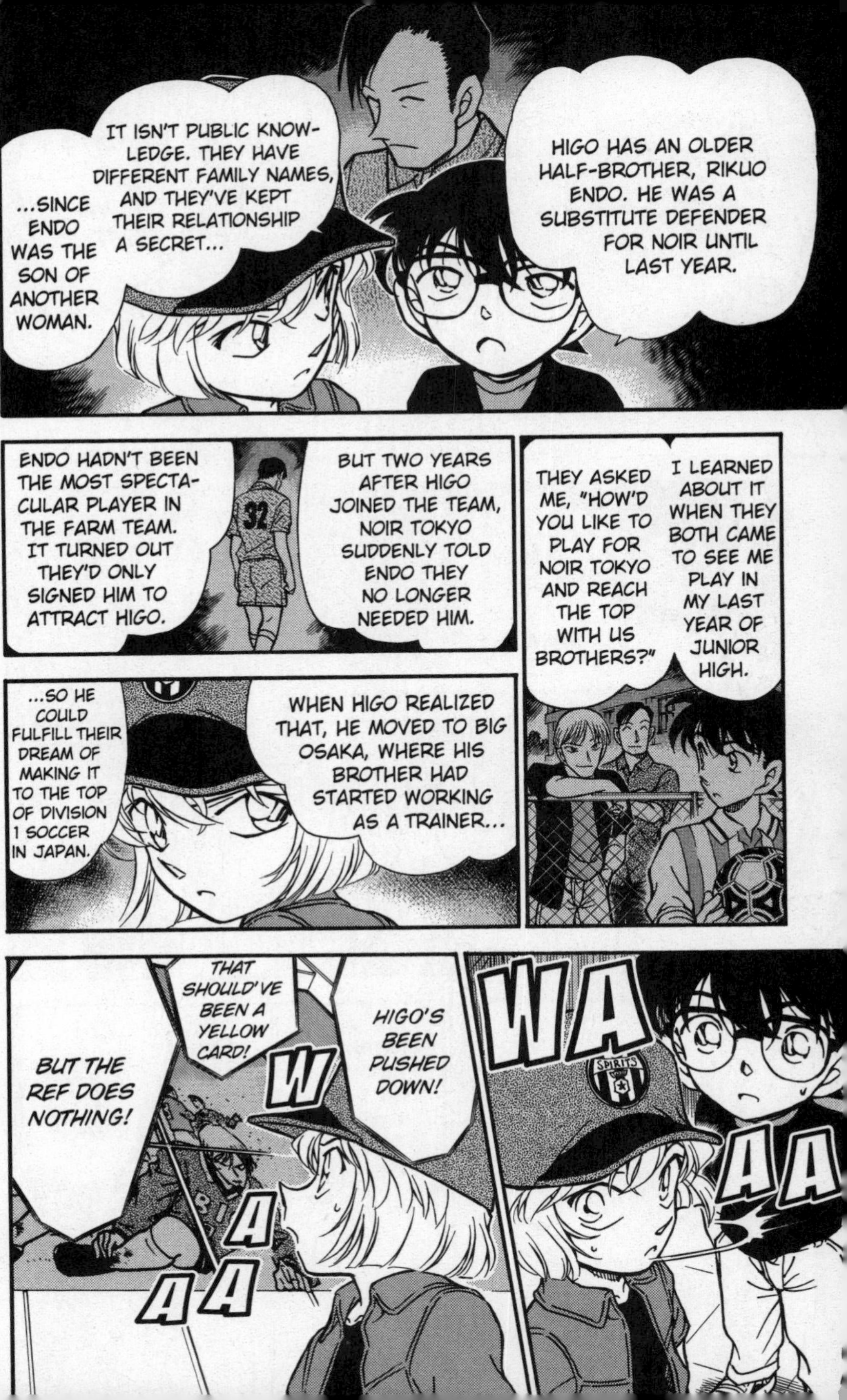
HIGO HAS AN OLDER HALF-BROTHER, RIKUO ENDO. HE WAS A SUBSTITUTE DEFENDER FOR NOIR UNTIL LAST YEAR.
IT ISN'T PUBLIC KNOWLEDGE. THEY HAVE DIFFERENT FAMILY NAMES, AND THEY'VE KEPT THEIR RELATIONSHIP A SECRET...
...SINCE ENDO WAS THE SON OF ANOTHER WOMAN.
I LEARNED ABOUT IT WHEN THEY BOTH CAME TO SEE ME PLAY IN MY LAST YEAR OF JUNIOR HIGH.
THEY ASKED ME, "HOW'D YOU LIKE TO PLAY FOR NOIR TOKYO AND REACH THE TOP WITH US BROTHERS?"
BUT TWO YEARS AFTER HIGO JOINED THE TEAM, NOIR TOKYO SUDDENLY TOLD ENDO THEY NO LONGER NEEDED HIM.
ENDO HADN'T BEEN THE MOST SPECTACULAR PLAYER IN THE FARM TEAM. IT TURNED OUT THEY'D ONLY SIGNED HIM TO ATTRACT HIGO.
WHEN HIGO REALIZED THAT, HE MOVED TO BIG OSAKA, WHERE HIS BROTHER HAD STARTED WORKING AS A TRAINER...
...SO HE COULD FULFILL THEIR DREAM OF MAKING IT TO THE TOP OF DIVISION 1 SOCCER IN JAPAN.
WA
AA
HIGO'S BEEN PUSHED DOWN!
THAT SHOULD'VE BEEN A YELLOW CARD!
W
BUT THE REF DOES NOTHING!
A
A
AA

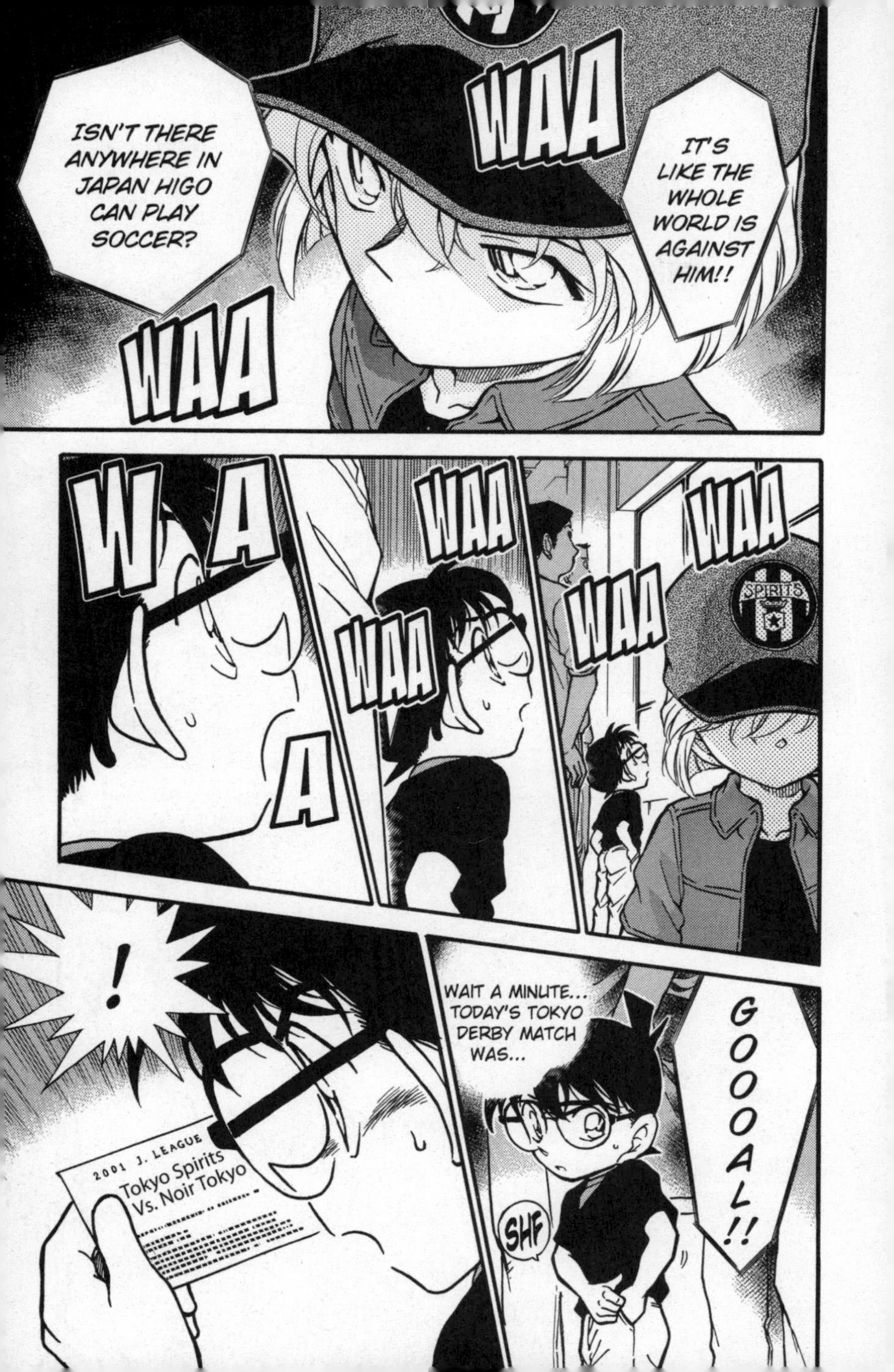
WAA
IT'S LIKE THE WHOLE WORLD IS AGAINST HIM!!
ISN'T THERE ANYWHERE IN JAPAN HIGO CAN PLAY SOCCER?
WAA
WAA
WAA
SPIRITS
WAA
WAA
W A
A
GOOOOAL!!
WAIT A MINUTE... TODAY'S TOKYO DERBY MATCH WAS...
SHF
!
2001 J. LEAGUE
Tokyo Spirits Vs. Noir Tokyo

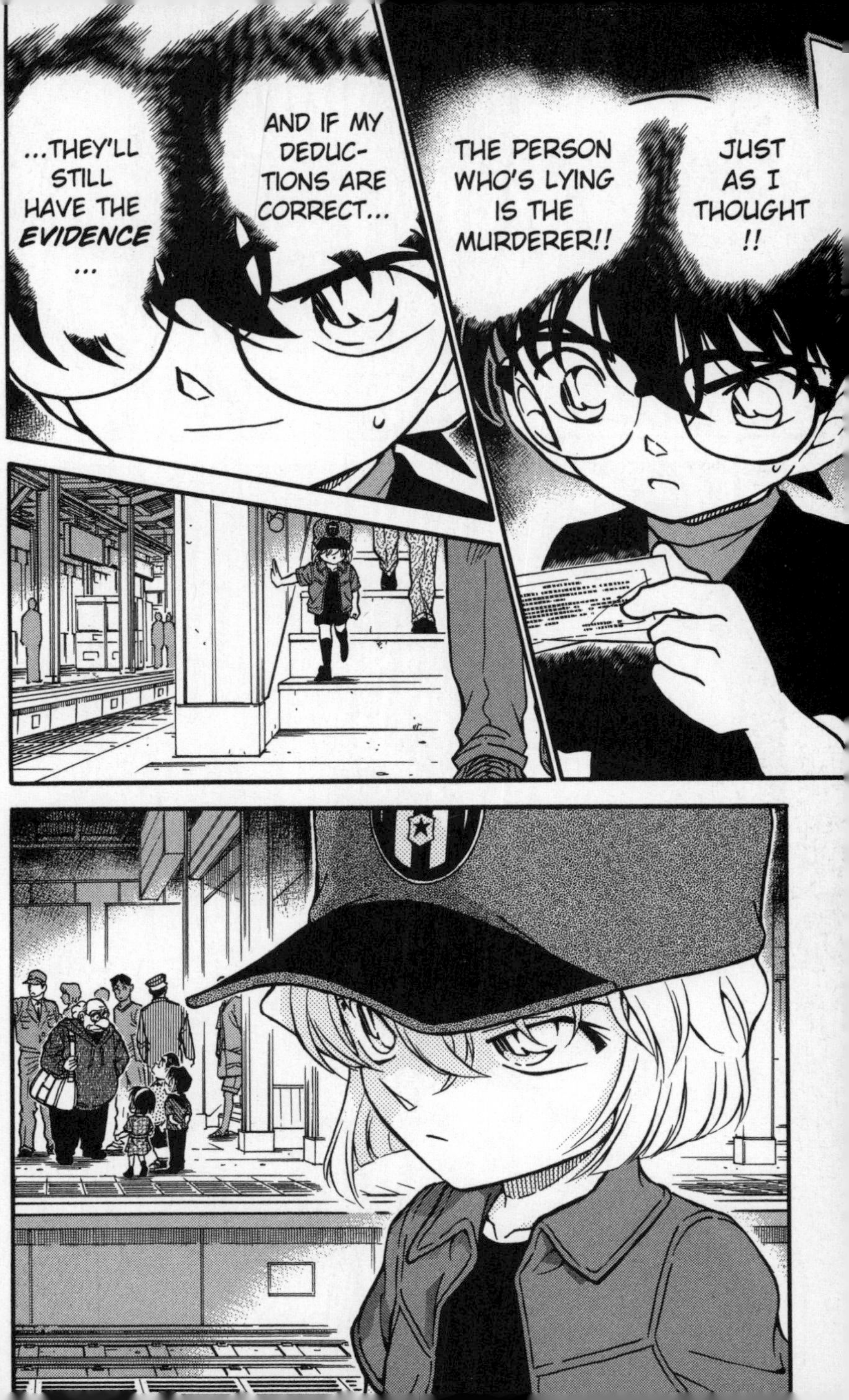
JUST AS I THOUGHT!!
THE PERSON WHO'S LYING IS THE MURDERER!!
AND IF MY DEDUC-TIONS ARE CORRECT...
...THEY'LL STILL HAVE THE *EVIDENCE*...

FILE 7: THE FAKE FAN

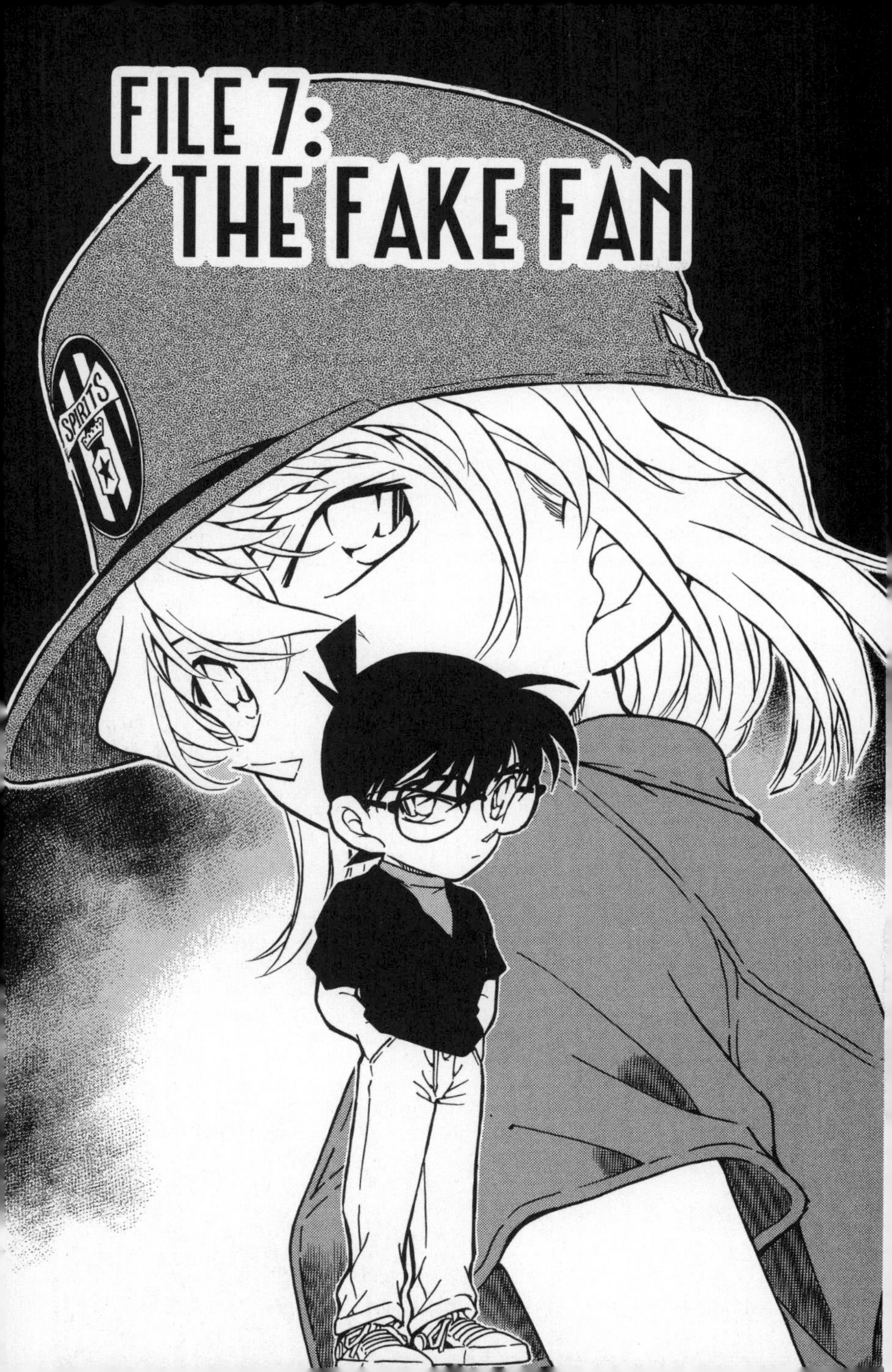
SPIRITS

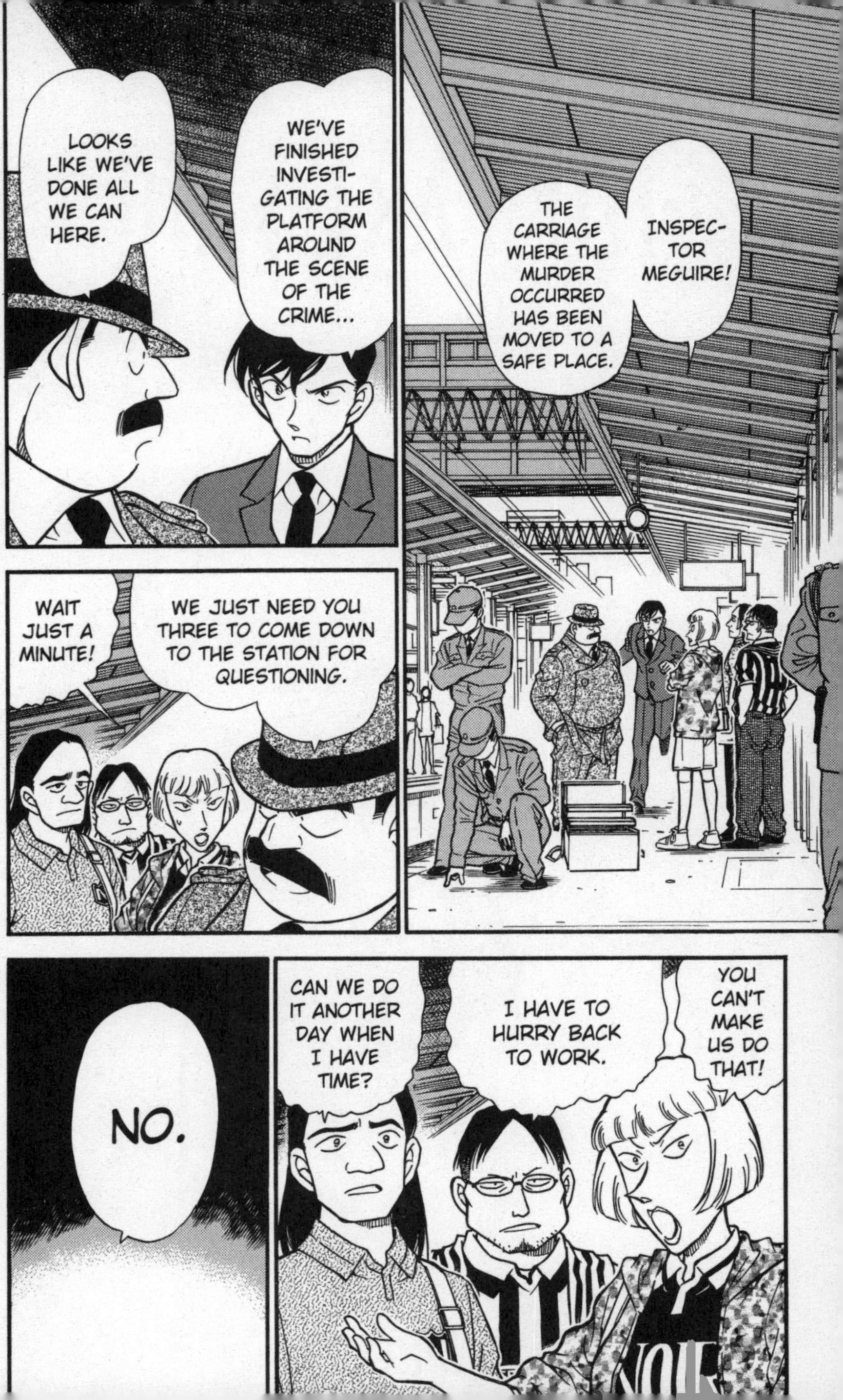
INSPECTOR MEGUIRE!
THE CARRIAGE WHERE THE MURDER OCCURRED HAS BEEN MOVED TO A SAFE PLACE.
WE'VE FINISHED INVESTIGATING THE PLATFORM AROUND THE SCENE OF THE CRIME...
LOOKS LIKE WE'VE DONE ALL WE CAN HERE.
WE JUST NEED YOU THREE TO COME DOWN TO THE STATION FOR QUESTIONING.
WAIT JUST A MINUTE!
YOU CAN'T MAKE US DO THAT!
I HAVE TO HURRY BACK TO WORK.
CAN WE DO IT ANOTHER DAY WHEN I HAVE TIME?
NO.

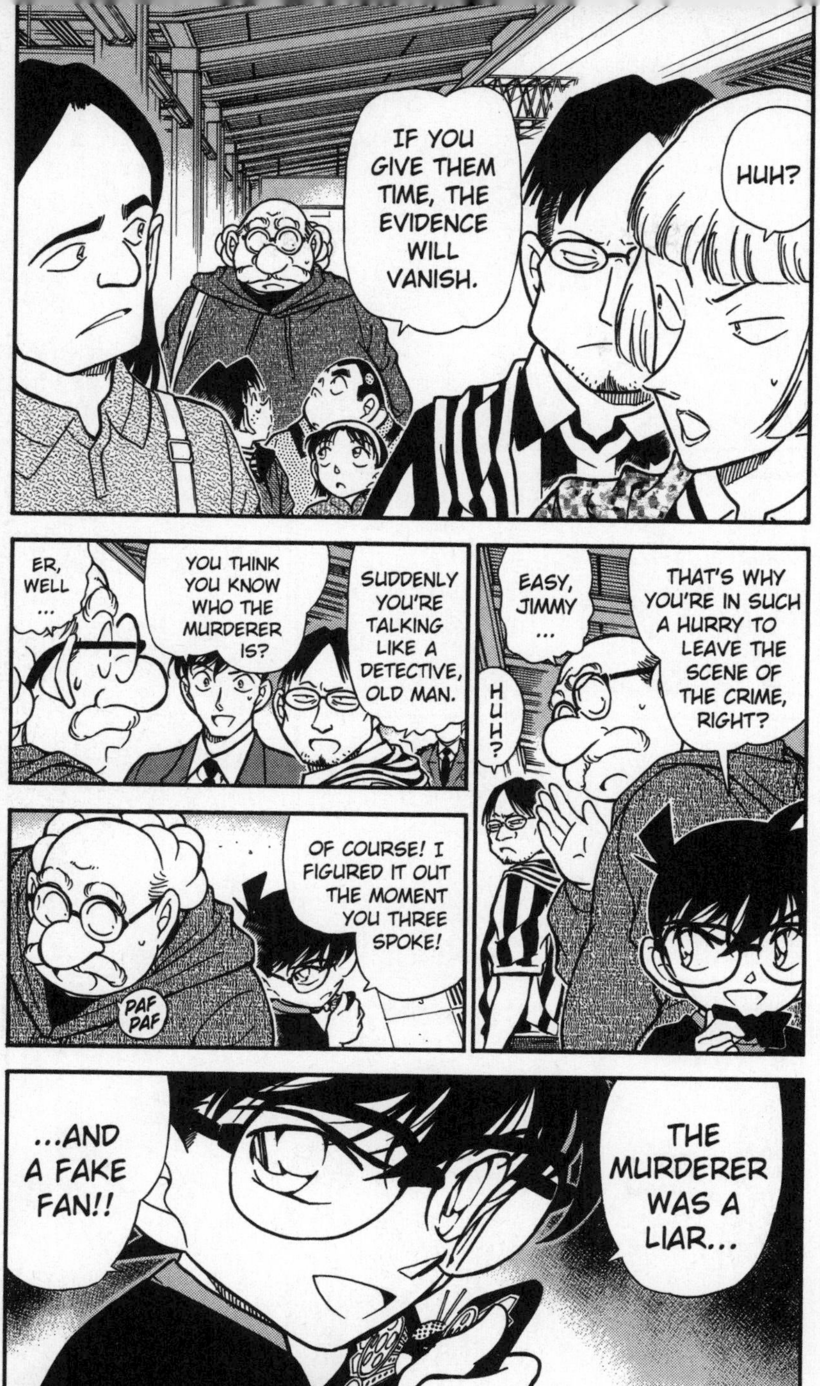

IF YOU GIVE THEM TIME, THE EVIDENCE WILL VANISH.
HUH?
THAT'S WHY YOU'RE IN SUCH A HURRY TO LEAVE THE SCENE OF THE CRIME, RIGHT?
EASY, JIMMY ...
HUH?
SUDDENLY YOU'RE TALKING LIKE A DETECTIVE, OLD MAN.
YOU THINK YOU KNOW WHO THE MURDERER IS?
ER, WELL ...
OF COURSE! I FIGURED IT OUT THE MOMENT YOU THREE SPOKE!
PAF PAF
THE MURDERER WAS A LIAR...
...AND A FAKE FAN!!

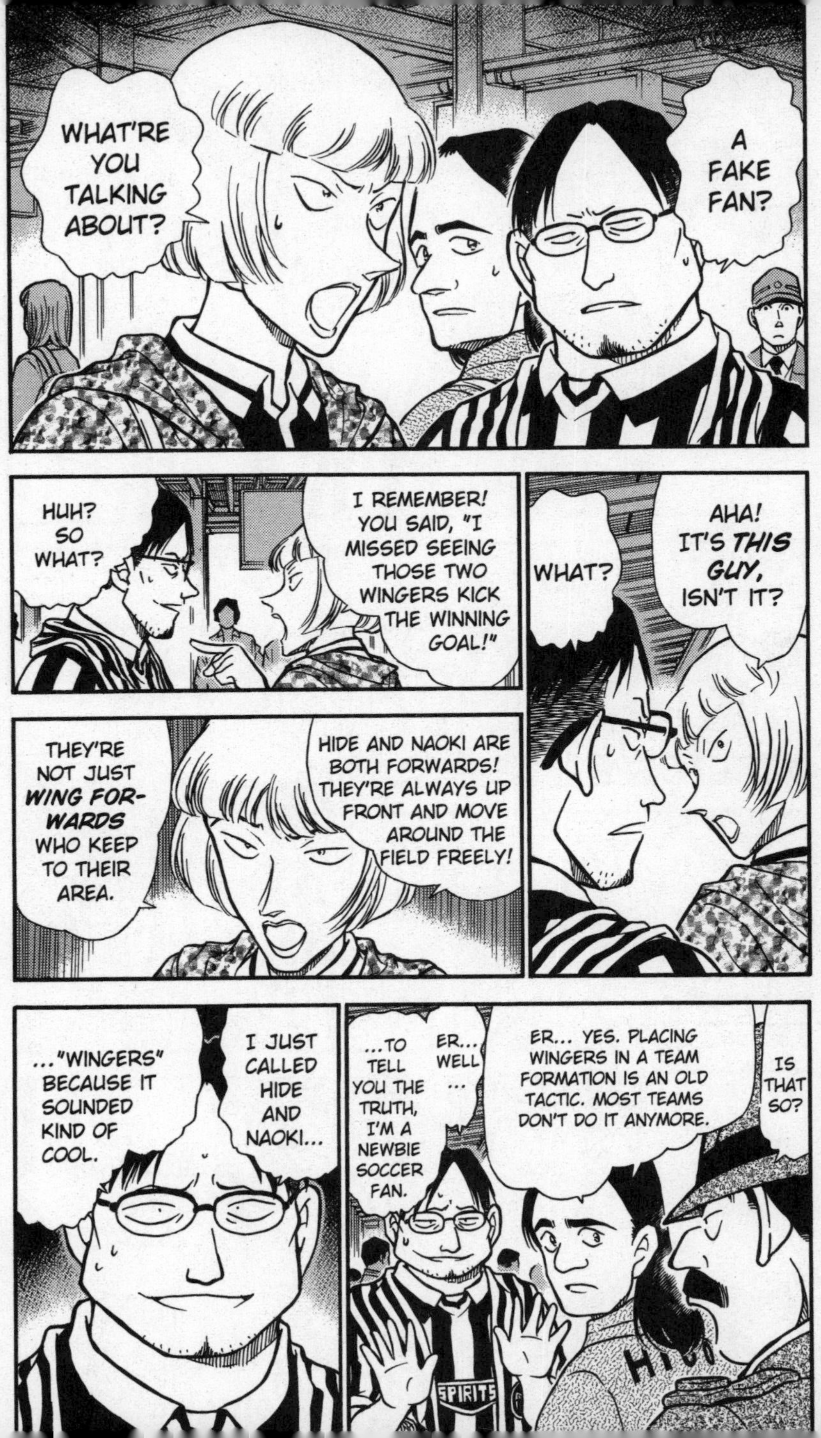
A FAKE FAN?
WHAT'RE YOU TALKING ABOUT?
AHA! IT'S *THIS GUY*, ISN'T IT?
WHAT?
I REMEMBER! YOU SAID, "I MISSED SEEING THOSE TWO WINGERS KICK THE WINNING GOAL!"
HUH? SO WHAT?
HIDE AND NAOKI ARE BOTH FORWARDS! THEY'RE ALWAYS UP FRONT AND MOVE AROUND THE FIELD FREELY!
THEY'RE NOT JUST ***WING FORWARDS*** WHO KEEP TO THEIR AREA.
IS THAT SO?
ER... YES. PLACING WINGERS IN A TEAM FORMATION IS AN OLD TACTIC. MOST TEAMS DON'T DO IT ANYMORE.
ER... WELL ...
...TO TELL YOU THE TRUTH, I'M A NEWBIE SOCCER FAN.
SPIRITS
I JUST CALLED HIDE AND NAOKI...
..."WINGERS" BECAUSE IT SOUNDED KIND OF COOL.

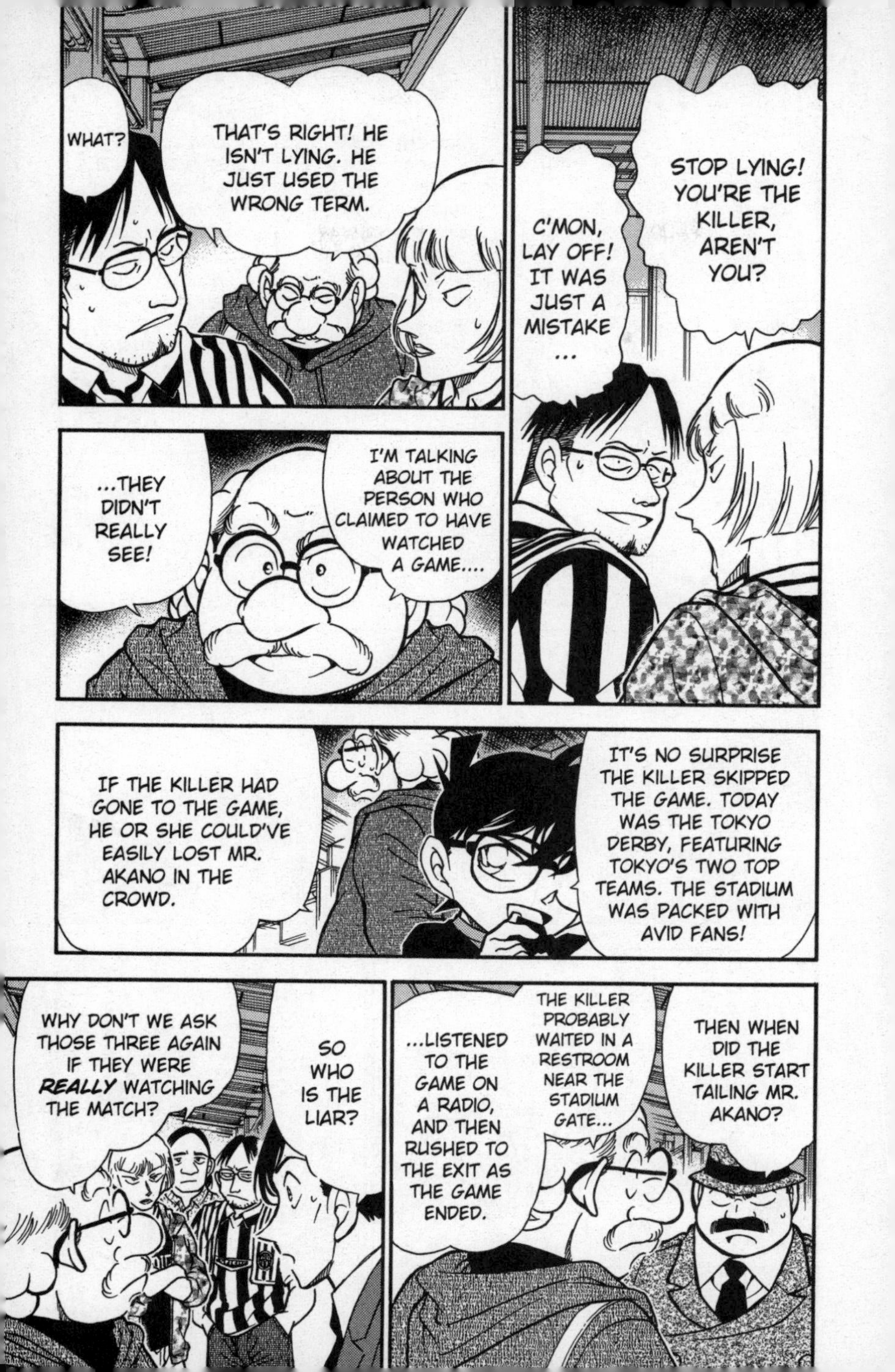
STOP LYING! YOU'RE THE KILLER, AREN'T YOU?
C'MON, LAY OFF! IT WAS JUST A MISTAKE ...
THAT'S RIGHT! HE ISN'T LYING. HE JUST USED THE WRONG TERM.
WHAT?
I'M TALKING ABOUT THE PERSON WHO CLAIMED TO HAVE WATCHED A GAME....
...THEY DIDN'T REALLY SEE!
IT'S NO SURPRISE THE KILLER SKIPPED THE GAME. TODAY WAS THE TOKYO DERBY, FEATURING TOKYO'S TWO TOP TEAMS. THE STADIUM WAS PACKED WITH AVID FANS!
IF THE KILLER HAD GONE TO THE GAME, HE OR SHE COULD'VE EASILY LOST MR. AKANO IN THE CROWD.
THEN WHEN DID THE KILLER START TAILING MR. AKANO?
THE KILLER PROBABLY WAITED IN A RESTROOM NEAR THE STADIUM GATE...
...LISTENED TO THE GAME ON A RADIO, AND THEN RUSHED TO THE EXIT AS THE GAME ENDED.
SO WHO IS THE LIAR?
WHY DON'T WE ASK THOSE THREE AGAIN IF THEY WERE *REALLY* WATCHING THE MATCH?

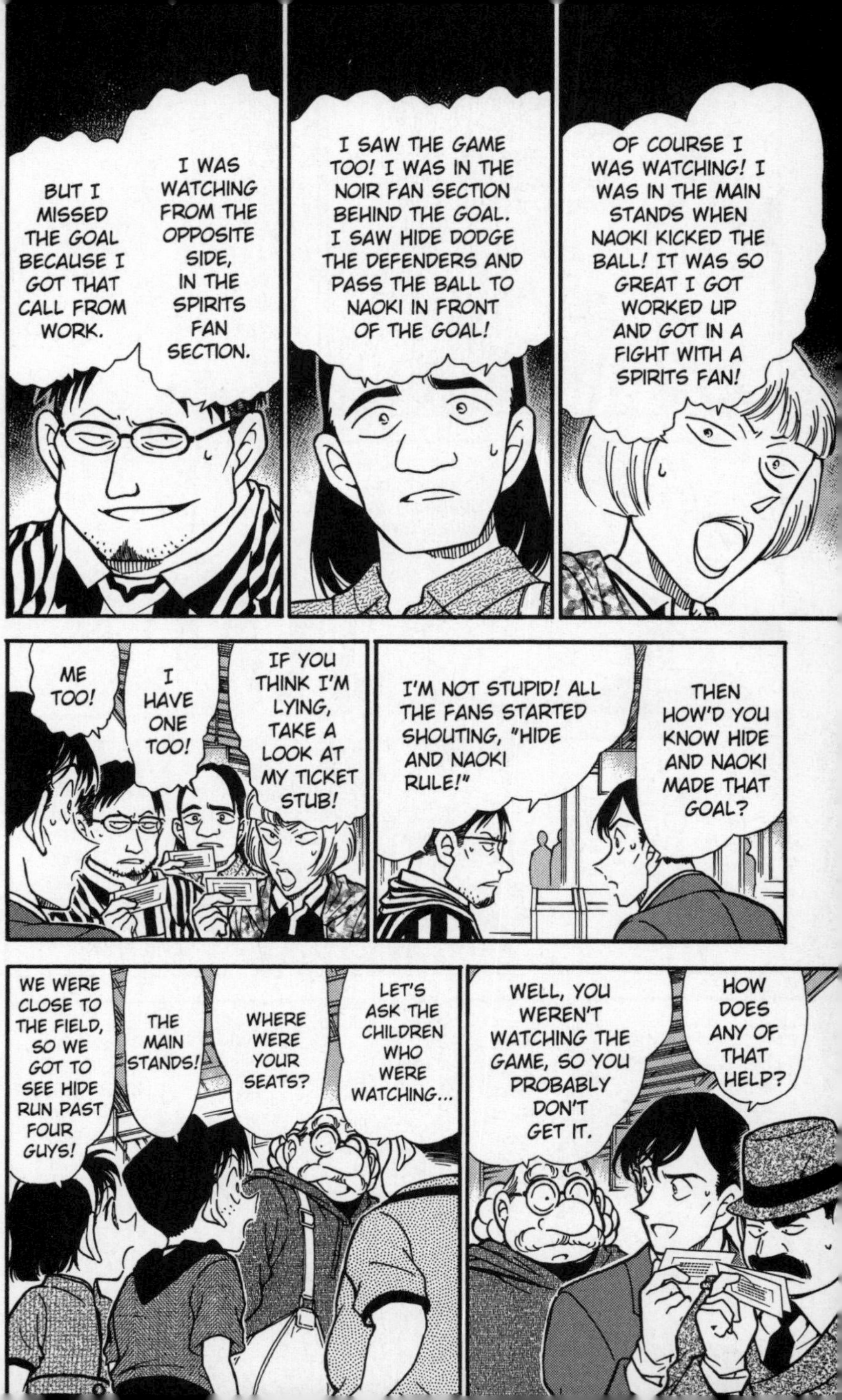
OF COURSE I WAS WATCHING! I WAS IN THE MAIN STANDS WHEN NAOKI KICKED THE BALL! IT WAS SO GREAT I GOT WORKED UP AND GOT IN A FIGHT WITH A SPIRITS FAN!
I SAW THE GAME TOO! I WAS IN THE NOIR FAN SECTION BEHIND THE GOAL. I SAW HIDE DODGE THE DEFENDERS AND PASS THE BALL TO NAOKI IN FRONT OF THE GOAL!
I WAS WATCHING FROM THE OPPOSITE SIDE, IN THE SPIRITS FAN SECTION.
BUT I MISSED THE GOAL BECAUSE I GOT THAT CALL FROM WORK.
THEN HOW'D YOU KNOW HIDE AND NAOKI MADE THAT GOAL?
I'M NOT STUPID! ALL THE FANS STARTED SHOUTING, "HIDE AND NAOKI RULE!"
IF YOU THINK I'M LYING, TAKE A LOOK AT MY TICKET STUB!
I HAVE ONE TOO!
ME TOO!
HOW DOES ANY OF THAT HELP?
WELL, YOU WEREN'T WATCHING THE GAME, SO YOU PROBABLY DON'T GET IT.
LET'S ASK THE CHILDREN WHO WERE WATCHING...
WHERE WERE YOUR SEATS?
THE MAIN STANDS!
WE WERE CLOSE TO THE FIELD, SO WE GOT TO SEE HIDE RUN PAST FOUR GUYS!

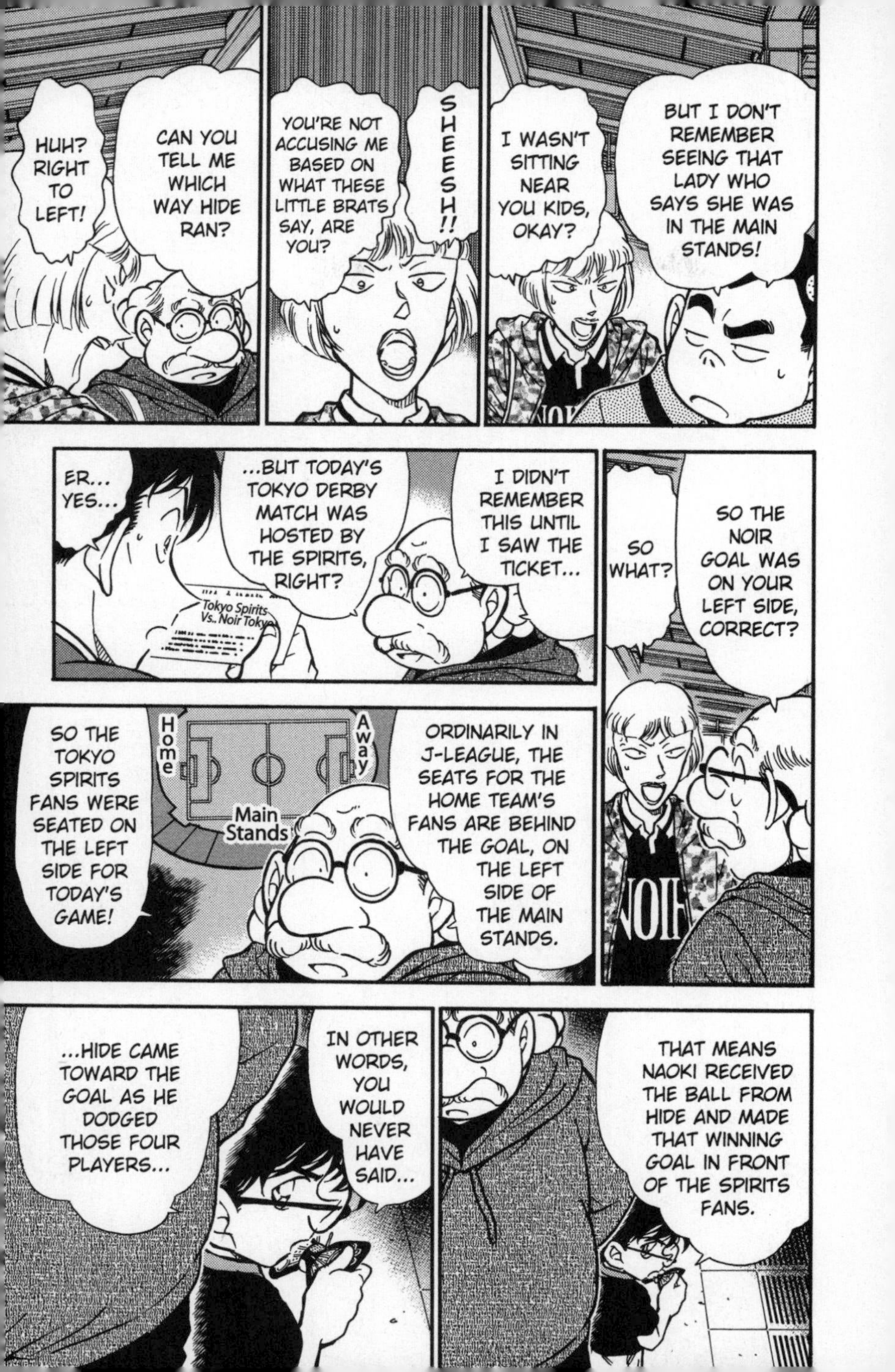
BUT I DON'T REMEMBER SEEING THAT LADY WHO SAYS SHE WAS IN THE MAIN STANDS!
I WASN'T SITTING NEAR YOU KIDS, OKAY?
SHEESH!!
YOU'RE NOT ACCUSING ME BASED ON WHAT THESE LITTLE BRATS SAY, ARE YOU?
CAN YOU TELL ME WHICH WAY HIDE RAN?
HUH? RIGHT TO LEFT!
SO THE NOIR GOAL WAS ON YOUR LEFT SIDE, CORRECT?
SO WHAT?
I DIDN'T REMEMBER THIS UNTIL I SAW THE TICKET...
...BUT TODAY'S TOKYO DERBY MATCH WAS HOSTED BY THE SPIRITS, RIGHT?
Tokyo Spirits
ER... YES...
ORDINARILY IN J-LEAGUE, THE SEATS FOR THE HOME TEAM'S FANS ARE BEHIND THE GOAL, ON THE LEFT SIDE OF THE MAIN STANDS.
Away
Home
Main Stands
SO THE TOKYO SPIRITS FANS WERE SEATED ON THE LEFT SIDE FOR TODAY'S GAME!
THAT MEANS NAOKI RECEIVED THE BALL FROM HIDE AND MADE THAT WINNING GOAL IN FRONT OF THE SPIRITS FANS.
IN OTHER WORDS, YOU WOULD NEVER HAVE SAID...
...HIDE CAME TOWARD THE GOAL AS HE DODGED THOSE FOUR PLAYERS...

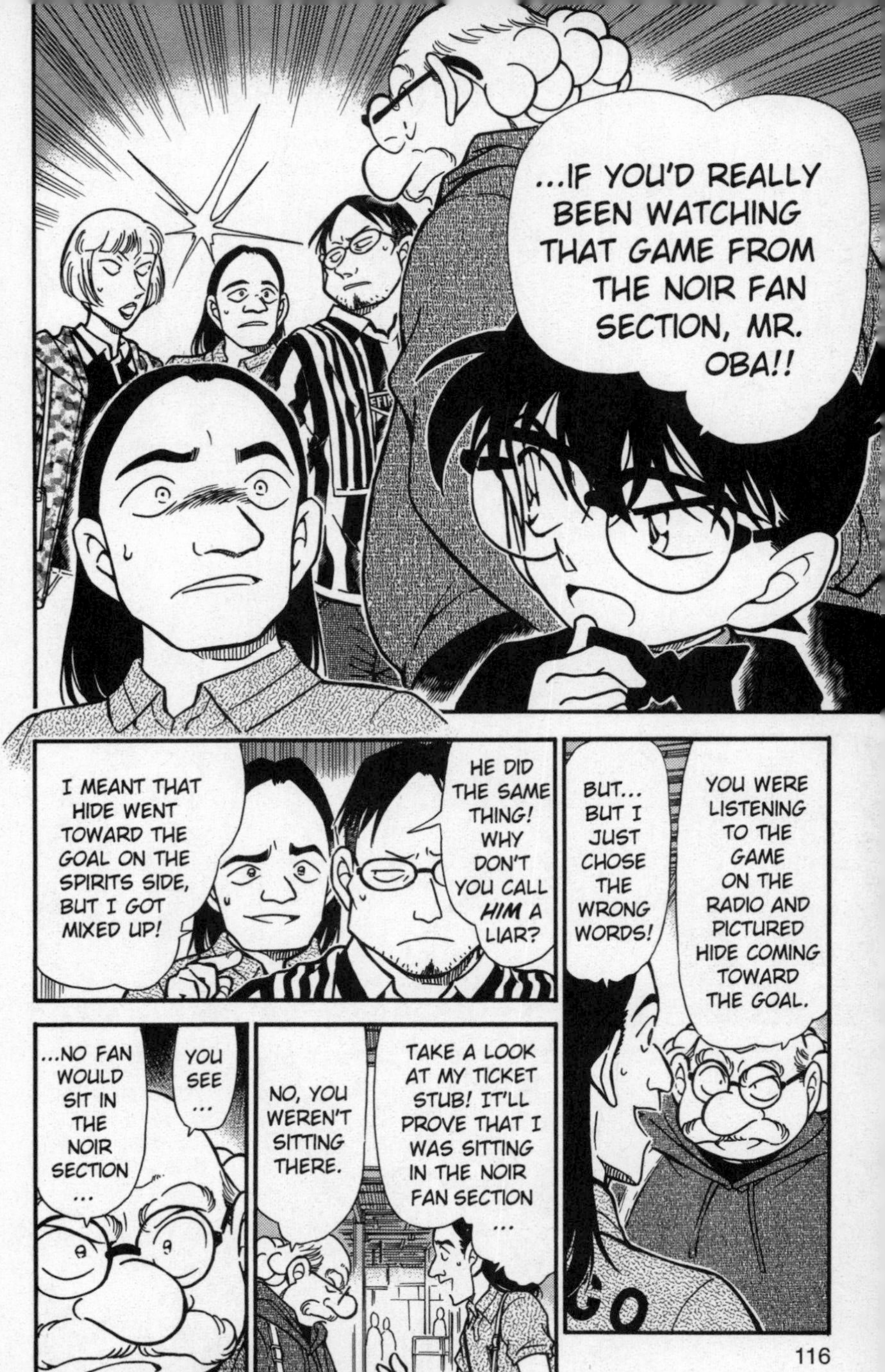
...IF YOU'D REALLY BEEN WATCHING THAT GAME FROM THE NOIR FAN SECTION, MR. OBA!!
YOU WERE LISTENING TO THE GAME ON THE RADIO AND PICTURED HIDE COMING TOWARD THE GOAL.
BUT... BUT I JUST CHOSE THE WRONG WORDS!
HE DID THE SAME THING! WHY DON'T YOU CALL *HIM* A LIAR?
I MEANT THAT HIDE WENT TOWARD THE GOAL ON THE SPIRITS SIDE, BUT I GOT MIXED UP!
TAKE A LOOK AT MY TICKET STUB! IT'LL PROVE THAT I WAS SITTING IN THE NOIR FAN SECTION...
NO, YOU WEREN'T SITTING THERE.
YOU SEE...
...NO FAN WOULD SIT IN THE NOIR SECTION...
GO

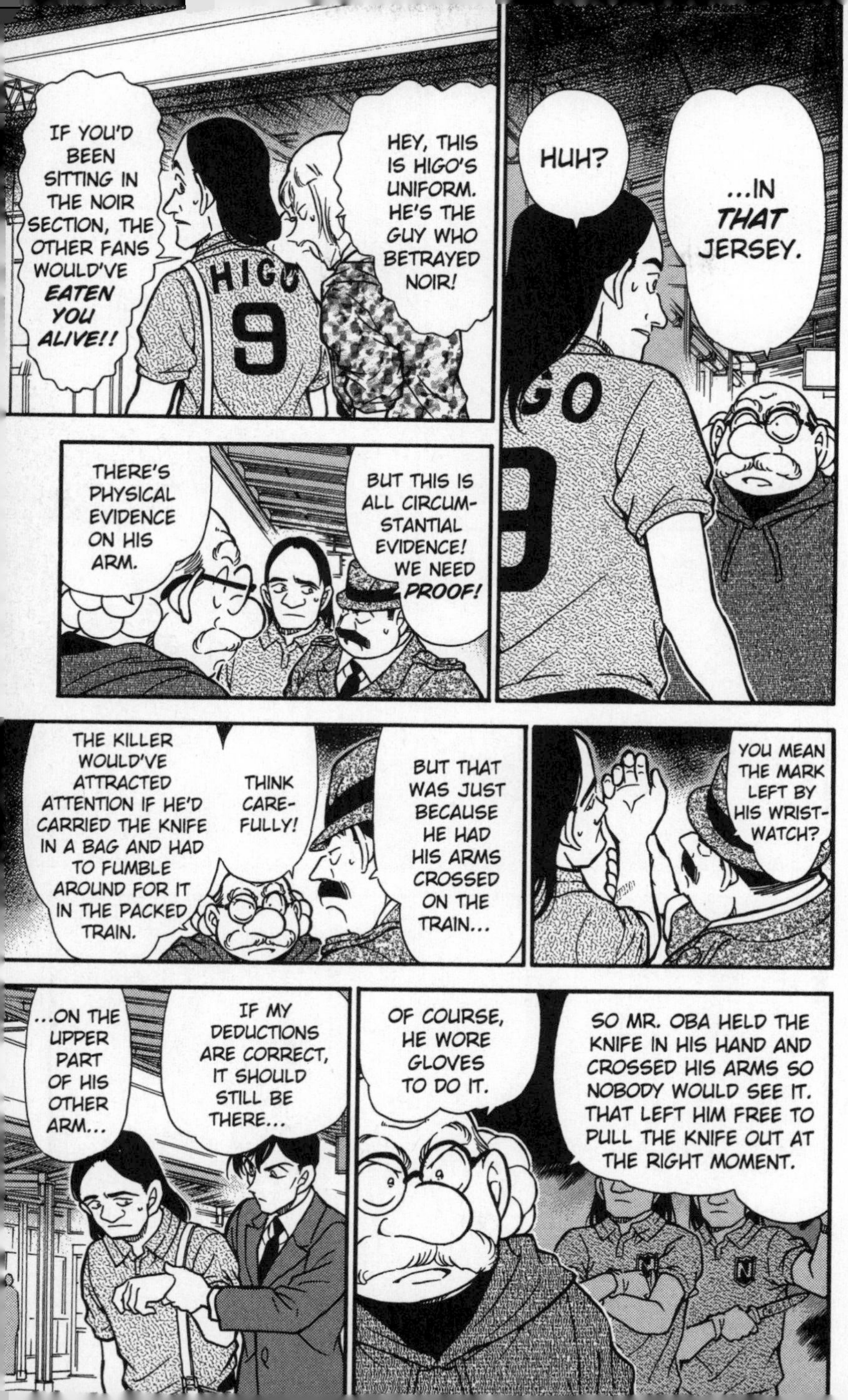
...IN *THAT* JERSEY.
HUH?
HEY, THIS IS HIGO'S UNIFORM. HE'S THE GUY WHO BETRAYED NOIR!
IF YOU'D BEEN SITTING IN THE NOIR SECTION, THE OTHER FANS WOULD'VE *EATEN YOU ALIVE!!*
BUT THIS IS ALL CIRCUM-STANTIAL EVIDENCE! WE NEED *PROOF!*
THERE'S PHYSICAL EVIDENCE ON HIS ARM.
YOU MEAN THE MARK LEFT BY HIS WRIST-WATCH?
BUT THAT WAS JUST BECAUSE HE HAD HIS ARMS CROSSED ON THE TRAIN...
THINK CARE-FULLY!
THE KILLER WOULD'VE ATTRACTED ATTENTION IF HE'D CARRIED THE KNIFE IN A BAG AND HAD TO FUMBLE AROUND FOR IT IN THE PACKED TRAIN.
SO MR. OBA HELD THE KNIFE IN HIS HAND AND CROSSED HIS ARMS SO NOBODY WOULD SEE IT. THAT LEFT HIM FREE TO PULL THE KNIFE OUT AT THE RIGHT MOMENT.
OF COURSE, HE WORE GLOVES TO DO IT.
IF MY DEDUCTIONS ARE CORRECT, IT SHOULD STILL BE THERE...
...ON THE UPPER PART OF HIS OTHER ARM...

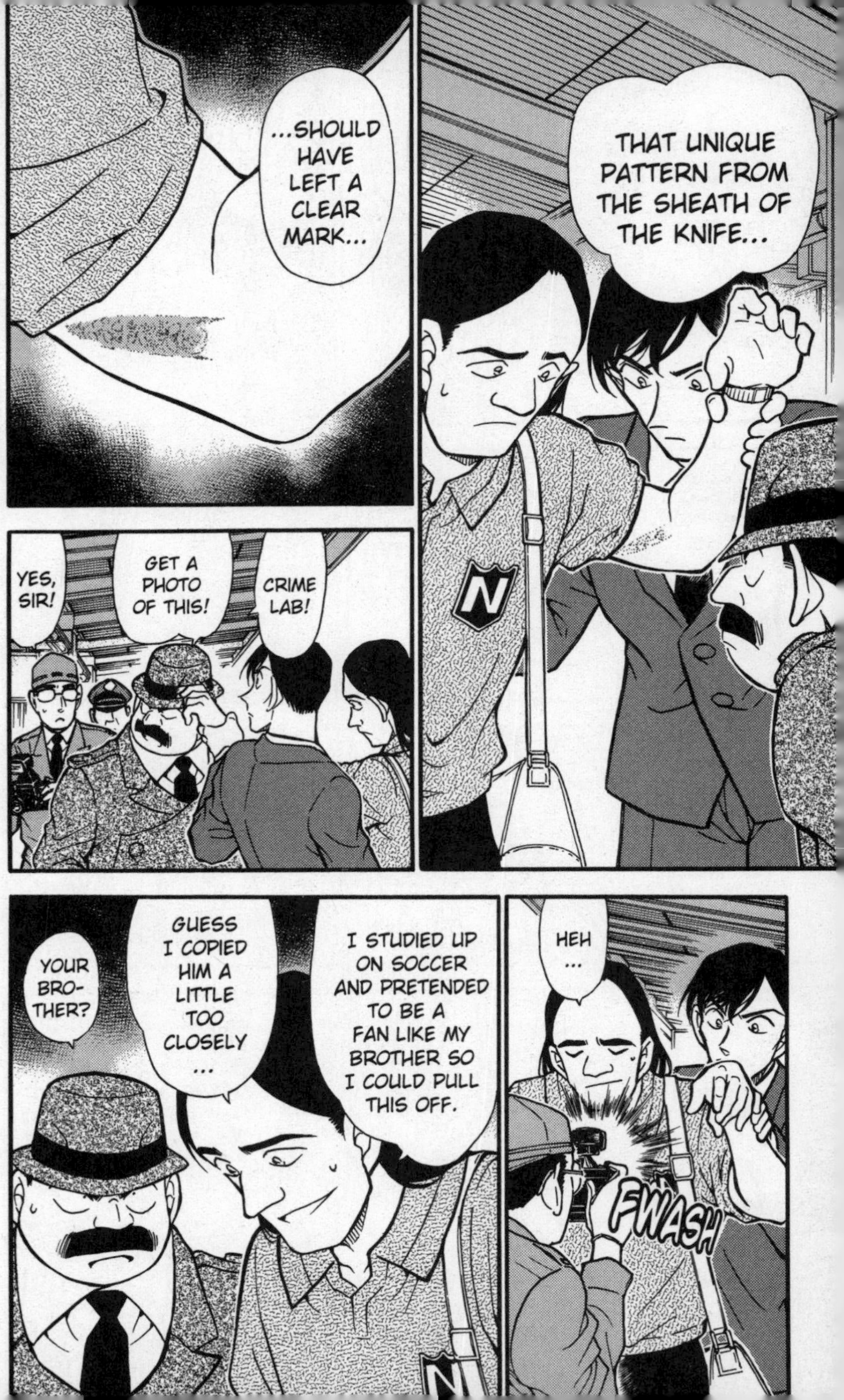
THAT UNIQUE PATTERN FROM THE SHEATH OF THE KNIFE...
...SHOULD HAVE LEFT A CLEAR MARK...
CRIME LAB!
GET A PHOTO OF THIS!
YES, SIR!
HEH ...
FWASH
I STUDIED UP ON SOCCER AND PRETENDED TO BE A FAN LIKE MY BROTHER SO I COULD PULL THIS OFF.
GUESS I COPIED HIM A LITTLE TOO CLOSELY ...
YOUR BRO-THER?

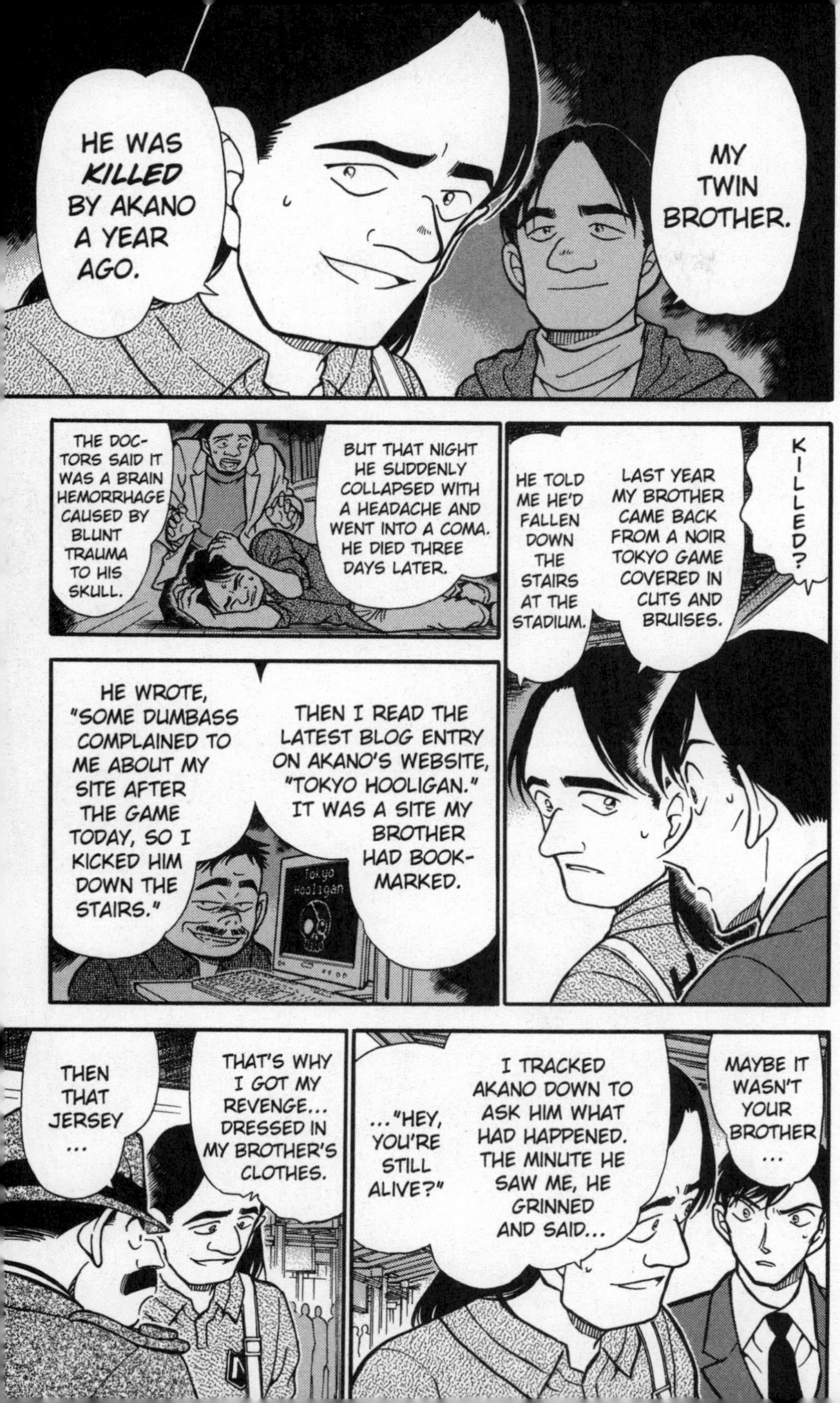
MY TWIN BROTHER.
HE WAS *KILLED* BY AKANO A YEAR AGO.
KILLED?
LAST YEAR MY BROTHER CAME BACK FROM A NOIR TOKYO GAME COVERED IN CUTS AND BRUISES.
HE TOLD ME HE'D FALLEN DOWN THE STAIRS AT THE STADIUM.
BUT THAT NIGHT HE SUDDENLY COLLAPSED WITH A HEADACHE AND WENT INTO A COMA. HE DIED THREE DAYS LATER.
THE DOCTORS SAID IT WAS A BRAIN HEMORRHAGE CAUSED BY BLUNT TRAUMA TO HIS SKULL.
THEN I READ THE LATEST BLOG ENTRY ON AKANO'S WEBSITE, "TOKYO HOOLIGAN." IT WAS A SITE MY BROTHER HAD BOOKMARKED.
HE WROTE, "SOME DUMBASS COMPLAINED TO ME ABOUT MY SITE AFTER THE GAME TODAY, SO I KICKED HIM DOWN THE STAIRS."
Tokyo Hooligan
MAYBE IT WASN'T YOUR BROTHER...
I TRACKED AKANO DOWN TO ASK HIM WHAT HAD HAPPENED. THE MINUTE HE SAW ME, HE GRINNED AND SAID...
..."HEY, YOU'RE STILL ALIVE?"
THAT'S WHY I GOT MY REVENGE... DRESSED IN MY BROTHER'S CLOTHES.
THEN THAT JERSEY ...

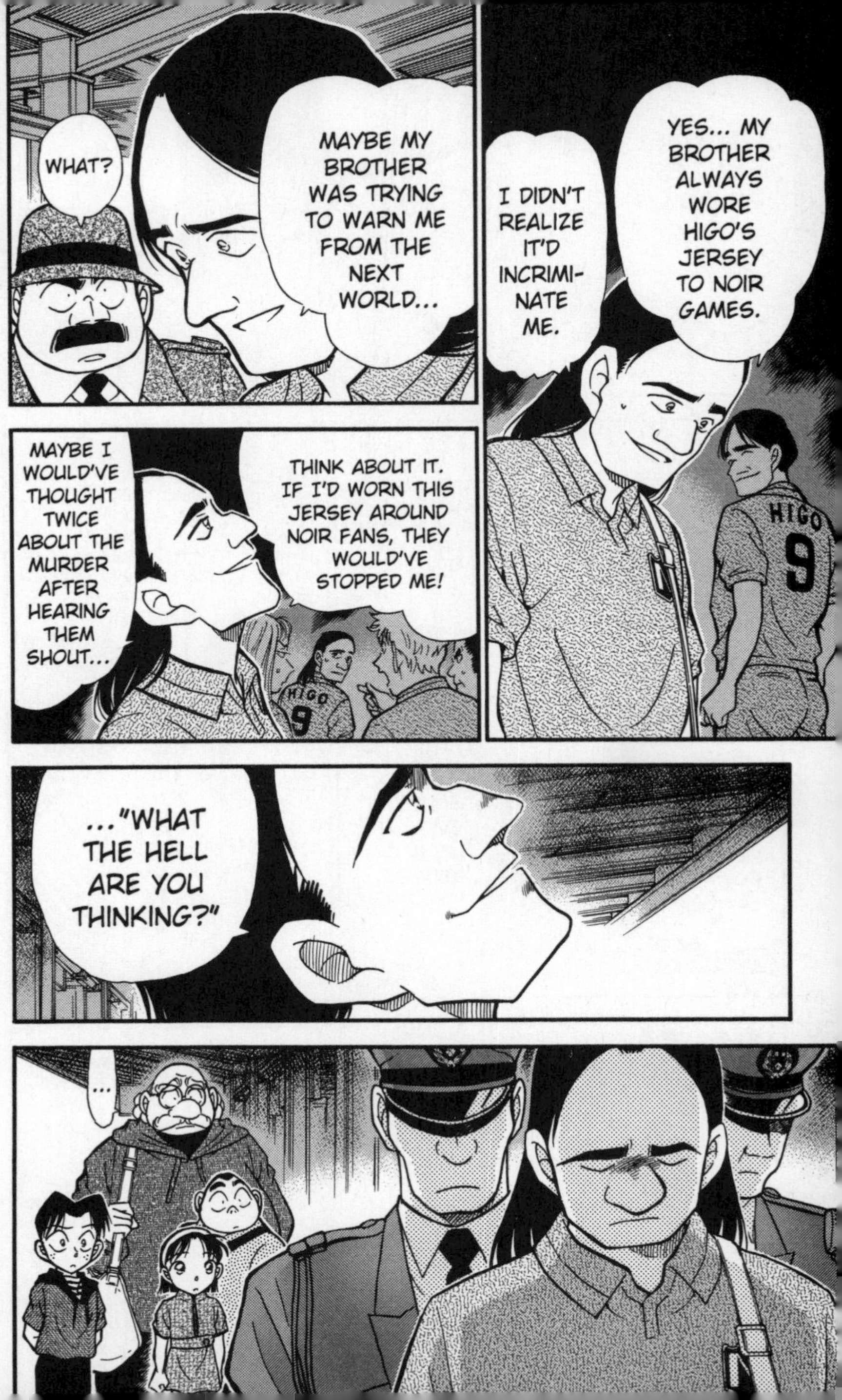
YES... MY BROTHER ALWAYS WORE HIGO'S JERSEY TO NOIR GAMES.
I DIDN'T REALIZE IT'D INCRIMINATE ME.
HIGO 9
MAYBE MY BROTHER WAS TRYING TO WARN ME FROM THE NEXT WORLD...
WHAT?
THINK ABOUT IT. IF I'D WORN THIS JERSEY AROUND NOIR FANS, THEY WOULD'VE STOPPED ME!
MAYBE I WOULD'VE THOUGHT TWICE ABOUT THE MURDER AFTER HEARING THEM SHOUT...
HIGO 9
..."WHAT THE HELL ARE YOU THINKING?"
...

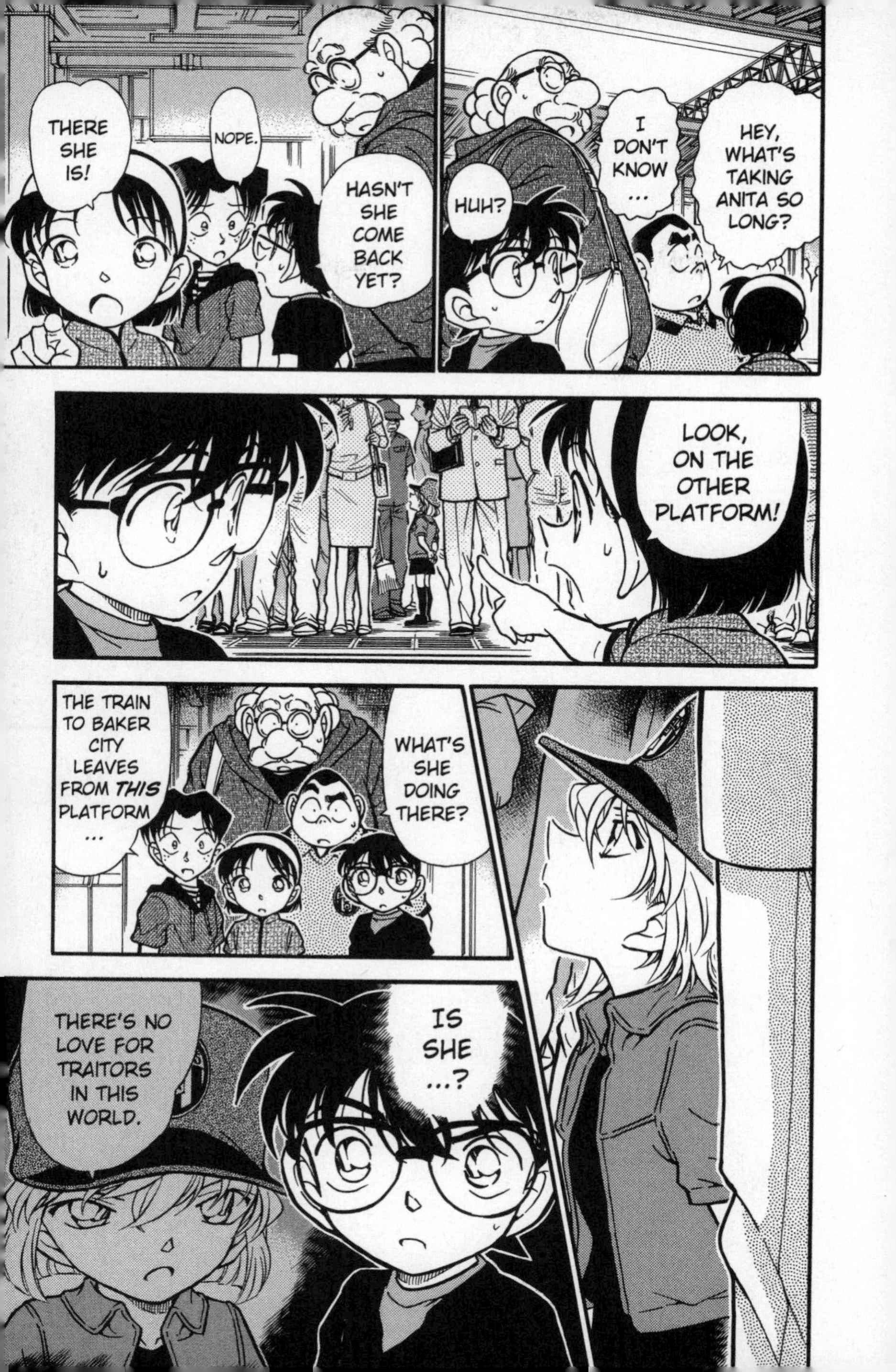
HEY, WHAT'S TAKING ANITA SO LONG?
I DON'T KNOW ...
HUH?
HASN'T SHE COME BACK YET?
NOPE.
THERE SHE IS!
LOOK, ON THE OTHER PLATFORM!
WHAT'S SHE DOING THERE?
THE TRAIN TO BAKER CITY LEAVES FROM *THIS* PLATFORM ...
IS SHE ...?
THERE'S NO LOVE FOR TRAITORS IN THIS WORLD.

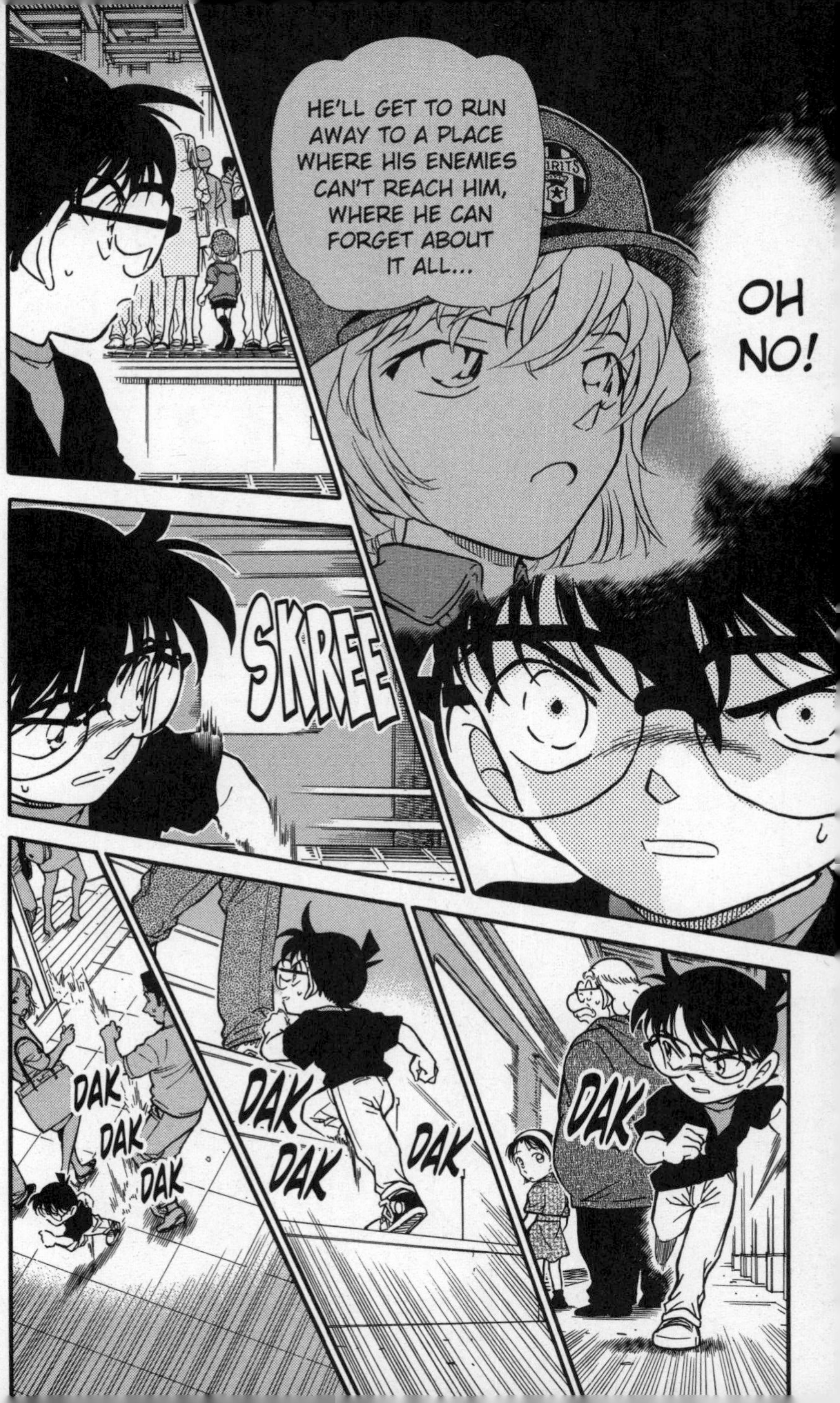
HE'LL GET TO RUN AWAY TO A PLACE WHERE HIS ENEMIES CAN'T REACH HIM, WHERE HE CAN FORGET ABOUT IT ALL...
OH NO!
SKREE
DAK
DAK
DAK
DAK
DAK
DAK
DAK

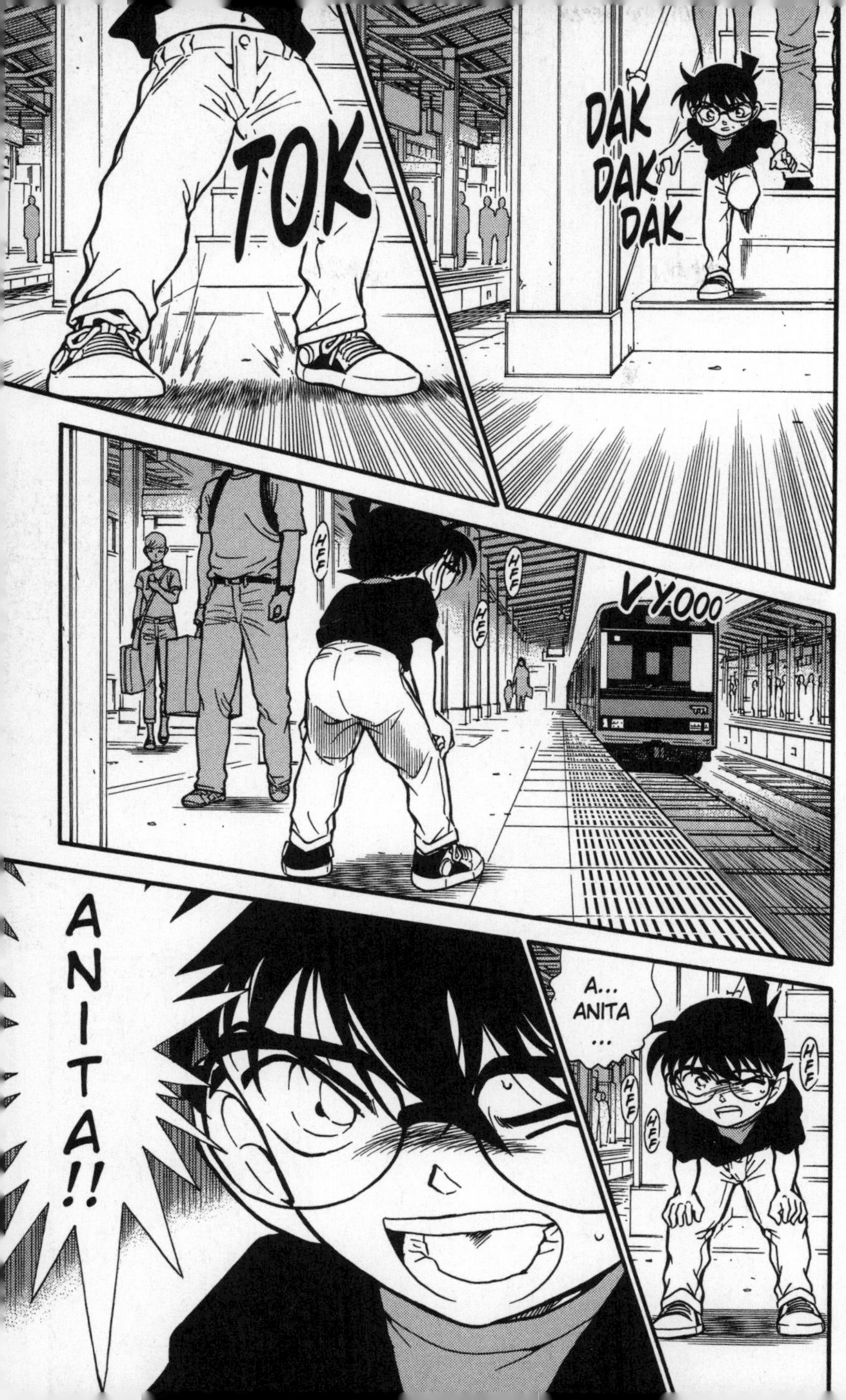
DAK DAK DAK
TOK
VYOOO
HFF
HFF
HFF
A... ANITA ...
HFF
HFF
HFF
ANITA!!

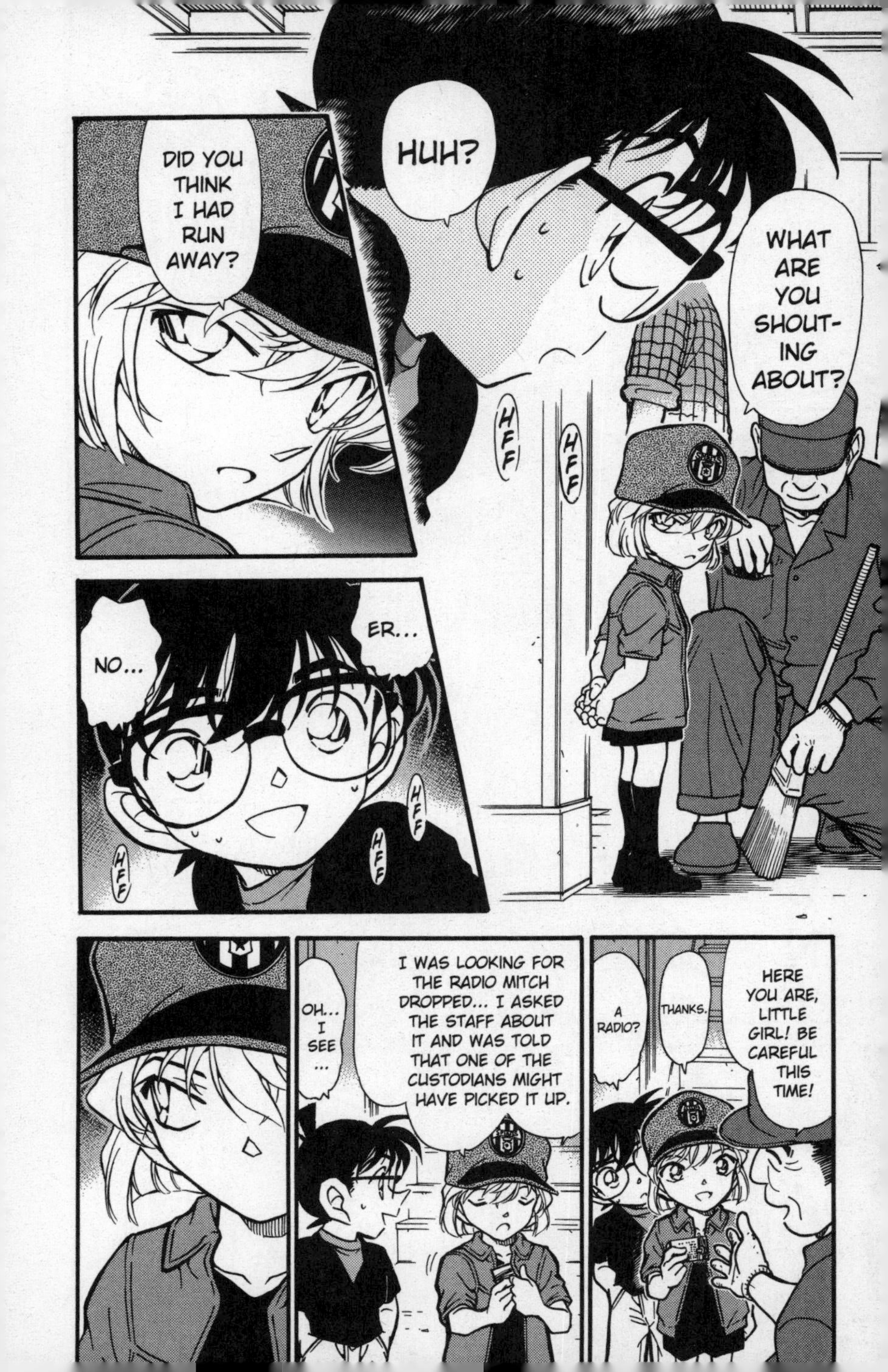
WHAT ARE YOU SHOUTING ABOUT?
HUH?
HFF
HFF
DID YOU THINK I HAD RUN AWAY?
ER...
NO...
HFF
HFF
HFF
HERE YOU ARE, LITTLE GIRL! BE CAREFUL THIS TIME!
THANKS.
A RADIO?
I WAS LOOKING FOR THE RADIO MITCH DROPPED... I ASKED THE STAFF ABOUT IT AND WAS TOLD THAT ONE OF THE CUSTODIANS MIGHT HAVE PICKED IT UP.
OH... I SEE...

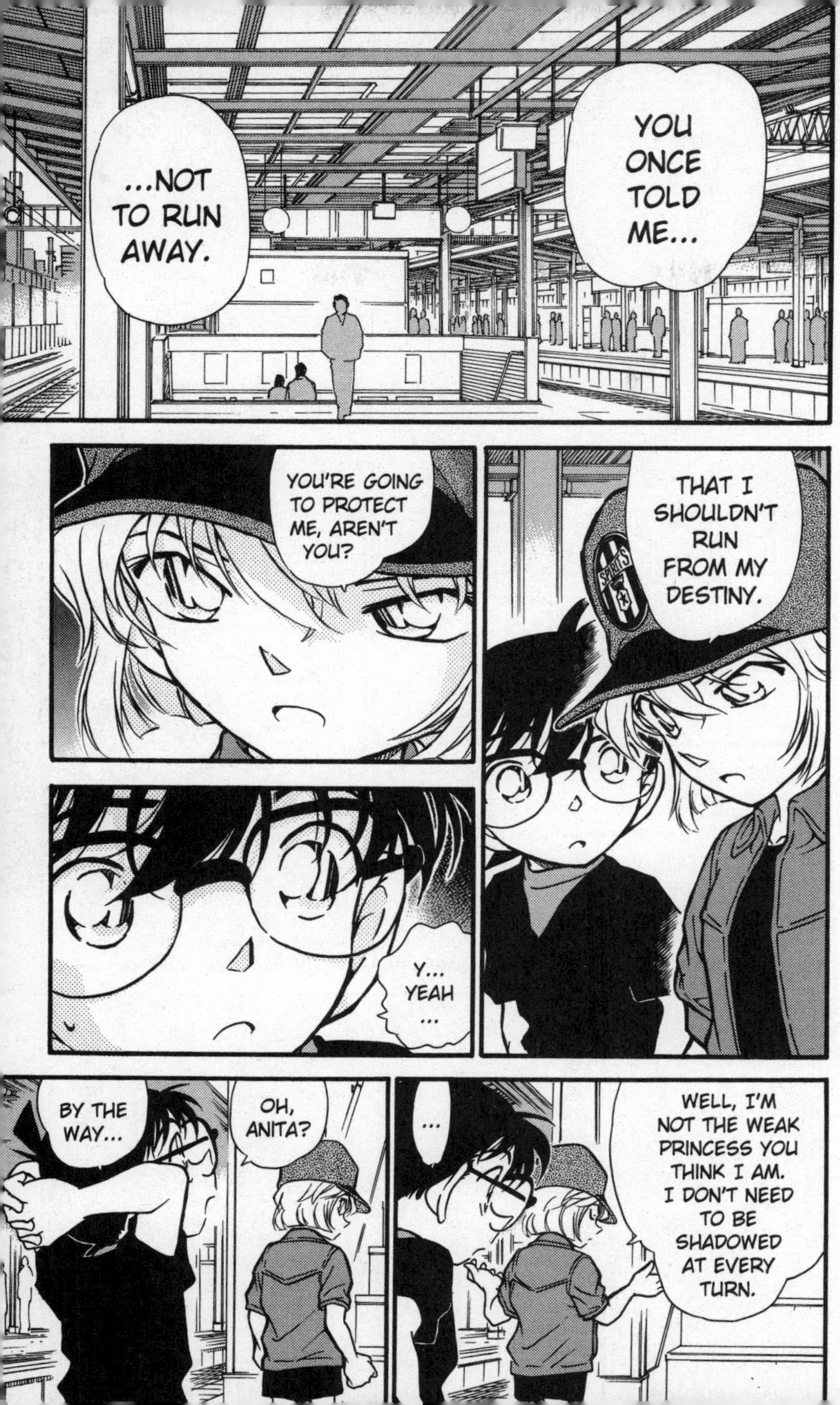
YOU ONCE TOLD ME...
...NOT TO RUN AWAY.
THAT I SHOULDN'T RUN FROM MY DESTINY.
YOU'RE GOING TO PROTECT ME, AREN'T YOU?
Y... YEAH ...
WELL, I'M NOT THE WEAK PRINCESS YOU THINK I AM. I DON'T NEED TO BE SHADOWED AT EVERY TURN.
...
OH, ANITA?
BY THE WAY...

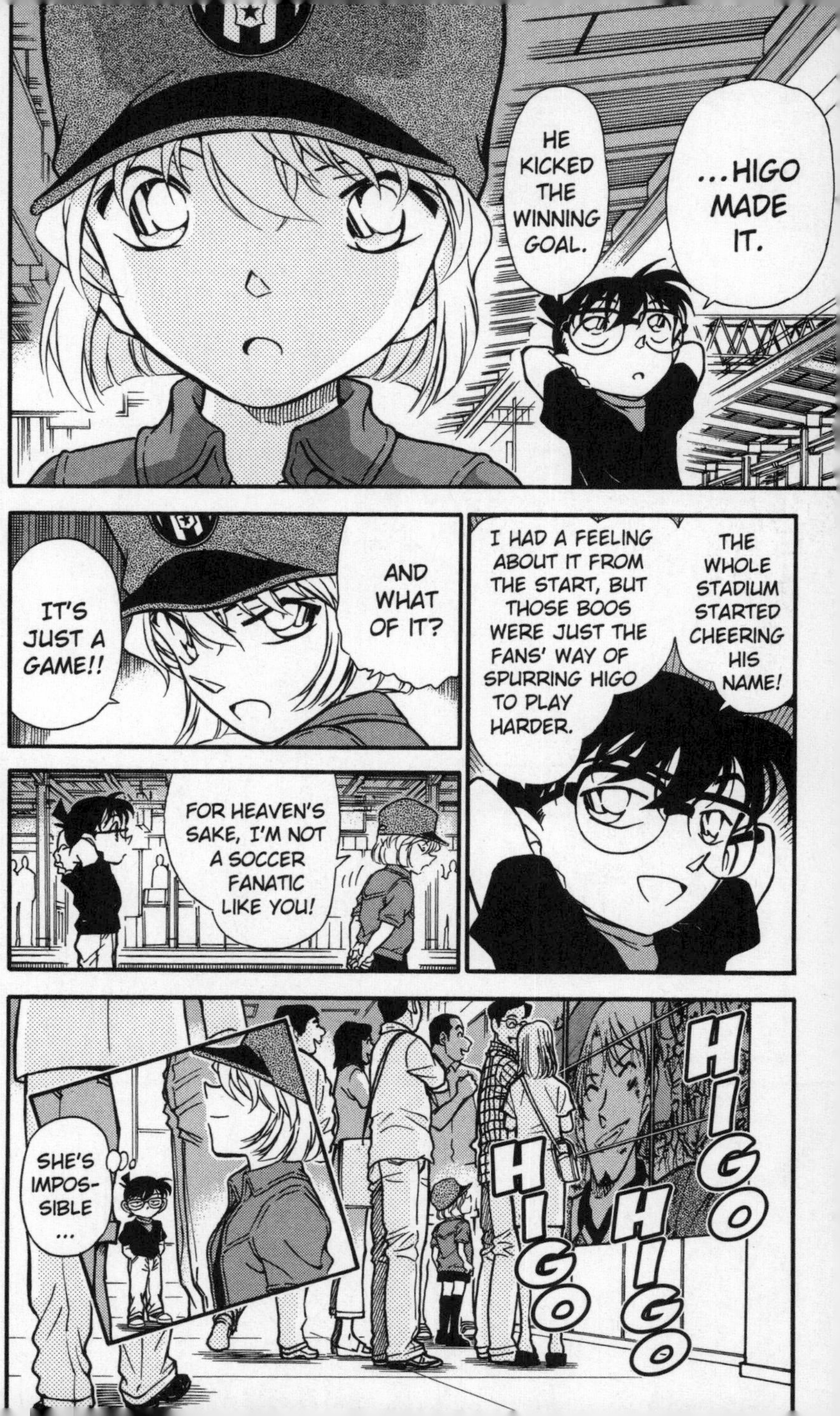
...HIGO MADE IT.
HE KICKED THE WINNING GOAL.
THE WHOLE STADIUM STARTED CHEERING HIS NAME!
I HAD A FEELING ABOUT IT FROM THE START, BUT THOSE BOOS WERE JUST THE FANS' WAY OF SPURRING HIGO TO PLAY HARDER.
AND WHAT OF IT?
IT'S JUST A GAME!!
FOR HEAVEN'S SAKE, I'M NOT A SOCCER FANATIC LIKE YOU!
HIGO
HIGO
HIGO
HIGO
SHE'S IMPOS-SIBLE ...

FILE 8: DÉJÀ VU IN THE RAIN

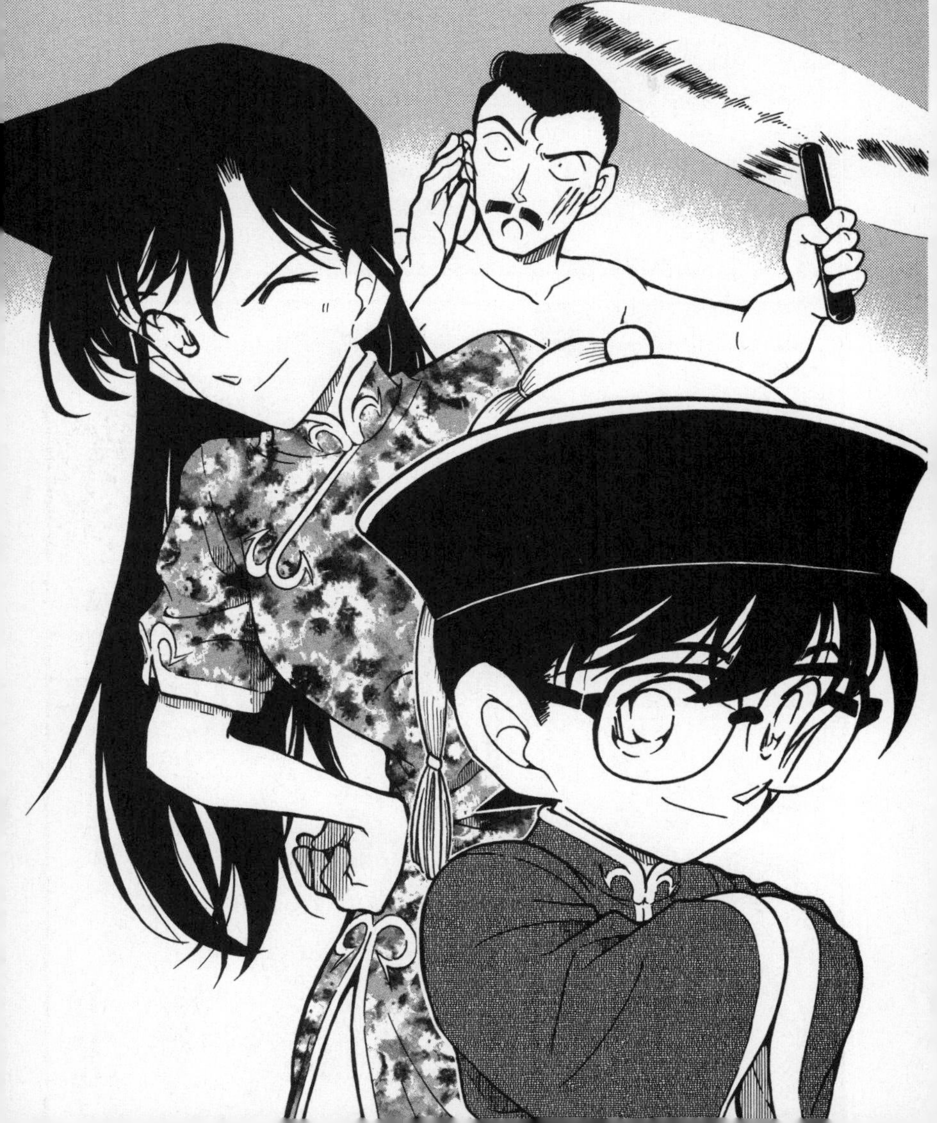

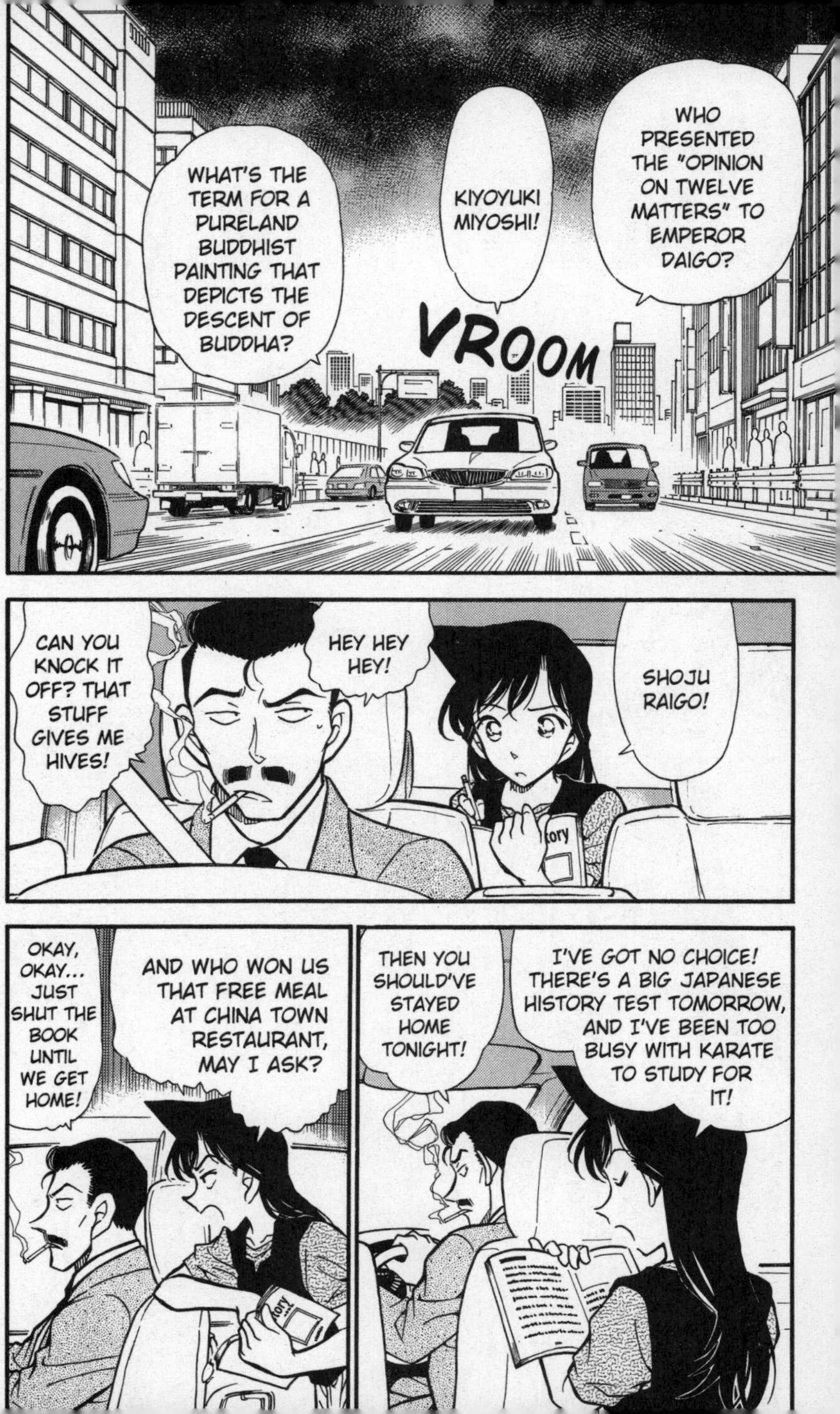
WHO PRESENTED THE "OPINION ON TWELVE MATTERS" TO EMPEROR DAIGO?
KIYOYUKI MIYOSHI!
WHAT'S THE TERM FOR A PURELAND BUDDHIST PAINTING THAT DEPICTS THE DESCENT OF BUDDHA?
VROOM
SHOJU RAIGO!
HEY HEY HEY!
CAN YOU KNOCK IT OFF? THAT STUFF GIVES ME HIVES!
I'VE GOT NO CHOICE! THERE'S A BIG JAPANESE HISTORY TEST TOMORROW, AND I'VE BEEN TOO BUSY WITH KARATE TO STUDY FOR IT!
THEN YOU SHOULD'VE STAYED HOME TONIGHT!
AND WHO WON US THAT FREE MEAL AT CHINA TOWN RESTAURANT, MAY I ASK?
OKAY, OKAY... JUST SHUT THE BOOK UNTIL WE GET HOME!

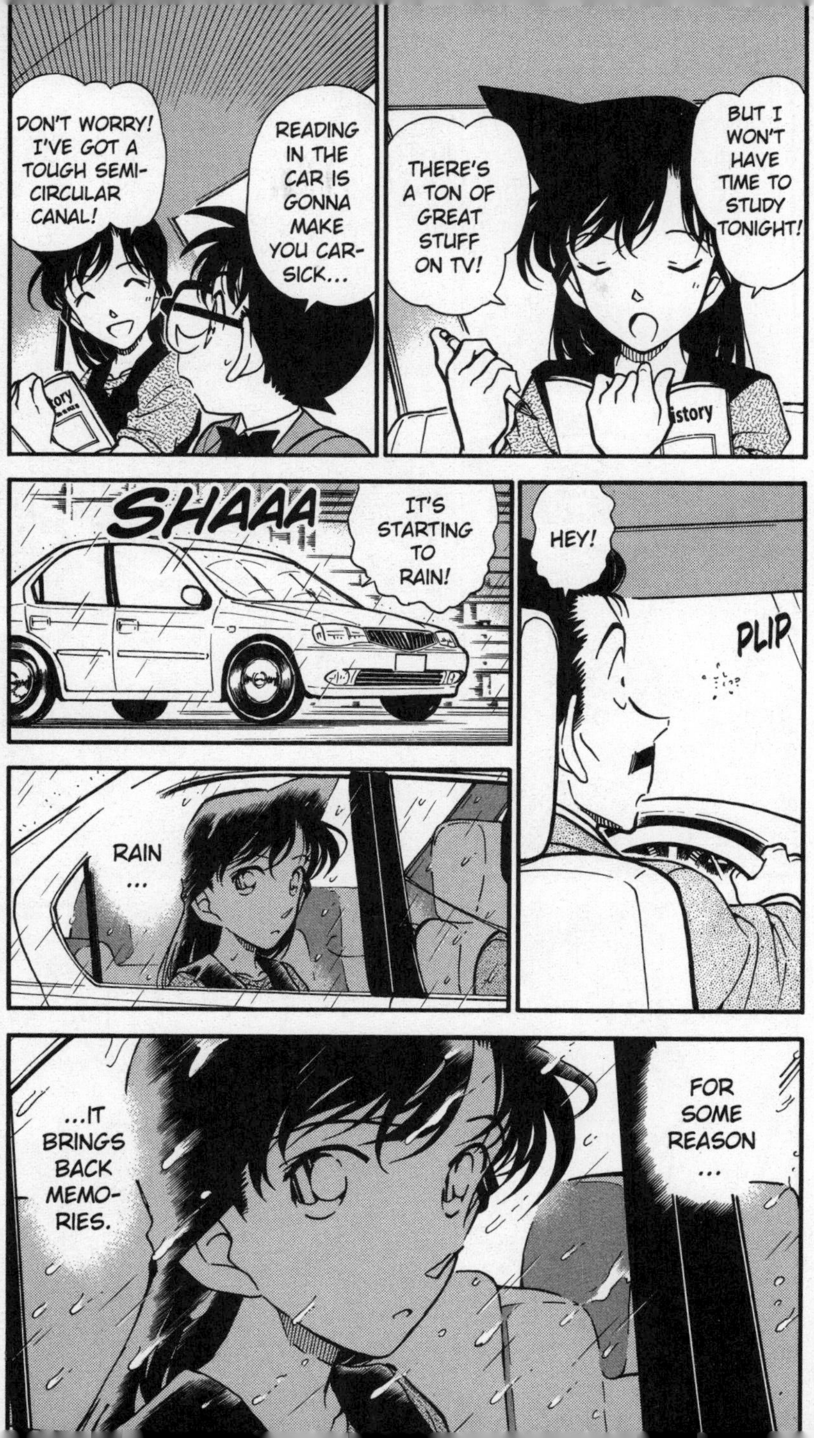
BUT I WON'T HAVE TIME TO STUDY TONIGHT!
THERE'S A TON OF GREAT STUFF ON TV!
READING IN THE CAR IS GONNA MAKE YOU CAR-SICK...
DON'T WORRY! I'VE GOT A TOUGH SEMI-CIRCULAR CANAL!
HEY!
PLIP
SHAAA
IT'S STARTING TO RAIN!
RAIN ...
FOR SOME REASON ...
...IT BRINGS BACK MEMO-RIES.

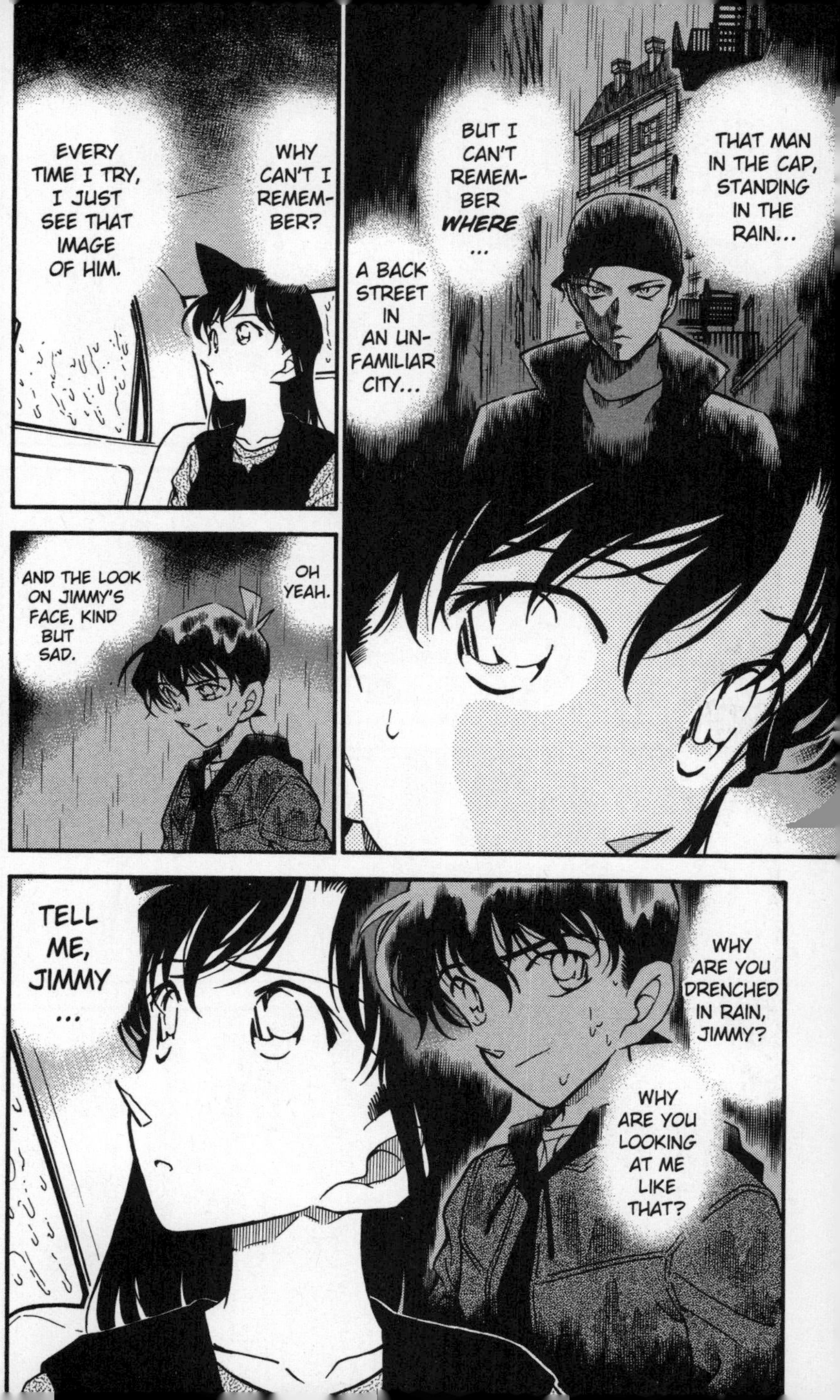
THAT MAN IN THE CAP, STANDING IN THE RAIN...
BUT I CAN'T REMEMBER *WHERE*...
A BACK STREET IN AN UNFAMILIAR CITY...
WHY CAN'T I REMEMBER?
EVERY TIME I TRY, I JUST SEE THAT IMAGE OF HIM.
OH YEAH.
AND THE LOOK ON JIMMY'S FACE, KIND BUT SAD.
WHY ARE YOU DRENCHED IN RAIN, JIMMY?
WHY ARE YOU LOOKING AT ME LIKE THAT?
TELL ME, JIMMY...

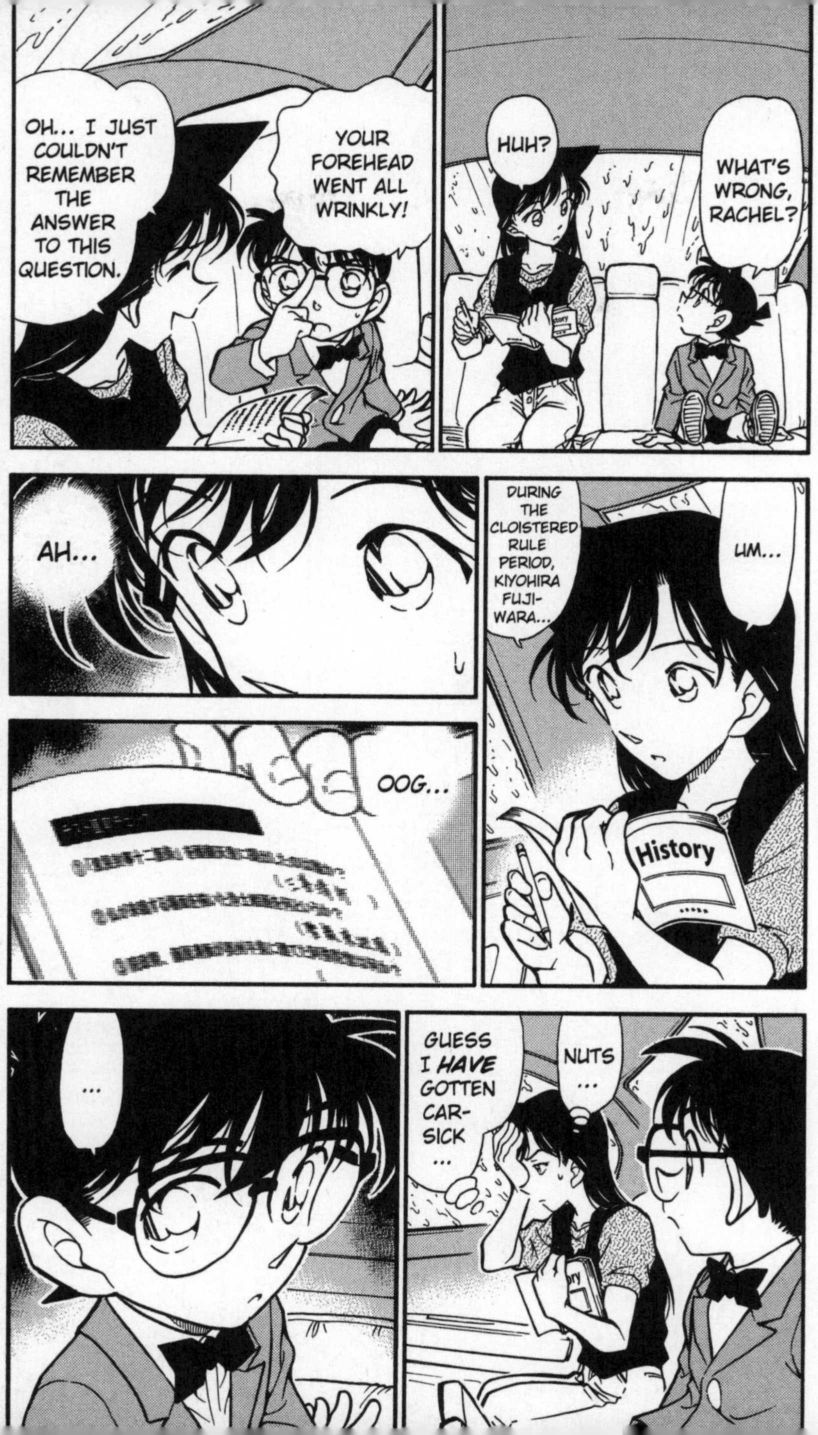
WHAT'S WRONG, RACHEL?
HUH?
YOUR FOREHEAD WENT ALL WRINKLY!
OH... I JUST COULDN'T REMEMBER THE ANSWER TO THIS QUESTION.
UM...
DURING THE CLOISTERED RULE PERIOD, KIYOHIRA FUJI-WARA...
History
AH...
OOG...
NUTS ...
GUESS I *HAVE* GOTTEN CAR-SICK ...
...

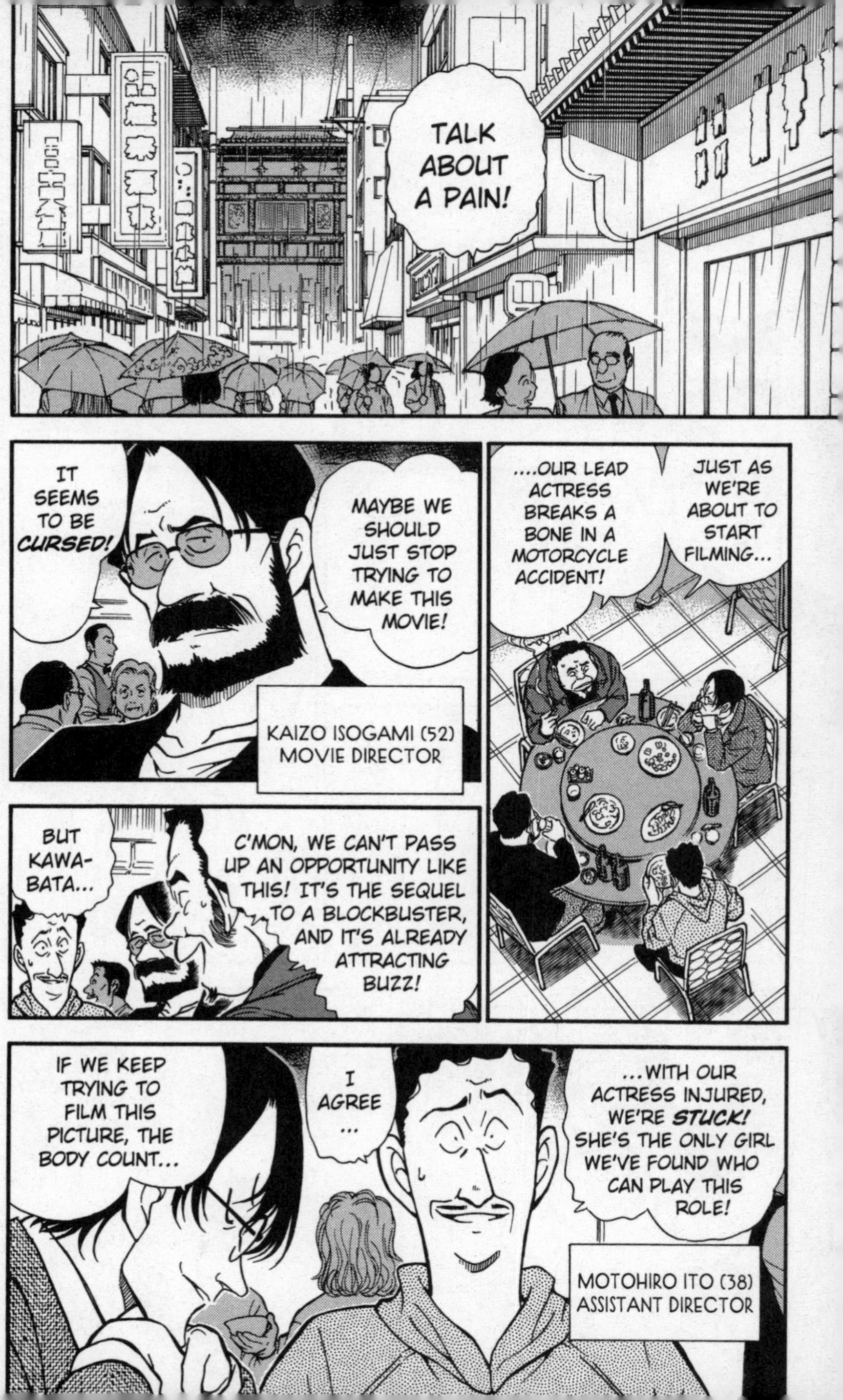
TALK ABOUT A PAIN!
JUST AS WE'RE ABOUT TO START FILMING...
....OUR LEAD ACTRESS BREAKS A BONE IN A MOTORCYCLE ACCIDENT!
MAYBE WE SHOULD JUST STOP TRYING TO MAKE THIS MOVIE!
IT SEEMS TO BE *CURSED!*
KAIZO ISOGAMI (52) MOVIE DIRECTOR
C'MON, WE CAN'T PASS UP AN OPPORTUNITY LIKE THIS! IT'S THE SEQUEL TO A BLOCKBUSTER, AND IT'S ALREADY ATTRACTING BUZZ!
BUT KAWA-BATA...
...WITH OUR ACTRESS INJURED, WE'RE *STUCK!* SHE'S THE ONLY GIRL WE'VE FOUND WHO CAN PLAY THIS ROLE!
MOTOHIRO ITO (38) ASSISTANT DIRECTOR
I AGREE ...
IF WE KEEP TRYING TO FILM THIS PICTURE, THE BODY COUNT...

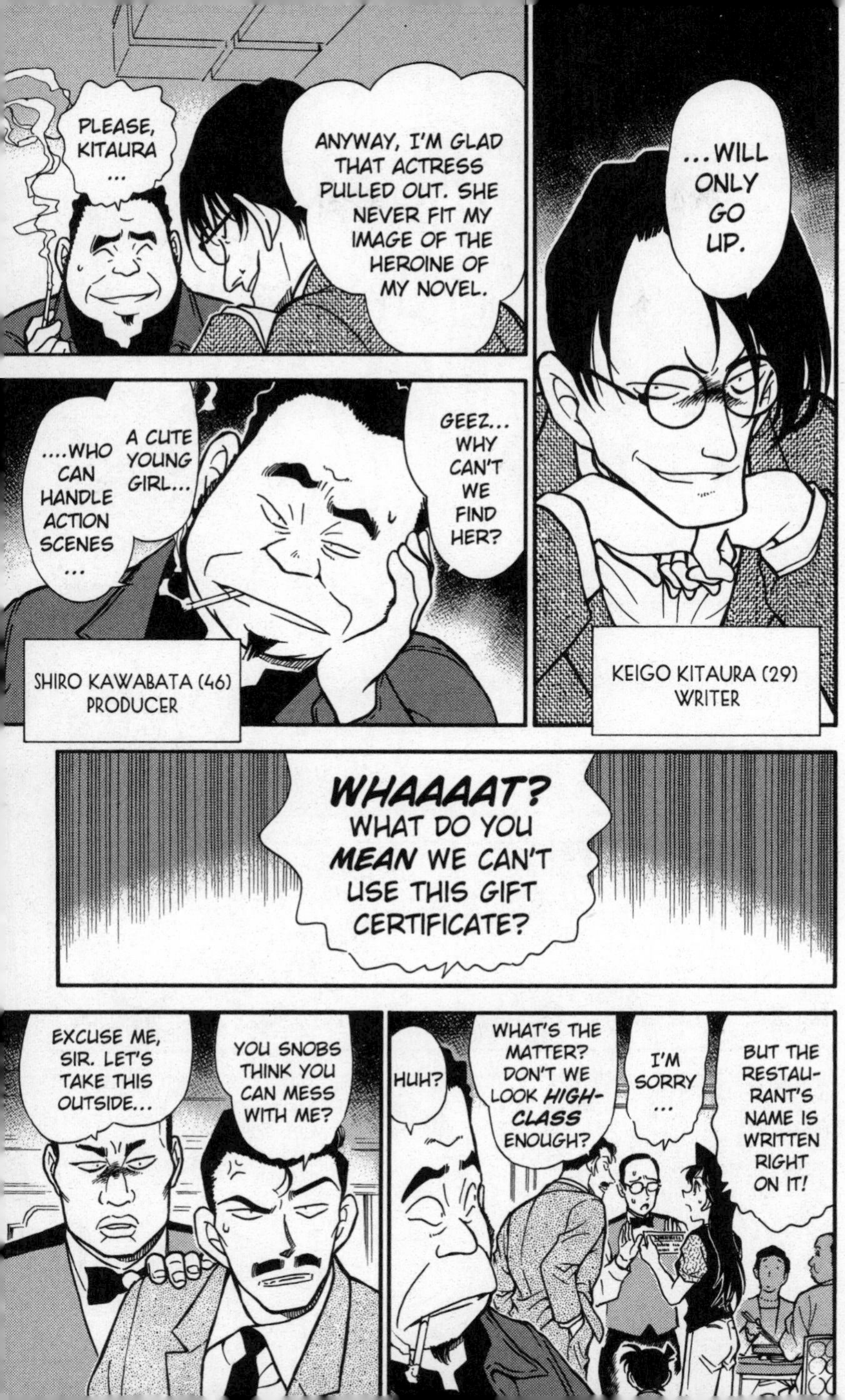
...WILL ONLY GO UP.
KEIGO KITAURA (29) WRITER
ANYWAY, I'M GLAD THAT ACTRESS PULLED OUT. SHE NEVER FIT MY IMAGE OF THE HEROINE OF MY NOVEL.
PLEASE, KITAURA ...
GEEZ... WHY CAN'T WE FIND HER?
A CUTE YOUNG GIRL...
....WHO CAN HANDLE ACTION SCENES ...
SHIRO KAWABATA (46) PRODUCER
WHAAAAT? WHAT DO YOU *MEAN* WE CAN'T USE THIS GIFT CERTIFICATE?
BUT THE RESTAU-RANT'S NAME IS WRITTEN RIGHT ON IT!
I'M SORRY ...
WHAT'S THE MATTER? DON'T WE LOOK *HIGH-CLASS* ENOUGH?
HUH?
YOU SNOBS THINK YOU CAN MESS WITH ME?
EXCUSE ME, SIR. LET'S TAKE THIS OUTSIDE...

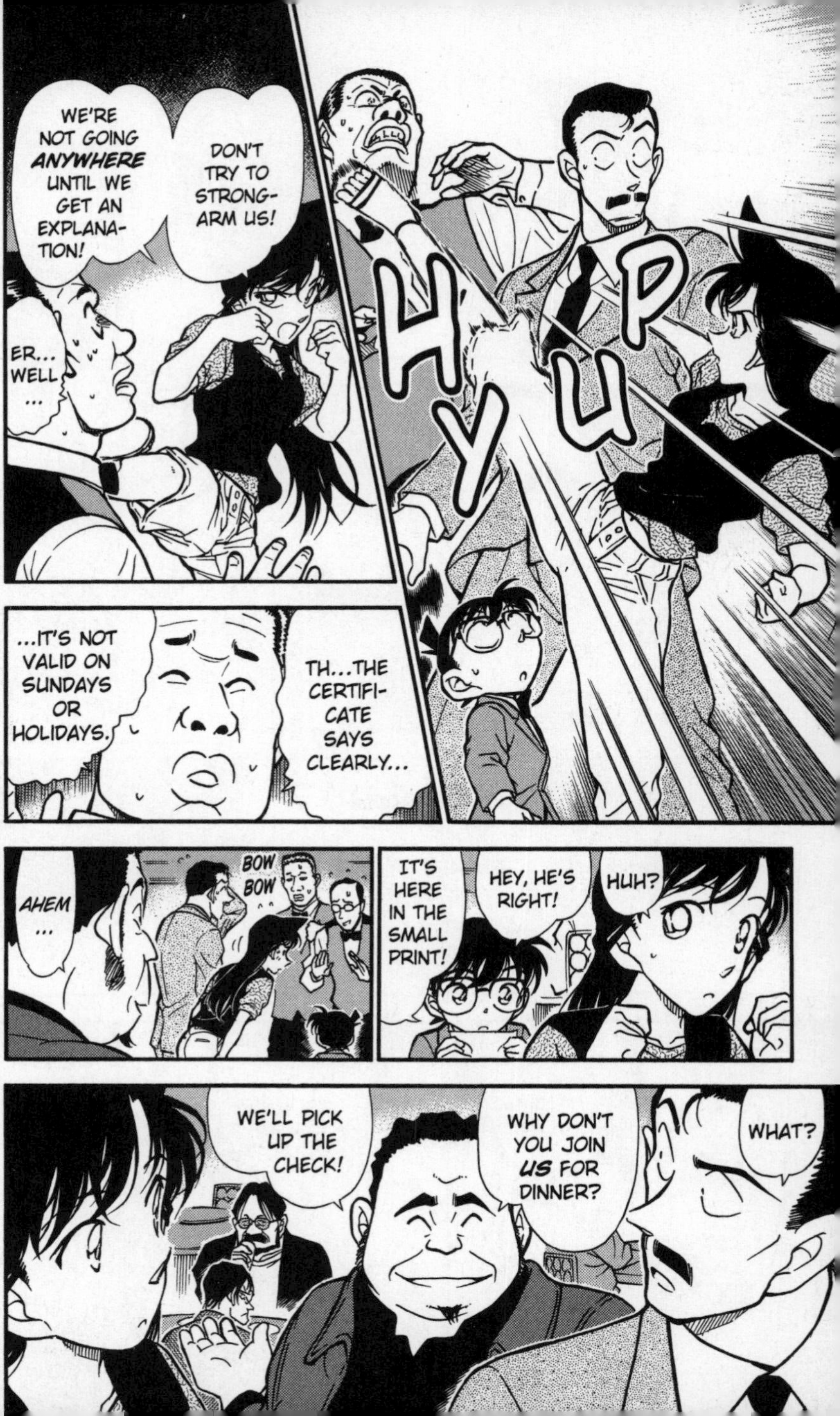
HYUP
DON'T TRY TO STRONG-ARM US!
WE'RE NOT GOING ANYWHERE UNTIL WE GET AN EXPLANATION!
ER... WELL...
TH...THE CERTIFICATE SAYS CLEARLY...
...IT'S NOT VALID ON SUNDAYS OR HOLIDAYS.
HUH?
HEY, HE'S RIGHT!
IT'S HERE IN THE SMALL PRINT!
BOW BOW
AHEM...
WHAT?
WHY DON'T YOU JOIN US FOR DINNER?
WE'LL PICK UP THE CHECK!

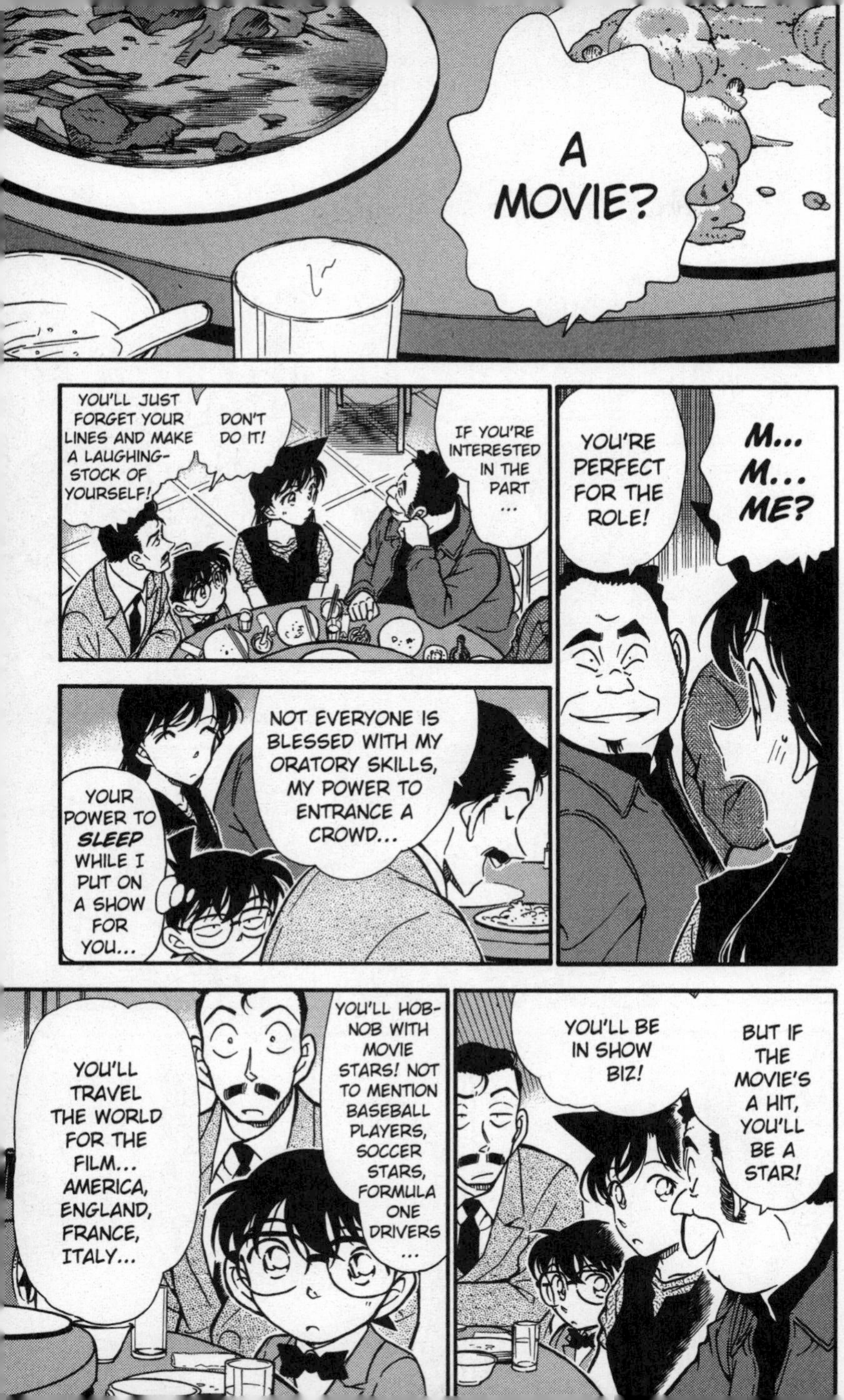
A MOVIE?
M... M... ME?
YOU'RE PERFECT FOR THE ROLE!
IF YOU'RE INTERESTED IN THE PART ...
DON'T DO IT!
YOU'LL JUST FORGET YOUR LINES AND MAKE A LAUGHING-STOCK OF YOURSELF!
NOT EVERYONE IS BLESSED WITH MY ORATORY SKILLS, MY POWER TO ENTRANCE A CROWD...
YOUR POWER TO *SLEEP* WHILE I PUT ON A SHOW FOR YOU...
BUT IF THE MOVIE'S A HIT, YOU'LL BE A STAR!
YOU'LL BE IN SHOW BIZ!
YOU'LL HOB-NOB WITH MOVIE STARS! NOT TO MENTION BASEBALL PLAYERS, SOCCER STARS, FORMULA ONE DRIVERS ...
YOU'LL TRAVEL THE WORLD FOR THE FILM... AMERICA, ENGLAND, FRANCE, ITALY...

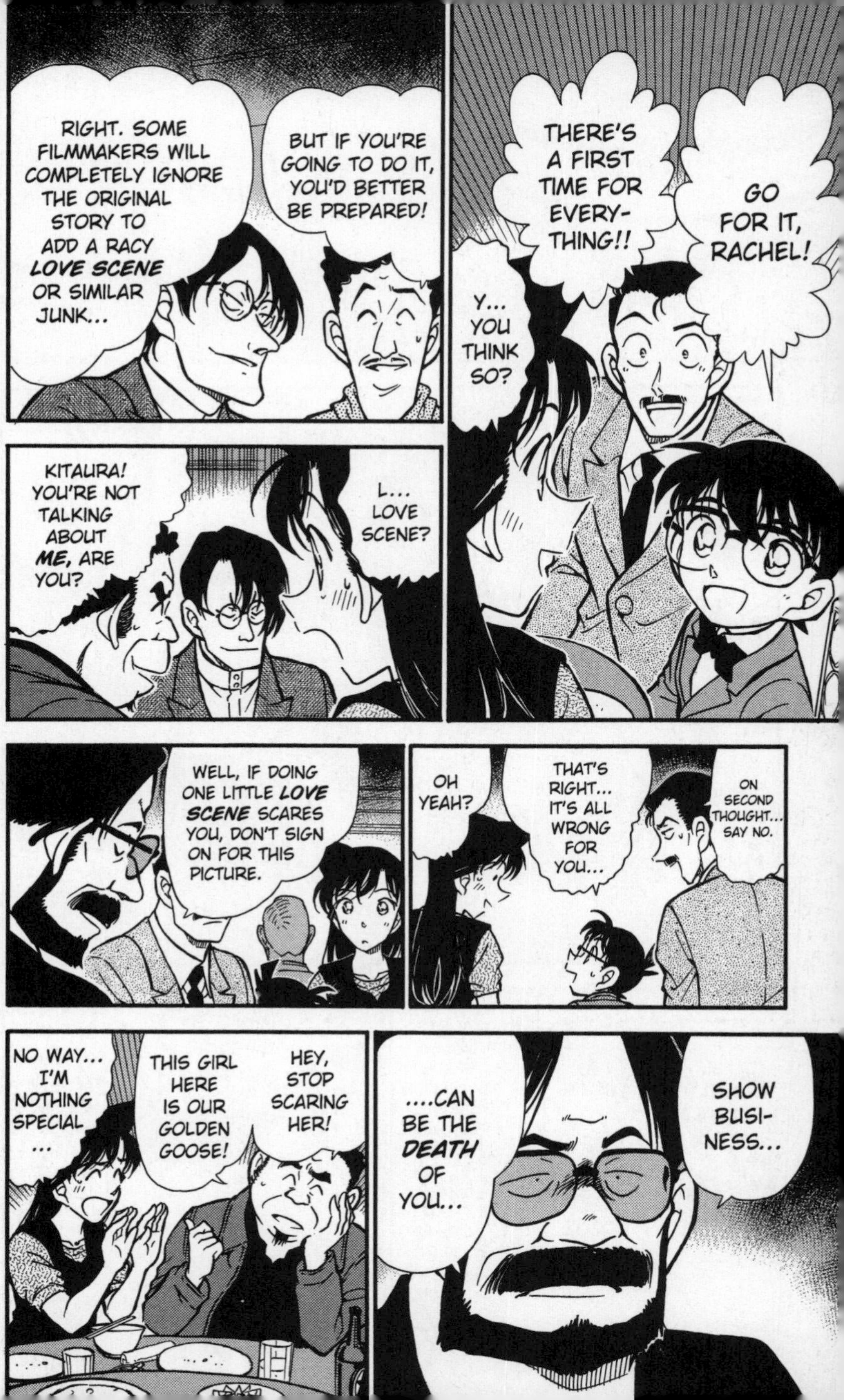
GO FOR IT, RACHEL!
THERE'S A FIRST TIME FOR EVERY-THING!!
Y... YOU THINK SO?
BUT IF YOU'RE GOING TO DO IT, YOU'D BETTER BE PREPARED!
RIGHT. SOME FILMMAKERS WILL COMPLETELY IGNORE THE ORIGINAL STORY TO ADD A RACY *LOVE SCENE* OR SIMILAR JUNK...
L... LOVE SCENE?
KITAURA! YOU'RE NOT TALKING ABOUT *ME*, ARE YOU?
ON SECOND THOUGHT... SAY NO.
THAT'S RIGHT... IT'S ALL WRONG FOR YOU...
OH YEAH?
WELL, IF DOING ONE LITTLE *LOVE SCENE* SCARES YOU, DON'T SIGN ON FOR THIS PICTURE.
SHOW BUSI-NESS...
....CAN BE THE *DEATH* OF YOU...
HEY, STOP SCARING HER!
THIS GIRL HERE IS OUR GOLDEN GOOSE!
NO WAY... I'M NOTHING SPECIAL ...

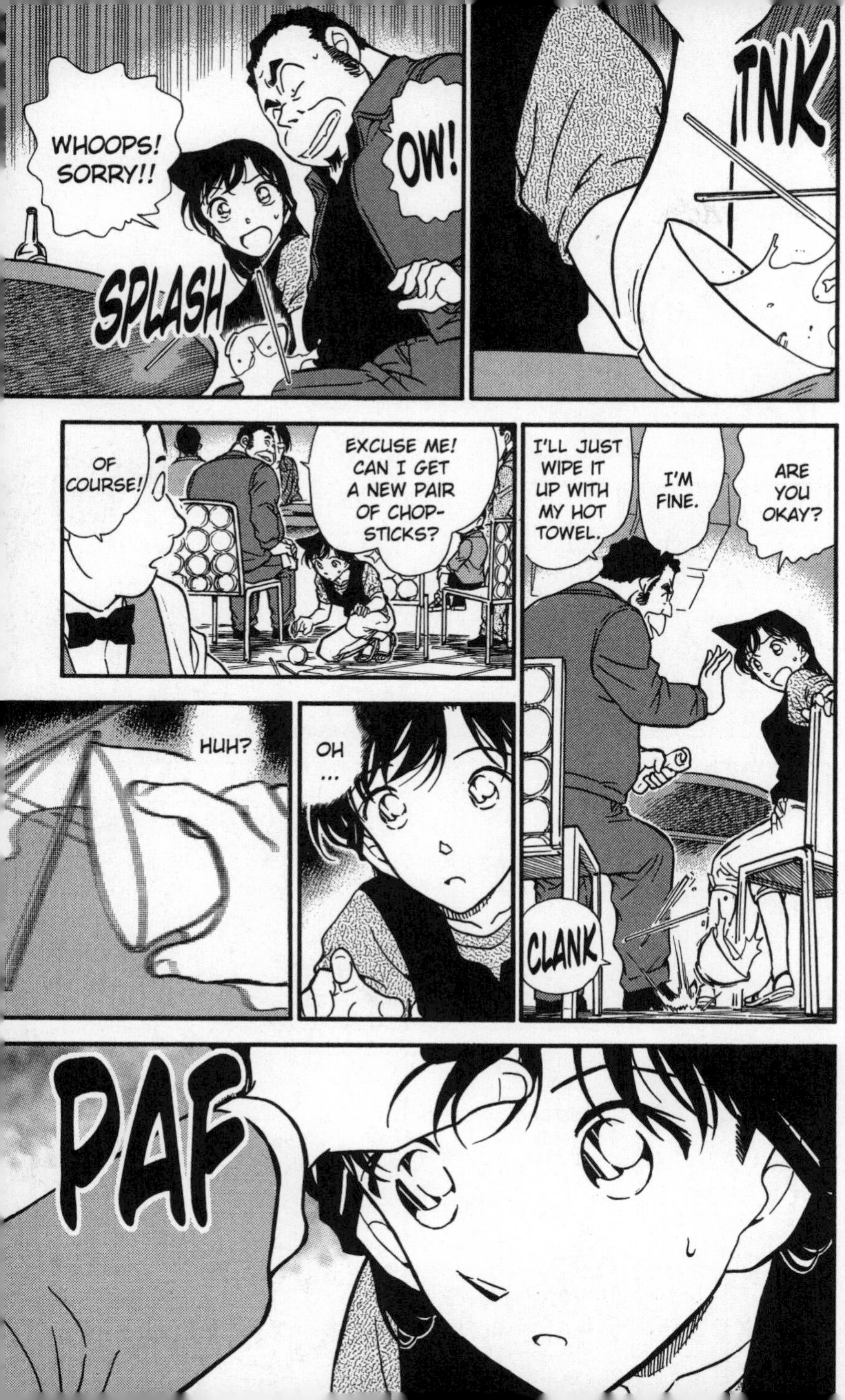
TNK
OW!
WHOOPS! SORRY!!
SPLASH
ARE YOU OKAY?
I'M FINE.
I'LL JUST WIPE IT UP WITH MY HOT TOWEL.
CLANK
EXCUSE ME! CAN I GET A NEW PAIR OF CHOP-STICKS?
OF COURSE!
OH ...
HUH?
PAF

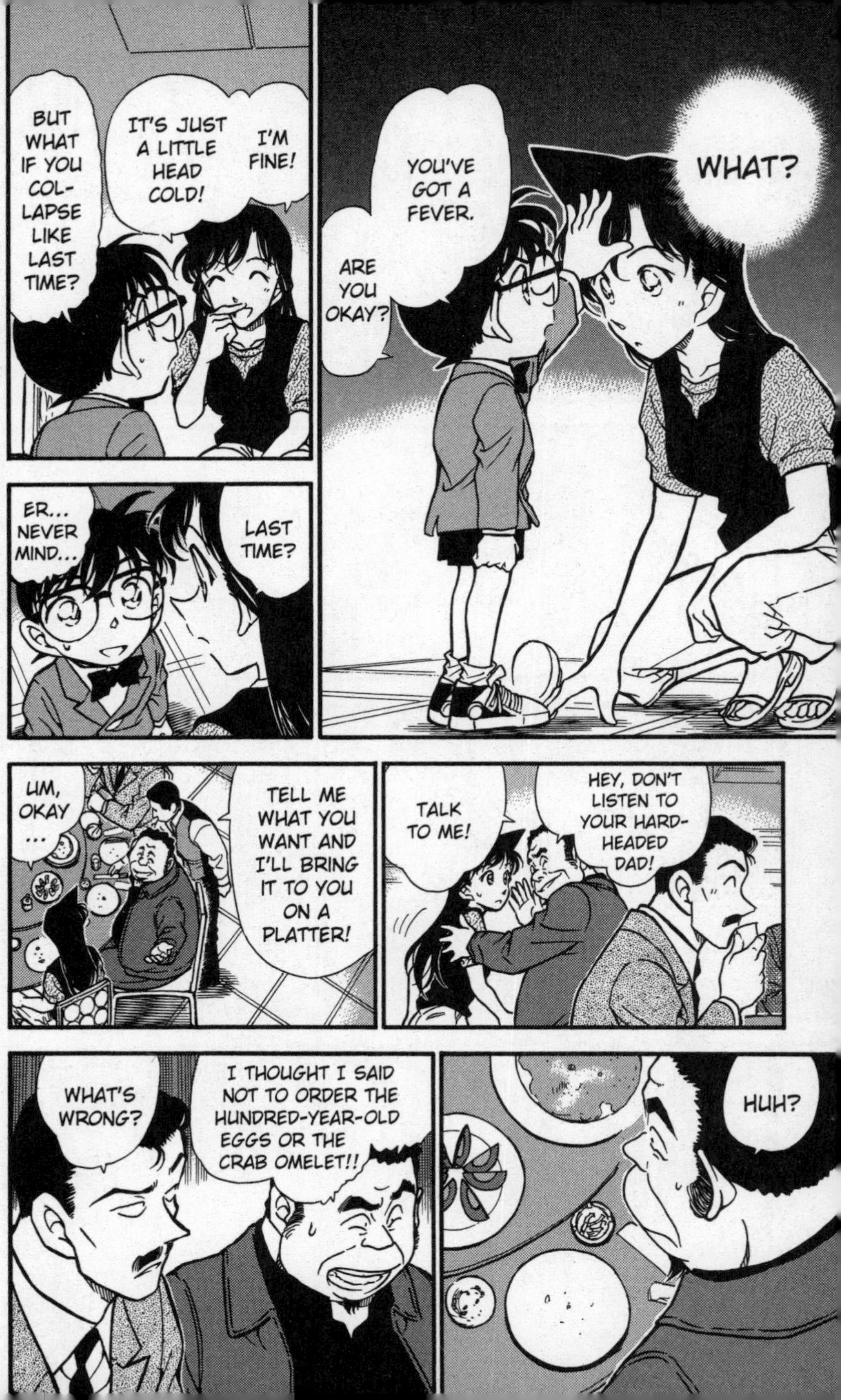
WHAT?
YOU'VE GOT A FEVER.
ARE YOU OKAY?
I'M FINE!
IT'S JUST A LITTLE HEAD COLD!
BUT WHAT IF YOU COL-LAPSE LIKE LAST TIME?
LAST TIME?
ER... NEVER MIND...
HEY, DON'T LISTEN TO YOUR HARD-HEADED DAD!
TALK TO ME!
TELL ME WHAT YOU WANT AND I'LL BRING IT TO YOU ON A PLATTER!
UM, OKAY ...
HUH?
I THOUGHT I SAID NOT TO ORDER THE HUNDRED-YEAR-OLD EGGS OR THE CRAB OMELET!!
WHAT'S WRONG?

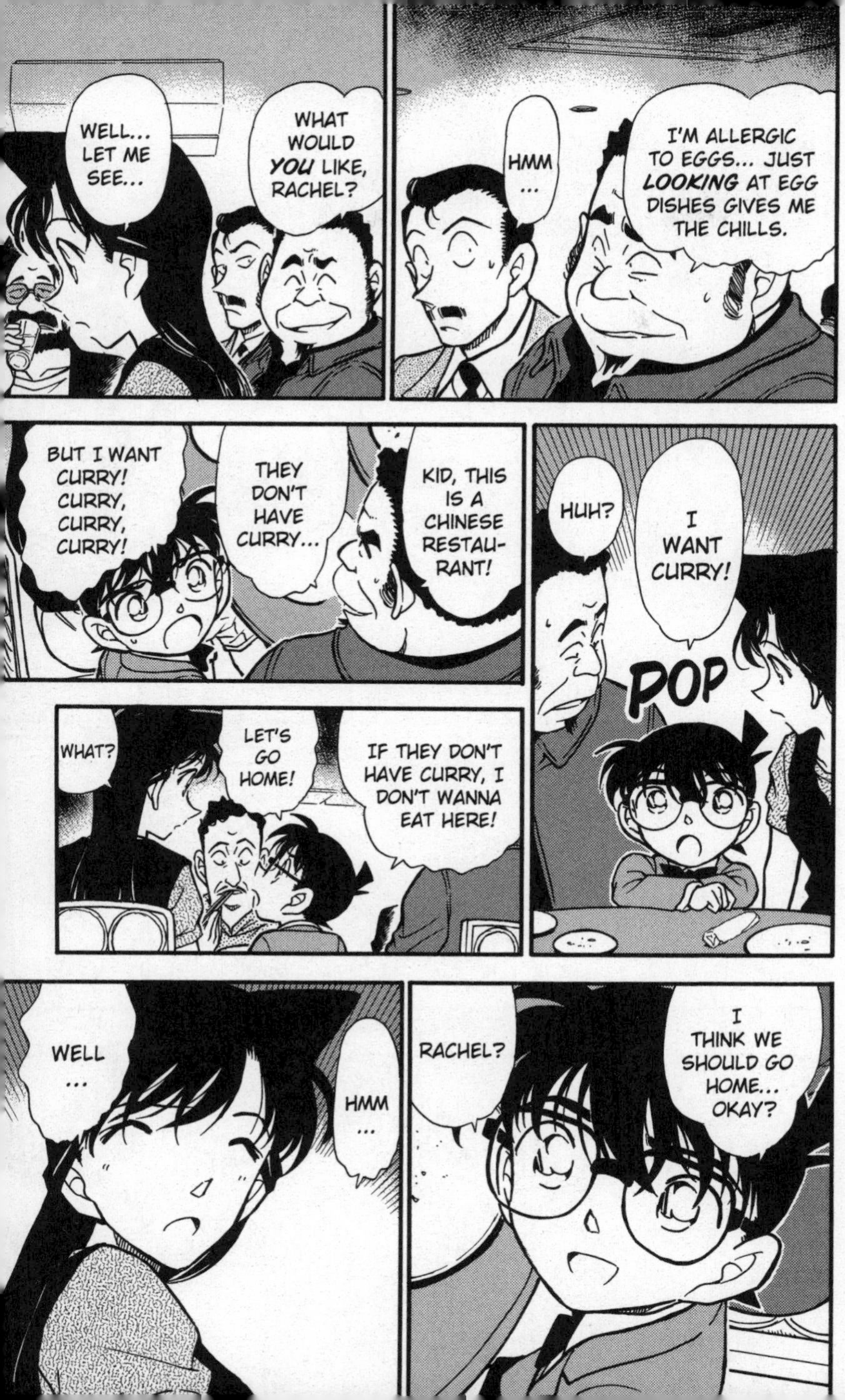
I'M ALLERGIC TO EGGS... JUST LOOKING AT EGG DISHES GIVES ME THE CHILLS.
HMM...
WHAT WOULD YOU LIKE, RACHEL?
WELL... LET ME SEE...
I WANT CURRY!
HUH?
POP
KID, THIS IS A CHINESE RESTAURANT!
THEY DON'T HAVE CURRY...
BUT I WANT CURRY! CURRY, CURRY, CURRY!
IF THEY DON'T HAVE CURRY, I DON'T WANNA EAT HERE!
LET'S GO HOME!
WHAT?
I THINK WE SHOULD GO HOME... OKAY?
RACHEL?
HMM...
WELL...

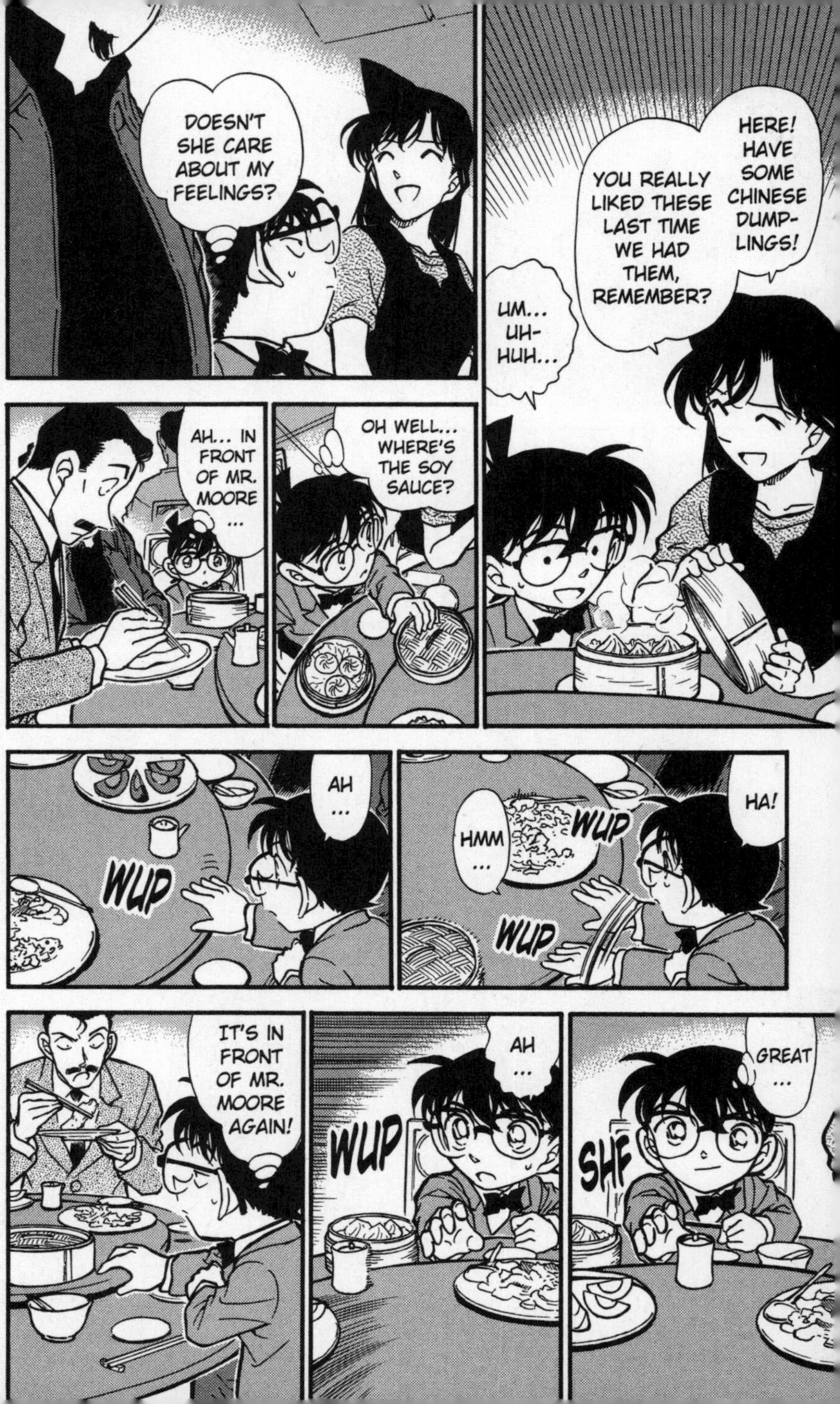
HERE! HAVE SOME CHINESE DUMPLINGS!
YOU REALLY LIKED THESE LAST TIME WE HAD THEM, REMEMBER?
UM... UH-HUH...
DOESN'T SHE CARE ABOUT MY FEELINGS?
OH WELL... WHERE'S THE SOY SAUCE?
AH... IN FRONT OF MR. MOORE ...
HA!
WUP
HMM ...
WUP
AH ...
WUP
GREAT ...
SHF
AH ...
WUP
IT'S IN FRONT OF MR. MOORE AGAIN!

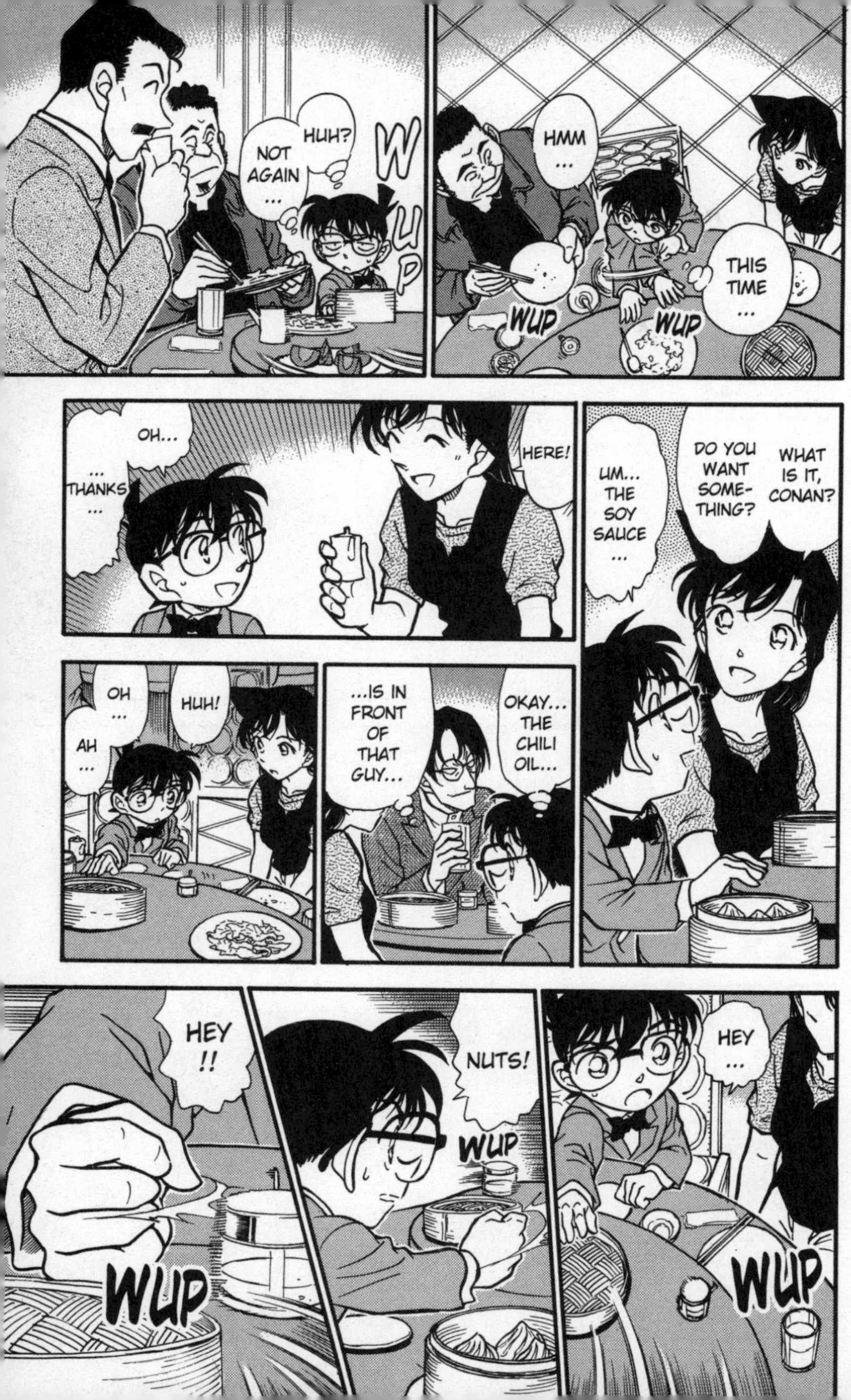
HMM ...
THIS TIME ...
WUP
WUP
HUH?
NOT AGAIN ...
WUP
WHAT IS IT, CONAN?
DO YOU WANT SOME-THING?
UM... THE SOY SAUCE ...
HERE!
OH...
... THANKS ...
OKAY... THE CHILI OIL...
...IS IN FRONT OF THAT GUY...
HUH!
OH ...
AH ...
HEY ...
WUP
NUTS!
WUP
HEY !!
WUP

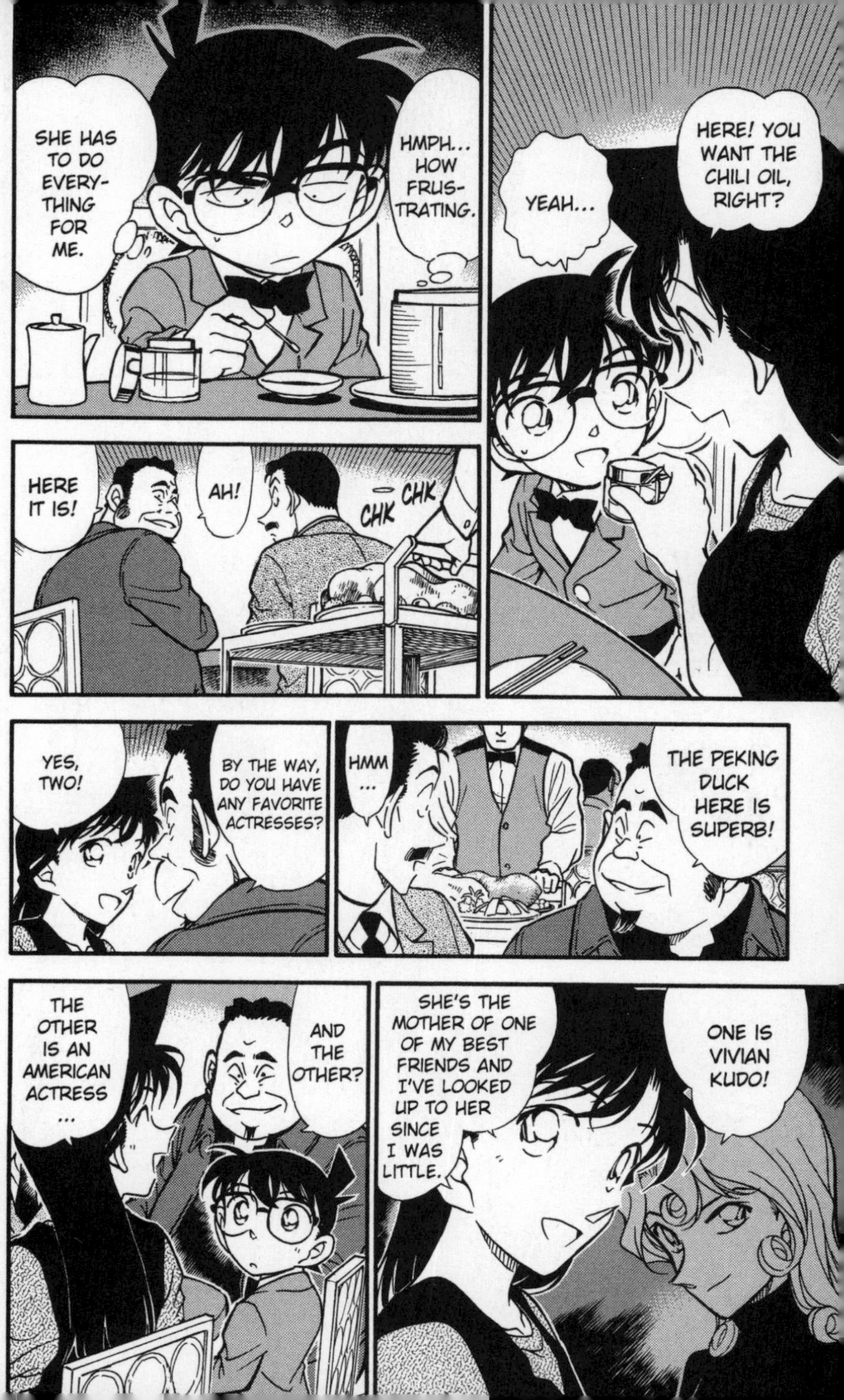
HERE! YOU WANT THE CHILI OIL, RIGHT?
YEAH...
HMPH... HOW FRUS-TRATING.
SHE HAS TO DO EVERY-THING FOR ME.
CHK CHK
AH!
HERE IT IS!
THE PEKING DUCK HERE IS SUPERB!
HMM ...
BY THE WAY, DO YOU HAVE ANY FAVORITE ACTRESSES?
YES, TWO!
ONE IS VIVIAN KUDO!
SHE'S THE MOTHER OF ONE OF MY BEST FRIENDS AND I'VE LOOKED UP TO HER SINCE I WAS LITTLE.
AND THE OTHER?
THE OTHER IS AN AMERICAN ACTRESS ...

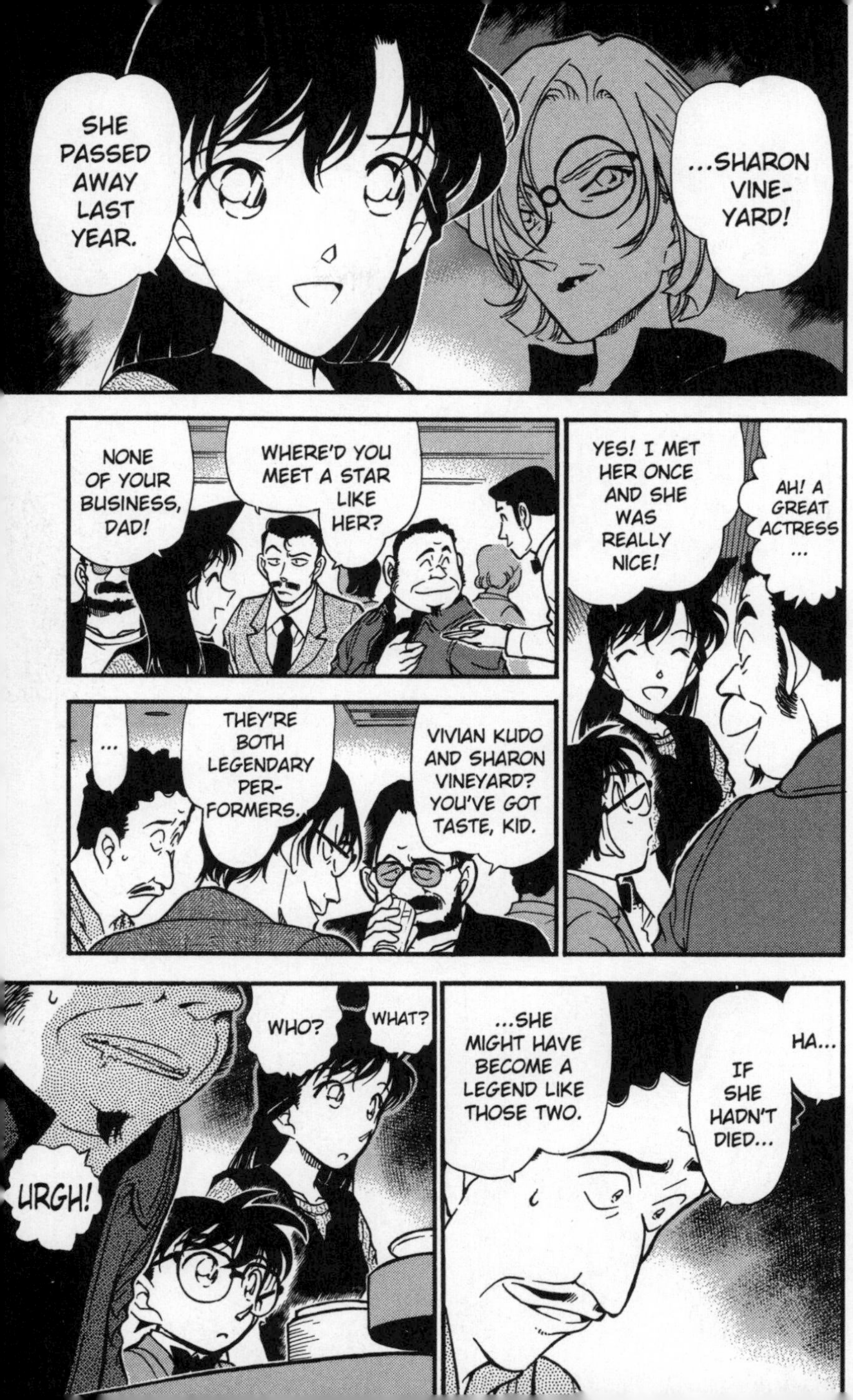
...SHARON VINE-YARD!
SHE PASSED AWAY LAST YEAR.
AH! A GREAT ACTRESS ...
YES! I MET HER ONCE AND SHE WAS REALLY NICE!
WHERE'D YOU MEET A STAR LIKE HER?
NONE OF YOUR BUSINESS, DAD!
VIVIAN KUDO AND SHARON VINEYARD? YOU'VE GOT TASTE, KID.
THEY'RE BOTH LEGENDARY PER-FORMERS.
...
HA...
IF SHE HADN'T DIED...
...SHE MIGHT HAVE BECOME A LEGEND LIKE THOSE TWO.
WHAT?
WHO?
URGH!

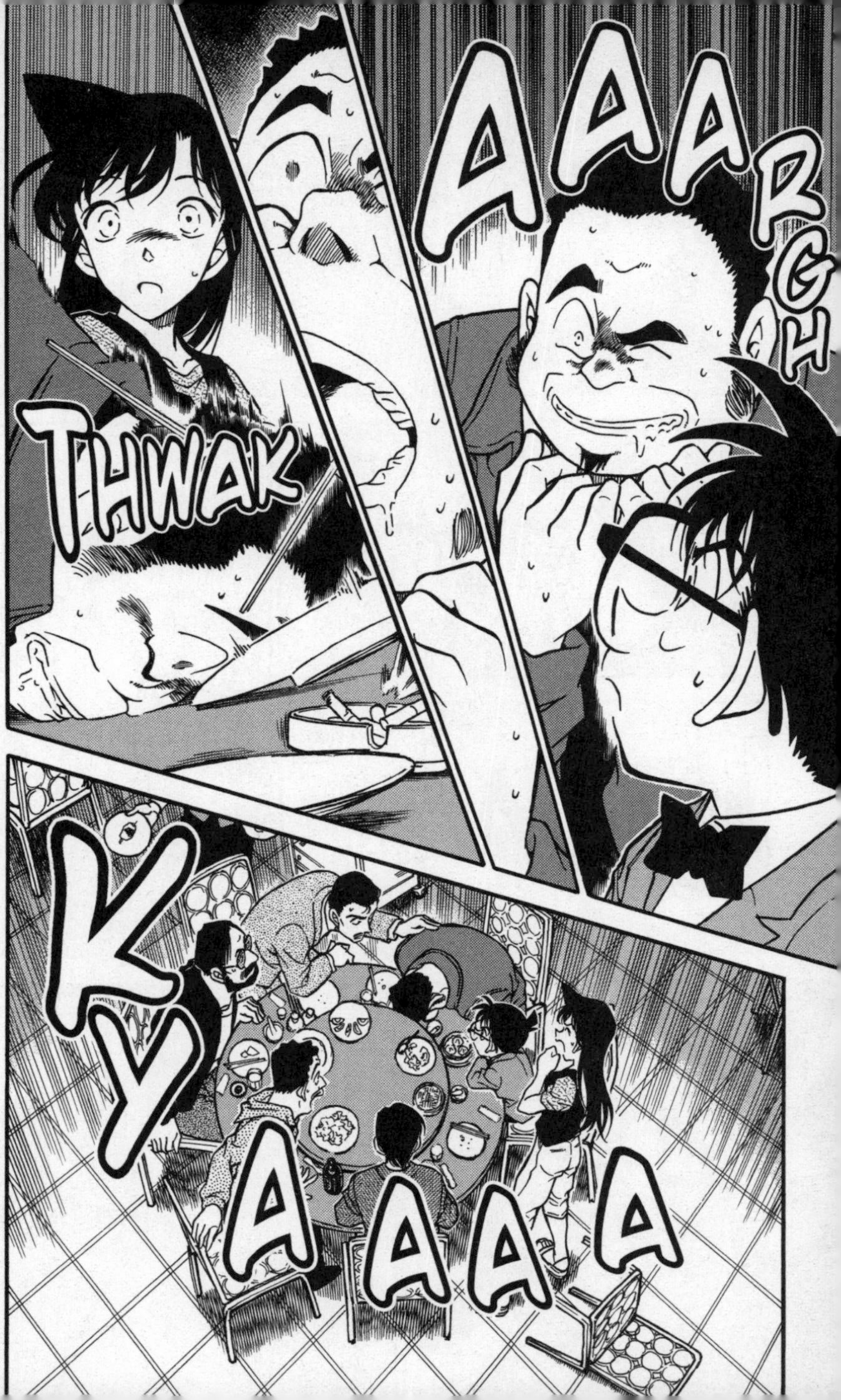
AAARGH
THWAK
KYAAAA

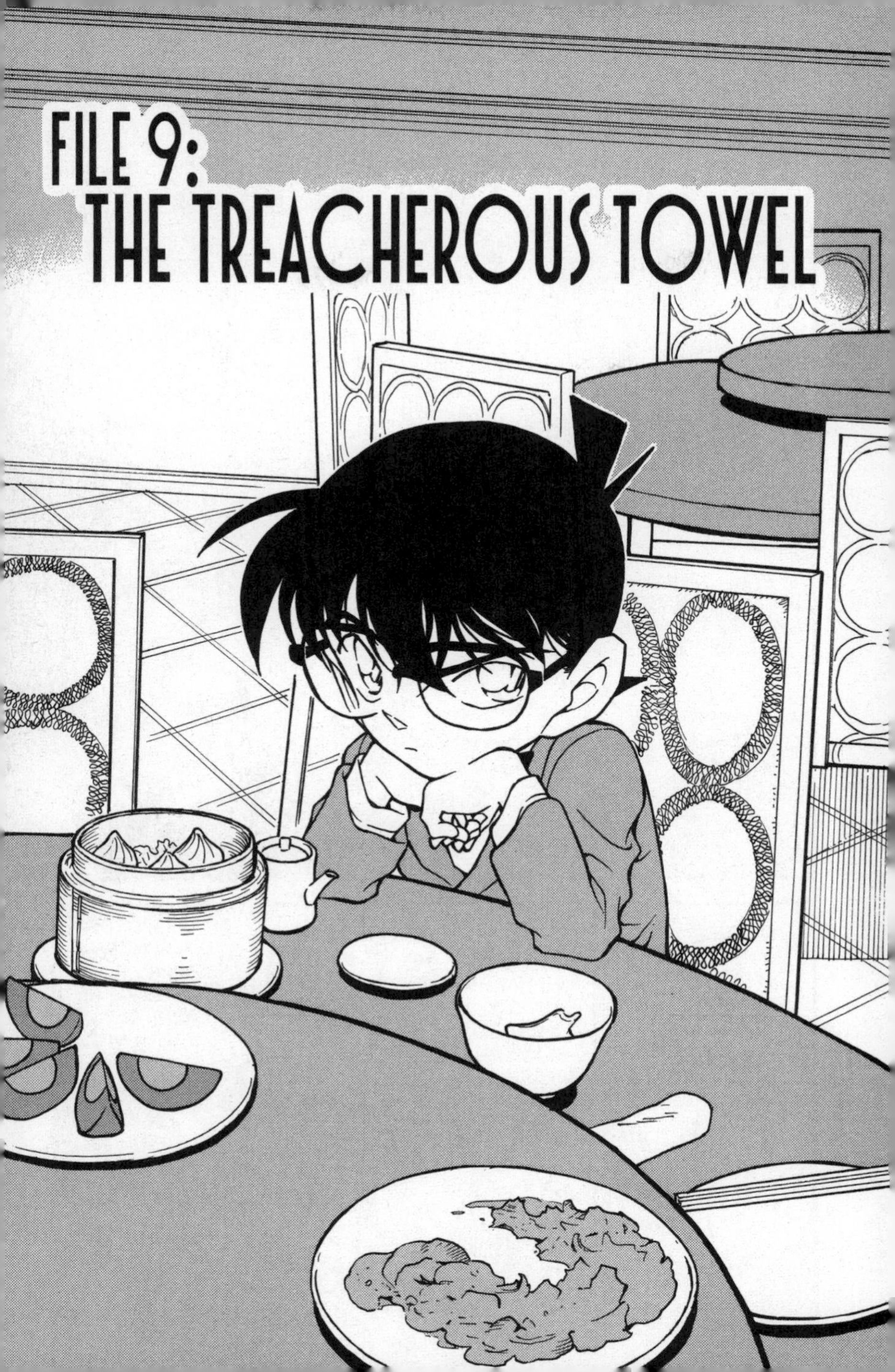
FILE 9:
THE TREACHEROUS TOWEL

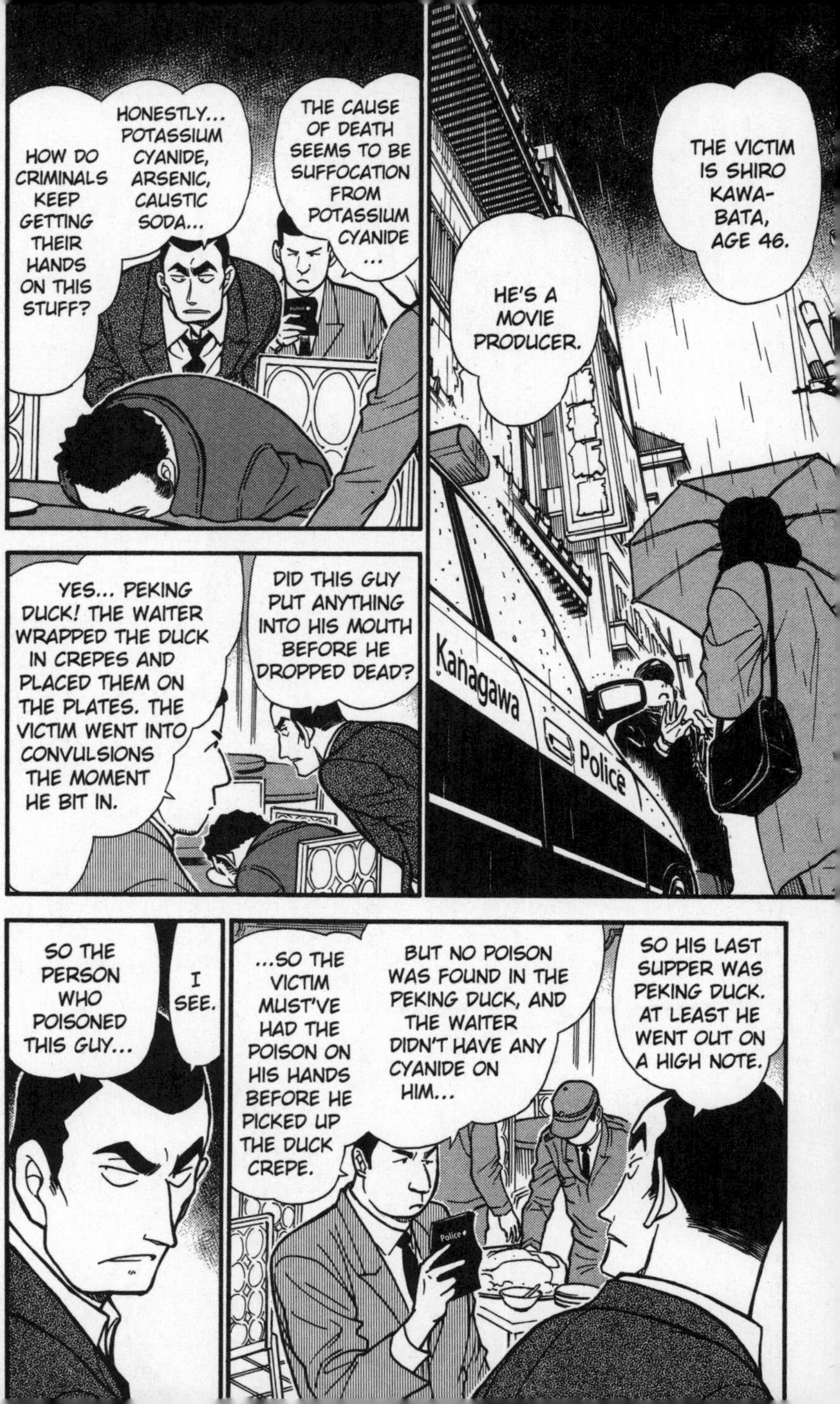
THE VICTIM IS SHIRO KAWA-BATA, AGE 46.
HE'S A MOVIE PRODUCER.
Kanagawa
Police
THE CAUSE OF DEATH SEEMS TO BE SUFFOCATION FROM POTASSIUM CYANIDE...
HONESTLY... POTASSIUM CYANIDE, ARSENIC, CAUSTIC SODA...
HOW DO CRIMINALS KEEP GETTING THEIR HANDS ON THIS STUFF?
DID THIS GUY PUT ANYTHING INTO HIS MOUTH BEFORE HE DROPPED DEAD?
YES... PEKING DUCK! THE WAITER WRAPPED THE DUCK IN CREPES AND PLACED THEM ON THE PLATES. THE VICTIM WENT INTO CONVULSIONS THE MOMENT HE BIT IN.
SO HIS LAST SUPPER WAS PEKING DUCK. AT LEAST HE WENT OUT ON A HIGH NOTE.
BUT NO POISON WAS FOUND IN THE PEKING DUCK, AND THE WAITER DIDN'T HAVE ANY CYANIDE ON HIM...
...SO THE VICTIM MUST'VE HAD THE POISON ON HIS HANDS BEFORE HE PICKED UP THE DUCK CREPE.
I SEE.
SO THE PERSON WHO POISONED THIS GUY...

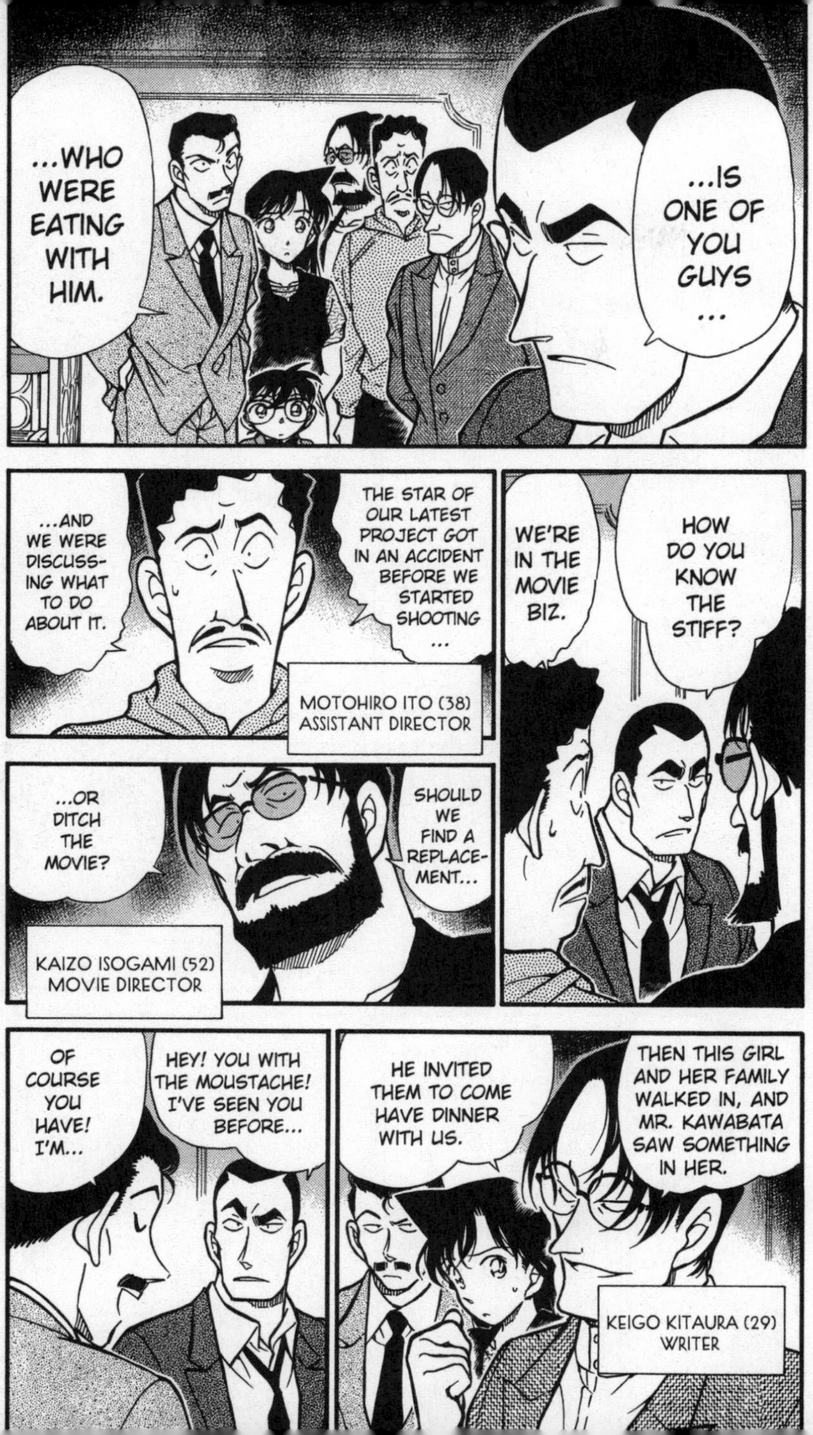
...IS ONE OF YOU GUYS ...
...WHO WERE EATING WITH HIM.
HOW DO YOU KNOW THE STIFF?
WE'RE IN THE MOVIE BIZ.
THE STAR OF OUR LATEST PROJECT GOT IN AN ACCIDENT BEFORE WE STARTED SHOOTING ...
...AND WE WERE DISCUSS-ING WHAT TO DO ABOUT IT.
MOTOHIRO ITO (38) ASSISTANT DIRECTOR
SHOULD WE FIND A REPLACE-MENT...
...OR DITCH THE MOVIE?
KAIZO ISOGAMI (52) MOVIE DIRECTOR
THEN THIS GIRL AND HER FAMILY WALKED IN, AND MR. KAWABATA SAW SOMETHING IN HER.
HE INVITED THEM TO COME HAVE DINNER WITH US.
KEIGO KITAURA (29) WRITER
HEY! YOU WITH THE MOUSTACHE! I'VE SEEN YOU BEFORE...
OF COURSE YOU HAVE! I'M...

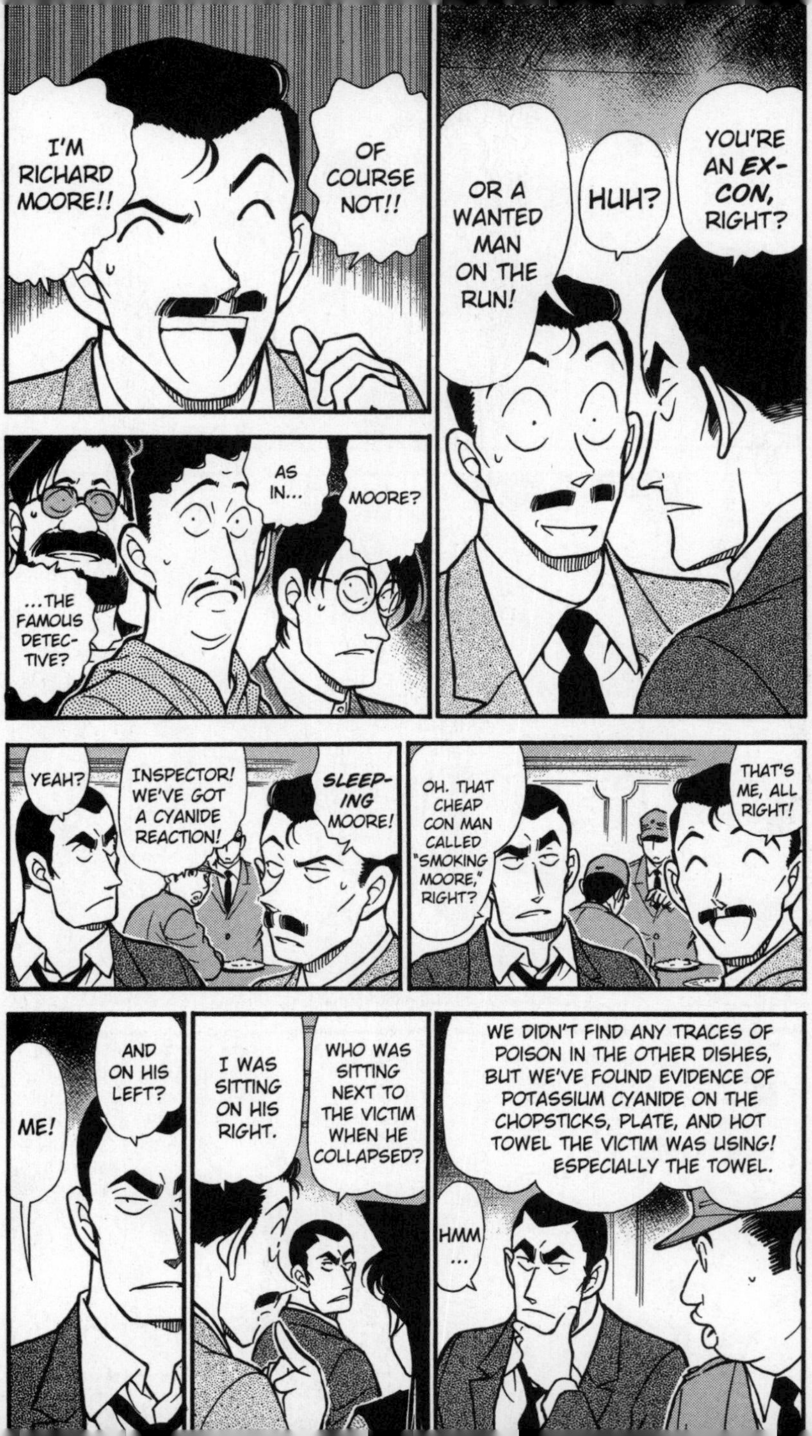
YOU'RE AN EX-CON, RIGHT?
HUH?
OR A WANTED MAN ON THE RUN!
OF COURSE NOT!!
I'M RICHARD MOORE!!
AS IN...
MOORE?
...THE FAMOUS DETECTIVE?
THAT'S ME, ALL RIGHT!
OH. THAT CHEAP CON MAN CALLED "SMOKING MOORE," RIGHT?
SLEEPING MOORE!
INSPECTOR! WE'VE GOT A CYANIDE REACTION!
YEAH?
WE DIDN'T FIND ANY TRACES OF POISON IN THE OTHER DISHES, BUT WE'VE FOUND EVIDENCE OF POTASSIUM CYANIDE ON THE CHOPSTICKS, PLATE, AND HOT TOWEL THE VICTIM WAS USING! ESPECIALLY THE TOWEL.
HMM...
WHO WAS SITTING NEXT TO THE VICTIM WHEN HE COLLAPSED?
I WAS SITTING ON HIS RIGHT.
AND ON HIS LEFT?
ME!

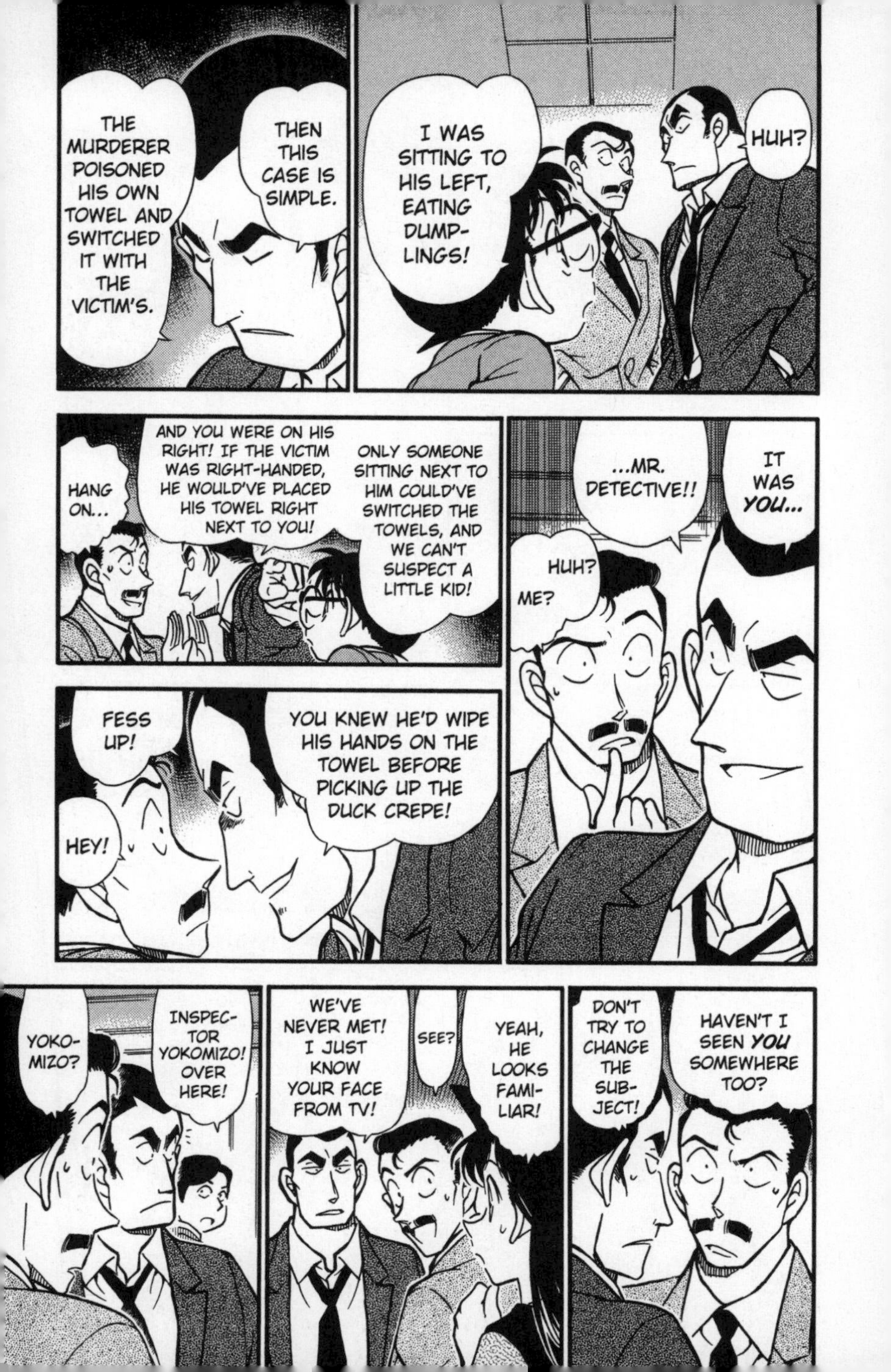
HUH?
I WAS SITTING TO HIS LEFT, EATING DUMP-LINGS!
THEN THIS CASE IS SIMPLE.
THE MURDERER POISONED HIS OWN TOWEL AND SWITCHED IT WITH THE VICTIM'S.
IT WAS *YOU...*
...MR. DETECTIVE!!
HUH? ME?
AND YOU WERE ON HIS RIGHT! IF THE VICTIM WAS RIGHT-HANDED, HE WOULD'VE PLACED HIS TOWEL RIGHT NEXT TO YOU!
ONLY SOMEONE SITTING NEXT TO HIM COULD'VE SWITCHED THE TOWELS, AND WE CAN'T SUSPECT A LITTLE KID!
HANG ON...
YOU KNEW HE'D WIPE HIS HANDS ON THE TOWEL BEFORE PICKING UP THE DUCK CREPE!
FESS UP!
HEY!
HAVEN'T I SEEN *YOU* SOMEWHERE TOO?
DON'T TRY TO CHANGE THE SUB-JECT!
YEAH, HE LOOKS FAMI-LIAR!
SEE?
WE'VE NEVER MET! I JUST KNOW YOUR FACE FROM TV!
INSPEC-TOR YOKOMIZO! OVER HERE!
YOKO-MIZO?

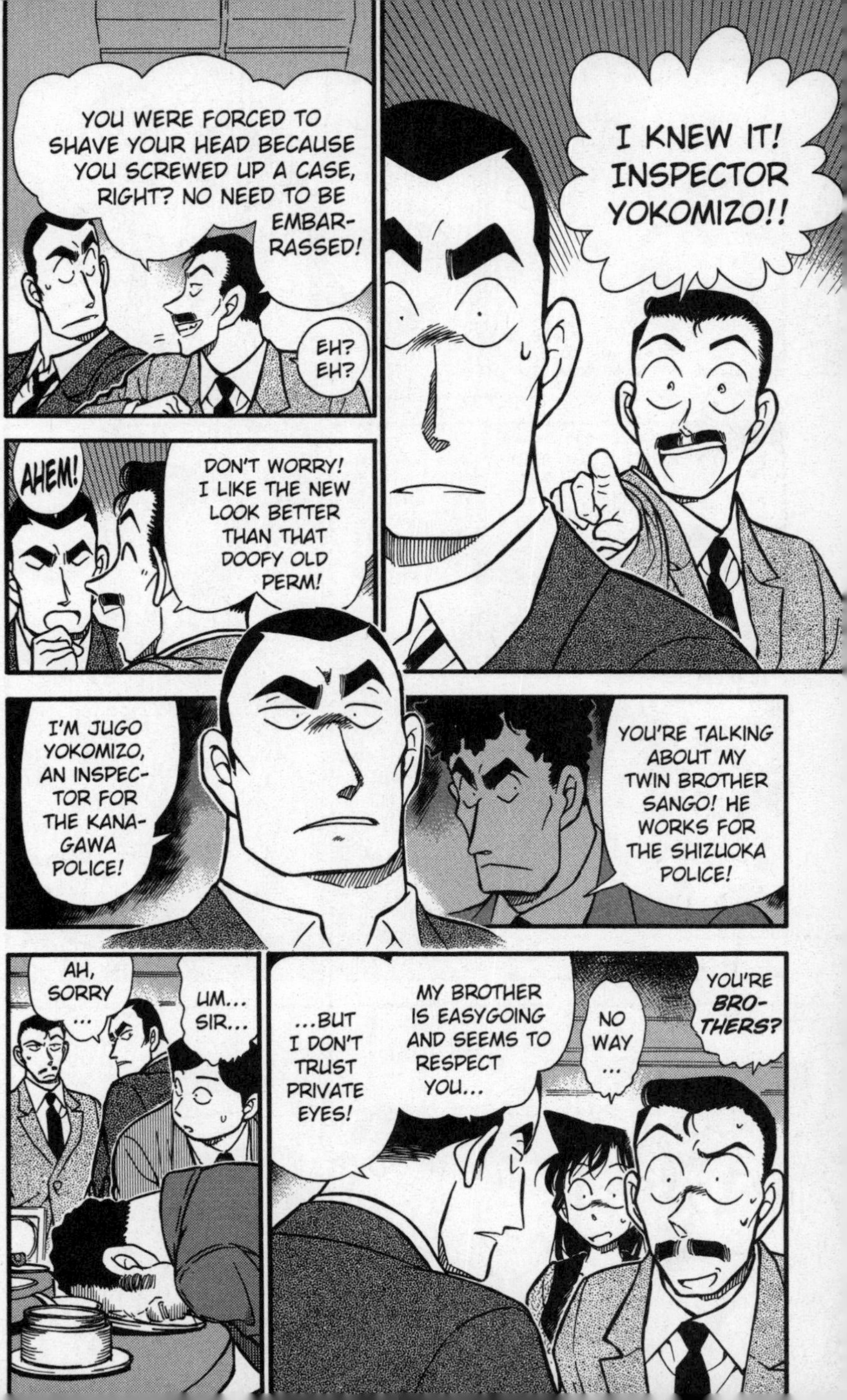

I KNEW IT! INSPECTOR YOKOMIZO!!
YOU WERE FORCED TO SHAVE YOUR HEAD BECAUSE YOU SCREWED UP A CASE, RIGHT? NO NEED TO BE EMBAR-RASSED!
EH? EH?
DON'T WORRY! I LIKE THE NEW LOOK BETTER THAN THAT DOOFY OLD PERM!
AHEM!
YOU'RE TALKING ABOUT MY TWIN BROTHER SANGO! HE WORKS FOR THE SHIZUOKA POLICE!
I'M JUGO YOKOMIZO, AN INSPEC-TOR FOR THE KANA-GAWA POLICE!
YOU'RE BRO-THERS?
NO WAY...
MY BROTHER IS EASYGOING AND SEEMS TO RESPECT YOU...
...BUT I DON'T TRUST PRIVATE EYES!
UM... SIR...
AH, SORRY...

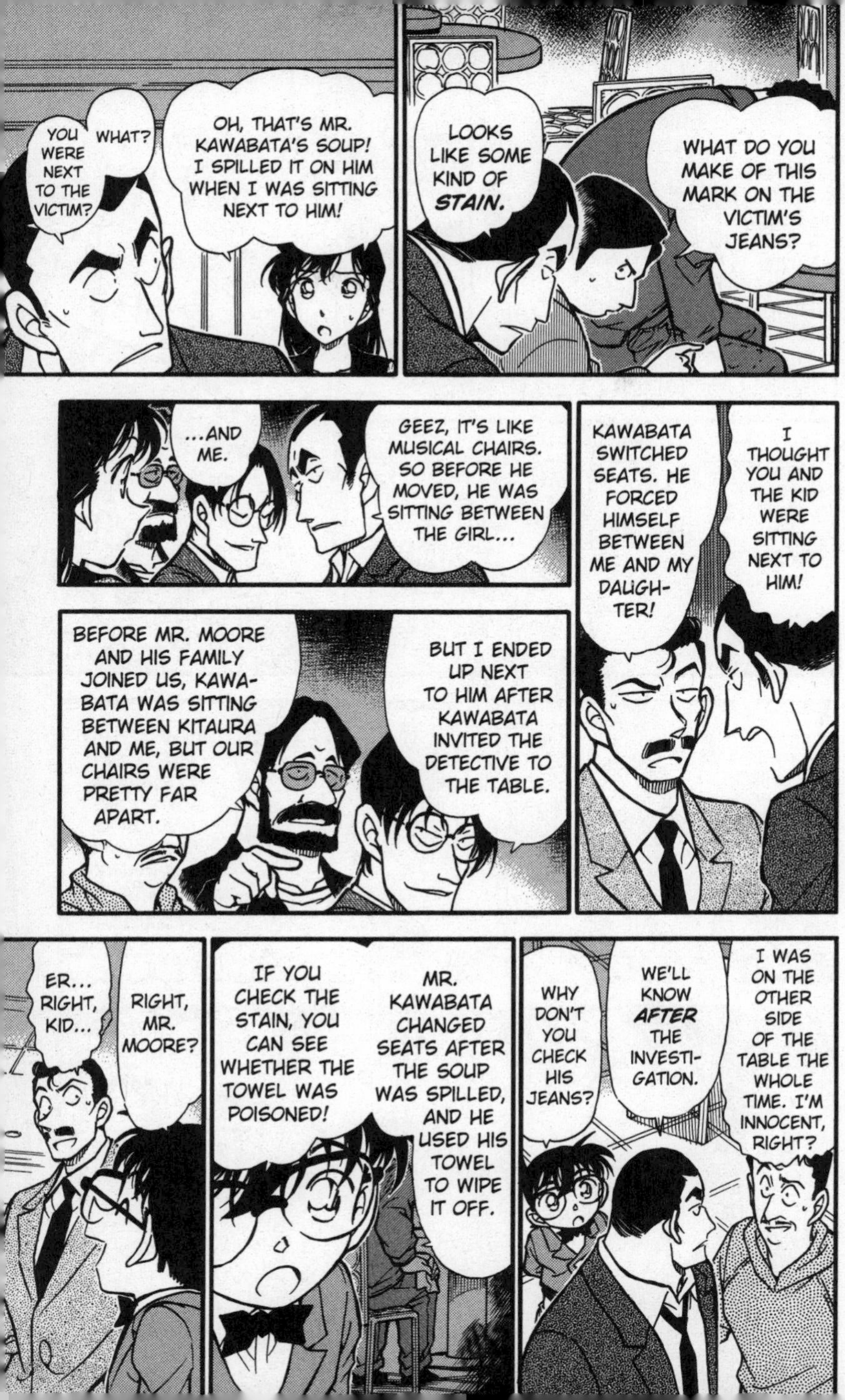
WHAT DO YOU MAKE OF THIS MARK ON THE VICTIM'S JEANS?
LOOKS LIKE SOME KIND OF *STAIN.*
OH, THAT'S MR. KAWABATA'S SOUP! I SPILLED IT ON HIM WHEN I WAS SITTING NEXT TO HIM!
WHAT?
YOU WERE NEXT TO THE VICTIM?
I THOUGHT YOU AND THE KID WERE SITTING NEXT TO HIM!
KAWABATA SWITCHED SEATS. HE FORCED HIMSELF BETWEEN ME AND MY DAUGHTER!
GEEZ, IT'S LIKE MUSICAL CHAIRS. SO BEFORE HE MOVED, HE WAS SITTING BETWEEN THE GIRL...
...AND ME.
BUT I ENDED UP NEXT TO HIM AFTER KAWABATA INVITED THE DETECTIVE TO THE TABLE.
BEFORE MR. MOORE AND HIS FAMILY JOINED US, KAWABATA WAS SITTING BETWEEN KITAURA AND ME, BUT OUR CHAIRS WERE PRETTY FAR APART.
I WAS ON THE OTHER SIDE OF THE TABLE THE WHOLE TIME. I'M INNOCENT, RIGHT?
WE'LL KNOW *AFTER* THE INVESTIGATION.
WHY DON'T YOU CHECK HIS JEANS?
MR. KAWABATA CHANGED SEATS AFTER THE SOUP WAS SPILLED, AND HE USED HIS TOWEL TO WIPE IT OFF.
IF YOU CHECK THE STAIN, YOU CAN SEE WHETHER THE TOWEL WAS POISONED!
RIGHT, MR. MOORE?
ER... RIGHT, KID...

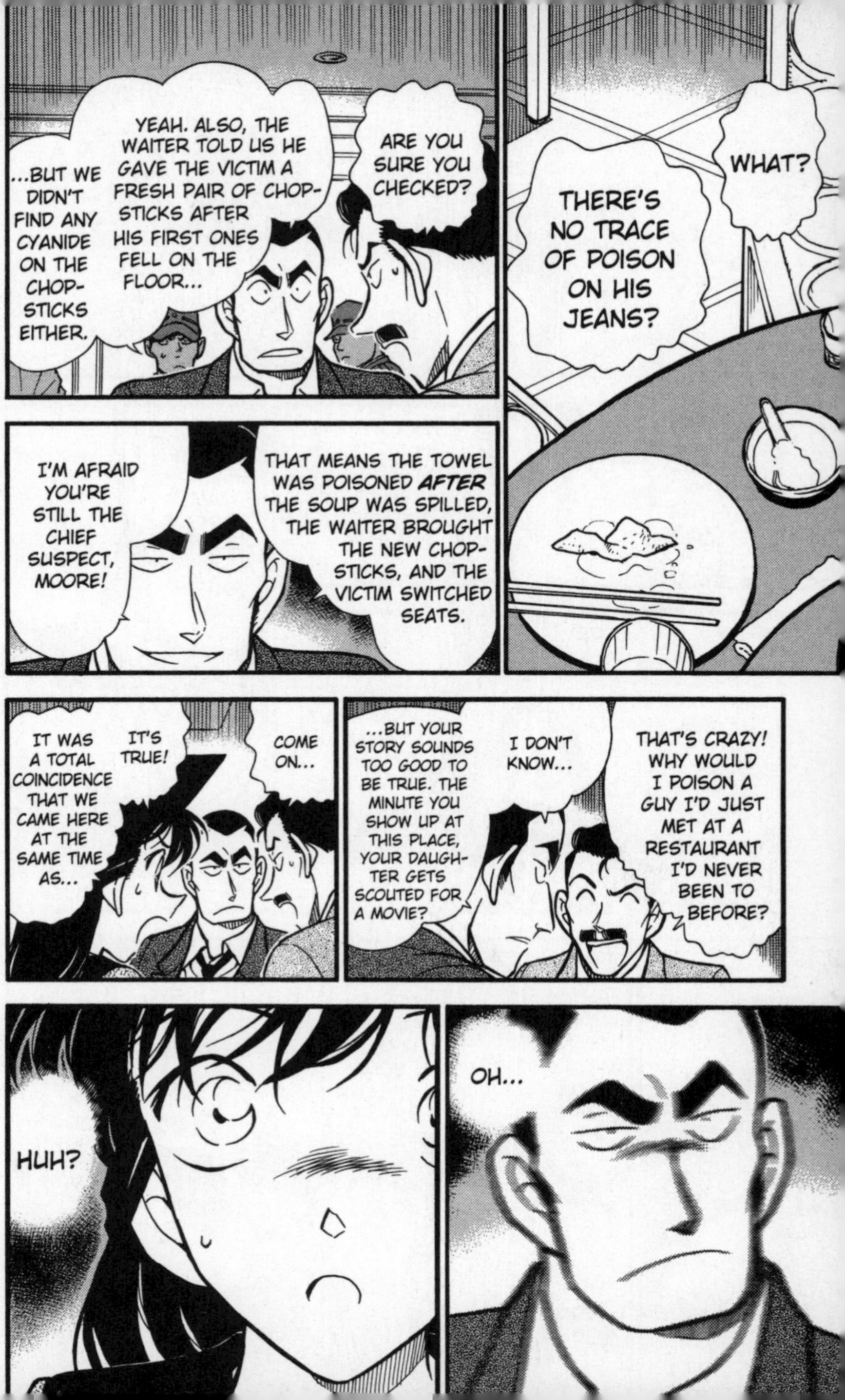
WHAT?
THERE'S NO TRACE OF POISON ON HIS JEANS?
ARE YOU SURE YOU CHECKED?
YEAH. ALSO, THE WAITER TOLD US HE GAVE THE VICTIM A FRESH PAIR OF CHOP-STICKS AFTER HIS FIRST ONES FELL ON THE FLOOR...
...BUT WE DIDN'T FIND ANY CYANIDE ON THE CHOP-STICKS EITHER.
THAT MEANS THE TOWEL WAS POISONED AFTER THE SOUP WAS SPILLED, THE WAITER BROUGHT THE NEW CHOP-STICKS, AND THE VICTIM SWITCHED SEATS.
I'M AFRAID YOU'RE STILL THE CHIEF SUSPECT, MOORE!
THAT'S CRAZY! WHY WOULD I POISON A GUY I'D JUST MET AT A RESTAURANT I'D NEVER BEEN TO BEFORE?
I DON'T KNOW...
...BUT YOUR STORY SOUNDS TOO GOOD TO BE TRUE. THE MINUTE YOU SHOW UP AT THIS PLACE, YOUR DAUGHTER GETS SCOUTED FOR A MOVIE?
COME ON...
IT'S TRUE!
IT WAS A TOTAL COINCIDENCE THAT WE CAME HERE AT THE SAME TIME AS...
OH...
HUH?

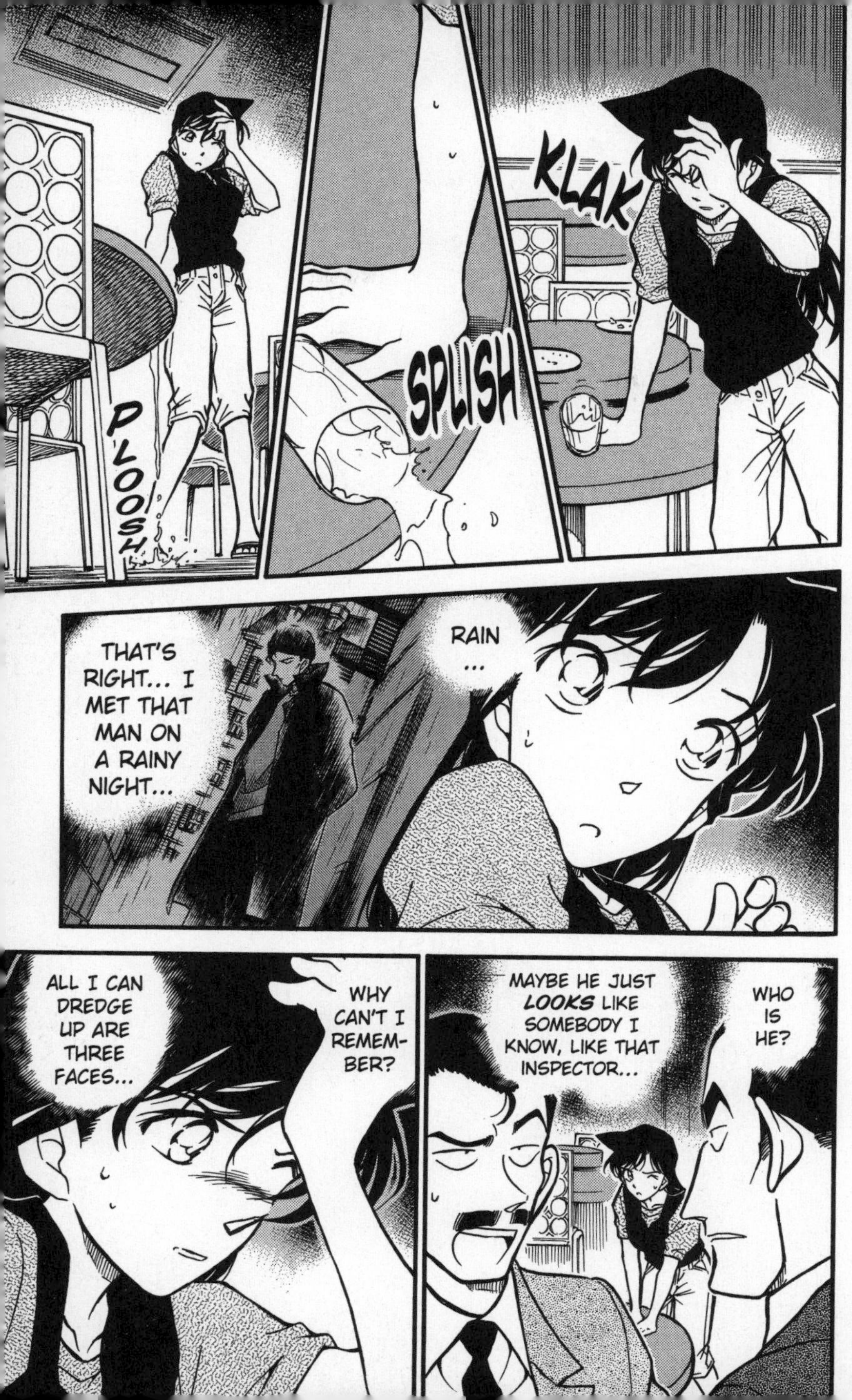
KLAK
SPLISH
P'LOOSH
RAIN ...
THAT'S RIGHT... I MET THAT MAN ON A RAINY NIGHT...
WHO IS HE?
MAYBE HE JUST **LOOKS** LIKE SOMEBODY I KNOW, LIKE THAT INSPECTOR...
WHY CAN'T I REMEMBER?
ALL I CAN DREDGE UP ARE THREE FACES...

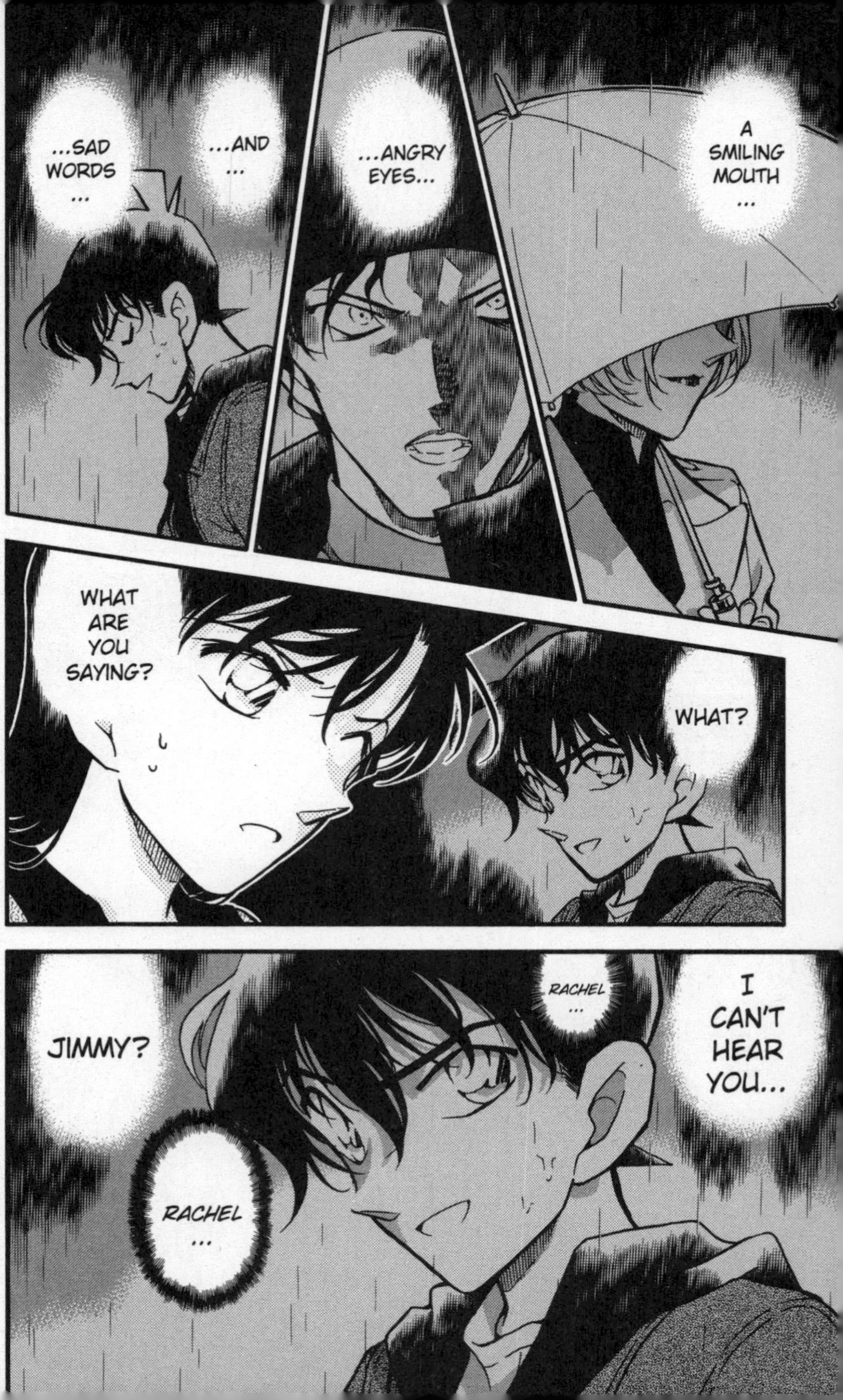
A SMILING MOUTH ...
...ANGRY EYES...
...AND ...
...SAD WORDS ...
WHAT?
WHAT ARE YOU SAYING?
I CAN'T HEAR YOU...
RACHEL ...
JIMMY?
RACHEL ...

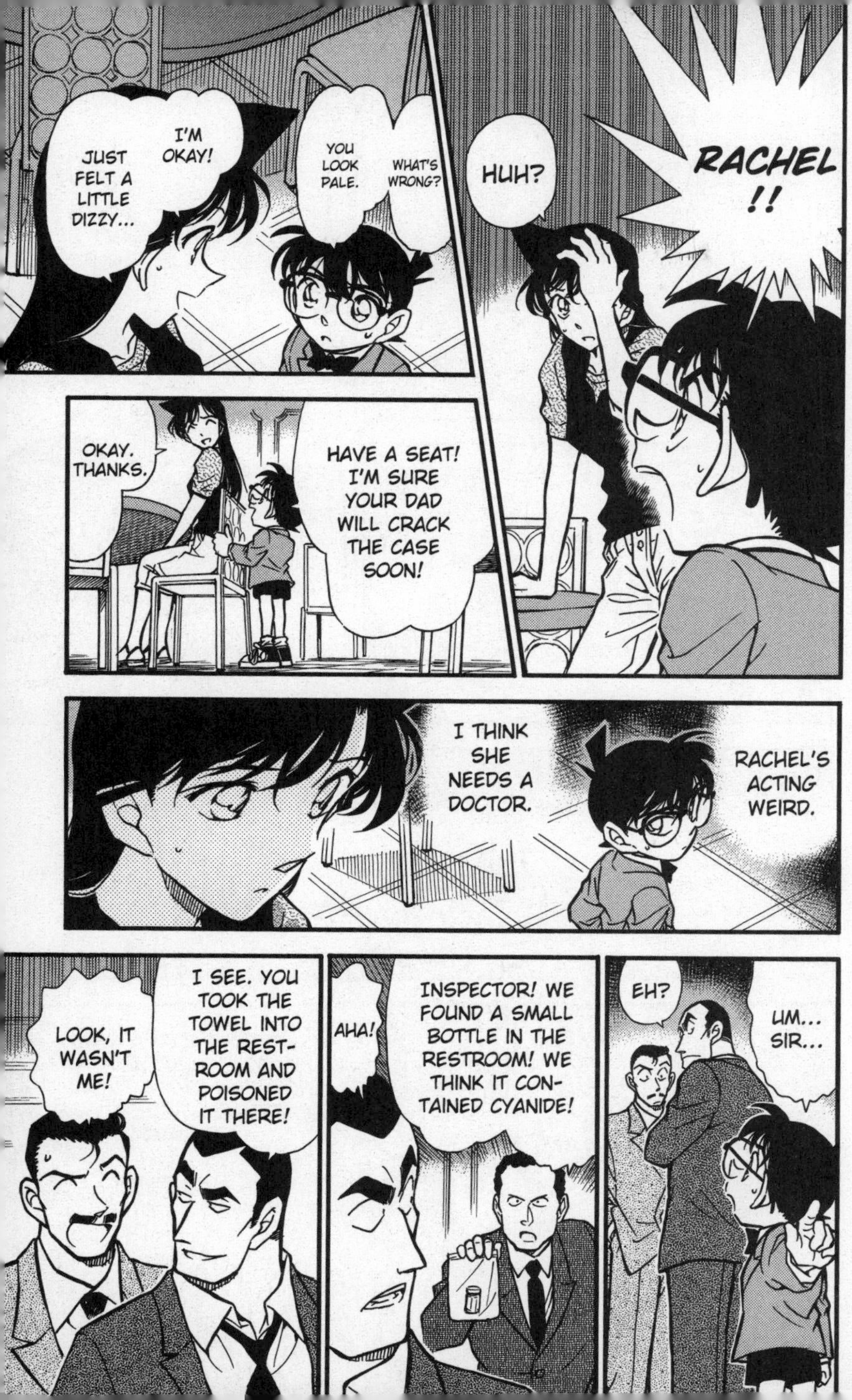
RACHEL !!
HUH?
WHAT'S WRONG?
YOU LOOK PALE.
I'M OKAY!
JUST FELT A LITTLE DIZZY...
HAVE A SEAT! I'M SURE YOUR DAD WILL CRACK THE CASE SOON!
OKAY. THANKS.
RACHEL'S ACTING WEIRD.
I THINK SHE NEEDS A DOCTOR.
UM... SIR...
EH?
INSPECTOR! WE FOUND A SMALL BOTTLE IN THE RESTROOM! WE THINK IT CONTAINED CYANIDE!
AHA!
I SEE. YOU TOOK THE TOWEL INTO THE REST-ROOM AND POISONED IT THERE!
LOOK, IT WASN'T ME!

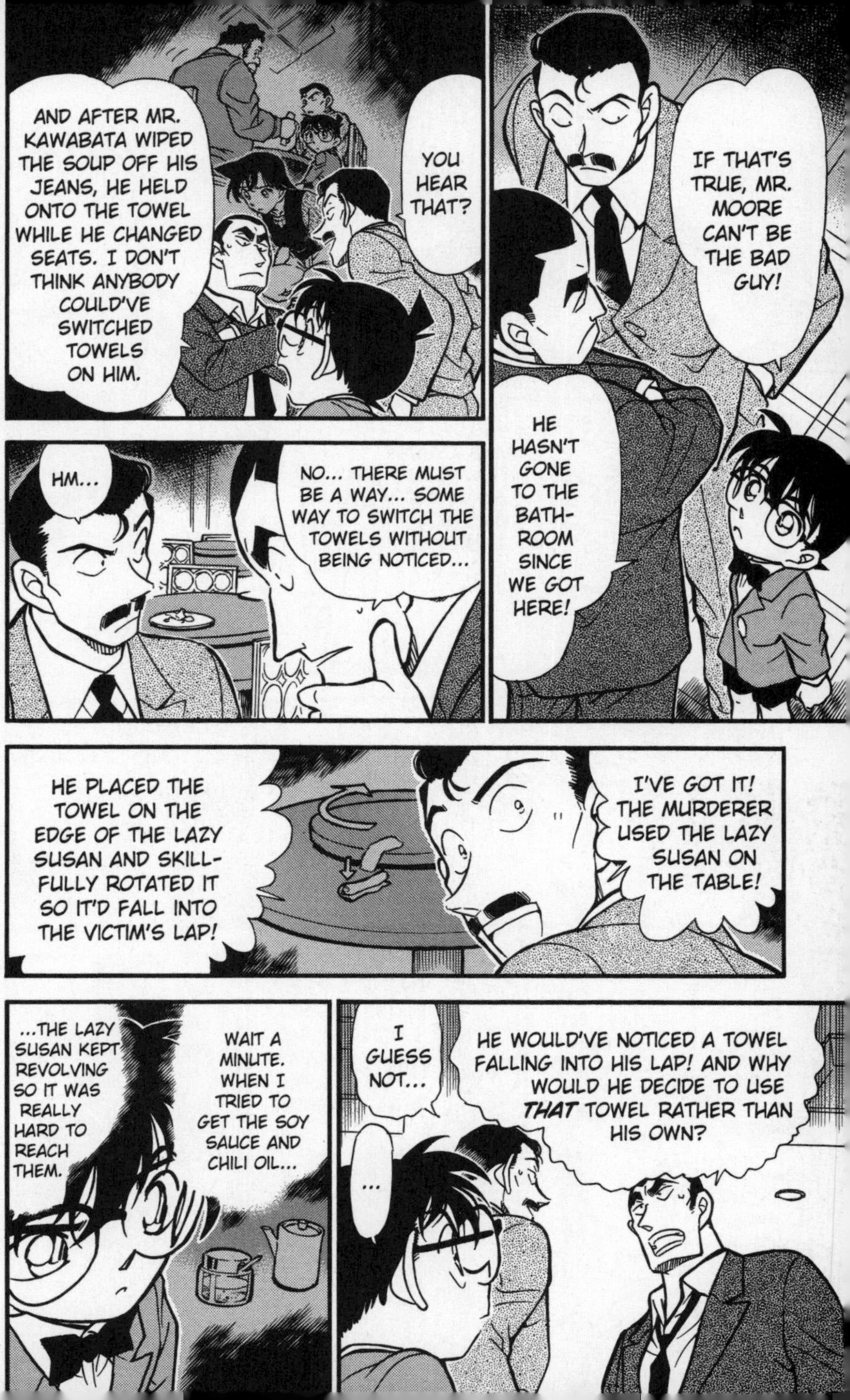
IF THAT'S TRUE, MR. MOORE CAN'T BE THE BAD GUY!
HE HASN'T GONE TO THE BATHROOM SINCE WE GOT HERE!
YOU HEAR THAT?
AND AFTER MR. KAWABATA WIPED THE SOUP OFF HIS JEANS, HE HELD ONTO THE TOWEL WHILE HE CHANGED SEATS. I DON'T THINK ANYBODY COULD'VE SWITCHED TOWELS ON HIM.
NO... THERE MUST BE A WAY... SOME WAY TO SWITCH THE TOWELS WITHOUT BEING NOTICED...
HM...
I'VE GOT IT! THE MURDERER USED THE LAZY SUSAN ON THE TABLE!
HE PLACED THE TOWEL ON THE EDGE OF THE LAZY SUSAN AND SKILLFULLY ROTATED IT SO IT'D FALL INTO THE VICTIM'S LAP!
HE WOULD'VE NOTICED A TOWEL FALLING INTO HIS LAP! AND WHY WOULD HE DECIDE TO USE *THAT* TOWEL RATHER THAN HIS OWN?
I GUESS NOT...
...
WAIT A MINUTE. WHEN I TRIED TO GET THE SOY SAUCE AND CHILI OIL...
...THE LAZY SUSAN KEPT REVOLVING SO IT WAS REALLY HARD TO REACH THEM.

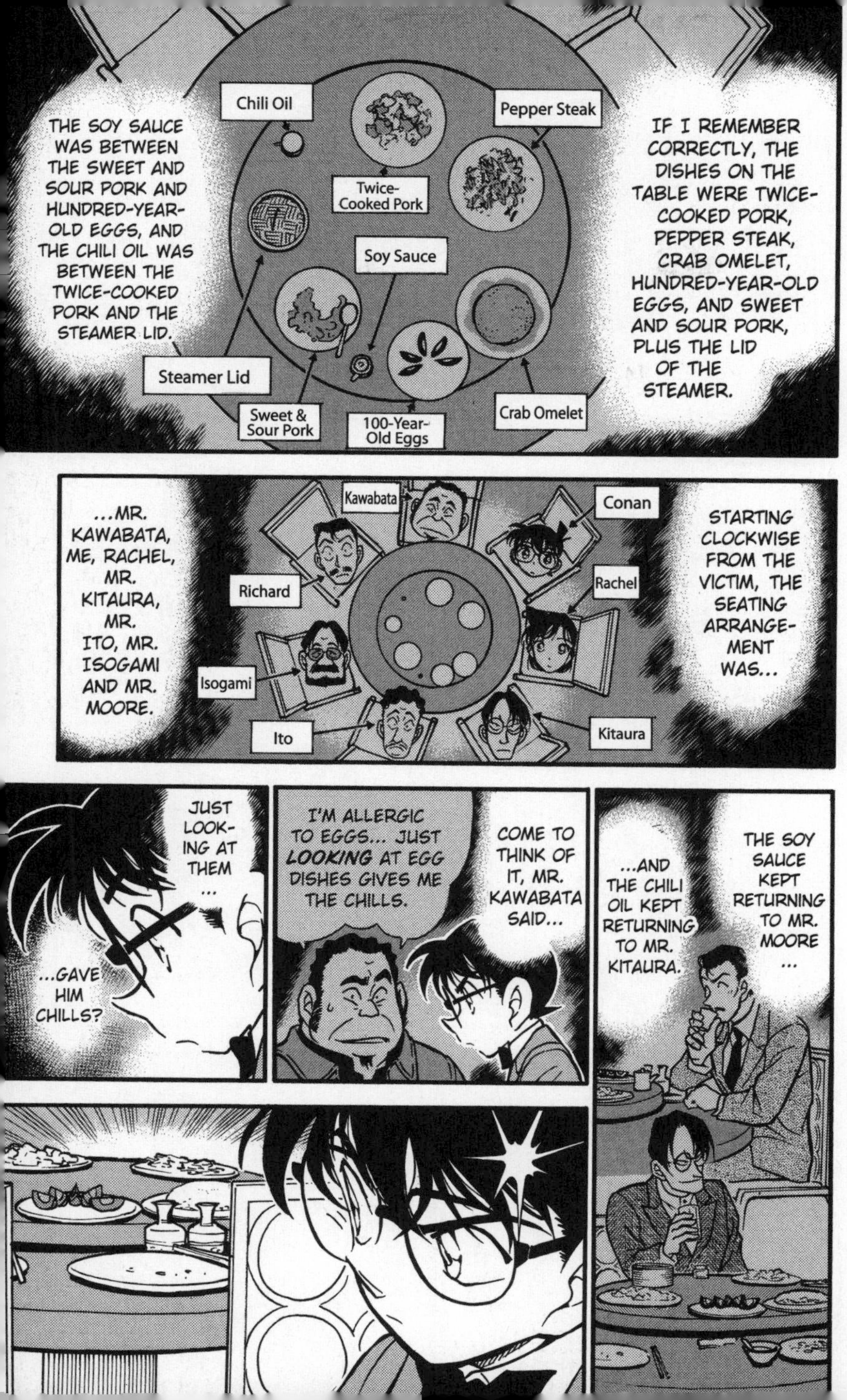
IF I REMEMBER CORRECTLY, THE DISHES ON THE TABLE WERE TWICE-COOKED PORK, PEPPER STEAK, CRAB OMELET, HUNDRED-YEAR-OLD EGGS, AND SWEET AND SOUR PORK, PLUS THE LID OF THE STEAMER.
Pepper Steak
Chili Oil
Twice-Cooked Pork
Soy Sauce
Crab Omelet
100-Year-Old Eggs
Sweet & Sour Pork
Steamer Lid
THE SOY SAUCE WAS BETWEEN THE SWEET AND SOUR PORK AND HUNDRED-YEAR-OLD EGGS, AND THE CHILI OIL WAS BETWEEN THE TWICE-COOKED PORK AND THE STEAMER LID.
STARTING CLOCKWISE FROM THE VICTIM, THE SEATING ARRANGE-MENT WAS...
Conan
Kawabata
Rachel
Richard
Kitaura
Isogami
Ito
...MR. KAWABATA, ME, RACHEL, MR. KITAURA, MR. ITO, MR. ISOGAMI AND MR. MOORE.
THE SOY SAUCE KEPT RETURNING TO MR. MOORE ...
...AND THE CHILI OIL KEPT RETURNING TO MR. KITAURA.
COME TO THINK OF IT, MR. KAWABATA SAID...
I'M ALLERGIC TO EGGS... JUST LOOKING AT EGG DISHES GIVES ME THE CHILLS.
JUST LOOKING AT THEM ...
...GAVE HIM CHILLS?

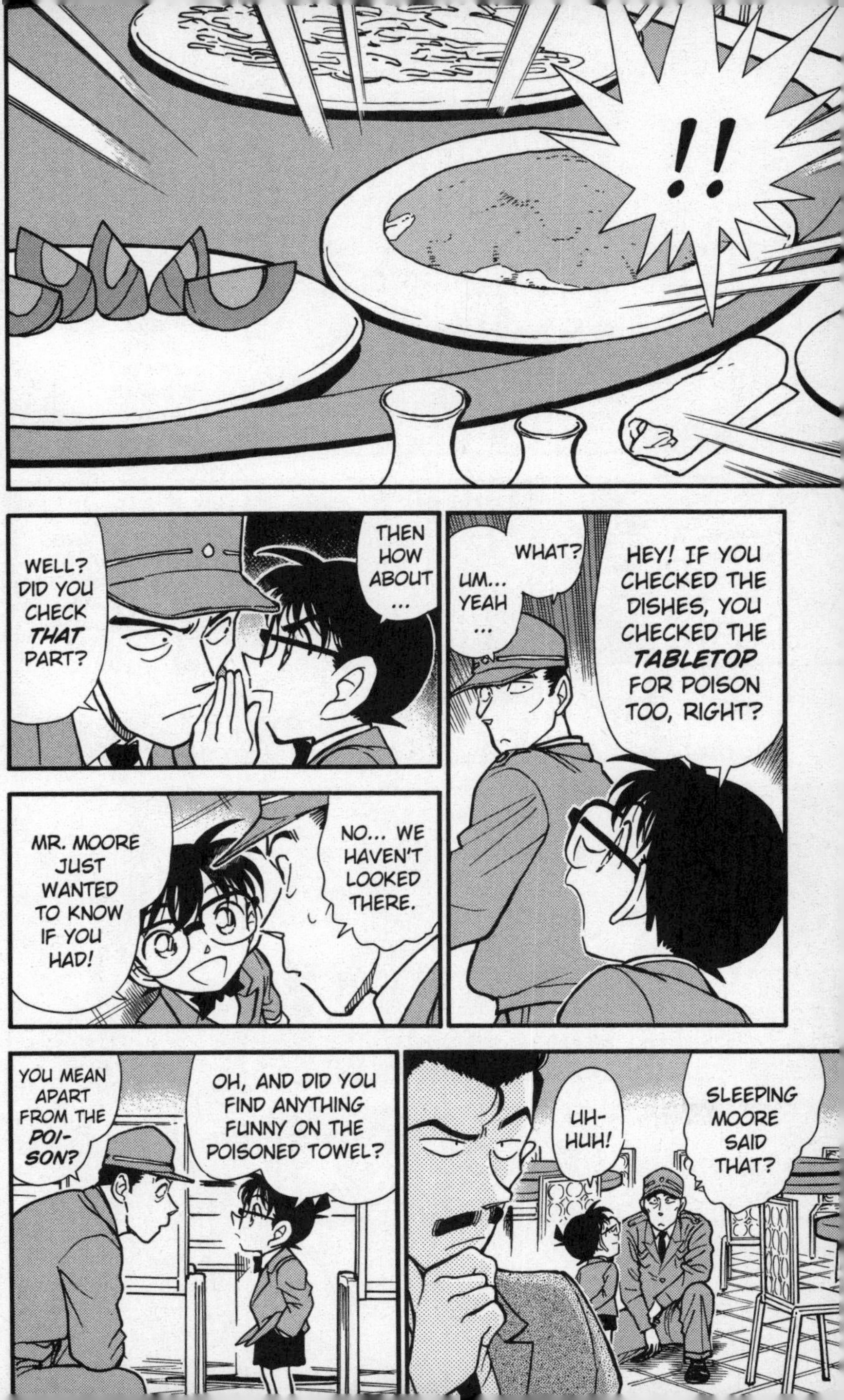
!!
HEY! IF YOU CHECKED THE DISHES, YOU CHECKED THE TABLETOP FOR POISON TOO, RIGHT?
WHAT?
UM... YEAH ...
THEN HOW ABOUT ...
WELL? DID YOU CHECK THAT PART?
NO... WE HAVEN'T LOOKED THERE.
MR. MOORE JUST WANTED TO KNOW IF YOU HAD!
SLEEPING MOORE SAID THAT?
UH-HUH!
OH, AND DID YOU FIND ANYTHING FUNNY ON THE POISONED TOWEL?
YOU MEAN APART FROM THE POI-SON?

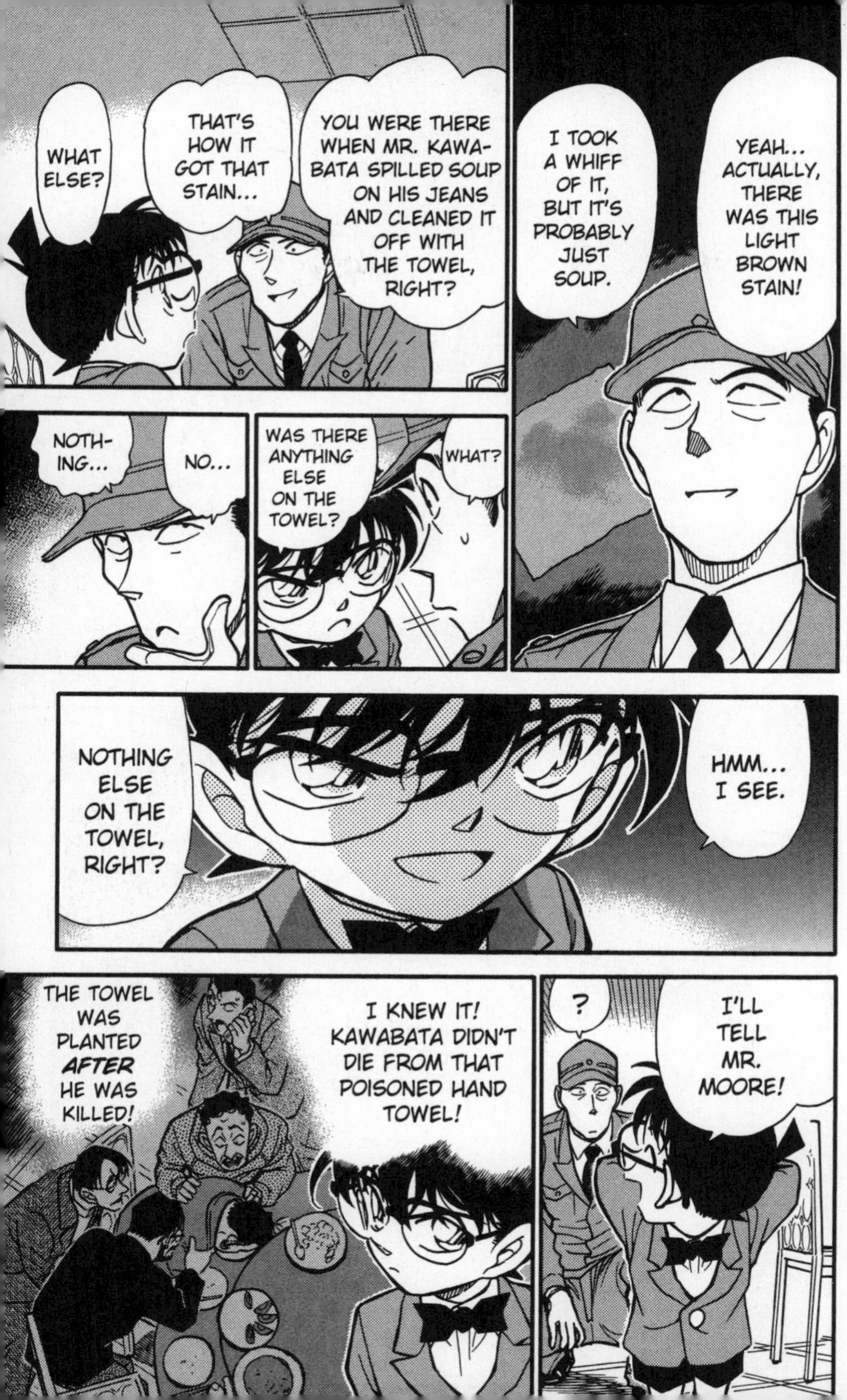
YEAH... ACTUALLY, THERE WAS THIS LIGHT BROWN STAIN!
I TOOK A WHIFF OF IT, BUT IT'S PROBABLY JUST SOUP.
YOU WERE THERE WHEN MR. KAWA-BATA SPILLED SOUP ON HIS JEANS AND CLEANED IT OFF WITH THE TOWEL, RIGHT?
THAT'S HOW IT GOT THAT STAIN...
WHAT ELSE?
WHAT?
WAS THERE ANYTHING ELSE ON THE TOWEL?
NO...
NOTH-ING...
HMM... I SEE.
NOTHING ELSE ON THE TOWEL, RIGHT?
I'LL TELL MR. MOORE!
?
I KNEW IT! KAWABATA DIDN'T DIE FROM THAT POISONED HAND TOWEL!
THE TOWEL WAS PLANTED AFTER HE WAS KILLED!

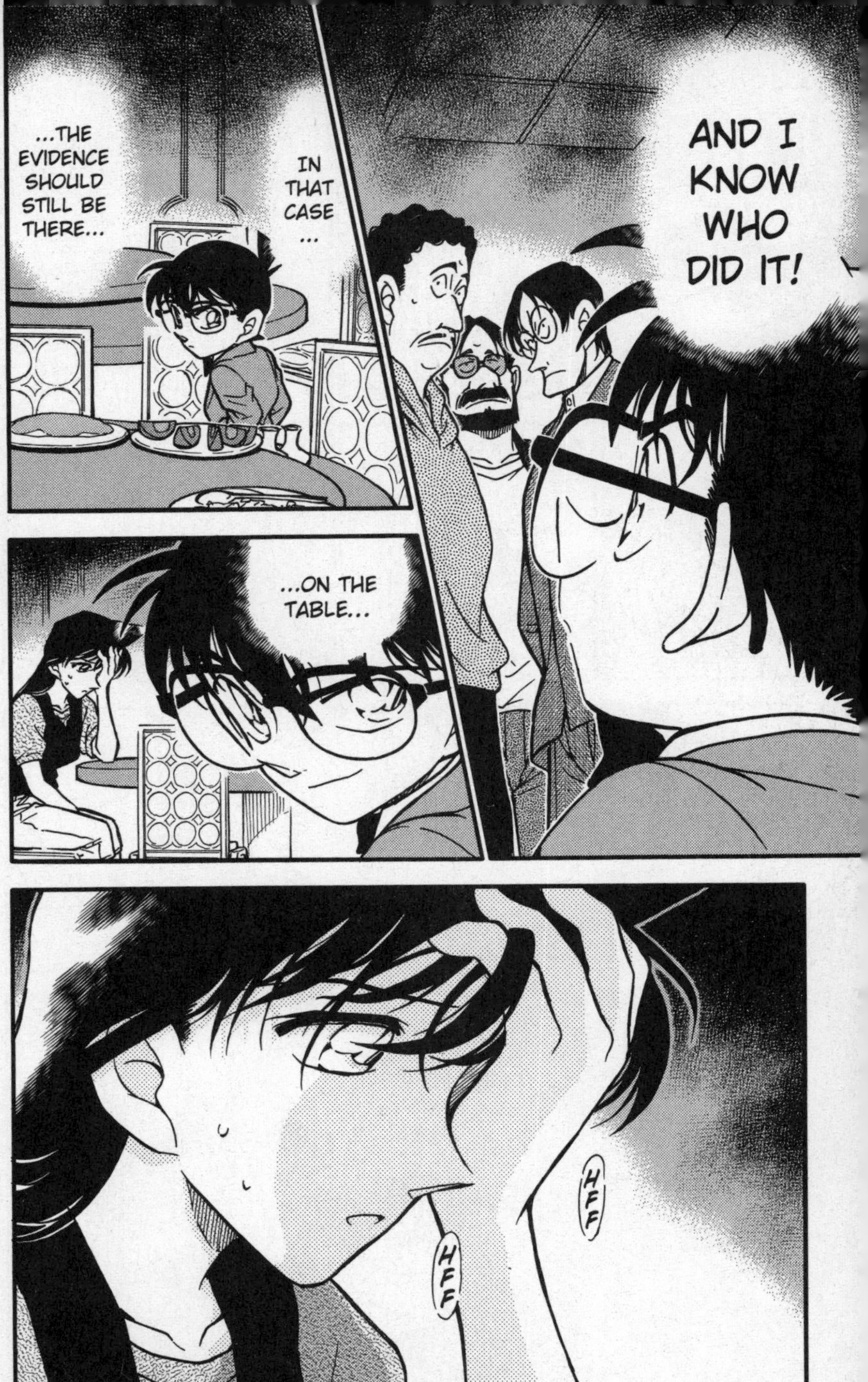
AND I KNOW WHO DID IT!
IN THAT CASE...
...THE EVIDENCE SHOULD STILL BE THERE...
...ON THE TABLE...
HFF
HFF

MEMORY REFRESHED

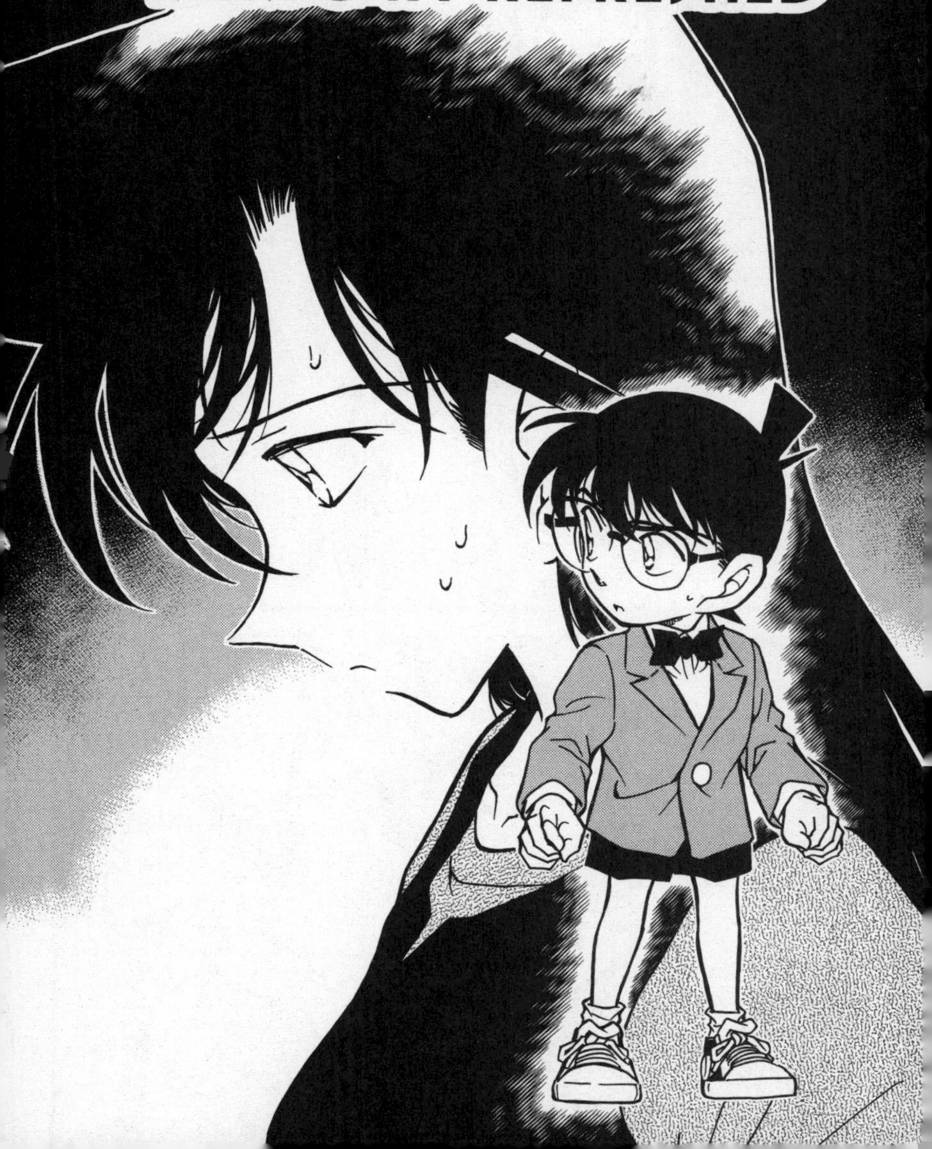

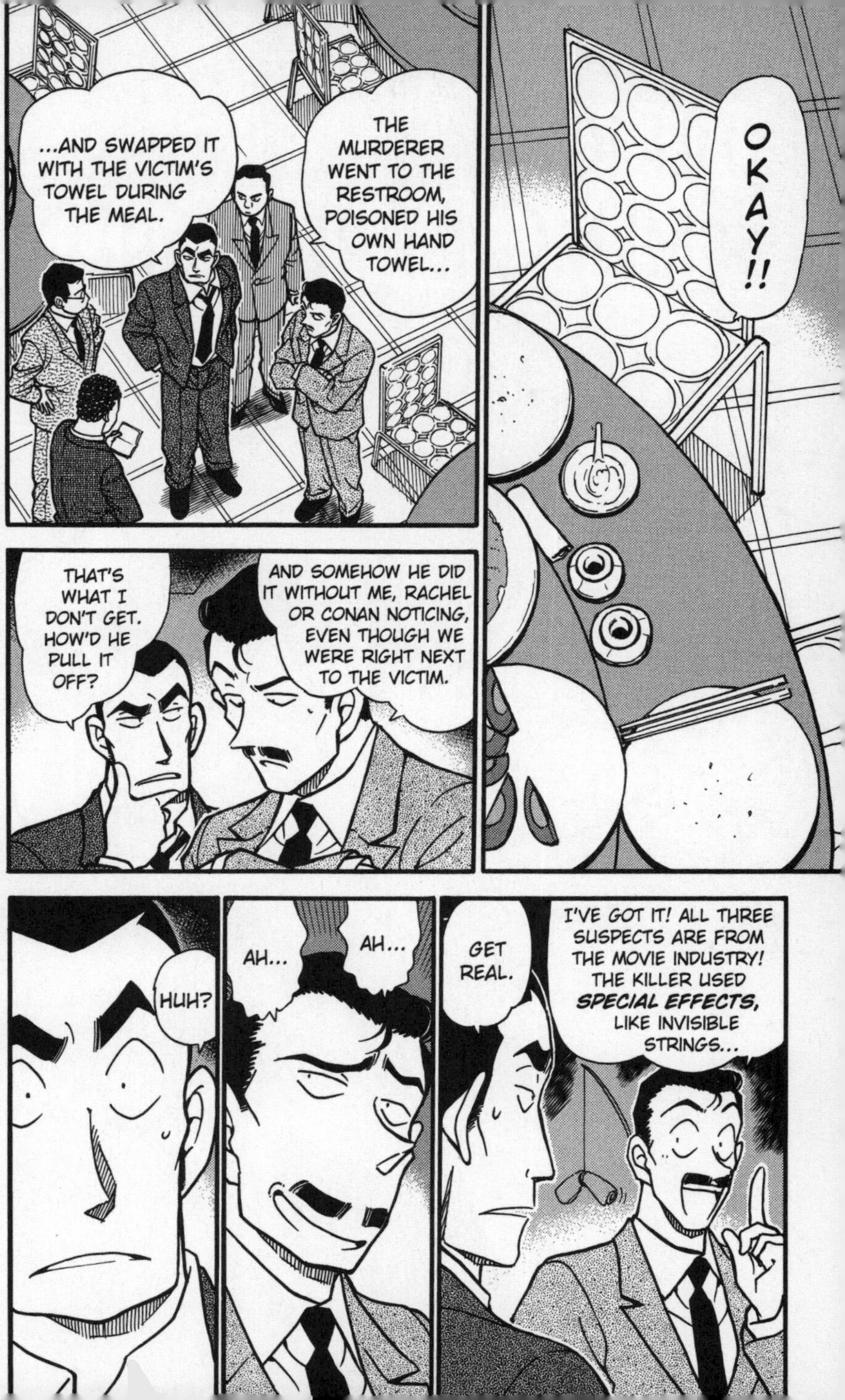
OKAY!!
THE MURDERER WENT TO THE RESTROOM, POISONED HIS OWN HAND TOWEL...
...AND SWAPPED IT WITH THE VICTIM'S TOWEL DURING THE MEAL.
AND SOMEHOW HE DID IT WITHOUT ME, RACHEL OR CONAN NOTICING, EVEN THOUGH WE WERE RIGHT NEXT TO THE VICTIM.
THAT'S WHAT I DON'T GET. HOW'D HE PULL IT OFF?
I'VE GOT IT! ALL THREE SUSPECTS ARE FROM THE MOVIE INDUSTRY! THE KILLER USED SPECIAL EFFECTS, LIKE INVISIBLE STRINGS...
GET REAL.
AH...
AH...
HUH?

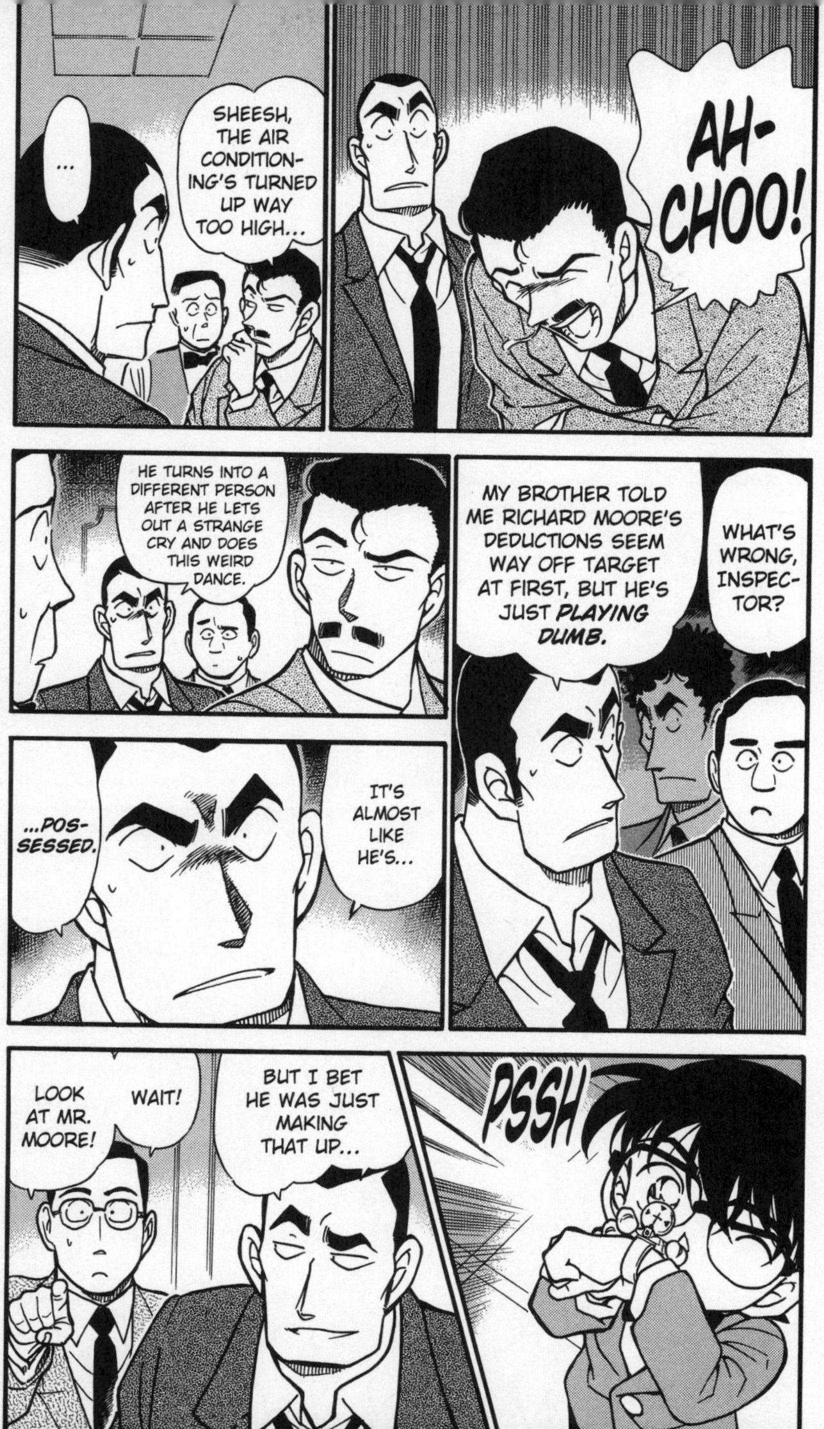
AH-CHOO!
SHEESH, THE AIR CONDITIONING'S TURNED UP WAY TOO HIGH...
...
WHAT'S WRONG, INSPECTOR?
MY BROTHER TOLD ME RICHARD MOORE'S DEDUCTIONS SEEM WAY OFF TARGET AT FIRST, BUT HE'S JUST **PLAYING DUMB.**
HE TURNS INTO A DIFFERENT PERSON AFTER HE LETS OUT A STRANGE CRY AND DOES THIS WEIRD DANCE.
IT'S ALMOST LIKE HE'S...
...POSSESSED.
PSSH
BUT I BET HE WAS JUST MAKING THAT UP...
WAIT!
LOOK AT MR. MOORE!

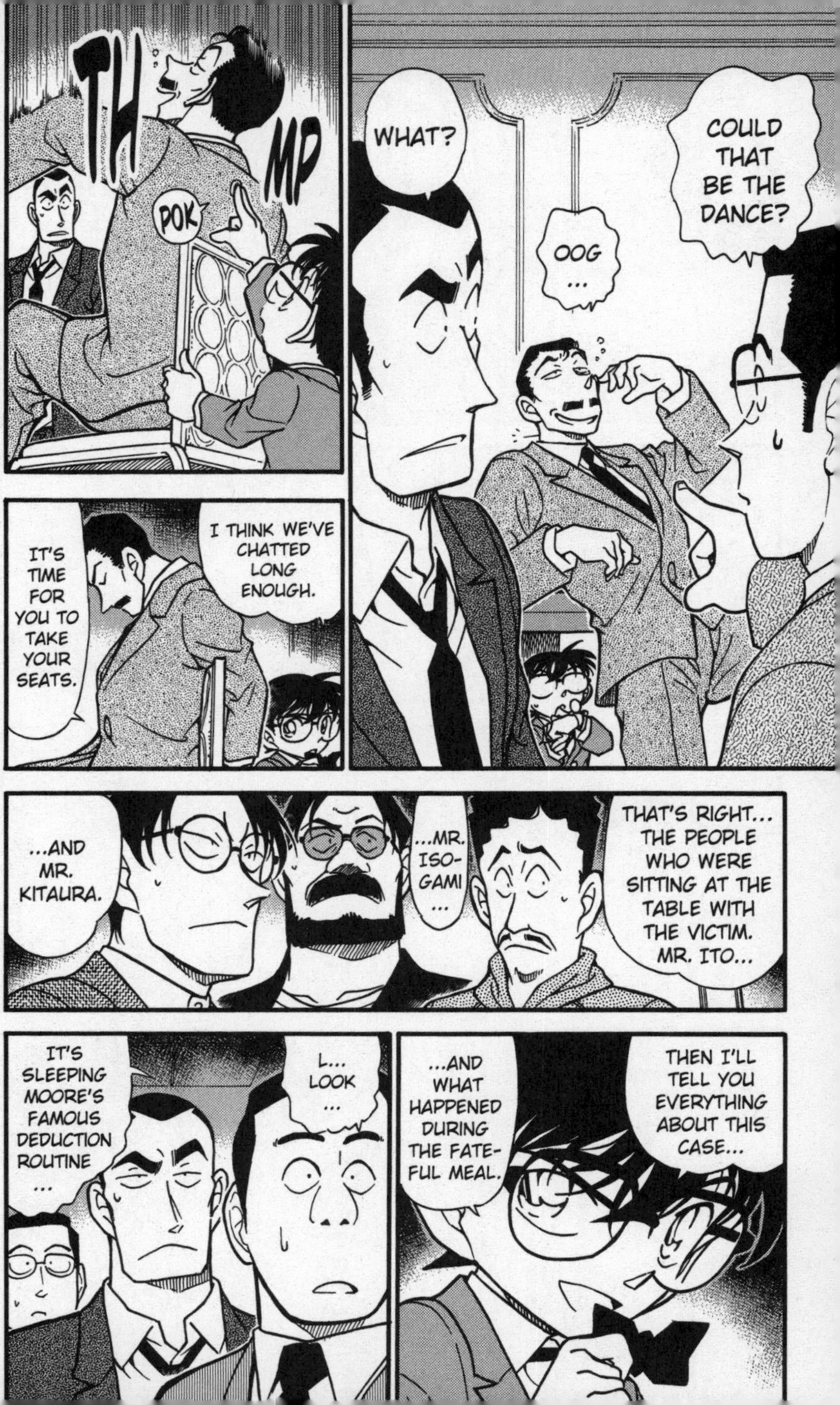
COULD THAT BE THE DANCE?
OOG ...
WHAT?
TH MP
POK
I THINK WE'VE CHATTED LONG ENOUGH.
IT'S TIME FOR YOU TO TAKE YOUR SEATS.
THAT'S RIGHT... THE PEOPLE WHO WERE SITTING AT THE TABLE WITH THE VICTIM. MR. ITO...
...MR. ISO-GAMI ...
...AND MR. KITAURA.
THEN I'LL TELL YOU EVERYTHING ABOUT THIS CASE...
...AND WHAT HAPPENED DURING THE FATE-FUL MEAL.
L... LOOK ...
IT'S SLEEPING MOORE'S FAMOUS DEDUCTION ROUTINE ...

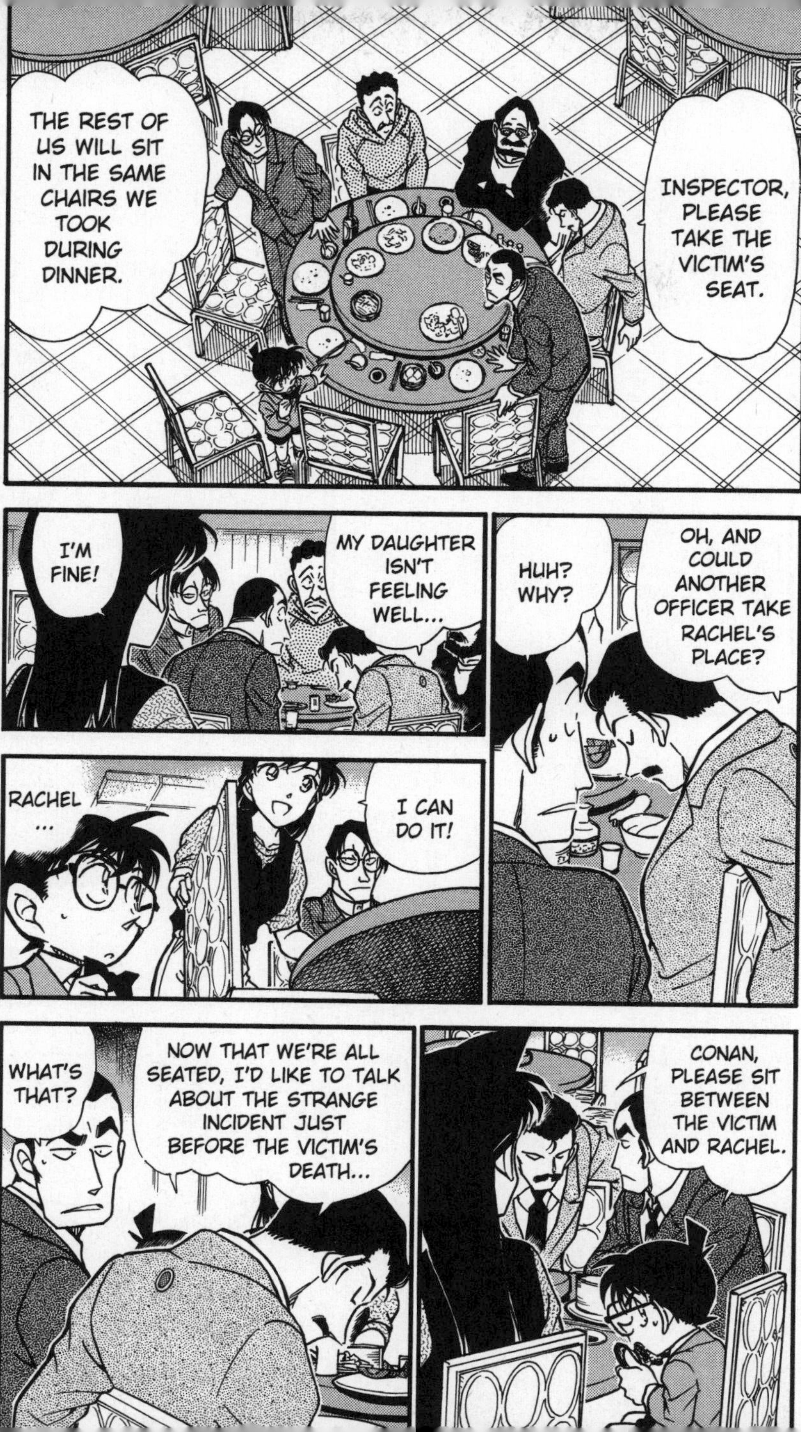
INSPECTOR, PLEASE TAKE THE VICTIM'S SEAT.
THE REST OF US WILL SIT IN THE SAME CHAIRS WE TOOK DURING DINNER.
OH, AND COULD ANOTHER OFFICER TAKE RACHEL'S PLACE?
HUH? WHY?
MY DAUGHTER ISN'T FEELING WELL...
I'M FINE!
I CAN DO IT!
RACHEL...
CONAN, PLEASE SIT BETWEEN THE VICTIM AND RACHEL.
NOW THAT WE'RE ALL SEATED, I'D LIKE TO TALK ABOUT THE STRANGE INCIDENT JUST BEFORE THE VICTIM'S DEATH...
WHAT'S THAT?

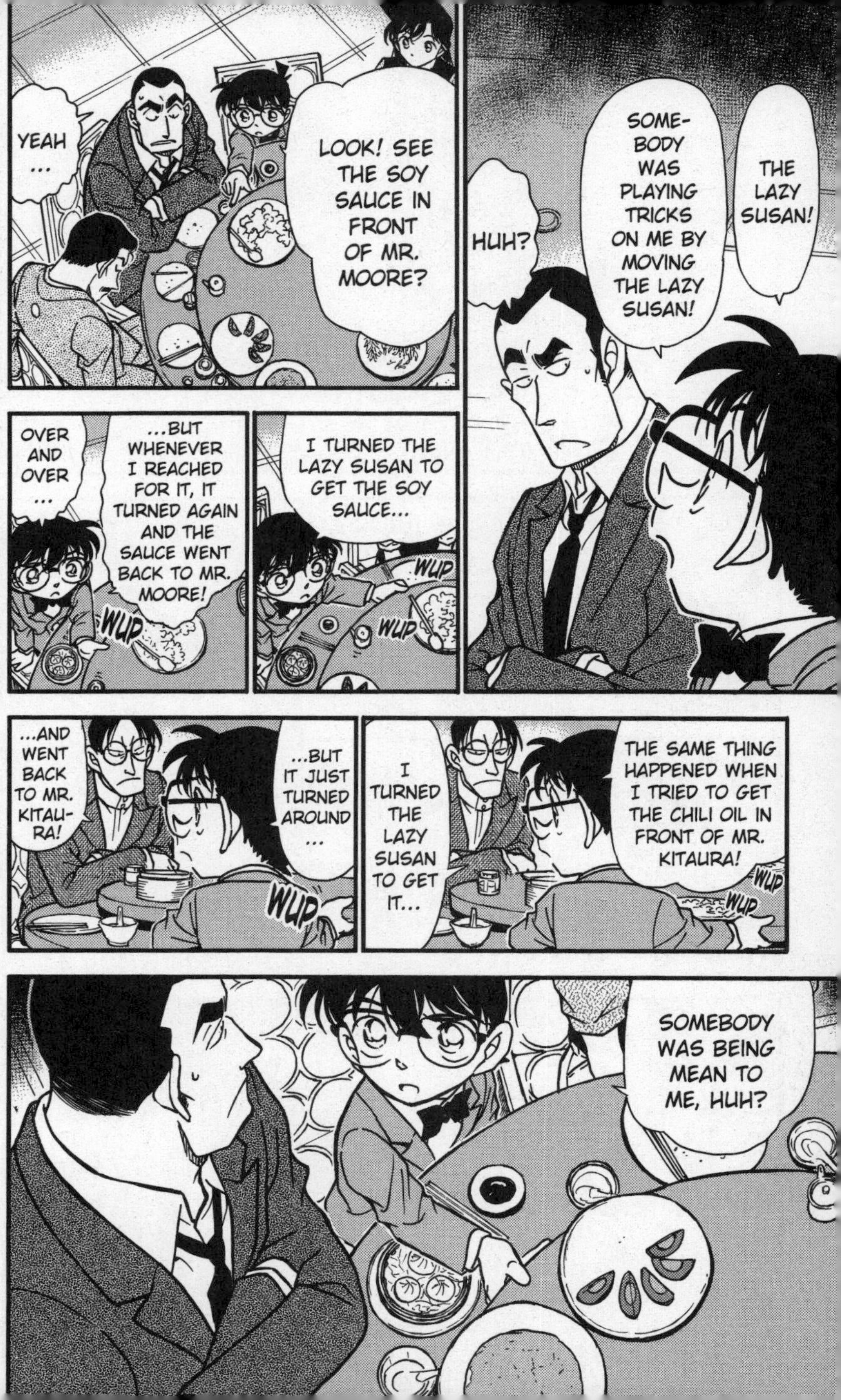
THE LAZY SUSAN!
SOME-BODY WAS PLAYING TRICKS ON ME BY MOVING THE LAZY SUSAN!
HUH?
LOOK! SEE THE SOY SAUCE IN FRONT OF MR. MOORE?
YEAH ...
I TURNED THE LAZY SUSAN TO GET THE SOY SAUCE...
WUP
WUP
...BUT WHENEVER I REACHED FOR IT, IT TURNED AGAIN AND THE SAUCE WENT BACK TO MR. MOORE!
OVER AND OVER ...
WUP
THE SAME THING HAPPENED WHEN I TRIED TO GET THE CHILI OIL IN FRONT OF MR. KITAURA!
WUP
WUP
I TURNED THE LAZY SUSAN TO GET IT...
...BUT IT JUST TURNED AROUND ...
WUP
...AND WENT BACK TO MR. KITAU-RA!
SOMEBODY WAS BEING MEAN TO ME, HUH?

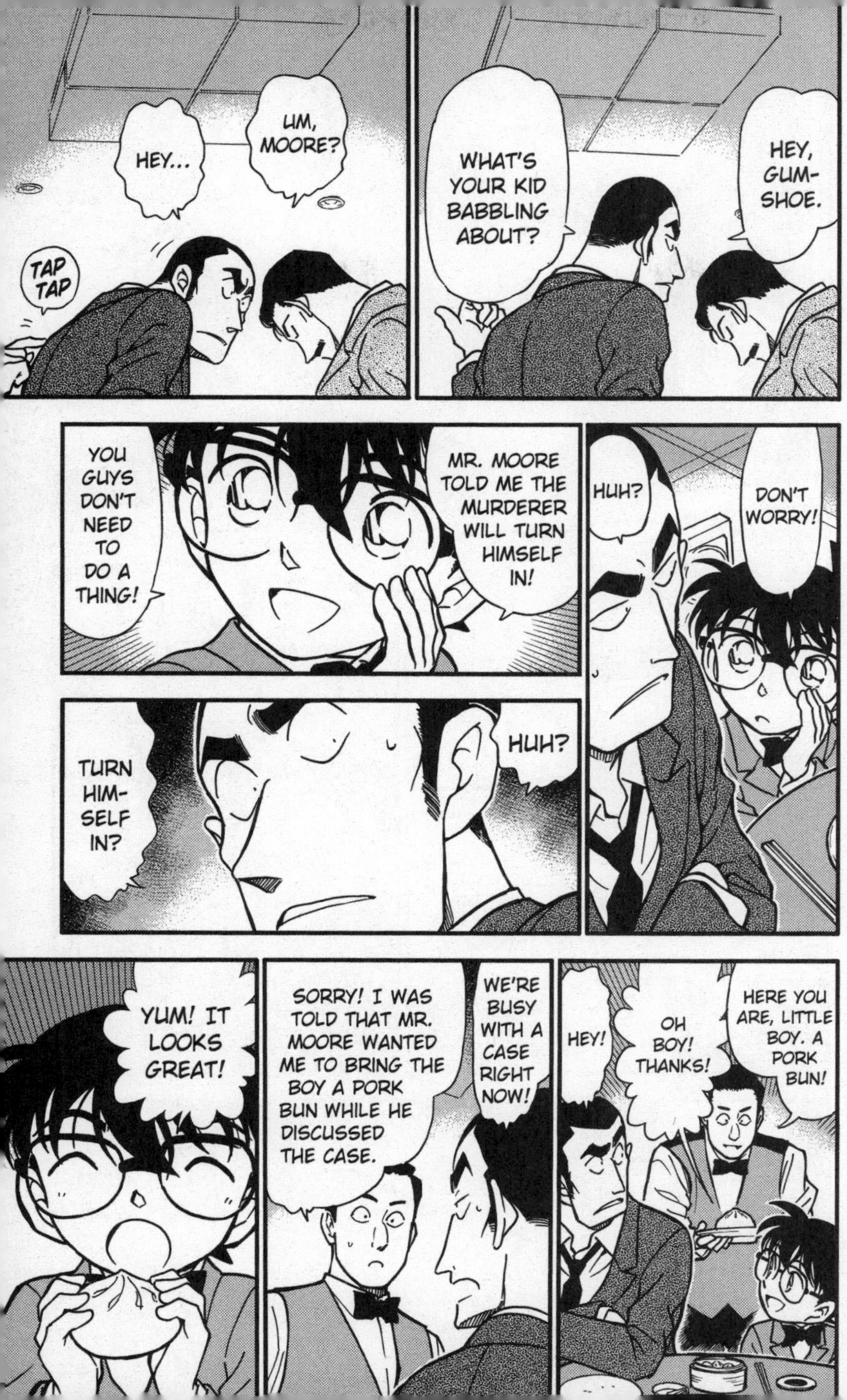
HEY, GUM-SHOE.
WHAT'S YOUR KID BABBLING ABOUT?
UM, MOORE?
HEY...
TAP TAP
DON'T WORRY!
HUH?
MR. MOORE TOLD ME THE MURDERER WILL TURN HIMSELF IN!
YOU GUYS DON'T NEED TO DO A THING!
HUH?
TURN HIM-SELF IN?
HERE YOU ARE, LITTLE BOY. A PORK BUN!
OH BOY! THANKS!
HEY!
WE'RE BUSY WITH A CASE RIGHT NOW!
SORRY! I WAS TOLD THAT MR. MOORE WANTED ME TO BRING THE BOY A PORK BUN WHILE HE DISCUSSED THE CASE.
YUM! IT LOOKS GREAT!

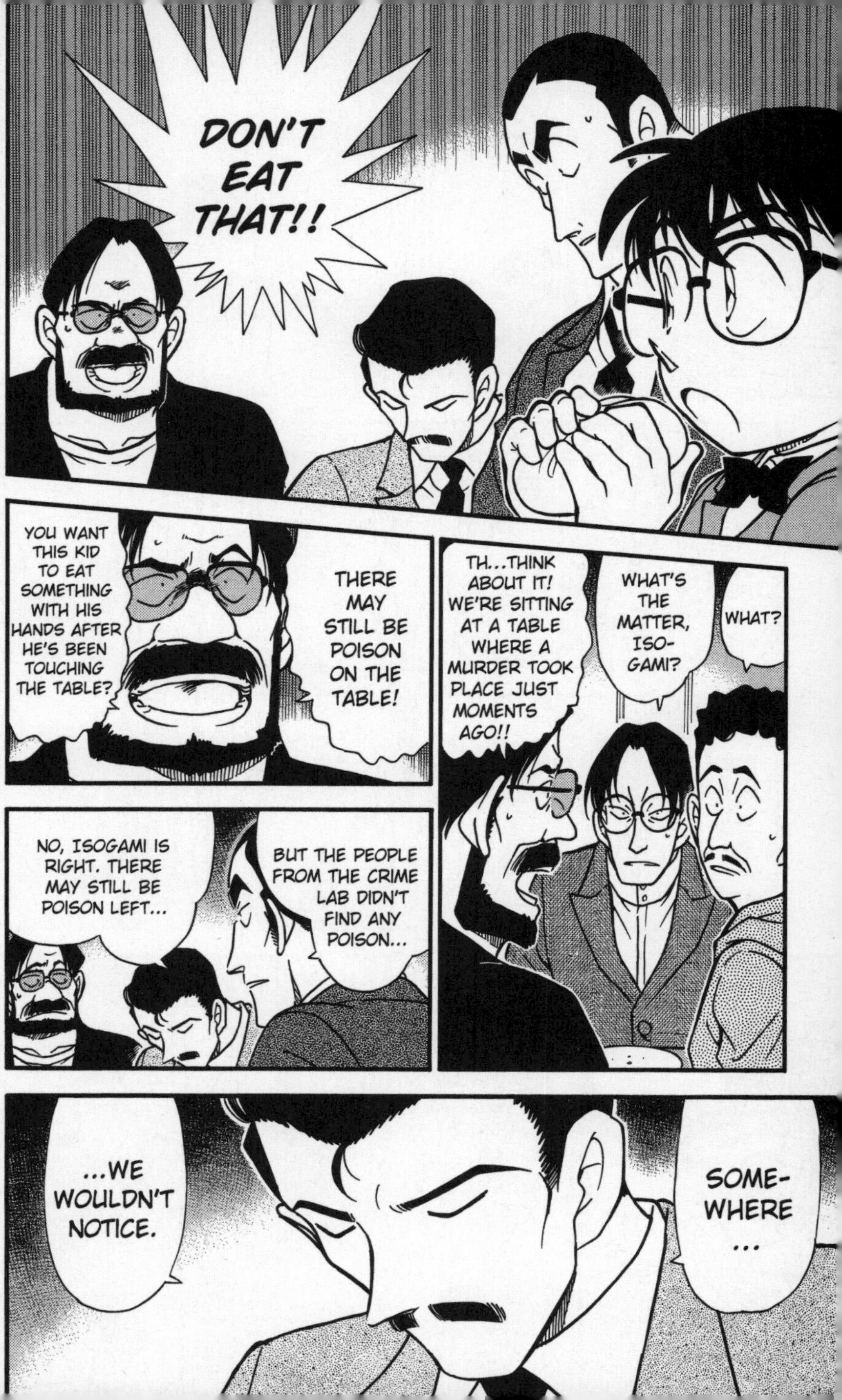
DON'T EAT THAT!!
WHAT?
WHAT'S THE MATTER, ISO-GAMI?
TH...THINK ABOUT IT! WE'RE SITTING AT A TABLE WHERE A MURDER TOOK PLACE JUST MOMENTS AGO!!
THERE MAY STILL BE POISON ON THE TABLE!
YOU WANT THIS KID TO EAT SOMETHING WITH HIS HANDS AFTER HE'S BEEN TOUCHING THE TABLE?
BUT THE PEOPLE FROM THE CRIME LAB DIDN'T FIND ANY POISON...
NO, ISOGAMI IS RIGHT. THERE MAY STILL BE POISON LEFT...
SOME-WHERE...
...WE WOULDN'T NOTICE.

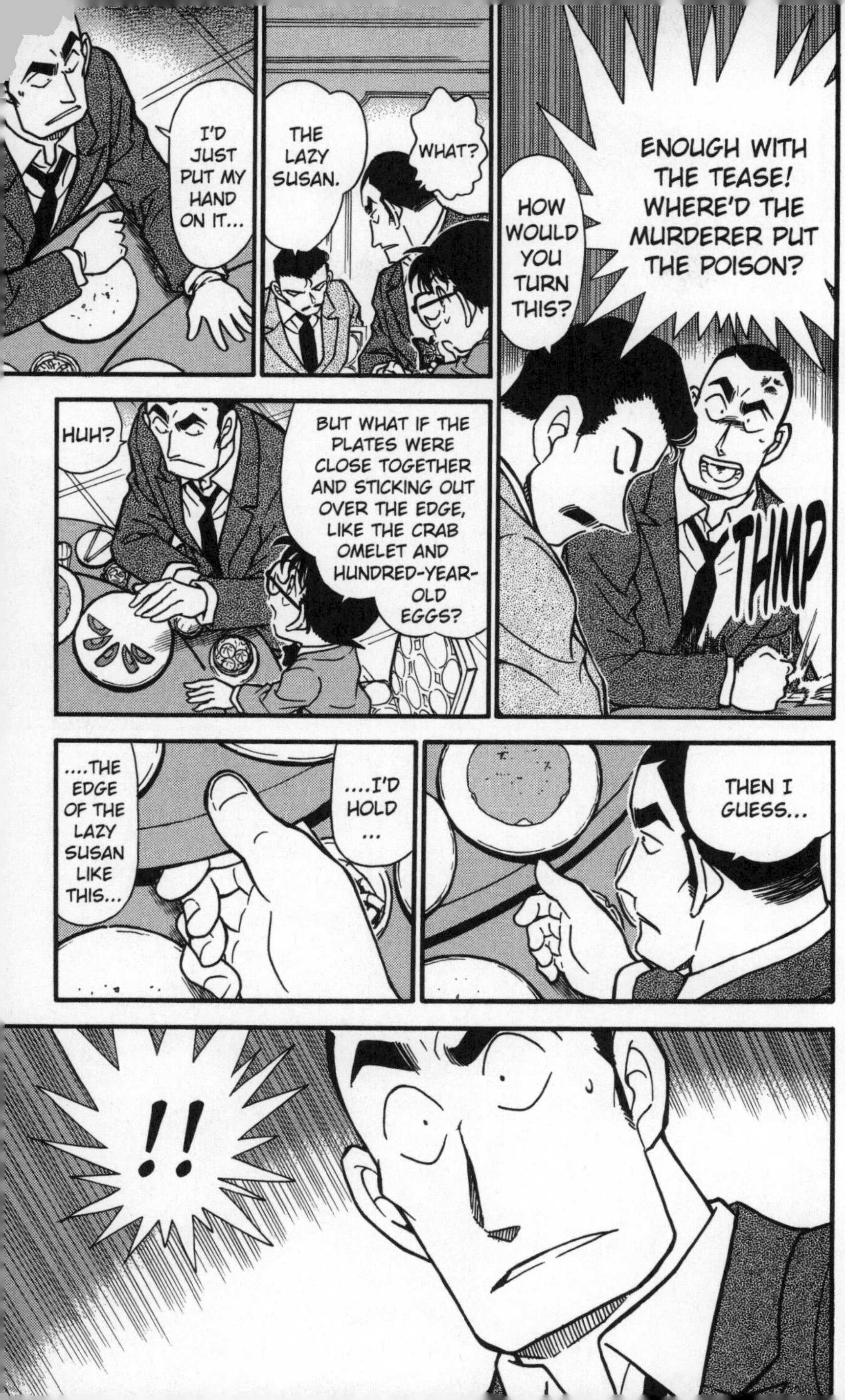
ENOUGH WITH THE TEASE! WHERE'D THE MURDERER PUT THE POISON?
HOW WOULD YOU TURN THIS?
THMP
WHAT?
THE LAZY SUSAN.
I'D JUST PUT MY HAND ON IT...
BUT WHAT IF THE PLATES WERE CLOSE TOGETHER AND STICKING OUT OVER THE EDGE, LIKE THE CRAB OMELET AND HUNDRED-YEAR-OLD EGGS?
HUH?
THEN I GUESS...
....I'D HOLD ...
....THE EDGE OF THE LAZY SUSAN LIKE THIS...
!!

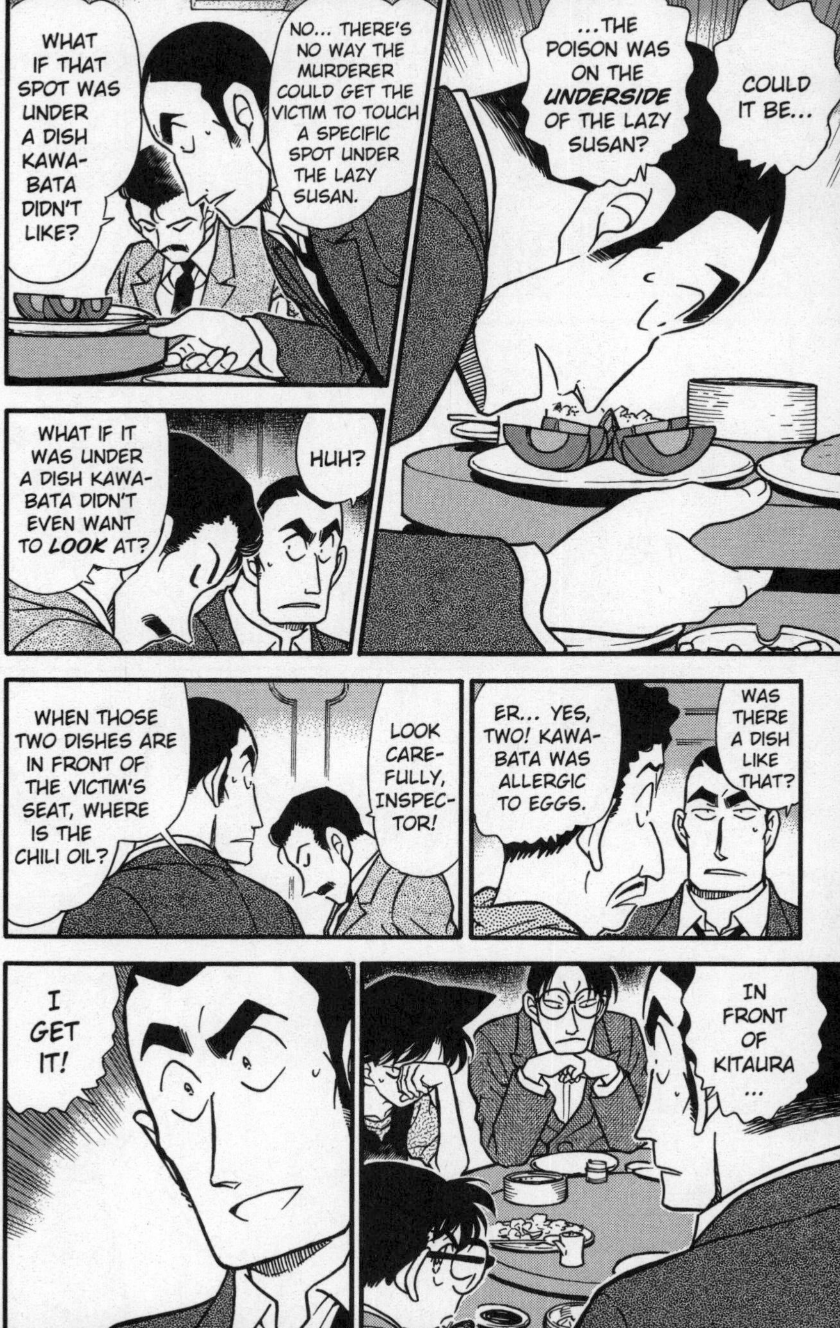
COULD IT BE...
...THE POISON WAS ON THE **UNDERSIDE** OF THE LAZY SUSAN?
NO... THERE'S NO WAY THE MURDERER COULD GET THE VICTIM TO TOUCH A SPECIFIC SPOT UNDER THE LAZY SUSAN.
WHAT IF THAT SPOT WAS UNDER A DISH KAWA-BATA DIDN'T LIKE?
HUH?
WHAT IF IT WAS UNDER A DISH KAWA-BATA DIDN'T EVEN WANT TO **LOOK** AT?
WAS THERE A DISH LIKE THAT?
ER... YES, TWO! KAWA-BATA WAS ALLERGIC TO EGGS.
LOOK CARE-FULLY, INSPEC-TOR!
WHEN THOSE TWO DISHES ARE IN FRONT OF THE VICTIM'S SEAT, WHERE IS THE CHILI OIL?
IN FRONT OF KITAURA ...
I GET IT!

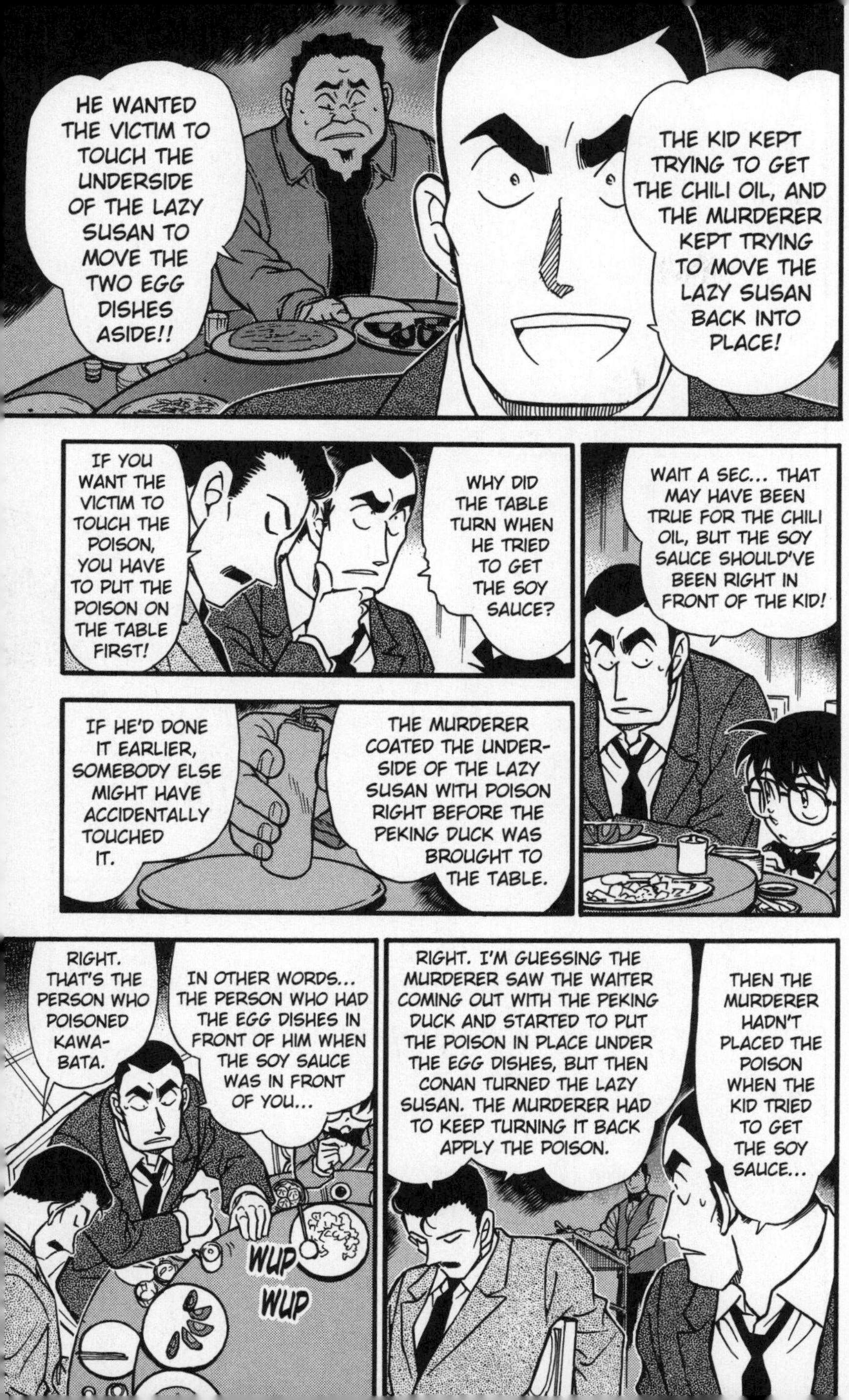
THE KID KEPT TRYING TO GET THE CHILI OIL, AND THE MURDERER KEPT TRYING TO MOVE THE LAZY SUSAN BACK INTO PLACE!
HE WANTED THE VICTIM TO TOUCH THE UNDERSIDE OF THE LAZY SUSAN TO MOVE THE TWO EGG DISHES ASIDE!!
WAIT A SEC... THAT MAY HAVE BEEN TRUE FOR THE CHILI OIL, BUT THE SOY SAUCE SHOULD'VE BEEN RIGHT IN FRONT OF THE KID!
WHY DID THE TABLE TURN WHEN HE TRIED TO GET THE SOY SAUCE?
IF YOU WANT THE VICTIM TO TOUCH THE POISON, YOU HAVE TO PUT THE POISON ON THE TABLE FIRST!
THE MURDERER COATED THE UNDER-SIDE OF THE LAZY SUSAN WITH POISON RIGHT BEFORE THE PEKING DUCK WAS BROUGHT TO THE TABLE.
IF HE'D DONE IT EARLIER, SOMEBODY ELSE MIGHT HAVE ACCIDENTALLY TOUCHED IT.
THEN THE MURDERER HADN'T PLACED THE POISON WHEN THE KID TRIED TO GET THE SOY SAUCE...
RIGHT. I'M GUESSING THE MURDERER SAW THE WAITER COMING OUT WITH THE PEKING DUCK AND STARTED TO PUT THE POISON IN PLACE UNDER THE EGG DISHES, BUT THEN CONAN TURNED THE LAZY SUSAN. THE MURDERER HAD TO KEEP TURNING IT BACK APPLY THE POISON.
IN OTHER WORDS... THE PERSON WHO HAD THE EGG DISHES IN FRONT OF HIM WHEN THE SOY SAUCE WAS IN FRONT OF YOU...
RIGHT. THAT'S THE PERSON WHO POISONED KAWA-BATA.
WUP
WUP

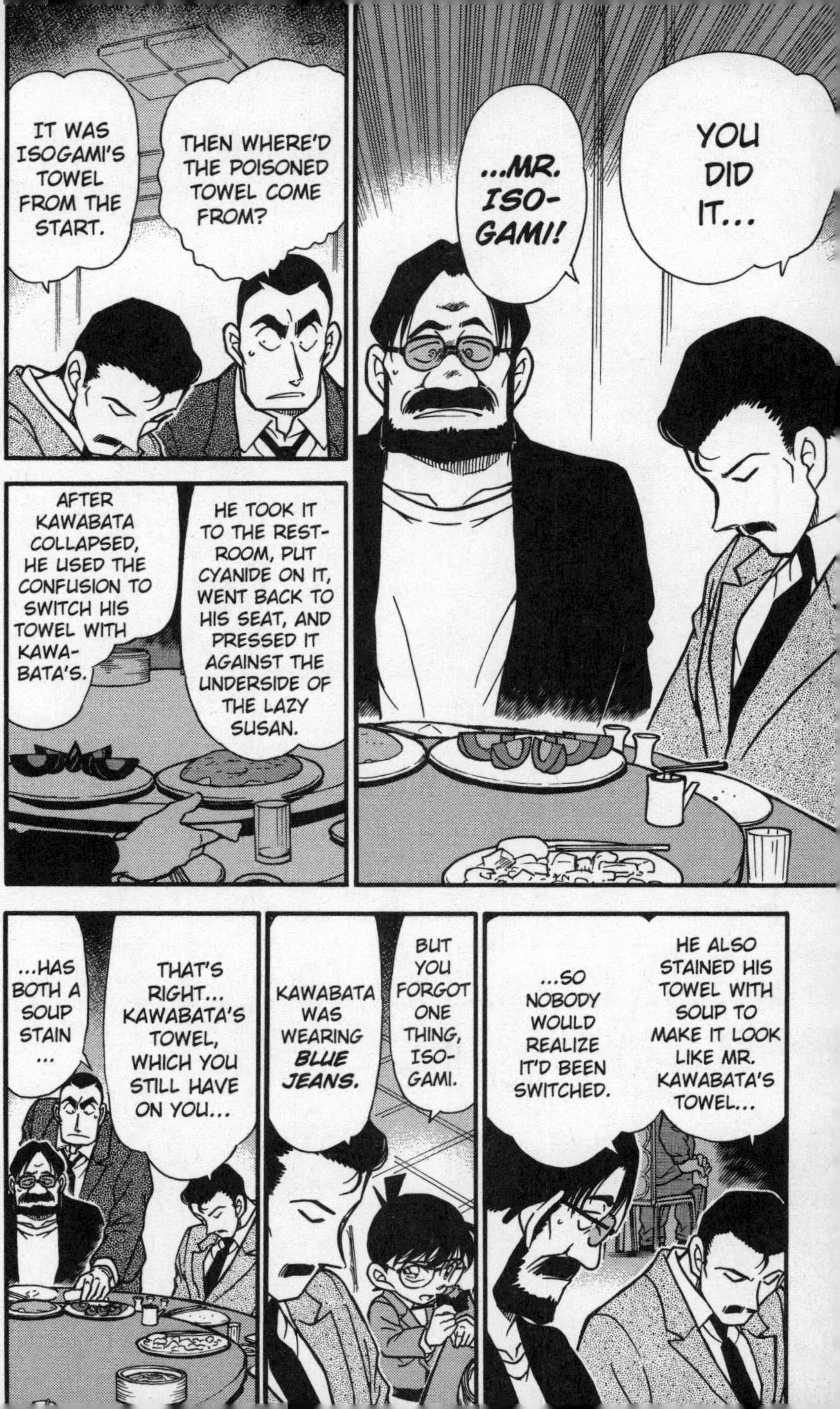
YOU DID IT...
...MR. ISO-GAMI!
THEN WHERE'D THE POISONED TOWEL COME FROM?
IT WAS ISOGAMI'S TOWEL FROM THE START.
HE TOOK IT TO THE REST-ROOM, PUT CYANIDE ON IT, WENT BACK TO HIS SEAT, AND PRESSED IT AGAINST THE UNDERSIDE OF THE LAZY SUSAN.
AFTER KAWABATA COLLAPSED, HE USED THE CONFUSION TO SWITCH HIS TOWEL WITH KAWA-BATA'S.
HE ALSO STAINED HIS TOWEL WITH SOUP TO MAKE IT LOOK LIKE MR. KAWABATA'S TOWEL...
...SO NOBODY WOULD REALIZE IT'D BEEN SWITCHED.
BUT YOU FORGOT ONE THING, ISO-GAMI.
KAWABATA WAS WEARING *BLUE JEANS.*
THAT'S RIGHT... KAWABATA'S TOWEL, WHICH YOU STILL HAVE ON YOU...
...HAS BOTH A SOUP STAIN ...

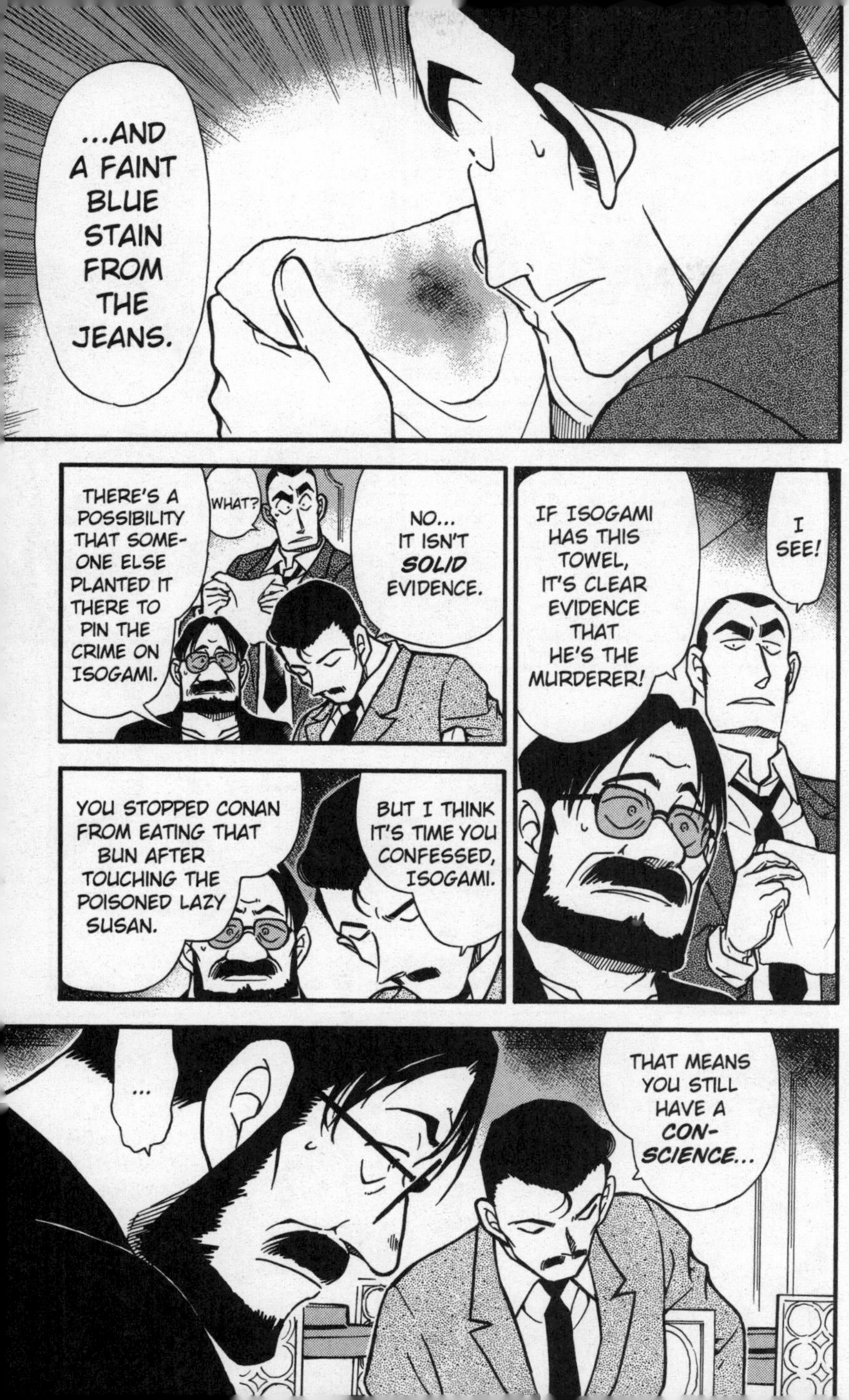
...AND A FAINT BLUE STAIN FROM THE JEANS.
I SEE!
IF ISOGAMI HAS THIS TOWEL, IT'S CLEAR EVIDENCE THAT HE'S THE MURDERER!
NO... IT ISN'T *SOLID* EVIDENCE.
WHAT?
THERE'S A POSSIBILITY THAT SOME-ONE ELSE PLANTED IT THERE TO PIN THE CRIME ON ISOGAMI.
BUT I THINK IT'S TIME YOU CONFESSED, ISOGAMI.
YOU STOPPED CONAN FROM EATING THAT BUN AFTER TOUCHING THE POISONED LAZY SUSAN.
THAT MEANS YOU STILL HAVE A *CON-SCIENCE*...
...

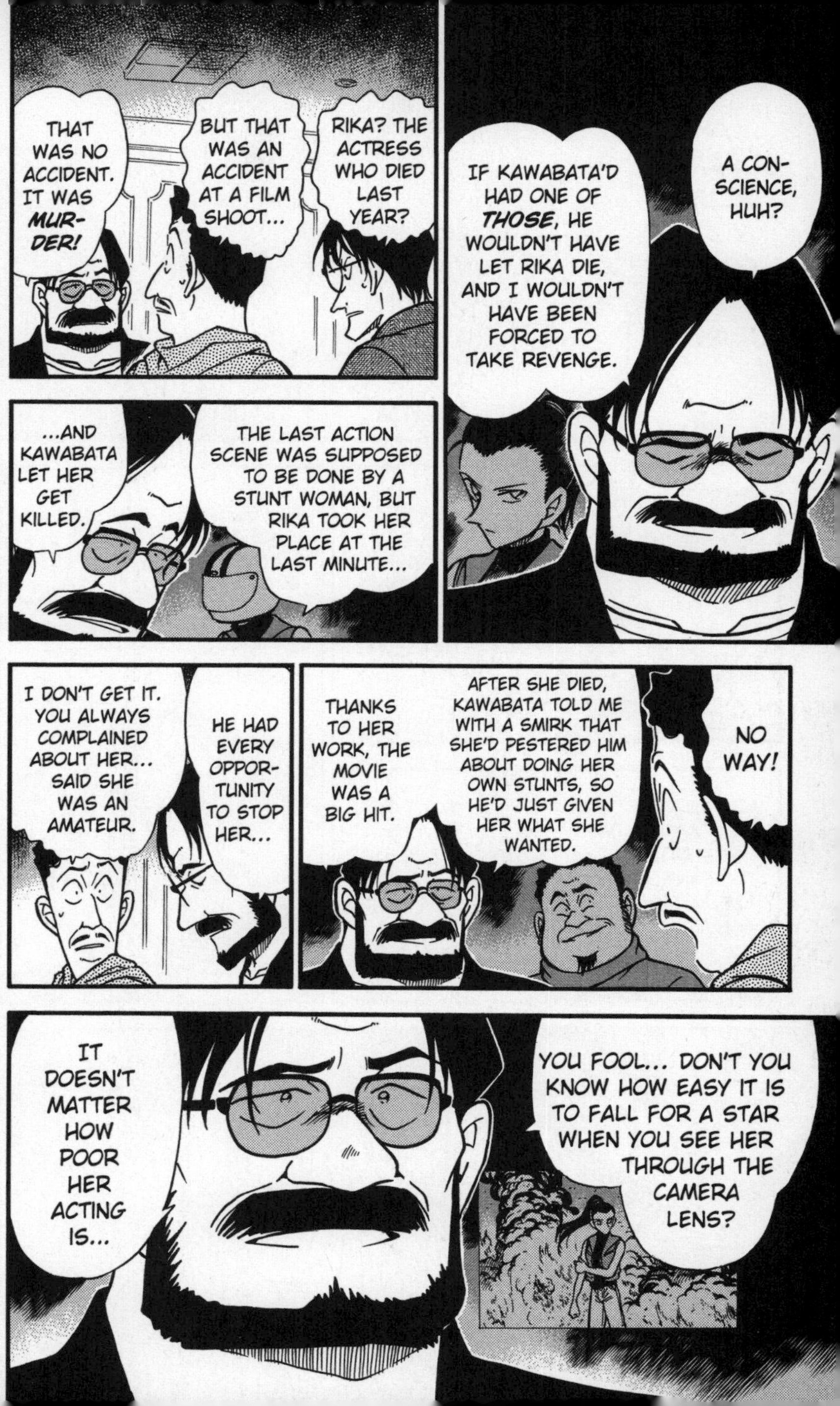
A CON-SCIENCE, HUH?
IF KAWABATA'D HAD ONE OF *THOSE*, HE WOULDN'T HAVE LET RIKA DIE, AND I WOULDN'T HAVE BEEN FORCED TO TAKE REVENGE.
RIKA? THE ACTRESS WHO DIED LAST YEAR?
BUT THAT WAS AN ACCIDENT AT A FILM SHOOT...
THAT WAS NO ACCIDENT. IT WAS *MUR-DER!*
THE LAST ACTION SCENE WAS SUPPOSED TO BE DONE BY A STUNT WOMAN, BUT RIKA TOOK HER PLACE AT THE LAST MINUTE...
...AND KAWABATA LET HER GET KILLED.
NO WAY!
AFTER SHE DIED, KAWABATA TOLD ME WITH A SMIRK THAT SHE'D PESTERED HIM ABOUT DOING HER OWN STUNTS, SO HE'D JUST GIVEN HER WHAT SHE WANTED.
THANKS TO HER WORK, THE MOVIE WAS A BIG HIT.
HE HAD EVERY OPPOR-TUNITY TO STOP HER...
I DON'T GET IT. YOU ALWAYS COMPLAINED ABOUT HER... SAID SHE WAS AN AMATEUR.
YOU FOOL... DON'T YOU KNOW HOW EASY IT IS TO FALL FOR A STAR WHEN YOU SEE HER THROUGH THE CAMERA LENS?
IT DOESN'T MATTER HOW POOR HER ACTING IS...

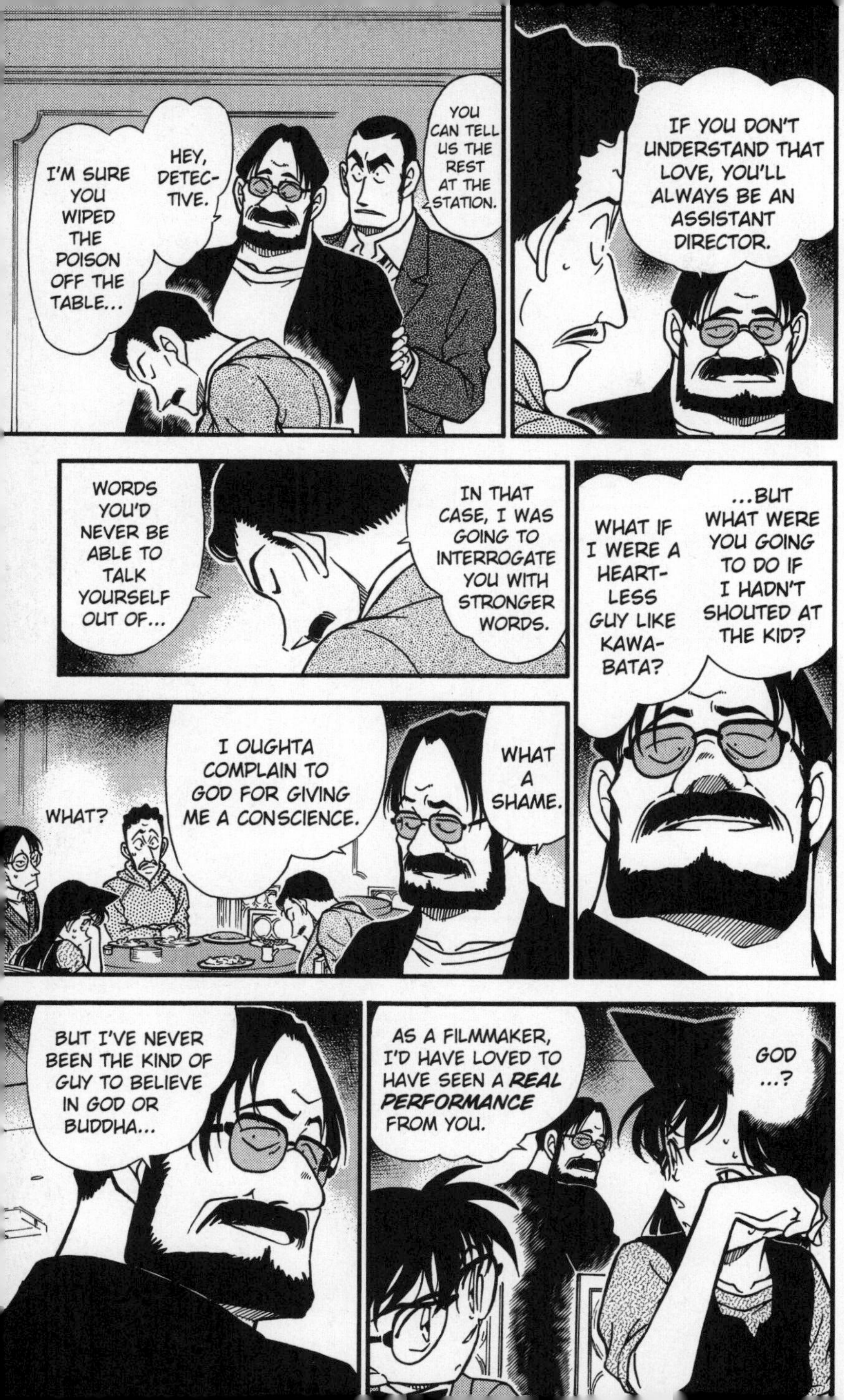
IF YOU DON'T UNDERSTAND THAT LOVE, YOU'LL ALWAYS BE AN ASSISTANT DIRECTOR.
YOU CAN TELL US THE REST AT THE STATION.
HEY, DETECTIVE.
I'M SURE YOU WIPED THE POISON OFF THE TABLE...
...BUT WHAT WERE YOU GOING TO DO IF I HADN'T SHOUTED AT THE KID?
WHAT IF I WERE A HEARTLESS GUY LIKE KAWABATA?
IN THAT CASE, I WAS GOING TO INTERROGATE YOU WITH STRONGER WORDS.
WORDS YOU'D NEVER BE ABLE TO TALK YOURSELF OUT OF...
WHAT A SHAME.
I OUGHTA COMPLAIN TO GOD FOR GIVING ME A CONSCIENCE.
WHAT?
GOD ...?
AS A FILMMAKER, I'D HAVE LOVED TO HAVE SEEN A *REAL PERFORMANCE* FROM YOU.
BUT I'VE NEVER BEEN THE KIND OF GUY TO BELIEVE IN GOD OR BUDDHA...

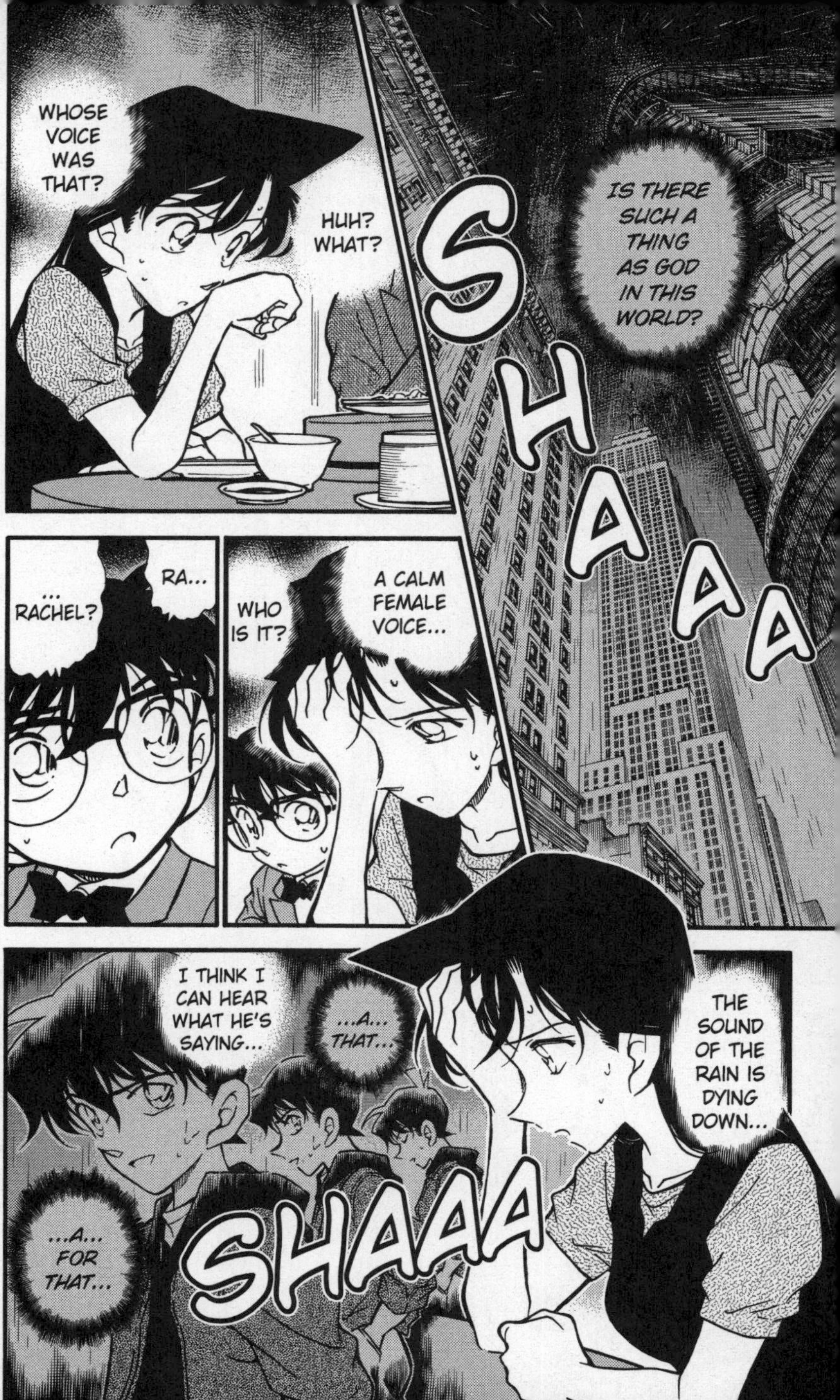
IS THERE SUCH A THING AS GOD IN THIS WORLD?
SHAAAA
HUH? WHAT?
WHOSE VOICE WAS THAT?
A CALM FEMALE VOICE...
WHO IS IT?
RA...
...RACHEL?
THE SOUND OF THE RAIN IS DYING DOWN...
...A... THAT...
I THINK I CAN HEAR WHAT HE'S SAYING...
SHAAAA
...A... FOR THAT...

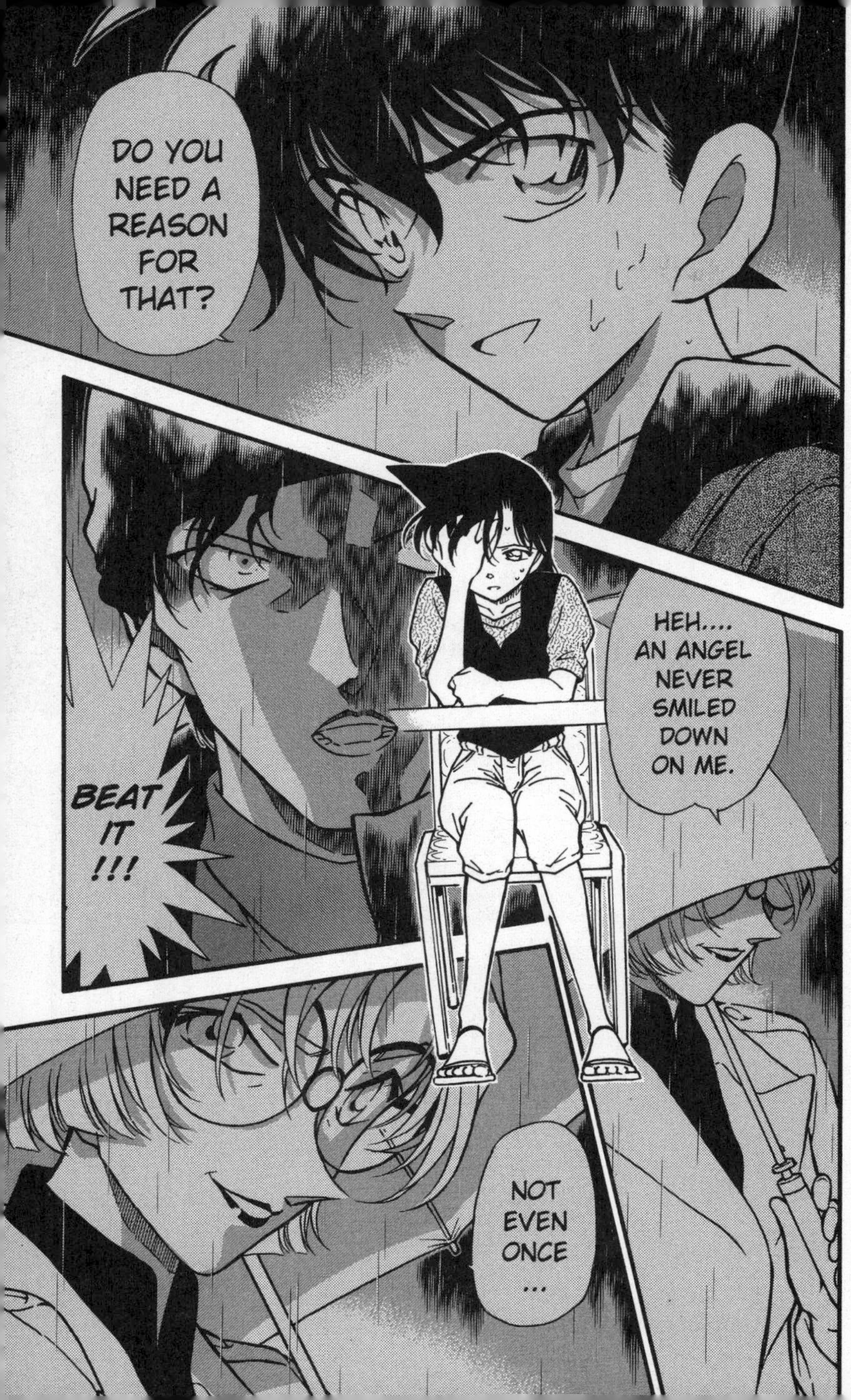
DO YOU NEED A REASON FOR THAT?
BEAT IT !!!
HEH.... AN ANGEL NEVER SMILED DOWN ON ME.
NOT EVEN ONCE ...

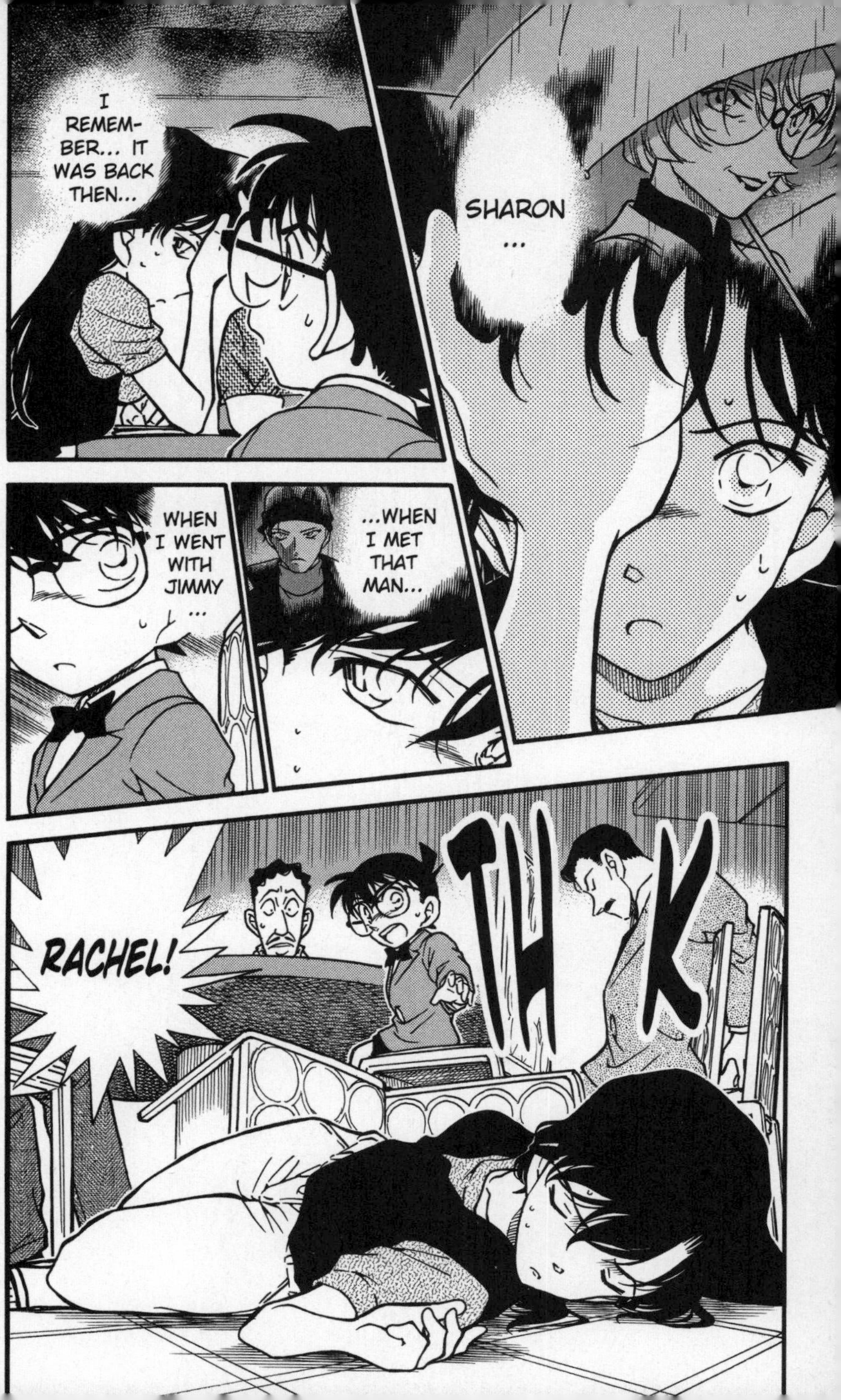
SHARON
...
I
REMEMBER... IT
WAS BACK
THEN...
...WHEN
I MET
THAT
MAN...
WHEN
I WENT
WITH
JIMMY
...
THK
RACHEL!

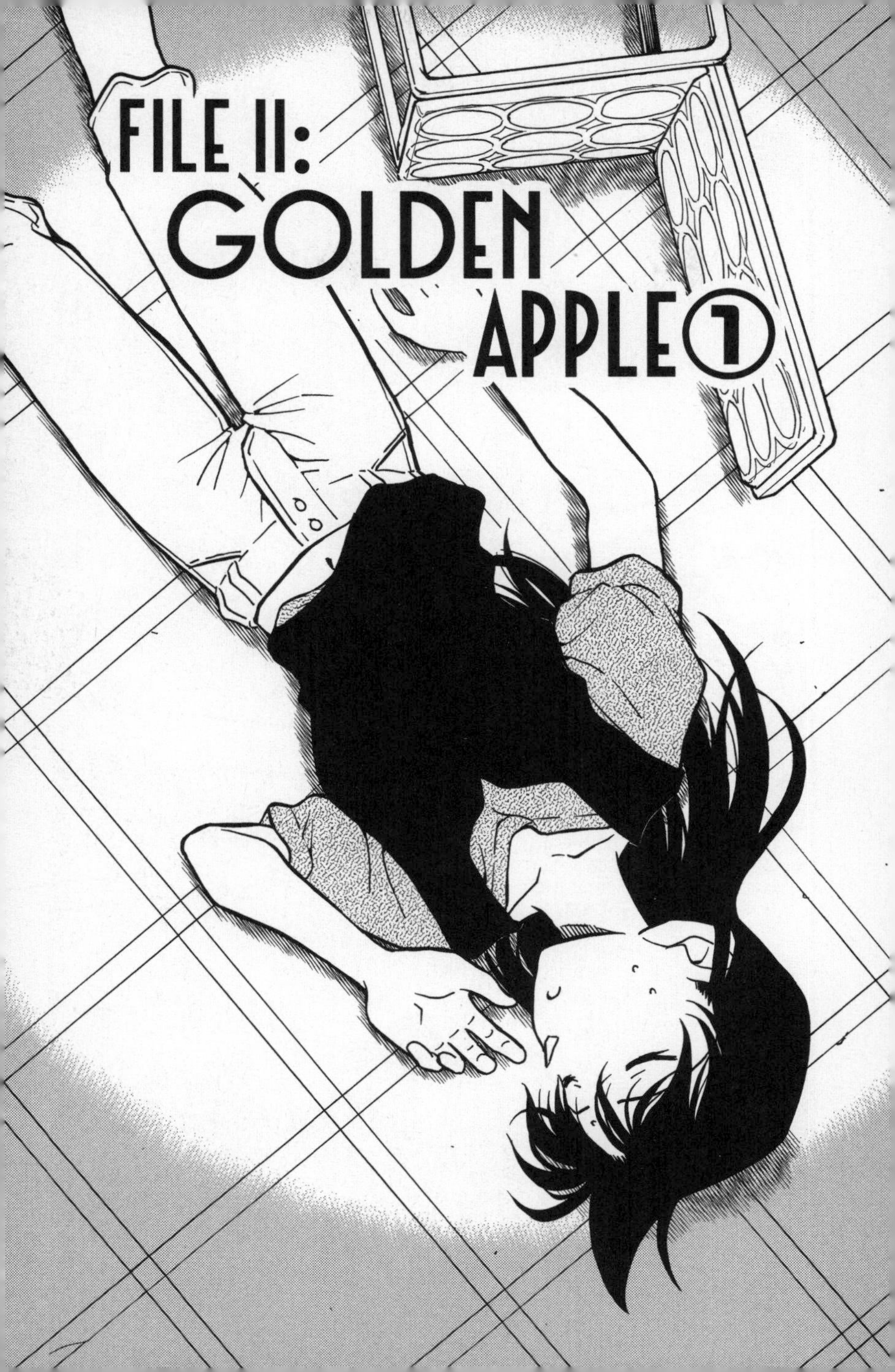
FILE 11:
GOLDEN
APPLE ①

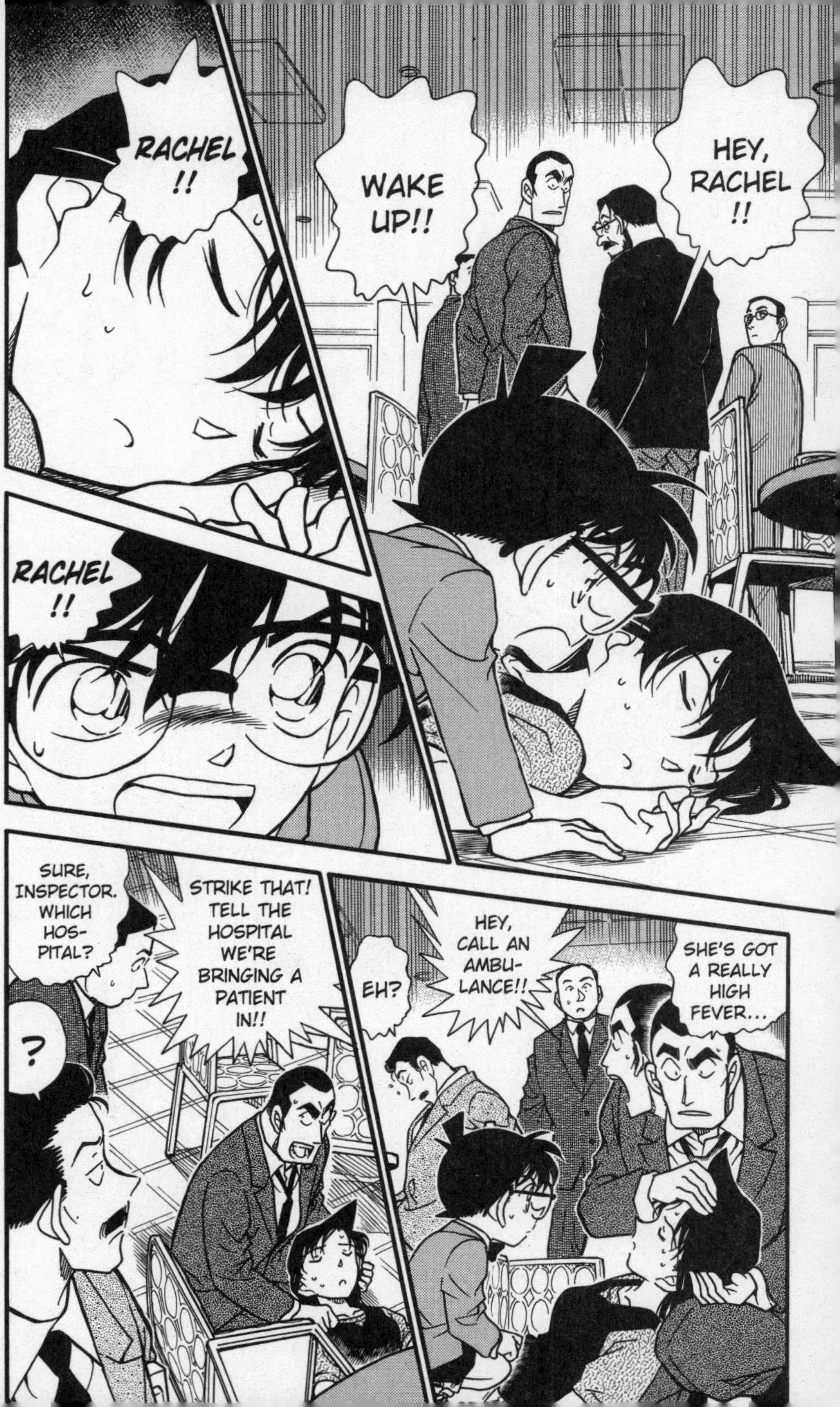
HEY, RACHEL!!
WAKE UP!!
RACHEL!!
RACHEL!!
SHE'S GOT A REALLY HIGH FEVER...
HEY, CALL AN AMBULANCE!!
EH?
SURE, INSPECTOR. WHICH HOSPITAL?
STRIKE THAT! TELL THE HOSPITAL WE'RE BRINGING A PATIENT IN!!
?

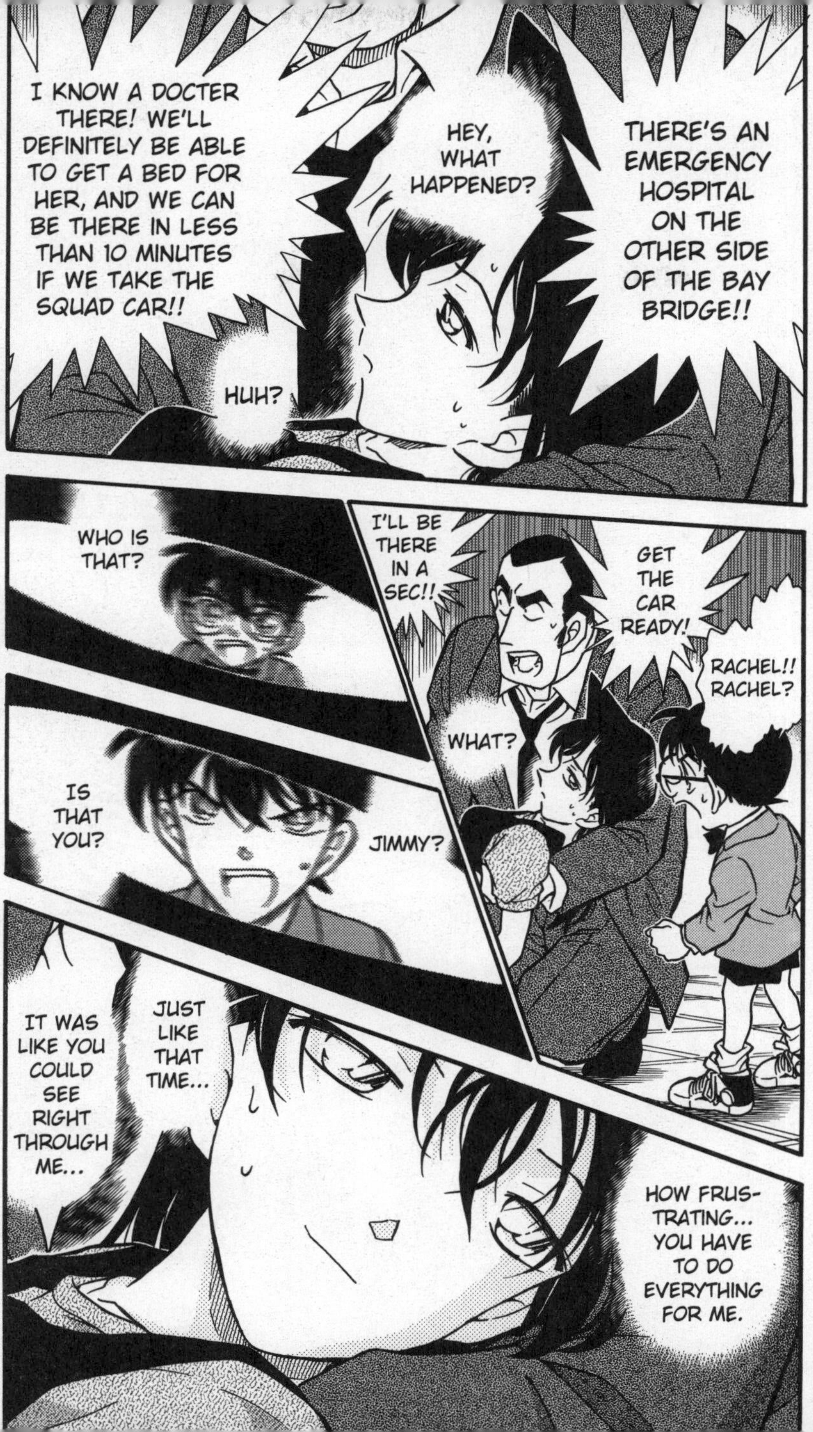
THERE'S AN EMERGENCY HOSPITAL ON THE OTHER SIDE OF THE BAY BRIDGE!!
HEY, WHAT HAPPENED?
I KNOW A DOCTER THERE! WE'LL DEFINITELY BE ABLE TO GET A BED FOR HER, AND WE CAN BE THERE IN LESS THAN 10 MINUTES IF WE TAKE THE SQUAD CAR!!
HUH?
GET THE CAR READY!
RACHEL!! RACHEL?
I'LL BE THERE IN A SEC!!
WHAT?
WHO IS THAT?
JIMMY?
IS THAT YOU?
JUST LIKE THAT TIME...
IT WAS LIKE YOU COULD SEE RIGHT THROUGH ME...
HOW FRUS-TRATING... YOU HAVE TO DO EVERYTHING FOR ME.

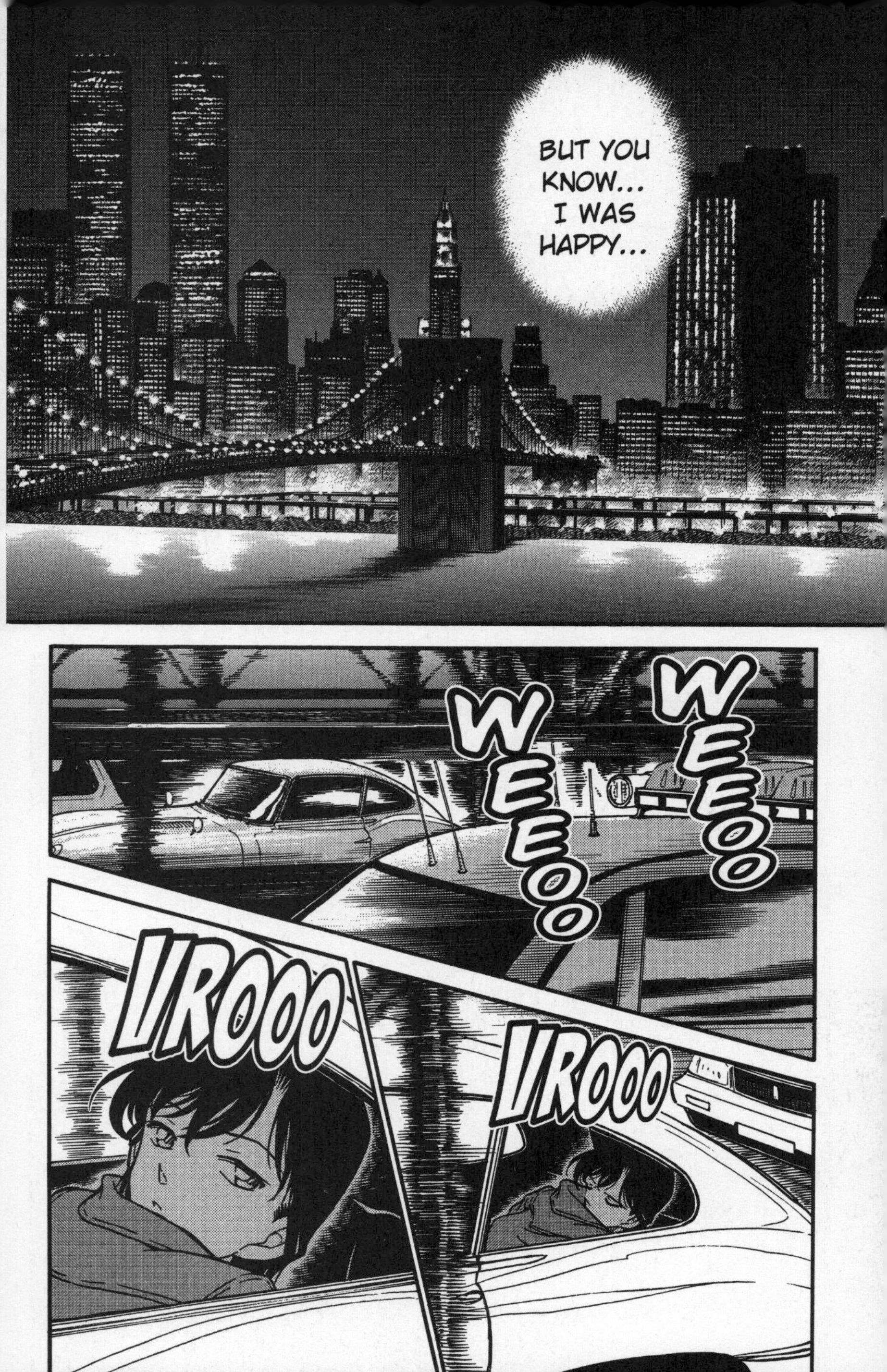
BUT YOU KNOW... I WAS HAPPY...
WEEOO
WEEOO
VROOO
VROOO

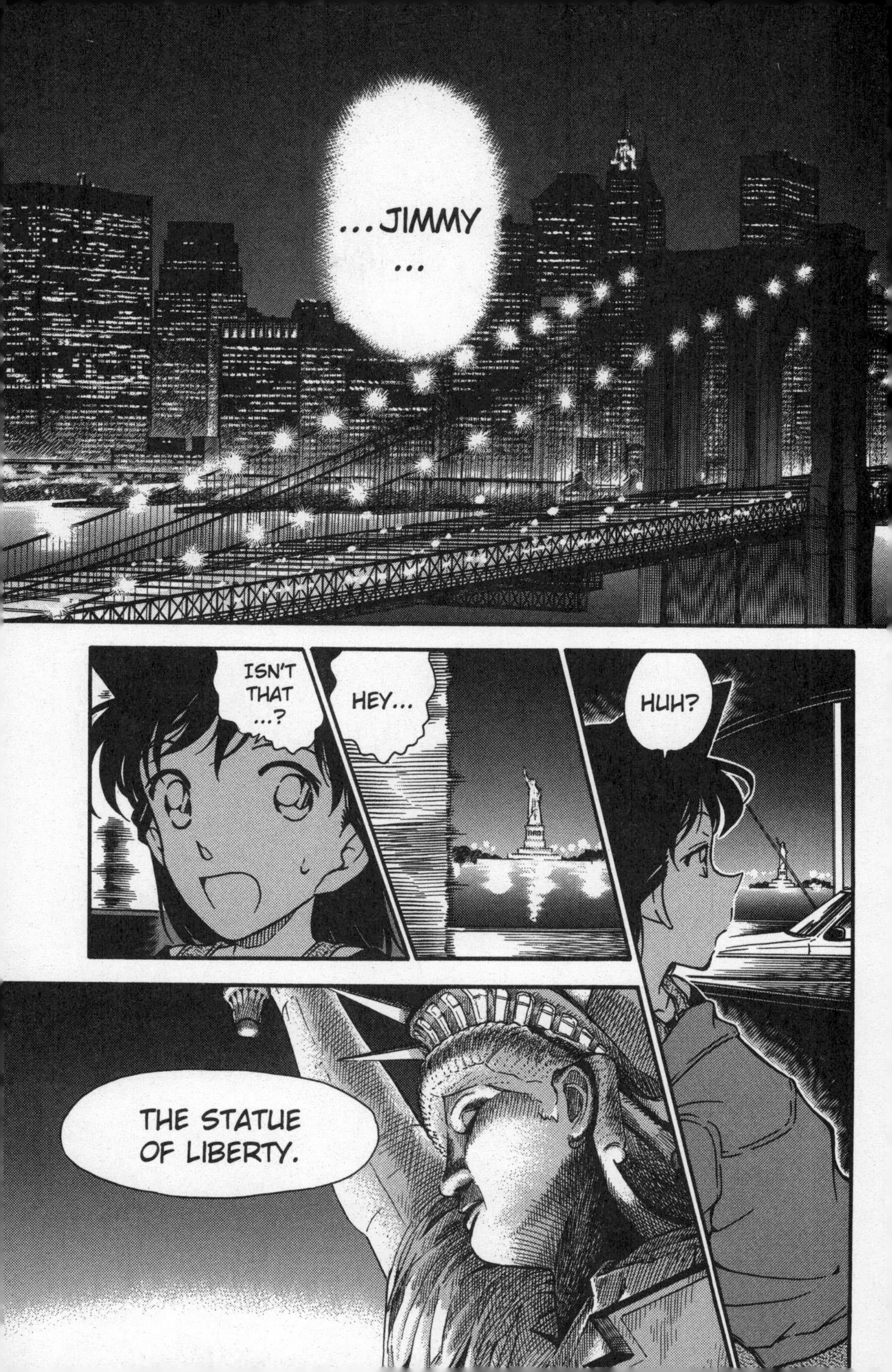
...JIMMY ...
HUH?
HEY...
ISN'T THAT ...?
THE STATUE OF LIBERTY.

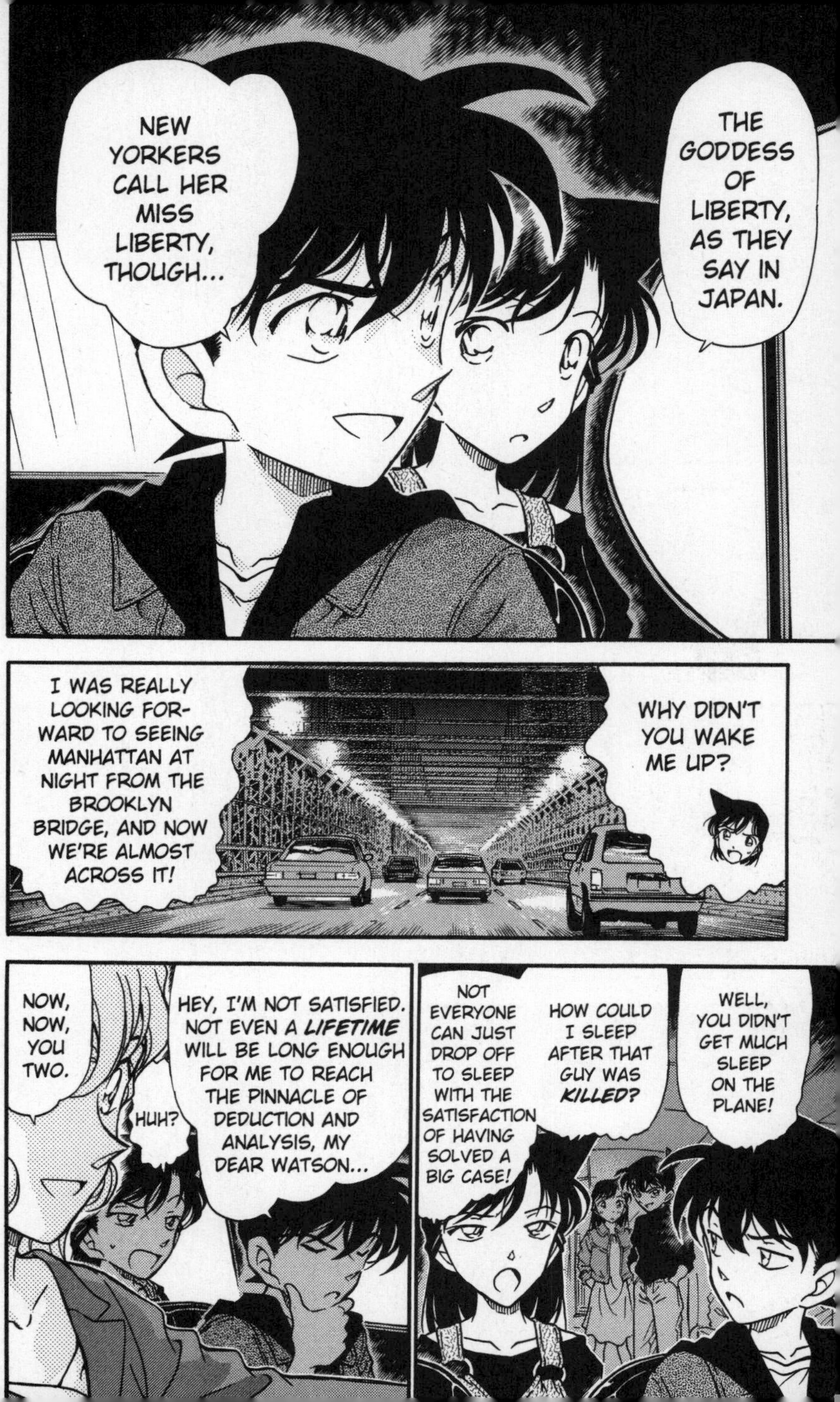
THE GODDESS OF LIBERTY, AS THEY SAY IN JAPAN.
NEW YORKERS CALL HER MISS LIBERTY, THOUGH...
WHY DIDN'T YOU WAKE ME UP?
I WAS REALLY LOOKING FOR-WARD TO SEEING MANHATTAN AT NIGHT FROM THE BROOKLYN BRIDGE, AND NOW WE'RE ALMOST ACROSS IT!
WELL, YOU DIDN'T GET MUCH SLEEP ON THE PLANE!
HOW COULD I SLEEP AFTER THAT GUY WAS *KILLED?*
NOT EVERYONE CAN JUST DROP OFF TO SLEEP WITH THE SATISFACTION OF HAVING SOLVED A BIG CASE!
HEY, I'M NOT SATISFIED. NOT EVEN A *LIFETIME* WILL BE LONG ENOUGH FOR ME TO REACH THE PINNACLE OF DEDUCTION AND ANALYSIS, MY DEAR WATSON...
HUH?
NOW, NOW, YOU TWO.

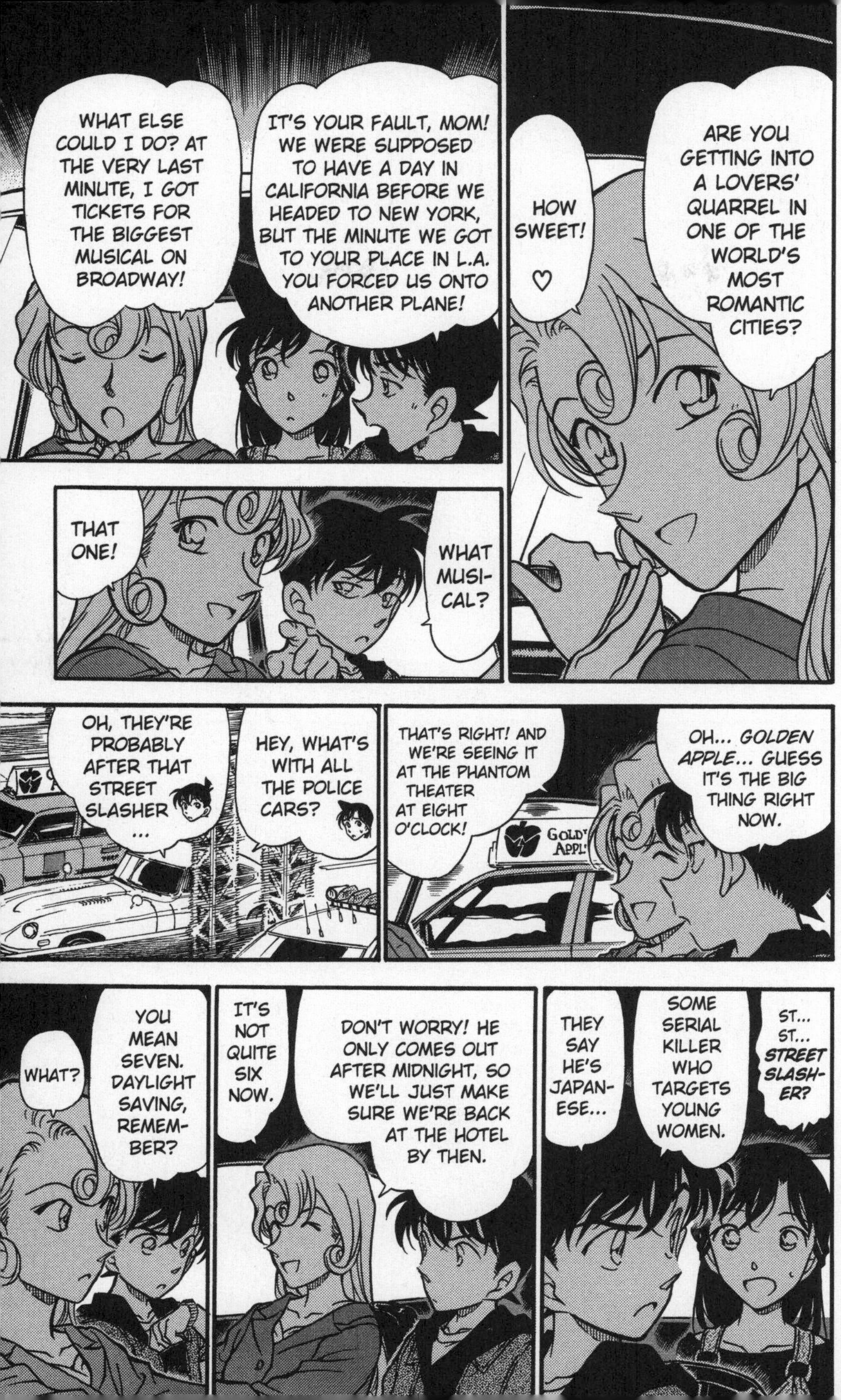
ARE YOU GETTING INTO A LOVERS' QUARREL IN ONE OF THE WORLD'S MOST ROMANTIC CITIES?
HOW SWEET! ♡
IT'S YOUR FAULT, MOM! WE WERE SUPPOSED TO HAVE A DAY IN CALIFORNIA BEFORE WE HEADED TO NEW YORK, BUT THE MINUTE WE GOT TO YOUR PLACE IN L.A. YOU FORCED US ONTO ANOTHER PLANE!
WHAT ELSE COULD I DO? AT THE VERY LAST MINUTE, I GOT TICKETS FOR THE BIGGEST MUSICAL ON BROADWAY!
WHAT MUSICAL?
THAT ONE!
OH... GOLDEN APPLE... GUESS IT'S THE BIG THING RIGHT NOW.
THAT'S RIGHT! AND WE'RE SEEING IT AT THE PHANTOM THEATER AT EIGHT O'CLOCK!
GOLD APPL
HEY, WHAT'S WITH ALL THE POLICE CARS?
OH, THEY'RE PROBABLY AFTER THAT STREET SLASHER...
ST... ST... STREET SLASHER?
SOME SERIAL KILLER WHO TARGETS YOUNG WOMEN.
THEY SAY HE'S JAPANESE...
DON'T WORRY! HE ONLY COMES OUT AFTER MIDNIGHT, SO WE'LL JUST MAKE SURE WE'RE BACK AT THE HOTEL BY THEN.
IT'S NOT QUITE SIX NOW.
YOU MEAN SEVEN. DAYLIGHT SAVING, REMEMBER?
WHAT?

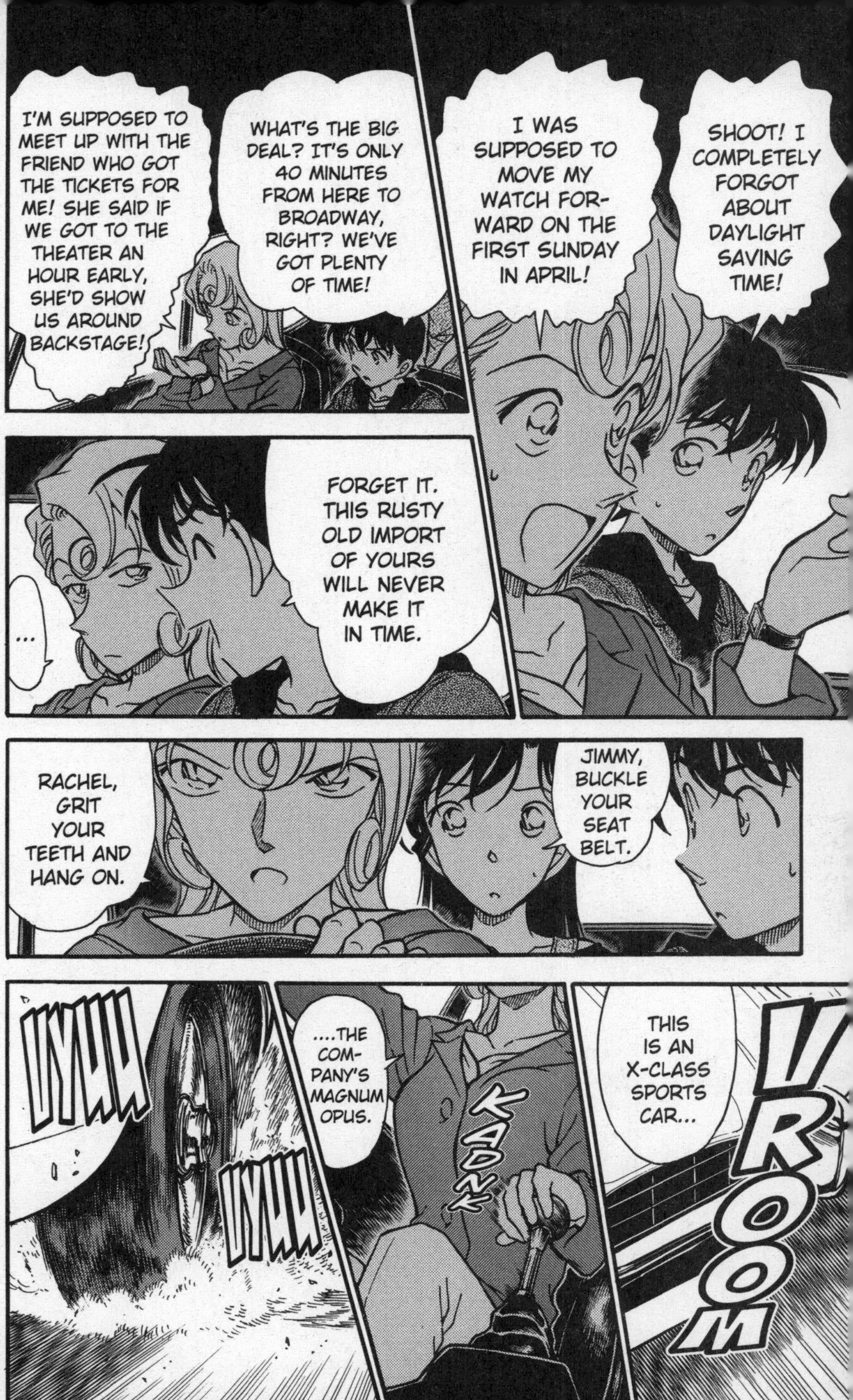
SHOOT! I COMPLETELY FORGOT ABOUT DAYLIGHT SAVING TIME!
I WAS SUPPOSED TO MOVE MY WATCH FOR-WARD ON THE FIRST SUNDAY IN APRIL!
WHAT'S THE BIG DEAL? IT'S ONLY 40 MINUTES FROM HERE TO BROADWAY, RIGHT? WE'VE GOT PLENTY OF TIME!
I'M SUPPOSED TO MEET UP WITH THE FRIEND WHO GOT THE TICKETS FOR ME! SHE SAID IF WE GOT TO THE THEATER AN HOUR EARLY, SHE'D SHOW US AROUND BACKSTAGE!
FORGET IT. THIS RUSTY OLD IMPORT OF YOURS WILL NEVER MAKE IT IN TIME.
...
JIMMY, BUCKLE YOUR SEAT BELT.
RACHEL, GRIT YOUR TEETH AND HANG ON.
VROOM
THIS IS AN X-CLASS SPORTS CAR...
KADNK
....THE COM-PANY'S MAGNUM OPUS.

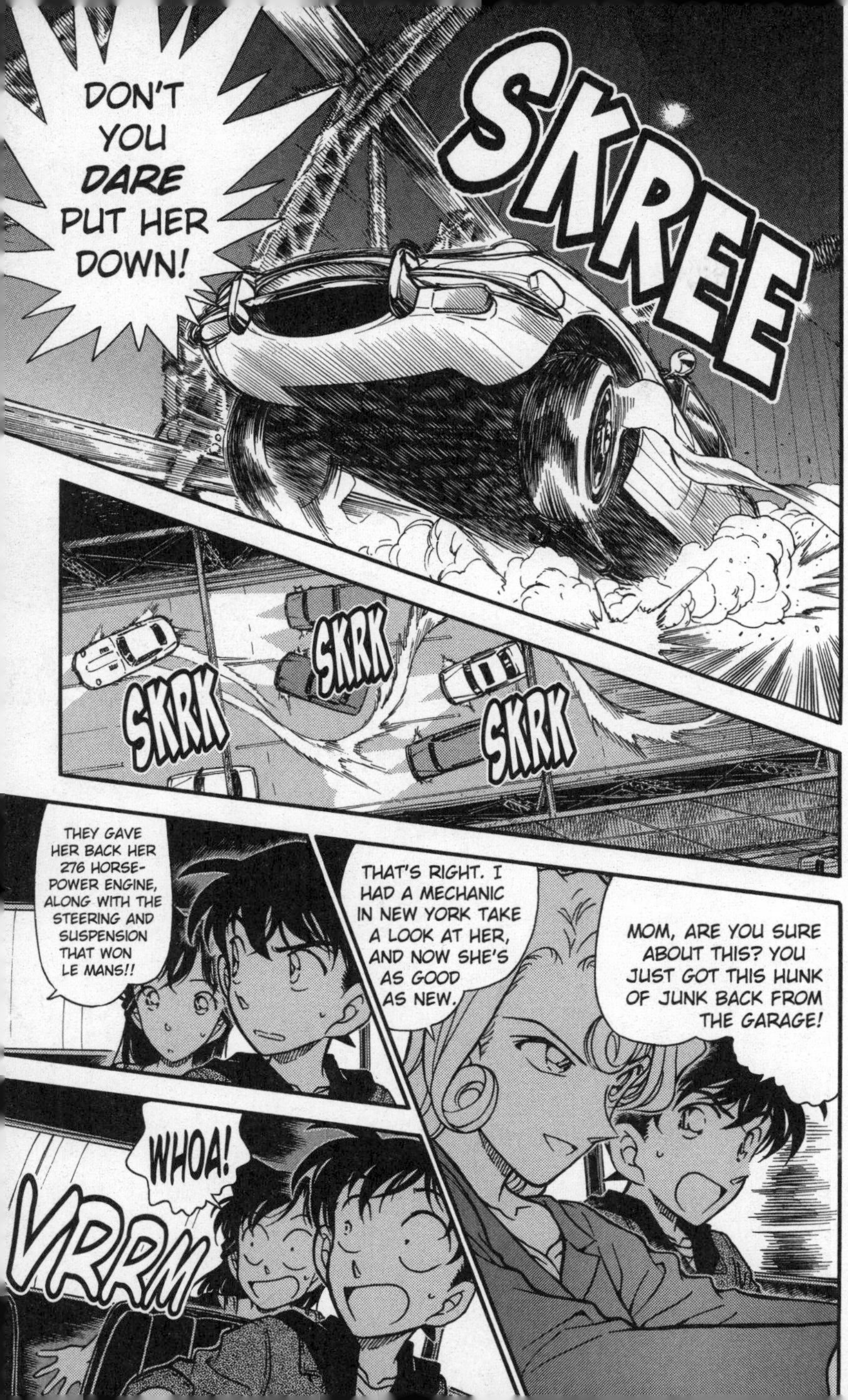
SKREE
DON'T YOU *DARE* PUT HER DOWN!
SKRK
SKRK
SKRK
MOM, ARE YOU SURE ABOUT THIS? YOU JUST GOT THIS HUNK OF JUNK BACK FROM THE GARAGE!
THAT'S RIGHT. I HAD A MECHANIC IN NEW YORK TAKE A LOOK AT HER, AND NOW SHE'S AS GOOD AS NEW.
THEY GAVE HER BACK HER 276 HORSE-POWER ENGINE, ALONG WITH THE STEERING AND SUSPENSION THAT WON LE MANS!!
WHOA!
VRRM

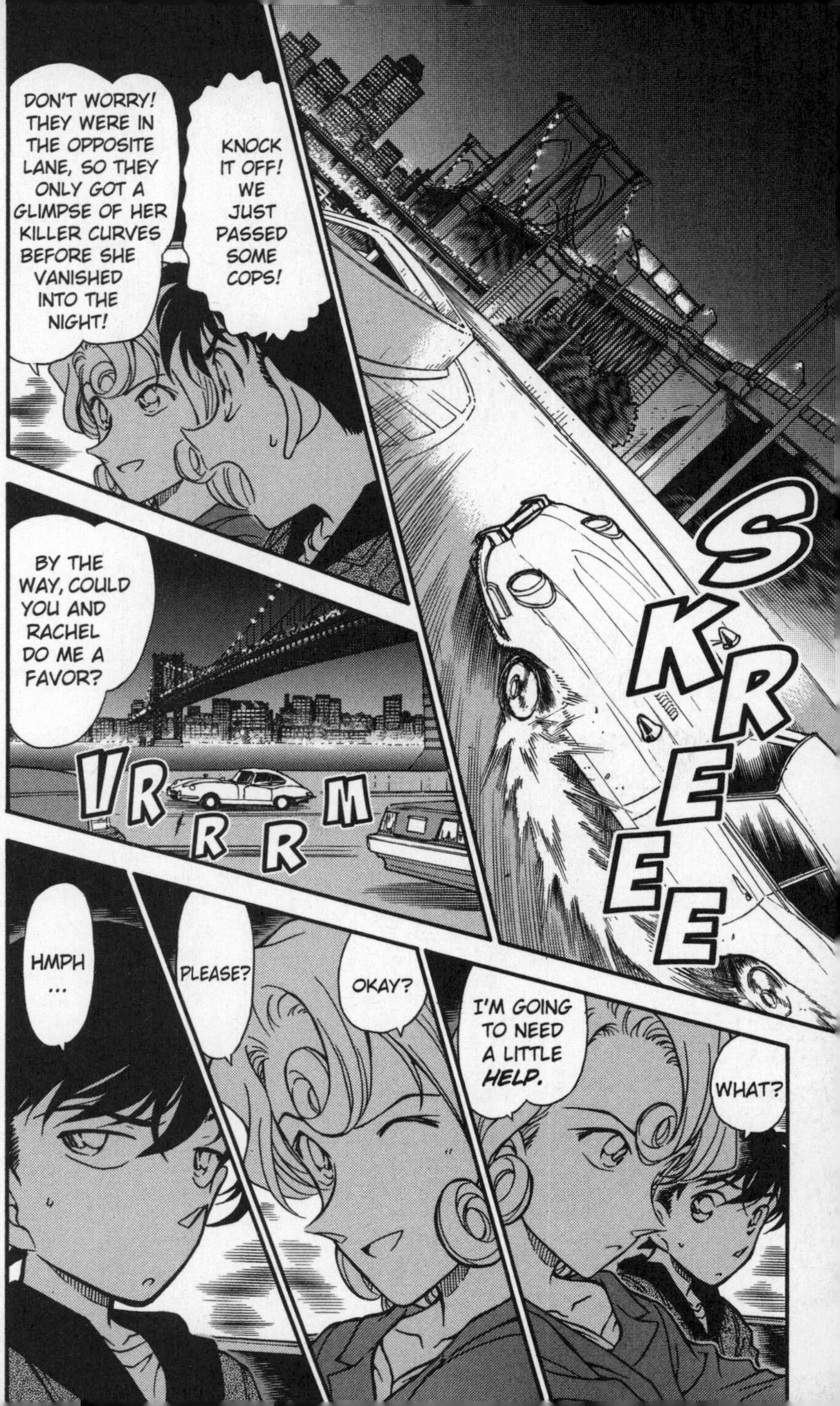
SKREEEE
KNOCK IT OFF! WE JUST PASSED SOME COPS!
DON'T WORRY! THEY WERE IN THE OPPOSITE LANE, SO THEY ONLY GOT A GLIMPSE OF HER KILLER CURVES BEFORE SHE VANISHED INTO THE NIGHT!
BY THE WAY, COULD YOU AND RACHEL DO ME A FAVOR?
VRRRM
WHAT?
I'M GOING TO NEED A LITTLE *HELP*.
OKAY?
PLEASE?
HMPH ...

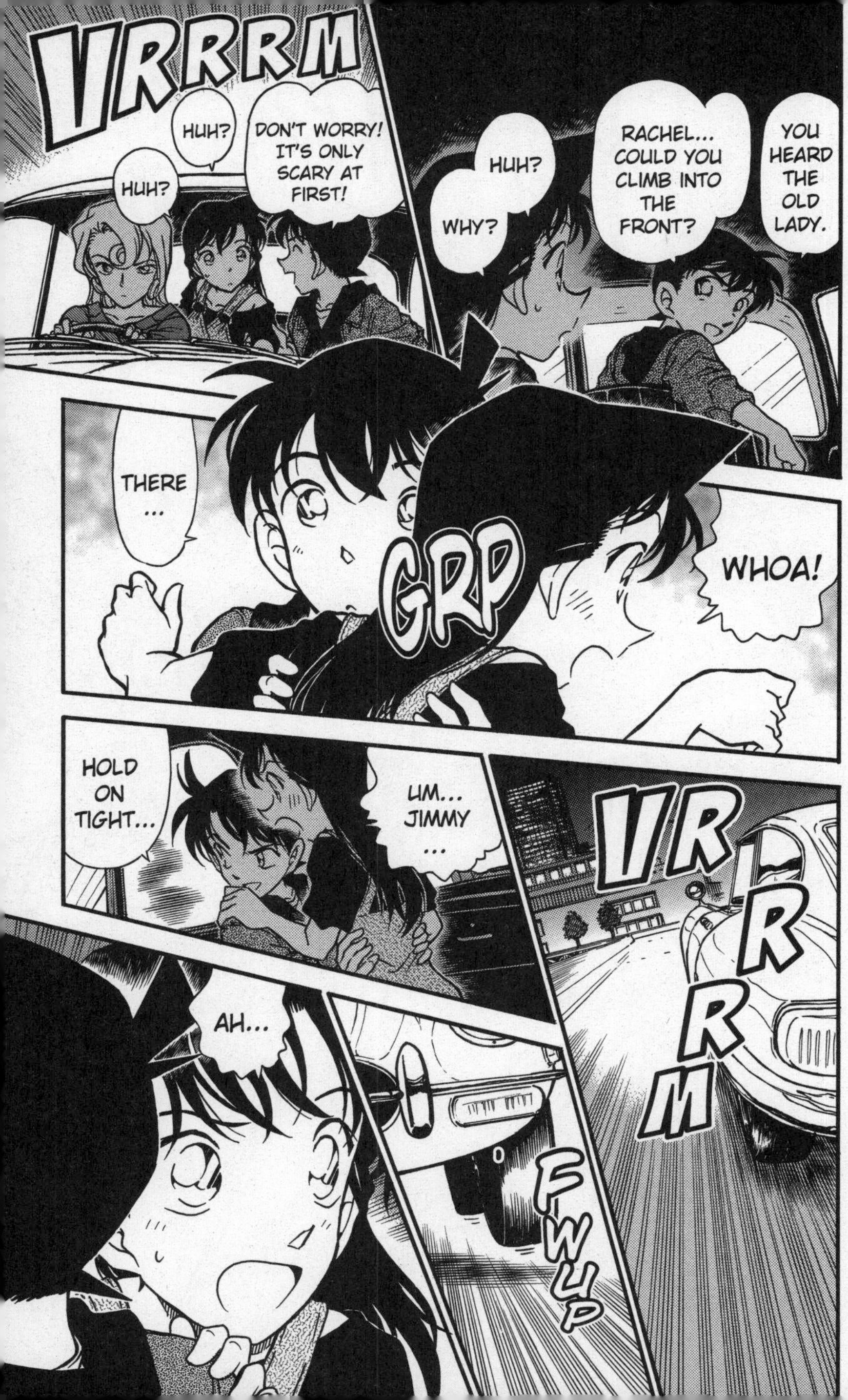
YOU HEARD THE OLD LADY.
RACHEL... COULD YOU CLIMB INTO THE FRONT?
HUH?
WHY?
VRRRM
DON'T WORRY! IT'S ONLY SCARY AT FIRST!
HUH?
HUH?
WHOA!
GRP
THERE ...
VRRRM
FWUP
UM... JIMMY ...
HOLD ON TIGHT...
AH...

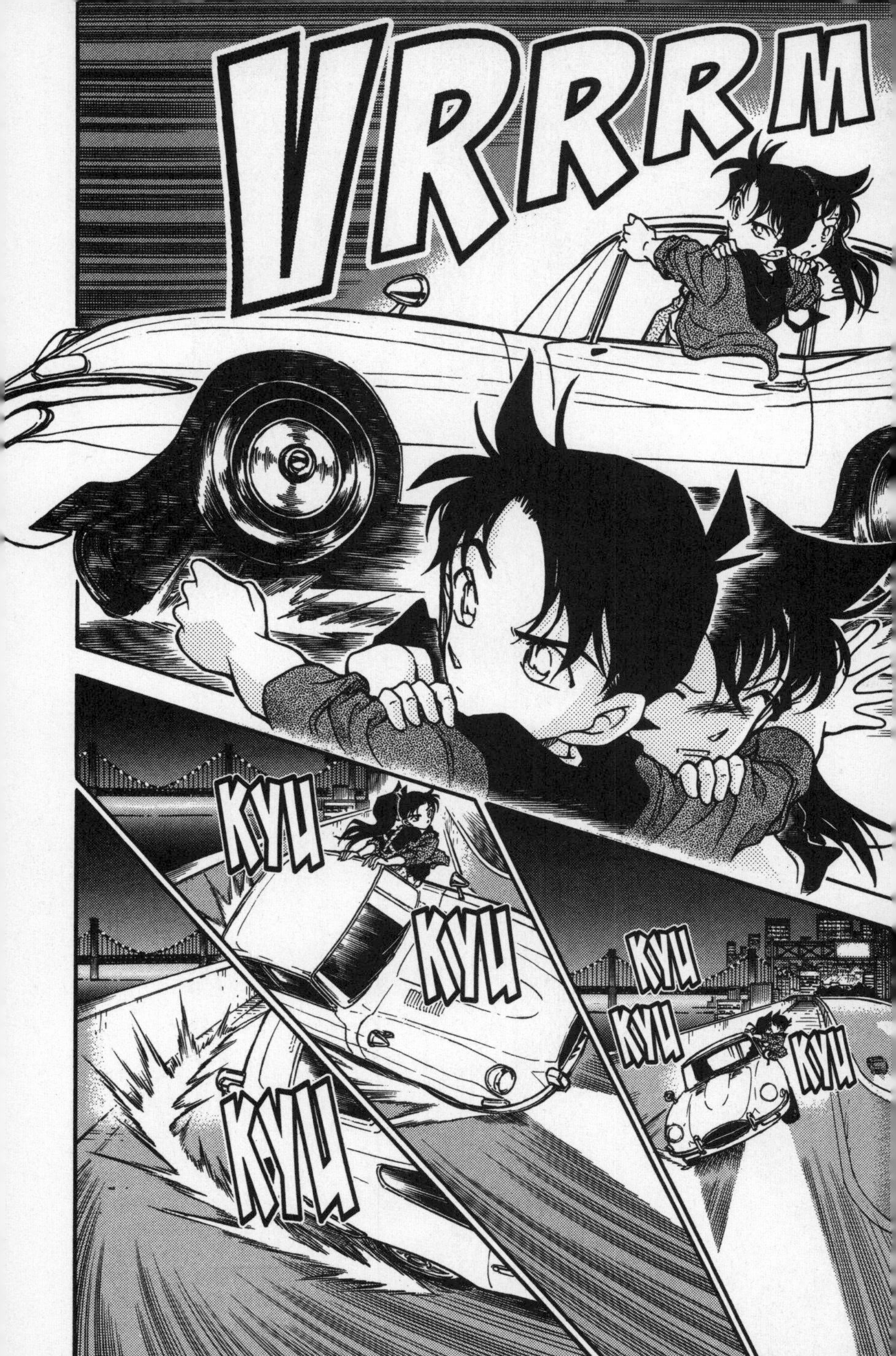
VRRRM
KYU
KYU
KYU
KYU
KYU
KYU

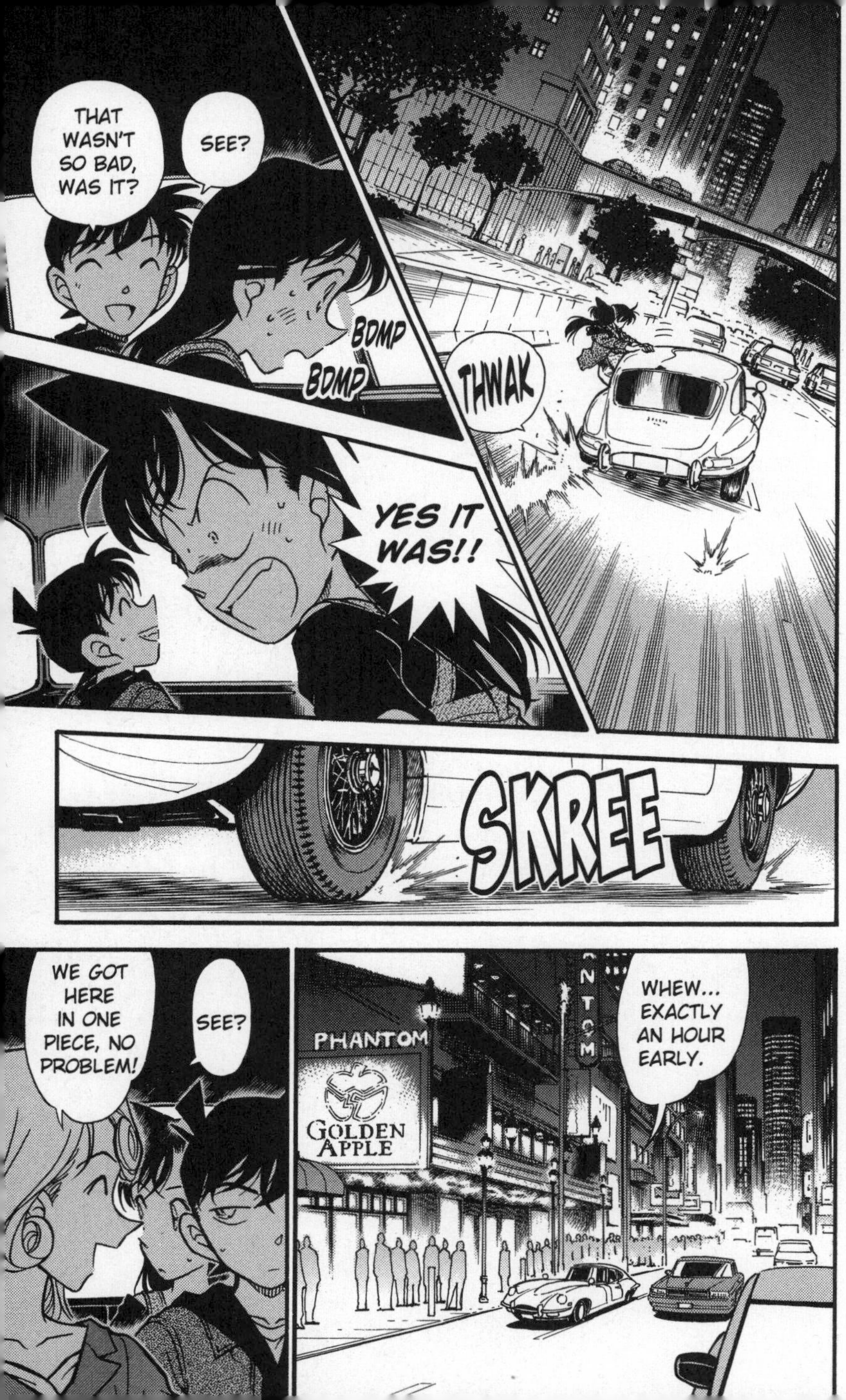
THWAK
SEE?
THAT WASN'T SO BAD, WAS IT?
BDMP
BDMP
YES IT WAS!!
SKREE
WHEW... EXACTLY AN HOUR EARLY.
PHANTOM
GOLDEN APPLE
SEE?
WE GOT HERE IN ONE PIECE, NO PROBLEM!

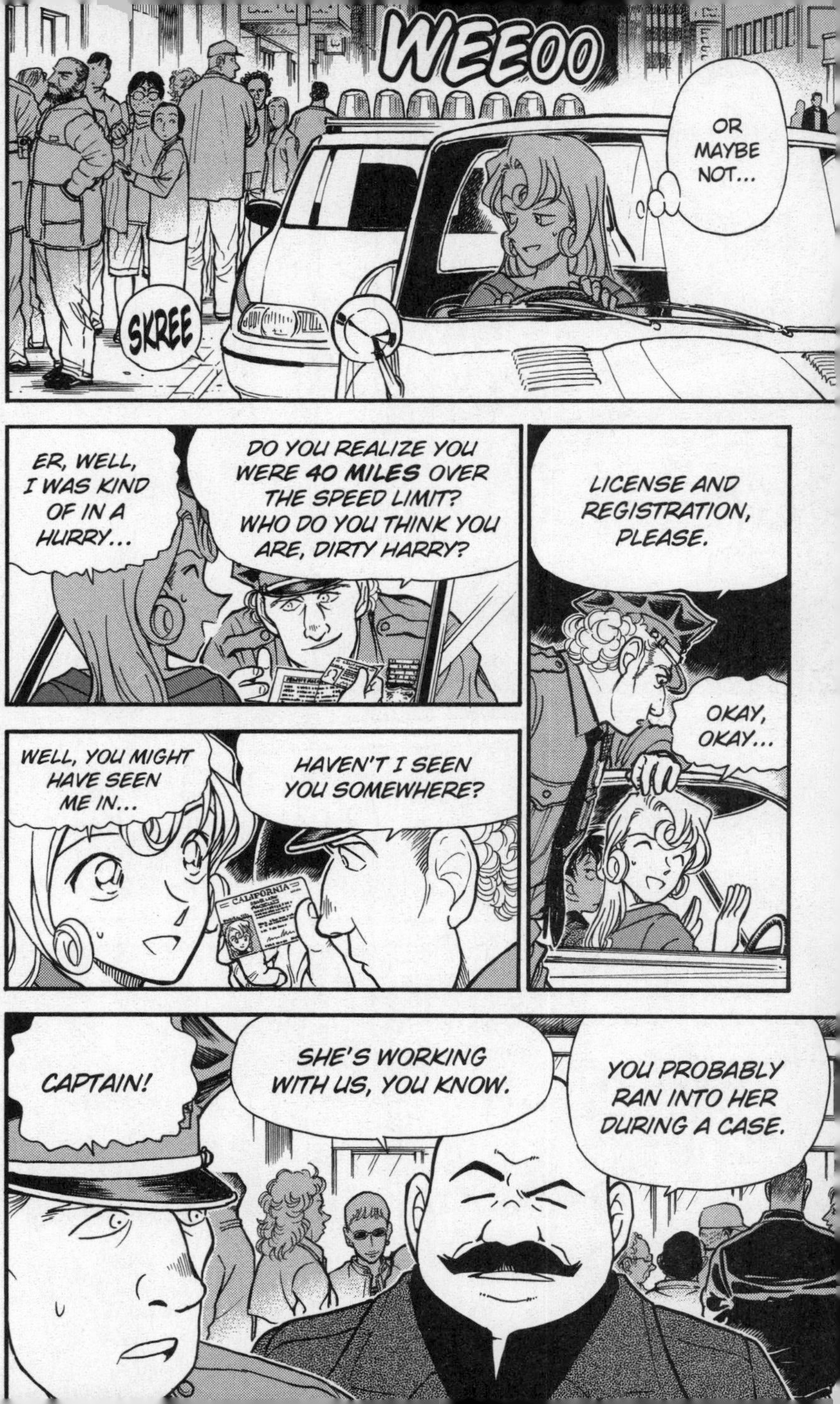
WEEOO
OR MAYBE NOT...
SKREE
LICENSE AND REGISTRATION, PLEASE.
OKAY, OKAY...
DO YOU REALIZE YOU WERE 40 MILES OVER THE SPEED LIMIT? WHO DO YOU THINK YOU ARE, DIRTY HARRY?
ER, WELL, I WAS KIND OF IN A HURRY...
HAVEN'T I SEEN YOU SOMEWHERE?
WELL, YOU MIGHT HAVE SEEN ME IN...
CALIFORNIA
YOU PROBABLY RAN INTO HER DURING A CASE.
SHE'S WORKING WITH US, YOU KNOW.
CAPTAIN!

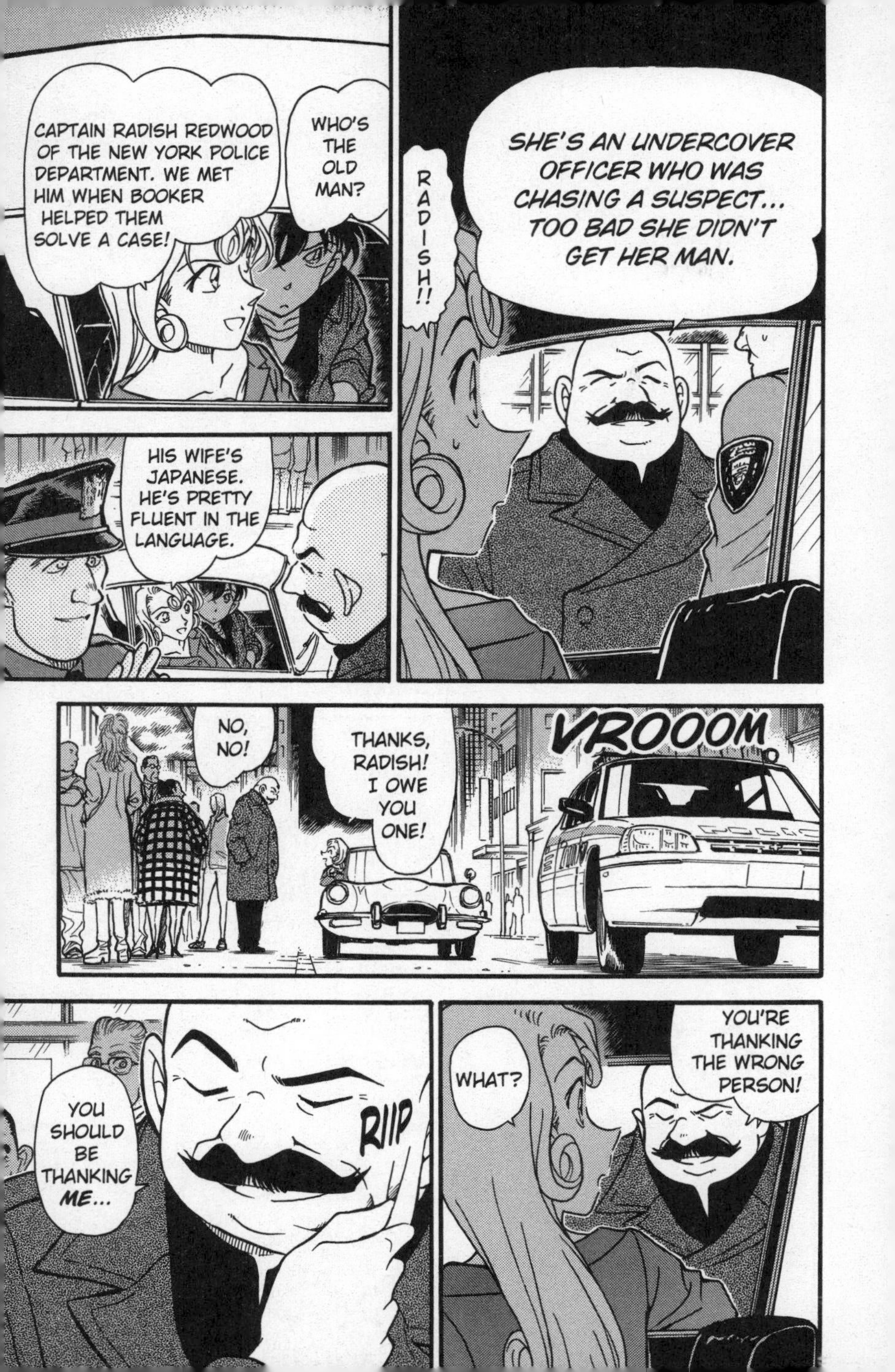
SHE'S AN UNDERCOVER OFFICER WHO WAS CHASING A SUSPECT... TOO BAD SHE DIDN'T GET HER MAN.
RADISH!!
WHO'S THE OLD MAN?
CAPTAIN RADISH REDWOOD OF THE NEW YORK POLICE DEPARTMENT. WE MET HIM WHEN BOOKER HELPED THEM SOLVE A CASE!
HIS WIFE'S JAPANESE. HE'S PRETTY FLUENT IN THE LANGUAGE.
VROOOM
THANKS, RADISH! I OWE YOU ONE!
NO, NO!
YOU'RE THANKING THE WRONG PERSON!
WHAT?
RIIP
YOU SHOULD BE THANKING ME...

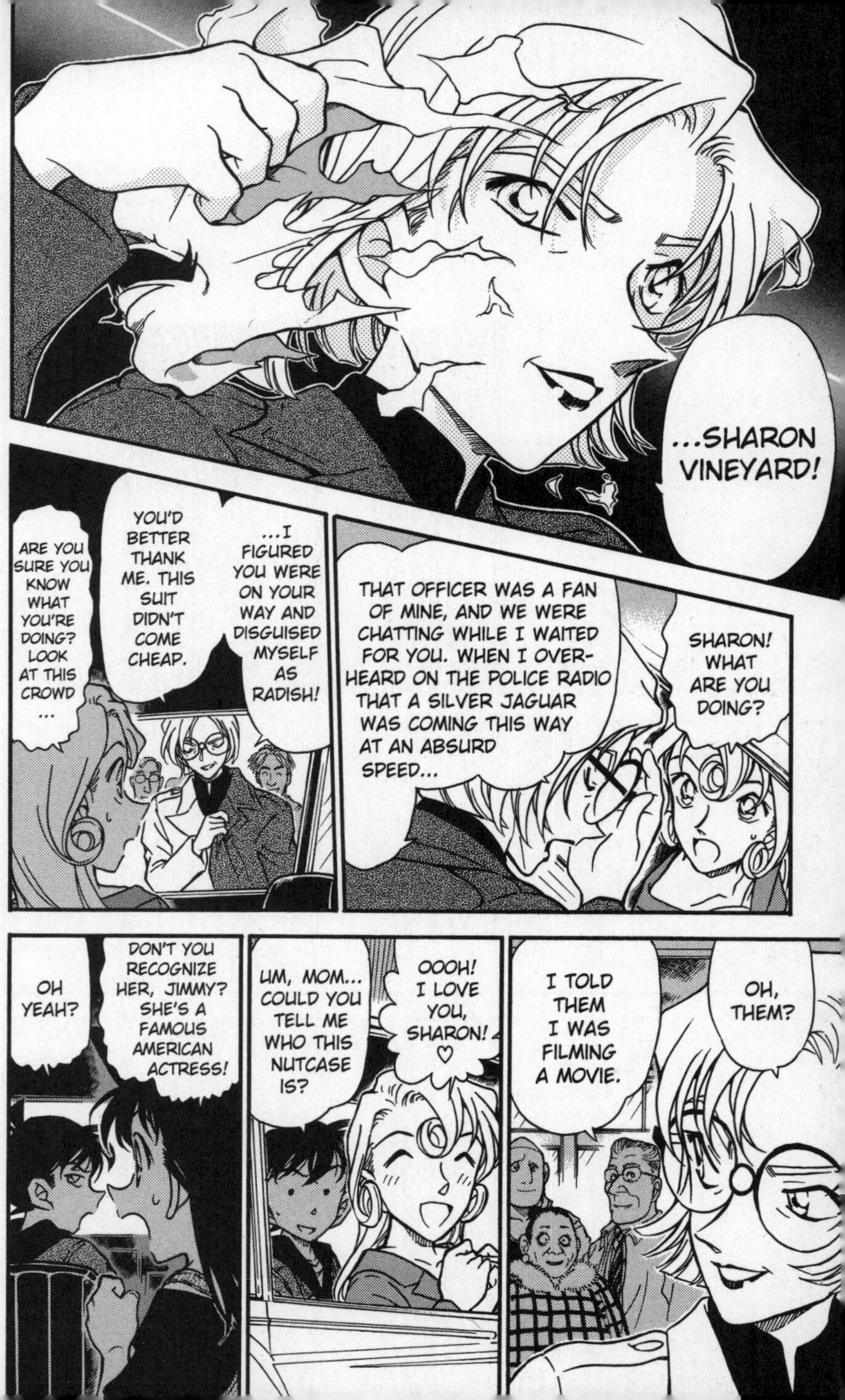
...SHARON VINEYARD!
SHARON! WHAT ARE YOU DOING?
THAT OFFICER WAS A FAN OF MINE, AND WE WERE CHATTING WHILE I WAITED FOR YOU. WHEN I OVER-HEARD ON THE POLICE RADIO THAT A SILVER JAGUAR WAS COMING THIS WAY AT AN ABSURD SPEED...
...I FIGURED YOU WERE ON YOUR WAY AND DISGUISED MYSELF AS RADISH!
YOU'D BETTER THANK ME. THIS SUIT DIDN'T COME CHEAP.
ARE YOU SURE YOU KNOW WHAT YOU'RE DOING? LOOK AT THIS CROWD ...
OH, THEM?
I TOLD THEM I WAS FILMING A MOVIE.
OOOH! I LOVE YOU, SHARON! ♡
UM, MOM... COULD YOU TELL ME WHO THIS NUTCASE IS?
DON'T YOU RECOGNIZE HER, JIMMY? SHE'S A FAMOUS AMERICAN ACTRESS!
OH YEAH?

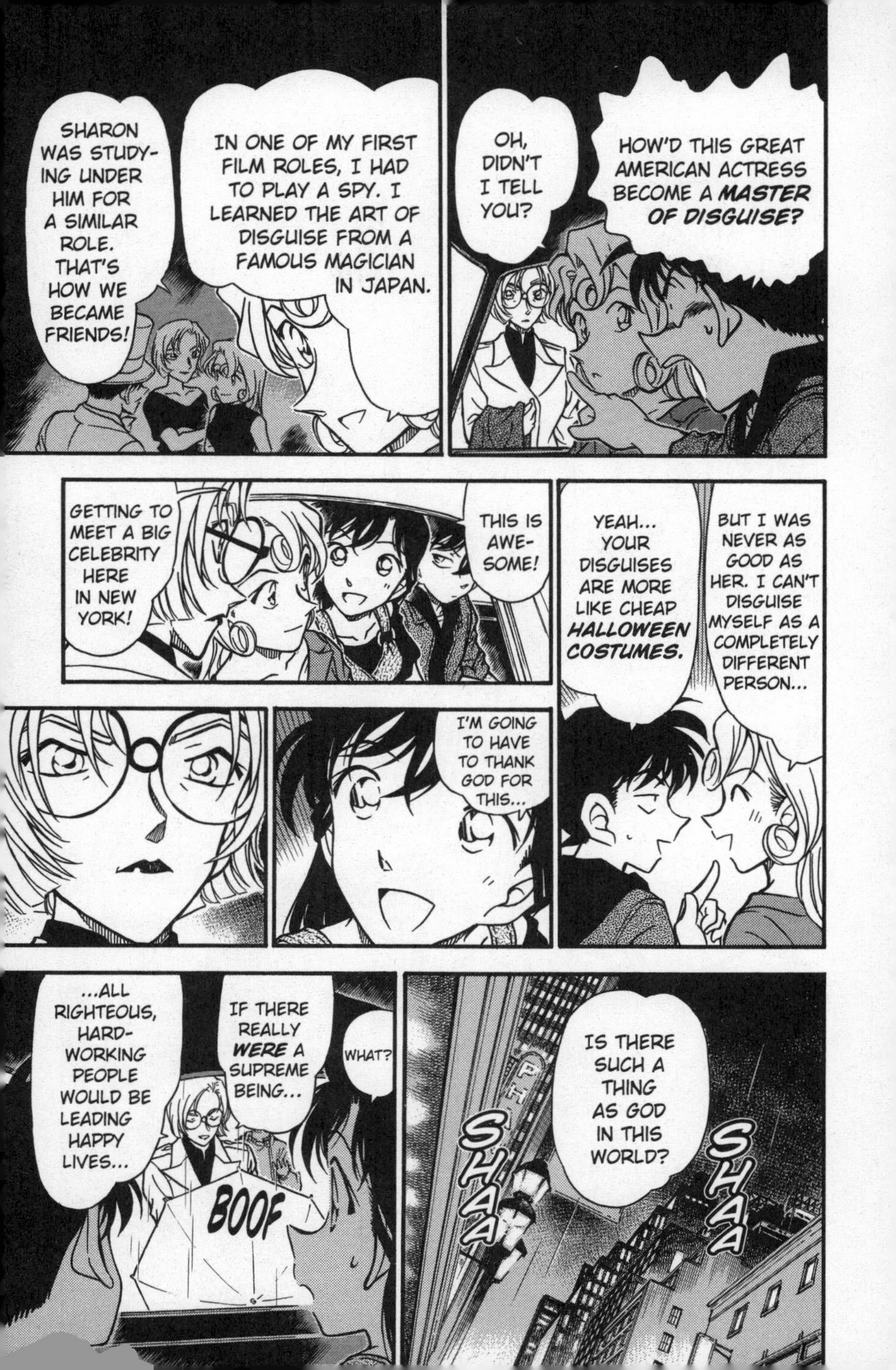
HOW'D THIS GREAT AMERICAN ACTRESS BECOME A ***MASTER OF DISGUISE?***
OH, DIDN'T I TELL YOU?
IN ONE OF MY FIRST FILM ROLES, I HAD TO PLAY A SPY. I LEARNED THE ART OF DISGUISE FROM A FAMOUS MAGICIAN IN JAPAN.
SHARON WAS STUDYING UNDER HIM FOR A SIMILAR ROLE. THAT'S HOW WE BECAME FRIENDS!
BUT I WAS NEVER AS GOOD AS HER. I CAN'T DISGUISE MYSELF AS A COMPLETELY DIFFERENT PERSON...
YEAH... YOUR DISGUISES ARE MORE LIKE CHEAP ***HALLOWEEN COSTUMES.***
THIS IS AWESOME!
GETTING TO MEET A BIG CELEBRITY HERE IN NEW YORK!
I'M GOING TO HAVE TO THANK GOD FOR THIS...
IS THERE SUCH A THING AS GOD IN THIS WORLD?
SHAA
SHAA
WHAT?
IF THERE REALLY ***WERE*** A SUPREME BEING...
...ALL RIGHTEOUS, HARD-WORKING PEOPLE WOULD BE LEADING HAPPY LIVES...
BOOF

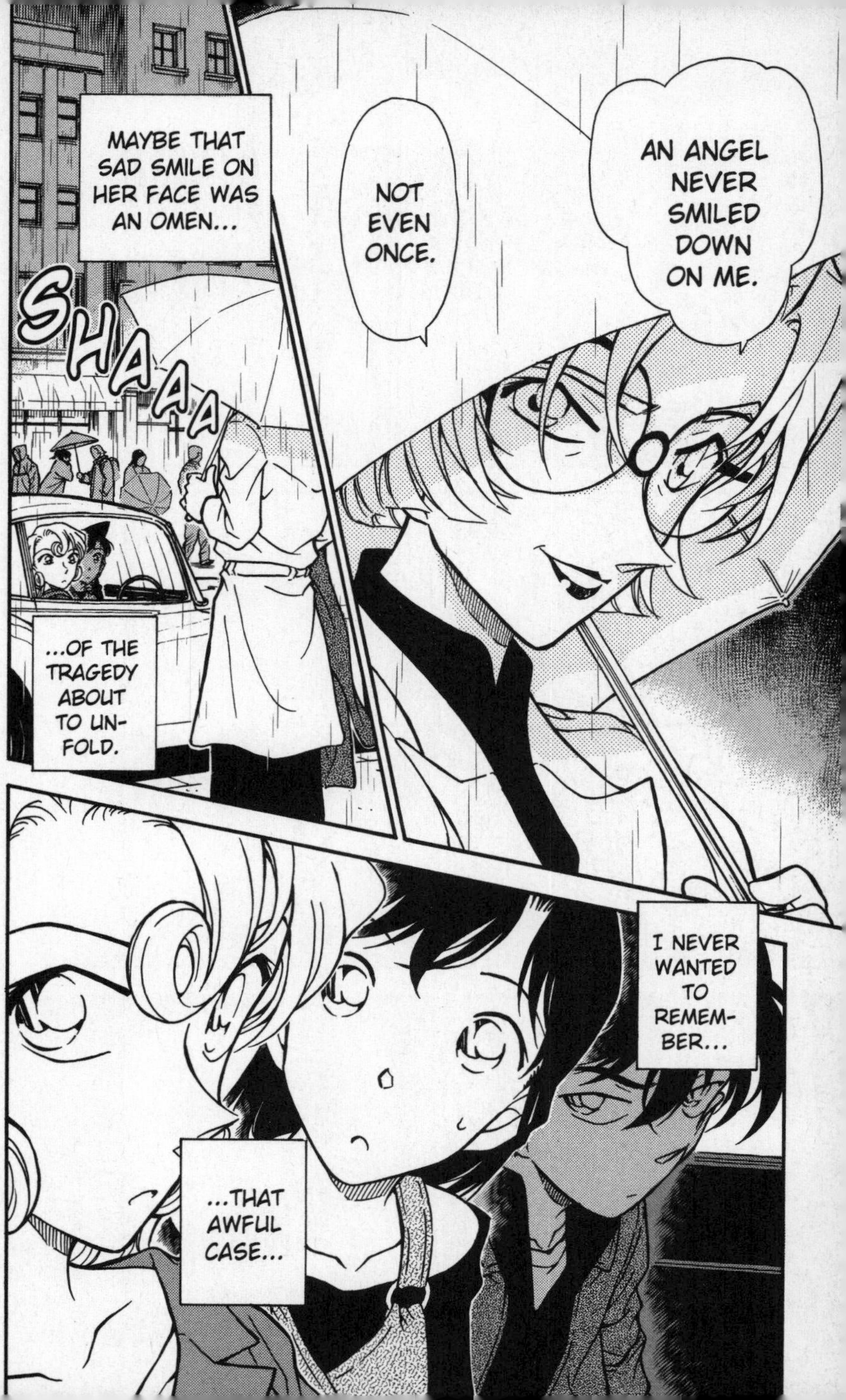
AN ANGEL NEVER SMILED DOWN ON ME.
NOT EVEN ONCE.
MAYBE THAT SAD SMILE ON HER FACE WAS AN OMEN...
SHAAAA
...OF THE TRAGEDY ABOUT TO UNFOLD.
I NEVER WANTED TO REMEMBER...
...THAT AWFUL CASE...

Hello, Aoyama here.

We've finally made it to the New York chapters! This story line is vital to the plot of *Case Closed*! It was also a lot of hard work because of all the English...

I traveled to New York City for a day to do research. Please enjoy these chapters drawn from my own blood and sweat!

Oops... but only the first chapter of the New York story is in this volume... Heh.

Gosho Aoyama's Mystery Library

34

SHIGERU HIRAGI

You may not recognize this detective's name, but I'm sure Japanese readers will know who I'm talking about when I call him "The Red Turnip Prosecutor." Hiragi spent years as an assistant officer and assistant prosecutor before finally becoming a prosecutor at age 50. A tall, thin man with wiry salt-and-pepper hair, he's famous for his "Yah, y'know" Nagoya dialect. After an incident where he spilled pickled red turnip all over a courtroom floor, he was nicknamed "The Red Turnip Prosecutor."

Hiragi works at a small district prosecution office, so he has to perform investigations, inquisitions, prosecutions and court proceedings all on his own. This allows him to see the whole case from start to finish. He works through deductions with the calmness he's attained from his long career. His creator, Shunzo Waku, became a lawyer for the express purpose of writing detective novels. I did the same thing to create this detective manga... well, not really. Heh.

I recommend *Utagawashiki wa Basseyo* (Guilty Until Proven Innocent).

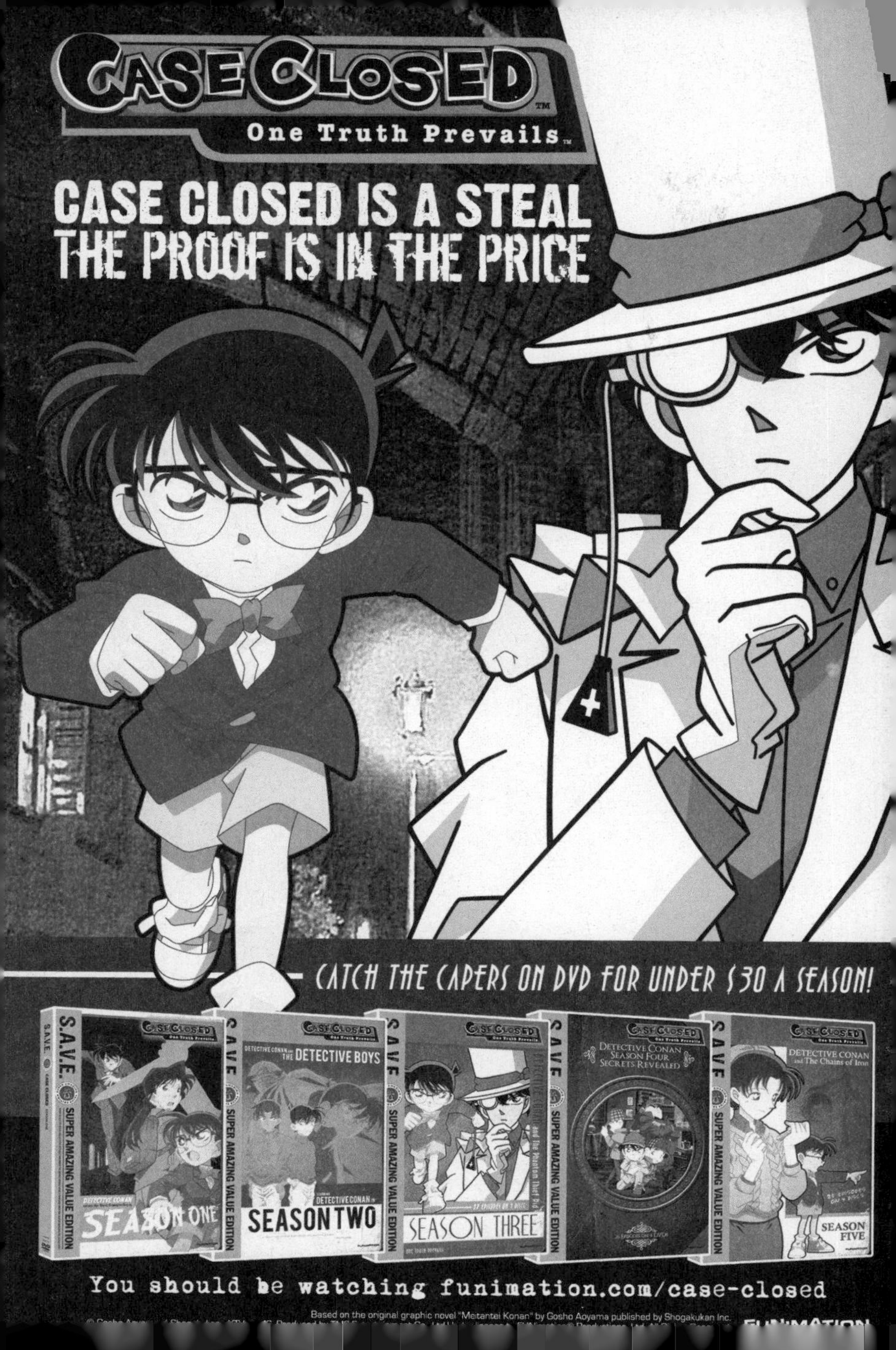

CASE CLOSED
One Truth Prevails
CASE CLOSED IS A STEAL
THE PROOF IS IN THE PRICE
CATCH THE CAPERS ON DVD FOR UNDER $30 A SEASON!
SEASON ONE
SEASON TWO
SEASON THREE
DETECTIVE CONAN SEASON FOUR SECRETS REVEALED
SEASON FIVE
SUPER AMAZING VALUE EDITION
You should be watching funimation.com/case-closed
Based on the original graphic novel "Meitantei Konan" by Gosho Aoyama published by Shogakukan Inc.

Hey! You're Reading in the Wrong Direction!

This is the **end** of this graphic novel!

To properly enjoy this VIZ graphic novel, please turn it around and begin reading from **right to left.** Unlike English, Japanese is read right to left, so Japanese comics are read in reverse order from the way English comics are typically read.

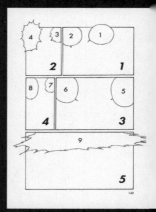

Follow the action this way

This book has been printed in the original Japanese format in order to preserve the orientation of the original artwork. Have fun with it!